RESTORING OUR COMPETITIVE EDGE

RESTORING OUR COMPETITIVE EDGE

COMPETING THROUGH MANUFACTURING

ROBERT H. HAYES
Graduate School of Business Administration
Harvard University

STEVEN C. WHEELWRIGHT
Graduate School of Business
Stanford University

JOHN WILEY & SONS
New York • Chichester • Brisbane • Toronto • Singapore

Library of Congress Cataloging in Publication Data:

Hayes, Robert H.
    Restoring our competitive edge:
    competing through manufacturing.

    Includes index.
    1. United States—Manufactures—Management.
2. Industrial management—United States.   3. Production
planning.   4. Manufacturing processes—Technological
innovations.   5. Competition, International.
I. Wheelwright, Steven C., 1943-   .   II. Title.

HD9725.H39   1984   658.5   84-3710
ISBN 0-471-05159-4

Printed in the United States of America

10   9   8   7   6   5   4

To

Priscilla and Margaret

Who kept us anchored to reality,
most of the time

Preface

In 1979, when we began discussing seriously the idea of writing a book together, the kind of book we were thinking about writing was very different from the one that finally emerged. For a number of years we and several of our colleagues, both individually and in various combinations, had been writing about the potential competitive vulnerability of U.S. manufacturing companies. We had been arguing that a large part of this vulnerability arose out of the failure of these companies to develop and manage their manufacturing capabilities effectively. In these articles and books, which we directed at both business managers and scholars, we tried to indicate the nature of the problem, as we saw it, and the steps that manufacturing managers should take in addressing it.

When we began writing this book in earnest, one of the authors had just returned from living in Europe for two years. After observing firsthand the emphasis on quality and technological leadership in many world class European manufacturing companies, we felt that it was time to sound the alarm again. The wolf, whom we earlier knew to exist only because of a few lonely howls in the distance, then appeared to be just outside the garden wall. We decided to try to rouse the household and help organize the defense; that was the purpose of the book we began writing.

Between then and now the world has changed faster than we had anticipated. Not only did the wolf arrive at the door—it was seen to be part of a pack. The household was wide awake. It didn't need another alarm, or a series of general guidelines for defending itself. It wanted specific advice regarding the steps it should take. We and our colleagues found ourselves spending a good deal of our time working with a variety of manufacturing companies, helping them gird their manufacturing organizations for battle.

In the process we learned a great deal that we had not known, or properly understood, when we began writing this book. We each had the opportunity to visit Japan at least twice, in the company of U.S. manufacturing managers, during this period. As we compared leading Japanese companies' approaches to managing manufacturing with those followed by their U.S. competitors, it became clear to us that the gap that had to be overcome was enormous. Learning to compete in the new competitive environment of the 1980s and beyond would be a long process.

For many companies the issue had become one of simple survival. The "secret weapon" of their international competitors was not superior product designs, marketing ingenuity, or financial strength, but manufacturing superiority—the ability to "make it better." Yet many of the companies that had come under attack suddenly came to realize that they had been systematically neglecting their manufacturing organizations over a long period of time. Their production equipment had been allowed to age, their management systems to become obsolete. The skills required to compete effectively against world class competitors had atrophied. In many cases top management did not even understand clearly what was required in order to rebuild their manufacturing capabilities. Until this was done, their companies were unlikely to be helped by more supportive government policies or union relationships.

In this new, more urgent environment, sounding the alarm and providing a framework for thinking about the problem, while useful, was only the first step. A variety of other changes had to be made—in bricks and mortar, in systems, and, above all, in competitive philosophy—before these endangered companies would be able to regain competitive parity with their attackers.

The book that finally emerged, therefore, devotes most of its attention to these issues. It is directed at both practicing managers and teachers of management, because the changes that have to be made require that both be involved. This can be a tricky business: academics like hard data and lots of footnotes; managers want to get at the heart of the matter quickly and value vignettes that "ring true" with their experience and illuminate their comprehension of things they already subconsciously understand. We have tried to serve both their needs, in the process teaching a little useful theory to the practitioners and some of the nuts and bolts of practice to the theorists.

Most of this book focuses on the *structural* kinds of changes that manufacturing companies have to make—in facilities, locations, manufacturing technologies, and sourcing arrangements. Only in the last few chapters do we devote much attention to *infrastructural* changes: the management policies and practices that enable a manufacturing structure to operate at its full potential. In most companies it is very difficult to disentangle structure from infrastructure, and we hesitated to separate them in this way because, by dealing with structure first, it might imply that these decisions are more important. Infrastructural issues are just as important (in fact, we are devoting most of our current research to these issues), but it is often easier and quicker for a company to make structural changes than changes in its organizational policies and attitudes.

In many respects this book is a collaborative enterprise, in that we were stimulated and tutored by many colleagues, past and present, as well as by literally hundreds of business managers with whom we have come into contact over the years. Where possible we try to indicate clearly who was the source of certain ideas or pieces of data, but in many cases it is unclear to us exactly where a particular insight came from. We would be remiss, however, if we did not acknowledge our debt to certain specific individuals.

First, Professor Wickham Skinner was the first to articulate and propound the concept of "manufacturing strategy." For many years he waged a rather lonely battle to get American managers to understand the difficulties that they were creating for themselves because of their unwillingness to develop and exploit their manufacturing capabilities. Some of his articles, written over a decade ago, are amazingly prescient; one squirms as one compares the problems facing many companies today with those Skinner predicted would occur if the necessary steps were not taken. They weren't and he was right. We are proud to be his students.

The late Professor William Abernathy taught us both much about the technological side of competition. His ideas surface throughout the book, particularly its second half. Also, much of Chapter 1 is drawn from things that he wrote with one of us: two working papers (which later were compressed into a *Harvard Business Review* article, "Managing Our Way to Economic Decline"), and two short articles in *The New York Times:* "Results Now: Pay Later?" and "Management Minus Invention."

Similarly, several of the ideas contained in Chapters 2, 3, and 4 derive from research conducted by Professor Roger Schmenner. In particular, Chapter 2 is based partially on a working paper that he wrote with one of us, which later became a *Harvard Business Review* article entitled "How Should You Organize Manufacturing?" A section of Chapter 10 similarly is based partially on a short *New York Times* article, "The Technology Gap," written with Professor Modesto Maidique; and much of Chapter 11 is drawn from a working paper written with Dr. Joseph Limprecht of the U.S. State Department (an edited version of which appeared in the *Harvard Business Review* as "Germany's World Class Manufacturers").

We also want to acknowledge the extent to which we have benefited from the insight and perspectives of Professors Kim Clark, Richard Rosenbloom, and Earl Sasser, and many others. This latter group includes the many MBA students and executives that we have taught over the years. Most of them took our courses because they thought they would learn something from us; what we tried to hide from them was that often we were learning more from them.

This reciprocal learning relationship was especially valuable in the case of the General Electric Company. Our work with its manufacturing development program, IMPACT, covered the same span of time as the writing of this book. We were challenged by GE's top management to help design a program that would change significantly the contribution that their manufacturing organizations could make to the success of their various businesses, and challenged by GE's manufacturing managers to help them deal with the organizational realities of their positions. This dual challenge forced us to continually sharpen, revise, and find ways to illustrate the ideas in this book. We owe special thanks to these managers, as well as those in many other firms, who allowed us to use their organizations (despite some initial skepticism) as research and test sites for many of the concepts presented here.

Finally, we must confess the tremendous debt we owe our secretaries, Sally Markham and Romayne Ponleithner. Again and again, usually under considerable pressure (which would not have been necessary if only we had met our own deadlines), they converted our half-legible scribblings into clean copy. Even the prospect of retyping something that they had just retyped a couple of weeks previously only rarely dampened their cheerfulness. They have been wonderful colleagues and cheerleaders.

ROBERT H. HAYES
STEVEN C. WHEELWRIGHT

Boston, Massachusetts
Stanford, California
March 1984

Contents

1

The New Competitive Challenge for Manufacturing

1-1 TAKING STOCK

As the 1970s evolved into the 1980s, American society experienced a deepening sense of malaise. During what had promised to be "the sizzling seventies," the United States had encountered a series of jolts—some external and some self-inflicted—that eroded both its role in the world and its self-image. Its industrial sector was of particular concern. In 1971, imports of manufactured goods into the United States exceeded manufactured exports for the first time in almost a century, and this imbalance persisted for 10 of the next 12 years. The U.S. dollar had weakened against most foreign currencies as inflation rose to double digits for the first time since the end of World War II. Several of the country's key industries were sent reeling by the onslaught of foreign competition.

One measure appeared to summarize the economic problems faced by the United States: the productivity of its private sector. After rising at an average rate of about 3 percent per year since World War II, U.S. productivity essentially stopped growing after 1976. As a result, the unit labor cost in the private sector increased more than 25 percent between 1976 and 1981. This deterioration in America's productivity growth rate—compared both with historical experience and with the current rates of its major foreign competitors—fueled inflation, undermined the country's ability to compete in international markets, and, ultimately, constrained improvements in its standard of living. Moreover, it called into question some of the basic attitudes and approaches that governed the way Americans managed their companies and their economic affairs.

1

This concern persisted even during the economic recovery that began in 1983, because this recovery was unlikely to have a long-term positive impact on U.S. manufacturers' competitive position in worldwide markets. U.S. inflation rates had dropped substantially, but so had those of other developed countries, and the strengthening of the dollar served to weaken U.S. manufacturers' relative cost position both domestically and in major foreign markets. Further, in many high-technology markets such as semiconductors, computers, and consumer electronics, where the United States traditionally had felt most secure, it was encountering significant challenges. Even labor productivity, despite its surge during the early stages of the economic recovery, showed little evidence of a sustained improvement.

Productivity, a concept that is almost as hard to explain as it is to measure, typically is calculated by dividing a country's (or an industry's) "output," adjusted for inflation, by the number of labor hours required to create it. Despite its imperfections as a measure of economic efficiency, Americans have used it for more than 30 years to monitor the vitality of their private sector. This is because the growth in labor productivity is a useful indicator of an economy's international competitiveness and long-term prospects, both of which affect the general sense of well-being of its people. A decline in this sense of well-being can profoundly alter a country's view of itself and its future. Ultimately it can unleash major destabilizing forces.

Americans were genuinely puzzled and dismayed to see large, powerful U.S. companies in a variety of industries suddenly struggling to compete with foreign producers—particularly since most of these new competitors were offering products that had originated in the United States. For example, by 1983 Japanese television manufacturers dominated several U.S. market segments even though many U.S. producers enjoyed the same low labor cost advantages of "offshore" production. Similarly, German machine tool and automotive producers continued their inroads into U.S. domestic markets even as their labor rates rose above those in the United States, and despite the fact that more than 20 percent of the famed German workers in German factories were non-German immigrants from southern Europe, Turkey, and northern Africa.

Why did the United States appear to be losing its vitality and capacity for organic growth? The usual explanations included (1) the growth of governmental regulation, taxes, and other forms of intrusion into business affairs; (2) a deterioration in the American work ethic which, combined with an adversary relationship between labor and business, had produced crippling strikes, inflexible work rules, and wage increases not justified by productivity increases; (3) interruptions in the supply, and rapid increases in the prices, of various forms of energy since the first OPEC oil shock in 1973; (4) a massive influx of new people into the workforce—teenagers, women, and minority groups—who had to be conditioned to work in an industrial environment and trained in new skills; and (5) the advent of unusually high capital costs brought on in part by high rates of inflation.

Some of these arguments lost their persuasiveness, however, when it was recognized that (1) the stagnation of American productivity growth predated the advent of certain of these "causes," and (2) most of the factors blamed for the U.S.'s economic deterioration operated just as powerfully in Europe and Japan. In fact, European managers looked to the United States as a land of relative freedom and opportunity! Yet Europe's productivity growth rate did not fall nearly as much during the 1970s as did that of the United States; in Germany and Belgium it actually increased during that decade, to well over 4 percent per year.

As one confronted the arguments and counterarguments and sifted the evidence for clues, it became apparent that one other variable could well be a key factor—management itself. American managers, in important ways, manage their firms differently from their European and Japanese counterparts. They have had different goals; they have made different assumptions about how competitors will react; and they have used different techniques in implementing their decisions.

Since World War II, the United States had taken for granted the superiority of its technology and management practices. This complacency (one might go so far as to call it arrogance) tended to blind U.S. managers, at least until the late 1970s, to the rapid improvements taking place elsewhere. It kept them from studying other countries or from making fundamental changes in their own approaches. The shock of suddenly discovering that the United States might not be the repository for all the best and the brightest approaches to managing either individual companies or the national economy undoubtedly contributed to American society's sense of malaise and its business community's loss of confidence.

Studies of manufacturing firms in a variety of countries have persuaded us that the economic problems facing U.S. companies in the 1980s—and particularly the productivity problem—have been due less to foreign pressure and governmental interference than to some critical weaknesses in the way that U.S. managers have guided their companies. These weaknesses have called into question some of the basic assumptions and practices that govern the way many top U.S. manufacturing companies have reacted to their strategic challenges.

We want to emphasize that these kinds of problems have not been uniquely American. They have afflicted manufacturing companies in all countries, although some countries (and some industries) seem to have been more susceptible to them than others. Therefore, while the U.S. situation, and our perspective on it, is used as the basic setting for this book, the ideas and approaches we discuss are applicable to manufacturing firms around the world. Wherever possible, therefore, examples are drawn from non–U.S. firms to complement those drawn from U.S. companies.

Our emphasis throughout is less on specific tools and techniques, which tend to be sensitive to cultural differences, than on an overall framework for thinking about the management of a firm's manufacturing function. Companies too often have treated manufacturing decisions on an ad hoc basis, as a series of technical problems that can be surmounted one by one without regard for the linkages between them. Such an approach may result in the creation of serviceable buildings, but it will not create manufacturing organizations that can endure and prevail against competitors whose every action is guided by an underlying consistency of purpose—a philosophy of competing through manufacturing.

1-2   PRODUCTIVITY AND INDUSTRIAL VIGOR— THE PROBLEM IN PERSPECTIVE

Contrary to popular belief, the rate of U.S. productivity growth did not drop suddenly during the late 1970s. It had been declining for roughly 15 years. Articles describing America's "long-term productivity problem" had appeared in business-oriented journals as early as 1971. For several years the decline had been dismissed as a consequence of the Vietnam War and the dislocations and recession that followed it. Then people blamed the 1973–1974 oil crisis and the dislocations and depression that followed that.

Such widely accepted explanations came under suspicion, however, in the late 1970s. In 1974–1975 the United States embarked on almost four years of relative stability and prosperity, during which its rate of growth and apparent economic prosperity surpassed those of most of its major European competitors. Still its rate of productivity growth declined, not only in absolute terms but also in relation to that of other countries. In the U.S. economy's manufacturing sector, which historically had experienced a higher rate of productivity growth than other sectors, the rate of increase collapsed from more than 3.5 percent per year in the mid-1960s to negative growth in 1979, 1980, and 1982.

The decline in the rate of productivity growth was not confined to just one or two economic sectors, as some believed; it was observed in almost every economic sector. If government intervention (through, for example, pollution control legislation and health and safety regulations), restrictions imposed by organized labor, and increases in energy costs were the primary causes of America's productivity slowdown, it might be expected that the greatest productivity decline would have occurred in the heavy manufacturing sector. In fact, the decline there was only slightly greater than the decline in light manufacturing, and neither manufacturing sector experienced as severe a decline as did wholesale and retail trade—a sector that was subject to less government intervention, used less energy, and was less heavily unionized.

Two other indicators of economic vigor warned of problems: investment in new capital equipment and investment in research and development. Neither type of investment actually decreased. Both, in fact, appeared to be increasing nicely until adjustments were made for inflation, for changes in the size of the workforce, or for increases in real GNP. Then the trends became more ominous.

For example, the ratio of the net book value of capital equipment to the number of labor hours worked had increased at a rate of about 3 percent per year between 1948 and 1973. In the decade following 1973—owing in part to the rising price of energy and world recession—it grew at only about 1 percent. Moreover, during the late 1970s the composition of investment shifted toward equipment and relatively short-term projects, and away from structures and other relatively long-lived investments. As a result, the U.S. industrial plant was slowly aging. In contrast, during the same period capital investment as a percentage of GNP in France and West Germany was more than 20 percent greater than that in the United States, and Japan's rate was almost double the United States'.

The significance of these trends was becoming apparent to many observers, regardless of their political persuasion. Economist Martin Feldstein (1981), who is usually placed to the right of the political center, worried that

> the rate of net investment is not only very low by international standards, but has fallen sharply in recent years. In the second half of the 1960s, the U.S. devoted 4.2% of GNP to increasing the stock of plant and equipment. By the second half of the 1970s, the investment share had fallen by 40% to only 2.6% of GNP.

And economist Lester Thurow (1981) from his left-of-center position added:

> In the U.S. the average employee works with $50,000 worth of plant and equipment. This means each new entrant into the labor force must be equipped with $50,000 worth of capital if he is to reach the average productivity level. If Americans decide to have a baby boom, as they did in the 1950s and early 1960s, they are making an implicit promise that they will, approximately 20 years later . . . cut their consumption and provide each of those babies with the $50,000 in plant and equipment he or she needs to enter the workforce as a productive worker. It is this implicit promise that Americans are failing to keep.

Spending on research and development (R&D) presented an equally depressing picture. Measured as a percentage of GNP, after reaching a high point in 1964 total U.S. investment in R&D had been on a downward trend for 15 years. This decline was due primarily to a drastic cutback in government-sponsored R&D, but private industry had failed to fill the void. In fact, as a percentage of GNP, industry-sponsored R&D fell slightly from its level of the late 1960s. Investment in basic research, which involved longer time horizons (typically more than 12 years between investment and initial payback), presented an even bleaker picture. In constant dollars, this investment peaked in the late 1960s, then dipped and did not regain its earlier level until 1978. By 1978 American companies were spending only two-thirds as much on basic R&D, as a percentage of GNP, as they had spent in the mid-1960s. During the same period, the percentage of GNP expended on R&D by West Germany and Japan continued to rise.

The number of patents granted in the United States also peaked in the early 1970s, and the "balance of patents" between the United States and most other developed countries deteriorated. By the early 1980s more patents were being granted in the United States to West German and Japanese firms than were being granted in West Germany and Japan to U.S. firms.

The vitality of one critical industry, machine tools, is of particular interest because it reflects the development and adoption of new process technology, while comparative export figures indicate the competitiveness of such technology. By 1981 the U.S. machine tool industry had fallen behind West Germany's in terms of total size and annual exports. As a percentage of GNP, it also ranked well below those of Japan, Italy, France, and the United Kingdom.

The common link behind such trends did not appear to be a lack of capital induced by lower profitability, high taxes, or government-required nonproductive expenditures (pollution control, safety, etc.). The inflation-adjusted return on equity of American business during the 1970s was roughly equal to what it had been during the 1950s, when spending on net capital equipment and R&D had been significantly higher as a percentage of GNP (Malkiel, 1979). What had changed was the ratio of shareholder dividends to total corporate operating cash flow (profit after tax plus depreciation), which was 30 percent higher in 1980 than it had been in the late 1960s. Moreover, the ratio of the amount invested in new capital equipment to corporate cash flow had edged downward since 1970, while the percentage spent on acquisitions almost quadrupled between 1971 and 1981, to more than $80 billion. The problem was not that U.S. business did not have the money to spend; it simply was not spending its money the way it used to.

1-3   THE ROLE OF MANAGEMENT IN DECLINING U.S. PRODUCTIVITY

The preceding sections provide a small part of the evidence that the decline in productivity growth in the United States has been both broadbased and deepseated. Several studies have failed to show much connection between this decline and forces external to individual firms (such as demographic changes or government regulation). Nor was it easy to explain why productivity continued to grow in other countries that faced similar external forces. Therefore, we are driven to consider another hypothesis: a significant part of the problem has been due to *internal* factors—the practices and policies that American managers have followed in managing their companies.

Productivity is a useful way of measuring the efficiency with which resources are consumed in producing goods and services, and that efficiency is primarily a management responsibility. Managers can increase efficiency through a combination of three basic approaches:

1. **Short term.** Use existing assets more efficiently on existing products; this requires toughness, determination, and attention to detail.

2. **Medium term.** Substitute a new set of resources for existing ones—such as equipment for labor, or high-skilled labor for less-skilled labor; this requires capital and willingness to take financial risks.
3. **Long term.** Develop new products and processes that readdress the same sequence of decisions at a higher level of productivity; this requires both imagination and daring.

Historically, U.S. managers had been greatly respected because of their aggressiveness along all three dimensions. During the early 1980s, although there was little criticism of their continued toughness and attention to short-term performance, Hayes and Abernathy (1980), Malkiel (1979, 1981), Reich (1983), and others, called into question U.S. managers' performance along the second and third dimensions.

It was somewhat surprising, however, to find that most of the prescriptions that economists such as Malkiel, or public policy analysts such as Reich, proposed for dealing with these problems were confined primarily to proposals for changes in the policies and practices of the U.S. government. Even those who did not believe that government was largely to blame for declining productivity were uneasy about entrusting the task of turning the situation around to that same government.

Our position is that the productivity decline in the United States has been more a management problem than a government problem. European managers (who bewail their lot at the hands of their own governments with just as much vigor, and at least as much justification, as do U.S. managers) have been increasingly critical of many American management practices. One commented that the U.S. companies in his industry acted like banks. "All they are interested in," he said, "is return on investment and getting their money back. In fact, sometimes they act like they are more interested in buying other companies than they are in selling products to customers."

Mr. Ryohei Suzuki of the Japan Trade Center (1979) reflected a similar view:

> Somehow or other, American business is losing confidence in itself, and especially confidence in its future. Instead of meeting the challenge of the changing world, American business today is making small, short-term adjustments by cutting costs and by turning to the government for temporary relief . . . Success in trade is the result of patient and meticulous preparations, with a long period of market preparation before the rewards are available . . . To undertake such commitments is hardly in the interest of a manager who is concerned with his or her next quarterly earnings report.

Although government policies that overconstrained or undersupported U.S. producers may have contributed to these problems, their long-term solution is not likely to be based on changing government tax laws, monetary policies, and regulatory practices, getting unions to "be more reasonable," or developing alternative energy sources. Instead, it will require fundamental changes in certain management attitudes and practices that have undermined American companies' ability to use technological strength—the ability to produce better products using better manufacturing processes—as a competitive weapon.

1-4 THE ROLE OF MODERN MANAGEMENT APPROACHES

It is unlikely that U.S. managers suddenly underwent some kind of profound psychological shift toward a "supersafe, no-risk" mind-set during the 1970s. This change in their behavior, we believe, is due to the fact that since the late 1950s U.S. managers have been adopting a new set of theories, replacing the conventional wisdom that underlay the management attitudes and practices prevailing earlier. These theories, and the techniques that emanated from them (usually referred to as "modern management approaches"), have permeated most of the management textbooks written in the United States since 1960, just as they currently permeate the curricula of most American business schools. At least three of these modern management approaches—organization and control theory, financial portfolio theory, and the "marketing concept"—have received disproportionate attention from practitioners and academics alike.

It is important to note that, despite the almost wholesale adoption of these theories and their extensions within the United States, many are viewed with profound mistrust by European and Japanese managers, who refer to them as "modern *American* management approaches." (Their only foothold abroad, if anywhere, has been in Great Britain.) These foreign critics suggest that this new management orthodoxy may have been a major factor in the deterioration of U.S. economic health—just as certain medicines that make one feel good for a short time can destroy one's physical health if used over too long a period. Pursuit of these modern management approaches has led American manufacturing companies to:

1. Emphasize analytical detachment and strategic elegance over hands-on experience and well-managed line operations.
2. Focus on short-term results rather than longer-term goals and capabilities.
3. Emphasize the management of marketing and financial resources at the expense of manufacturing and technological resources.

Over time, these changes in emphasis have eroded both the inclination and the capacity of American manufacturing companies to compete on the basis of technological superiority. Exploring some of these modern management approaches in detail will illustrate the subtle ways in which such shifts in emphasis have occurred.

1-4.1 Organization and Control Theory

Although "organization and control theory" comprises an extraordinarily broad set of issues, three ideas have been central to its use in U.S. firms: decentralized profit center–based organizations, management evaluation based primarily on financial measures, and "fast-track" career paths.

Profit Center Organizations

Modern management control theory has encouraged the adoption of organizational structures based on a number of relatively autonomous profit centers. Like any other organizational form, those built around a collection of profit centers are good at certain things and weak at others. On the good side, they are highly flexible—capable of responding quickly to growing markets, particularly when those markets are expanding geographically. They also tend to be very responsive to changes in consumer needs and competitive actions, and are effective at transmitting technology (product or process) that has been developed centrally, throughout the organization. Hence, profit center organizations tend to develop broad product lines with a host of incremental product improvements to meet the specialized needs of a number of small market segments. In short, this kind of organizational structure might be expected to have been effective during the late 1950s and early 1960s, when U.S. firms were growing rapidly (both geographically and through product line expansion) and most new technology was developed in the United States.

Unfortunately, such structures tend to be less effective when confronted with the need to make major product or process changes that cannibalize existing products and render existing assets obsolete. Many companies that have adopted profit center organizations have found that they have to overlay them with a centralized R&D activity whose purpose is to pursue the fundamental technological developments that are often slighted by profit center managers. But, since these new R&D projects seldom have "champions" in the line organization, they often find it difficult to get corporate headquarters to back them financially or to persuade profit center managers to bring them to market.

Worse, profit center organizations induce a peculiar kind of top management behavior. Profit center managers typically are required to submit comprehensive annual, quarterly, and often monthly reports on the performance of their operations. The problem for top management is how to evaluate all these data, particularly when they encompass 30–40 (not an unusual number for a billion-dollar company) profit centers in different parts of the world, operating in different economic environments, often in different industries. The usual reaction when top managers have little firsthand knowledge of the industry, technology, or geographic region in which a profit center manager operates has been to focus attention almost exclusively on financial results, particularly on "the bottom line"—the net profit for the period and the rate of return on the capital invested in that center.

Of course, profit center managers, aware of their superiors' preoccupation with these short-term financial results, have tended to react in predictable ways. This can be seen more clearly after identifying some of the other factors that influence the managers of these profit centers.

The rapid economic growth that characterized the 20 years after World War II, coupled with widespread adoption of profit center organizations and the relative shortage of well-trained general managers during this period (resulting from the low prewar birthrate and the interruptions in education and management development caused by the war), made it necessary for many companies to reduce the time required for a young manager to rise to general manager responsibilities. Compressing this time period, while still giving managers a variety of managerial experiences, led to the concept of the "fast track": a manager who was identified as a "comer" typically would spend only a year and a half to three years on a given assignment before moving up in the organization. This necessity, born of unusual economic and demographic circumstances, became the *norm,* so that young, ambitious managers came to feel that if they were not promoted within two to three years, they should look elsewhere for opportunities.

There have been two sides to this problem, both of them bad. On the one hand, managers tended to move rapidly from job to job, and even from company to company, before they had a chance to gain in-depth experience and before the long-term consequences of their managerial decisions had become evident. On the other hand, in comparison with companies in other countries, U.S. companies have made little commitment to their managers. In other words, managers have developed little company loyalty and in-depth experience, and companies have failed to provide the security that would encourage the learning and long-term thinking that are essential if technological capabilities are to be developed and deployed effectively.

European and Japanese managers have been astounded at the job-hopping they have observed in the United States. As one Japanese observer (Suzuki, 1979) put it:

> From my vantage point of lifetime employment, they seem to come and go and switch around as if playing a game of musical chairs at an "Alice in Wonderland" tea party. This surely must encourage the present tendency to avoid the burdens of long-term decisions and risks.

Another factor affecting the behavior of profit center managers has been compensation systems. In the United States, a major part of the total compensation received by top managers comes from bonuses based on near-term performance: last year's profits, last year's sales growth, last year's return on investment, and so forth. In contrast, in Japan bonuses based on recent performance constitute a large portion of the total compensation of *workers* (since their job is to maximize the productiveness of the assets provided them). Only small performance bonuses have been given to top managers—both because the status and perquisites provided them have been considered adequate and because of the strong desire to *avoid* the pressure to maximize short-term results.

Financial Measures of Managerial Performance

If the profit centers of U.S. companies were really "minicompanies," it seems logical that one should be able to evaluate their performance in the same way that the financial community has traditionally evaluated the performance of independent companies: through their quarterly financial reports. A corporate profit center is more difficult to evaluate, however, because it is not truly independent. Performance measurement is complicated by transfer prices, corporate charges, and bilateral agreements between corporate headquarters and the managers of the profit center. Yet the theory appears to make sense—until, that is, one examines its operation in practice.

If improving return on investment (ROI) is your goal, you may pursue it either by increasing the numerator of the equation (profit), which can be difficult and take a long time, or by decreasing the denominator (investment), which often is easier to do and takes less time. A profit center manager, who knows that he or she may not be in that position for more than a few years, is likely to focus considerable attention on the denominator. Note, for example, that if a profit center's normal tax rate is 50 percent, reducing its investment base by 10 percent has about the same impact on ROI as a 20 percent increase in profits before tax (achieved through, say, a 20 percent reduction in costs).

Reducing investment can be done in a variety of ways. The most obvious is to delay replacing old equipment, whose book value is low, with new equipment. Other, less obvious ways are to allow the performance of equipment to deteriorate by reducing maintenance or by replacing machinery, as it wears out, with less-productive (and usually less-expensive) equipment. Or, one can gradually obsolete a manufacturing process by persistently replacing worn-out equipment with machinery that is based on the same technology, rather than with machinery that incorporates newer technology. If one defines a firm's "capital stock" to encompass the earnings-generating capacity of its previous investments in R&D, advertising, and personnel development as well, a deterioration in this capital stock can result from reductions in spending, below historical standards, in any of these areas.

John Dearden discussed many of these problems in greater detail in his classic 1969 article, "The Case Against ROI Control." These brief excerpts summarize his argument:

> Many division managers will be reluctant to propose capital investments that do not have a rapid early payback, especially those who expect to be moved to another job within a few years . . . [also] it may take several years to evaluate a manager responsible for new product innovations . . . Because of the technical limitations of the ROI system, its use can result in serious mistakes unless the top managers are intimately familiar with division op-

erations. This familiarity is really the only adequate defense against the dysfunctional aspects of ROI.

Unfortunately, the very familiarity with divisional operations that Dearden felt to be so important was undermined during the 1960s and 1970s by the changing backgrounds of corporate managers and the rapid diversification of U.S. companies.

Top corporate executives have pointed to yet another reason for their preoccupation with short-term results: pressure from the financial community in general, and from investment fund managers in particular. To preserve the option of selling stock in order to raise additional capital, they reason, a company should cultivate the interest and respect of the people who manage the large funds. And how, in turn, are these investment fund managers evaluated and rewarded? Largely on the basis of the recent (six months to a year or two) performance of their funds, of course! Ironically, the net result of this natural desire of corporate managers to please the financial community appears to have been a deterioration in their price–earnings ratios throughout the 1970s.

Developing, Evaluating, and Rewarding Managers

The incentives for American managers have been shifting in a very important way since the 1960s. The "road to the top" formerly threaded up through the corporation with stops in several functional areas. This gave potential executives the opportunity to work in various departments and thus learn the details of their business. This approach to executive development had changed drastically by 1970, however. In the business community, as in academia, the concept of the "professional manager" took hold. Such a person was expected to be able, without special expertise in any particular market or technology, to step into an unfamiliar company or division and run it effectively. Industry expertise gained from in-depth experience acquired a "nonprogressive" stigma.

At the same time, American companies increasingly turned to people with financial, accounting, and legal backgrounds to fill their top positions. By the late 1970s the percentage of newly appointed CEOs with such backgrounds in the 100 largest U.S. corporations was up 50 percent from its level 30 years earlier. As a result, correspondingly fewer had hands-on experience in the more competitively oriented functions such as marketing, production, and engineering. The absolute change in numbers has not been as important as the change in attitude precipitated by this trend. Young managers searching for ways to get ahead tended to choose jobs and career paths that they perceived to be on the road to the top. If this road appeared to emphasize staff assignments, the best were attracted to staff positions.

In addition, top U.S. executives increasingly have been promoted into their positions from outside the company. As a result, they often have lacked sensitivity toward or insight about the consumers their companies serviced and the technologies upon which their products and processes were based. They were very different from top executives in Europe or Japan, where long-term involvement within the same company or division was generally the rule.

What kinds of philosophies and management practices did this new generation of managers sweep in with them as they began to dominate the competition for the top jobs? Three of the bedrock principles often espoused by this new breed of self-styled "professional managers" have been especially influential:

1. The top corporate manager, first and foremost, had to be a skilled strategist, able to cut through the complexities of messy problems while standing aloof from the nitty-gritty details that were the lot of the line manager.

2. The primary job of the senior executive was to oversee the complex *processes* and *systems* involved in managing a large organization: resource allocation, personnel assignment, compensation, and control. Specific, firsthand knowledge of an industry, or a technology, or of the competitive environment for specific products was less important.

3. Quickness and decisiveness were the keys to success. The most-admired executive was one who could move quickly in repositioning the company's assets, getting into attractive businesses and out of "losers" (like a portfolio manager of stocks and bonds), who could orchestrate a takeover or a divestment with equal aplomb.

This new philosophy of management led naturally to a new concept of the corporation.

1-4.2   The Concept of Corporate Portfolios

In the 1960s, U.S. corporate management increasingly exercised its expanding financial and legal skills. Senior managers spent a growing share of their time and resources in identifying and negotiating acquisition opportunities, learning to run unfamiliar businesses, fighting unwelcome merger attempts, and divesting business lines that were unprofitable or "didn't fit." Because of such outside interests, they had less time, and perhaps less interest, in deliberating critical internal decisions that involved complex technological and market tradeoffs.

Sadly, much (probably most) of this merger activity appears to have been wasted in terms of generating economic benefits to shareholders. Recent research has started to raise serious questions about the long-run value of very aggressive acquisition strategies. For example, Professor William Fruhan's empirically based, retrospective study (1979) of the financial returns from a variety of highly "creative" financial acquisition strategies showed very disappointing long-run returns to the shareholders. The 72 firms that Fruhan identified as *most* successful in long-range financial terms seemed to be characterized as powerful competitors in a small number of highly focused product

Table 1-1

Yardstick of Management Performance

(five-year averages)

	Return on Equity	Return on Total Capital	Sales Growth Rate
Conglomerates[a]	14.0	9.2	10.8
Multicompanies[b]	12.6	10.1	9.9
All industry medians	15.1	11.0	13.1

Source. Forbes Magazine, January 7, 1980.
[a]Examples: Gulf & Western, LTV, Tenneco, Textron, W. R. Grace, Rockwell International, IT&T, and Litton Industries.
[b]Examples: General Electric, Union Carbide, Bendix, FMC, Borg-Warner, and Westinghouse.

markets. Similarly, the five-year averages for growth, return on assets, and return on equity for 69 highly diversified firms listed in *Forbes Magazine*'s 1980 study (see Table 1-1) suggested that performance on all three measures was actually *degraded* by diversification, particularly unrelated diversification. The same pattern was reported in 1981, 1982 and 1983.

Why have senior executives spent so much of their time and energy on what may be an essentially valueless activity? The answer is threefold at least. First, it is natural for a financially (or legally) oriented CEO to concentrate primarily on financially and legally oriented activities. Second, it reduces total corporate riskiness—as perceived by management, although not necessarily as perceived by shareholders. Third, it is exciting and fun and attracts a lot of publicity and admiration in the business community. The moves in the game are bold and well-defined, the results quickly apparent and seemingly decisive. For such activities the financial community has awarded titles like "gunslingers," "white knights," and "black knights." In contrast, trying to win out through technological superiority in a long, tough, competitive game is much less glamorous or amenable to decisive and dramatic moves.

Despite the obvious appeal of such activities, over the long term they can seriously degrade a company's ability to compete. A basic fallacy underlies them all, the notion that there is no need to invest, build, or develop anything yourself. Given the capital and good (financial) management, anything of value can be bought and any problem can be divested, according to this view. A sense of commitment—to one's workers, customers, suppliers, even one's fellow managers—is an impediment. If something doesn't work, don't try to fix it—get rid of it and buy something else "off the shelf."

Stated so blatantly, such a belief seems naive and callous, yet it seems to be a basic American attitude, a heritage of its frontier movement: take up new land and resources, use them up, and move on. What this view fails to recognize, of course, is what European and Japanese critics have pointed out recently. When the frontier is gone, one must develop an environment that nurtures new technologies, opens new markets, and develops more productive people from the existing base.

1-4.3 The "Marketing Concept": Imitative versus Innovative Designs

These changes in management structure and style have subtly undermined many American firms' capacity for innovation. Consider the marketing concept: it suggests that new product ideas should flow from a consumer analysis, or should be tested exhaustively for consumer reaction before being introduced. Not only can such an approach be expensive and time consuming, but evidence is accumulating that it dampens the innovativeness of the products that finally do emerge.

For example, J. Hugh Davidson (1976) analyzed a sample of 100 major new consumer product entries into the U.K. market between 1960 and 1970. These products competed in existing product areas, like the Wilkinson Sword stainless steel razor blade and Polycolor hair color. All were offered through retail food stores, which according to conventional wisdom was a distribution channel where marketing, advertising, and pricing policy reigned supreme and product performance was secondary.

Yet of those that offered better performance to the customer, 74 percent were successful and 20 percent were failures, irrespective of the pricing policy followed. Conversely, of those offering no performance advantages, 80 percent failed and 20 percent succeeded. Davidson concluded that offering "me-too" new products was the primary cause of failure. Why then are so many new products imitative rather than innovative, including 53 percent of Davidson's sample?

Table 1-2 illustrates the tradeoffs that a manager has to make when choosing between innovative and imitative designs. By its very nature innovation is destructive of capital (as Joseph Schumpeter observed long ago), whether capital is in the form of labor skills, management systems, or manufacturing processes and equipment. It makes obsolete existing manufacturing investments, marketing policies, worker skills, and management intuition.

Not every category shown in Table 1-2 applies to every innovation, but many do. Typically, when a manager chooses a more innovative course of action, he or she is electing uncertainty over predictability and unsettled organizational relationships in place of a proven efficient structure. The investment required is likely to be much higher, and several years may elapse before a net profit is obtained.

Another set of data was compiled by Ralph Biggadike (1976), who compared the financial and market performance of 44 new products introduced into established product markets by 20 "Fortune 200" corporations. Among other factors, he contrasted innovative products with imitative products in terms of their return on investment and market share penetration. The average

Table 1-2
Tradeoffs in Choice of Innovative Versus Imitative Product
(for an established product line)

Imitative Model	Innovative Model
Market Factors	
Market demand is relatively well known and predictable.	Potentially large but unpredictable demand; the risk of a flop is also large.
Market recognition and acceptance is rapid.	Market acceptance may be slow initially, but the imitative response of competitors may also be slowed.
Readily adaptable to existing marketing, sales, and distribution policies.	May require unique, tailored marketing, distribution, and sales policies, for example, to educate customers, or because of special repair and warranty problems.
Fits with existing market segmentation and product policies.	Demand may cut across traditional marketing segments, disrupting divisional responsibilities and cannibalizing other products.
Production-Technology Factors	
Affords maximum use of existing facilities, processes, and vertical-integration investments.	Makes obsolete existing labor skills, manufacturing facilities, and vertical integration commitments, while requiring new investments for replacements.
Designs usually can be made compatible with existing product line modularization and standardization strategies.	May undermine successful product standardization and modularization policies.
Facilitates cost reduction through streamlined designs, production rationalization, and increased scale economies.	Unfamiliar technology, high start-up costs, and production uncertainties may conflict with ongoing cost reduction efforts.
Presents minimal manufacturability, product quality, and product liability risks.	Introduces large uncertainties in manufactured operations. Raises unanticipated problems in quality, cost, inventory control, and workforce planning.

Source. Adapted from Hayes and Abernathy, 1980.

results of these two groups, in the first and second of two biannual periods, are summarized in Table 1-3.

A striking feature of these results was the very long period needed to realize a positive return on investment, whether or not the new product was innovative. The relative success of innovative products in achieving market penetration was very pronounced. On the other hand, although their eventual

Table 1-3
Market and Financial Performance of 44 New Products

Measure	Innovative Product		Imitative Product	
	1st Period	2nd Period	1st Period	2nd Period
Market share penetration	62%	73%	13%	9%
Return on investment	−96%	−56%	−43%	−27%
Number of entries	26	18	14	10

Source. Biggadike, 1976.

market share was satisfactory, over the first four years they experienced a return on investment that was twice as negative as that of imitative products. Even though innovative products appear to offer the best long-run prospects, management resistance to their introduction can be understood if the experience of the large corporations in Biggadike's sample is typical.

When one combines the marketing concept with a "results now" ROI-oriented control system, other dangers arise. As two Canadian academics (Bennett and Cooper, 1979) pointed out, most great product innovations—the kind that create new markets and form the basis for new industries—have been the result of a technological triumph, a laboratory discovery, or an invention, rather than a response to an identified market need.

> Often these "great ideas" originated from men and women far removed from customers, from market needs and wants, and from the industry itself . . .

> Inventors, scientists, engineers, and academics, in the normal pursuit of scientific knowledge, gave the world the telephone, the phonograph, the electric light, and in more recent times the laser, xerography, instant photography, and the transistor. In contrast, worshipers of the marketing concept have bestowed upon mankind such products as newfangled potato chips, feminine hygiene deodorant, and the pet rock . . .

> Picture the would-be market researcher eighty years ago attempting to gauge market reaction to a proposed new product, the automobile. Respondents to any questionnaire would have assured the market-oriented innovator that cars would frighten horses, make too much noise, run too fast, and be generally unreliable. The competition of that time, the horse, would be judged just too strong for a potential market entry . . . Had it not been for tough-minded innovators and entrepreneurs who were driven by a vision of what they believed and who persisted in spite of negative market reaction, the automobile might never have come of age as quickly as it did . . . And the more innovative the product, the worse the problem.

We do not mean to imply that technology-driven product innovation is always better than market-driven innovation; a balance of the two is necessary.

Excessive reliance on a market-driven strategy, without sufficient attention to its limitations, implies opting for customer satisfaction and lower risk in the short run at the expense of superior products and market penetration in the long run.

Satisfying customers is critically important, of course, but not if the strategy for creating them is also responsible for unnecessary product proliferation, inflated costs, unfocused diversification, and a lagging commitment to new technology and new capital equipment. Customers may think they know what their needs are, but they often define those needs in terms of existing products, uses, markets, and prices. Those who listen *only* to customers slowly slip into an incremental, "me-too" mind-set.

1-4.4   Investing in Process Development

A lack of detailed familiarity with manufacturing technology and overreliance on buying solutions to manufacturing problems have led many companies to reduce their commitment to developing their own proprietary processes. This has further weakened the competitive position of many U.S. firms. When asked whether they invest in the development of new manufacturing processes, many U.S. managers—even those in very large firms—often have replied: "We can't afford to design new capital equipment just for our own manufacturing needs," or "The capital equipment producers develop much better designs and they can amortize their development costs over sales to many companies," or "Let others experiment in equipment manufacturing; we can buy it from them after they have gotten all the bugs out."

The rationale behind these arguments has been that essential advances in process technology can be appropriated through equipment purchase rather than through equipment design and skill development, that is, through learning by doing. This argument ignores the fact that if new products are produced with the firm's existing process technology—the same "cookie cutter" that everyone else can buy—the lead time for competitors who want to imitate and introduce a competing product is shortened. Proprietary processes are just as formidable competitive weapons as proprietary products, and more enduring competitive barriers are created when a firm couples product innovation with process innovation.

The U.S. companies that did invest in internal process development generally emphasized investments that reduced cost, displaced high-cost labor, or increased output, and therefore were able to evaluate such investment proposals using traditional capital budgeting evaluation methods. Our research suggests that U.S. managers have not paid sufficient attention (in comparison with their foreign competitors) to other important forms of process investment: those that would enhance their firm's ability to develop new products or improve other characteristics of an existing product, such as its quality or uniqueness.

The importance of internal process development has been supported by von Hipple's (1975) studies of industrial innovation, which showed that the innovations that led to new industrial equipment usually originated with the *user* of the equipment, not with the equipment producer. Olsen's investigation of the textile industry (1974) also suggested that the most innovative and successful companies were those which invested most heavily in advanced manufacturing capability.

How do U.S. firms compare with their foreign competitors in this regard? Recent interviews with managers of competitively successful technology-based German and Japanese firms have identified a strong pattern of commitment to the development of advanced process technology. Most of these firms designed and built critical elements of their own process equipment, and they have gained competitive advantage from unique products that depend upon proprietary developments in process technology, even though German and Japanese equipment suppliers are vigorous and responsive.

The apparent anemia of the U.S. machine tool industry in the 1970s may not stem entirely from its own lack of innovative vitality. It may also result from the lethargy of machine tool users who have not actively explored ways to improve their own manufacturing capability. This interpretation would be consistent with von Hippel's findings and explain the apparent paradox in German industry, where producers' emphasis on making their own capital equipment seems to have *strengthened* the German machine tool industry.

1-5 SUMMARY

The foregoing concerns about the internal causes of slowing industrial competitiveness in the United States and about the role of "modern management practices" can be summarized around five main points:

1. Financial considerations (and particularly short-term financial considerations based on such measures as ROI) have tended to dominate the thinking of U.S. managers much more than they have influenced the decisions of managers in other countries.

2. U.S. managers have been less sophisticated and imaginative in dealing with technological considerations than many of their international competitors. Many have focused their attention on financial and marketing issues. In so doing, they have mounted their competitive assaults on a two-legged stool, so to speak. Technology has its own inner logic and imperatives; it cannot be analyzed "in general."

3. U.S. managers have tended to separate complicated issues into simpler, specialized ones to a greater degree than their foreign counterparts. The object of organizational design, of course, is to divide responsibilities in such a way that individuals have relatively simple tasks to perform. But these differentiated responsibilities must be pulled together by sophisticated, broadly gauged integrators who can deal with the total picture. If these top managers are trained only in one or two areas or, worse, are simplifiers themselves, who will do the integrating? Who will resolve complicated issues instead of trying to "uncomplicate" them? A process technology decision is no more a "pure production problem" than a corporate merger is a "pure financial problem."

4. The U.S. penchant for separating and simplifying has led many American firms to diversify away from their core technologies and markets to a much greater degree than do European or Japanese firms (or, indeed than do the most successful U.S. corporations). U.S. managers apparently have accepted the validity of the portfolio "law of large numbers"—that if one amasses enough product lines, technologies, and businesses, one will be cushioned against the random setbacks that occur in life. This might be true for portfolios of stocks and bonds, where there is considerable evidence that setbacks are random. Businesses, however, are subject not only to random setbacks (strikes, shortages, etc.) but also to carefully orchestrated attacks by competitors who are focusing all their resources and energies on one set of activities in order to achieve a lasting competitive advantage.

5. There appears to have been a tacit agreement between firms in a number of important U.S. manufacturing industries over the past 15–20 years to compete primarily on dimensions other than manufacturing ability. The United States thought it had, as John Kenneth Galbraith (1958) phrased it, "solved the problem of production." Therefore, attention and resources have been directed toward mass distribution, packaging, advertising, and the development of incremental new products to round out existing product lines or to attack specific market segments, instead of toward improving manufacturing capabilities.

As a result, U.S. plants and equipment have been allowed to age. The country's technological advantage has been eroded by the decline in expenditures for new product R&D and for new processing technologies. The best managerial talent has been directed toward "fast tracks" that often ignored or excluded direct manufacturing experience. At the same time, promotions to top corporate positions increasingly have favored those who specialized in finance, marketing, accounting, or law.

For years this aging of plants and equipment and the adoption of the fast track as the route to the top did not seem to impair the competitiveness of most U.S. manufacturing firms. Then, beginning in the 1970s, they suddenly found themselves pitted against companies who *did* compete on such mundane dimensions as defect-free products, process innovation, and delivery dependability. Increasingly, they found themselves displaced, first in international markets and then in their home market as well. The recognition of their apparent vulnerability came as a shock to many American managers, who began to seek equally quick and dramatic "solutions"—preferably those that were easy to copy, such as quality circles, governmental assistance, and robotics.

1-6 OVERVIEW OF THIS BOOK

It would be an oversimplification to assert that the decline in the competitiveness of U.S. manufacturing companies has been due to the fact that their managers, under the influence of a few modern theories of management, have devoted too much of their attention and energy to the first of the three approaches for improving efficiency (utilizing existing resources more efficiently), and neglected the second and third approaches. It would also oversimplify the issue, although possibly to a lesser extent, to say that American manufacturers have fallen behind because they have neglected technology as a competitive weapon.

It would be more accurate, but possibly less quotable, to say that they have lost sight of the need to understand the complex interplay and tradeoffs between *all* the participants in the "productive confederation" of manufacturers, customers, competitors, materials suppliers, and equipment producers. Too often companies have acted as if they were driven by market and competitive forces alone, and as if manufacturing's role was simply to respond to those forces by enlisting and coordinating the adjustments and resources provided by suppliers of parts and equipment. Suppliers and users—in fact, *all* members of the productive confederation—must actively *pressure and accommodate one another* if the tension and creativity needed for long-run productivity growth are to flourish.

Very pervasive changes in corporate thinking would be required if a competitive strategy were adopted that emphasized productivity growth and technological competition. Firms cannot become more innovative simply by increasing R&D spending or conducting more basic research. Each decision described in this chapter directly affects several functional areas of management, and major conflicts can be reconciled only at senior executive levels. The benefits favoring the more innovative, aggressive option in each case depend more on intangible factors than do their efficiency-oriented alternative. Senior managers who are less informed about their industry and its productive confederation, or who have less time to consider the long-run implications of the complex interactions among its members, are likely to exhibit a noninnovative bias in their choices. Tight financial controls with an emphasis on short-run resulsts will also bias choices toward the less innovative and less technologically aggressive alternatives. To use an analogy from the automotive industry: In their preoccupation with braking systems and dashboard trim, U.S. managers have been neglecting the drive trains of their corporations.

This book focuses on that drive train—how to manage *strategically* the technological resources of a company, particularly its manufacturing function. It is written not only for people directly involved in manufacturing management, but also for those in other functions who must interact with, or oversee, manufacturing, because reforging manufacturing into a competitive weapon will require that *everybody* be involved. What is needed is not necessarily a wholesale replacement of existing practices, but a realignment of the basic philosophy of management underlying those practices. Over time this will lead to changes in policies that are tailored to the firm's specific competitive position.

Much of this book concentrates on how strategic manufacturing issues can be handled individually (making decisions) and collectively (using systems) to avoid the problems highlighted in this chapter. However, merely avoiding problems does not meet our definition of success. Manufacturing can and should contribute significantly to a firm's competitive strength. That is the basic philosophy underlying each of the following chapters.

SELECTED REFERENCES

Abernathy, William J., and Robert H. Hayes, "Management Minus Invention." *The New York Times,* August 20, 1980, p. D2.

Bennett, Roger, and Robert Cooper. "Beyond the Marketing Concept." *Business Horizons,* June 1979, pp. 76–83.

Biggadike, E. Ralph. *Corporate Diversification: Entry, Strategy, and Performance.* Boston: Harvard Business School, Division of Research, 1979.

Biggadike, E. Ralph. "Entry, Strategy and Performance." Ph.D. dissertation, Graduate School of Business Administration, Harvard University, 1976.

Clark, Peter K. "Investment in the 1970s: Theory, Performance, and Prediction." *Brookings Papers on Economic Activity,* Vol. 1, 1979, pp. 73–124.

Clark, Peter K. "Issues in the Analysis of Capital Formation and Productivity Growth." *Brookings Papers on Economic Activity,* Vol. 2, 1979, pp. 423–431.

Davidson, J. Hugh. "Why Most New Consumer Brands Fail." *Harvard Business Review,* March–April 1976, pp. 117–122.

Dearden, John. "The Case Against ROI Control." *Harvard Business Review,* May–June 1969, pp. 124–135.

Dennison, E. S. "Explanations of Declining Productivity Growth," Part II. *Survey of Current Business,* August 1979, pp. 1–24.

Ehrbar, A. F. "Unraveling the Mysteries of Corporate Profits." *Fortune,* August 27, 1979, pp. 90+.

Feldstein, Martin. "Reviewing Business Investment." *Wall Street Journal,* June 19, 1981.

Fruhan, William E., Jr. *Financial Strategy: Studies in the Creation, Transfer, and Destruction of Shareholder Value.* Homewood, IL: Richard D. Irwin, 1979.

Galbraith, John K. *The Affluent Society.* Boston: Houghton Mifflin, 1958.

Hayes, Robert H., and William J. Abernathy. "Managing Our Way to Economic Decline." *Harvard Business Review,* July–August 1980, pp. 67–77.

Hayes, Robert H., and William J. Abernathy. "Results Now: Pay Later?" *The New York Times,* August 22, 1980, p. D2.

Hayes, Robert H., and David A. Garvin. "Managing as if Tomorrow Mattered." *Harvard Business Review,* May–June 1982, pp. 70–79.

Malkiel, Burton G. "Productivity: The Problem Behind the Headlines." *Harvard Business Review,* May–June 1979, pp. 81+.

Malkiel, Burton G. "The Capital Formation Problem in the United States." *The Journal of Finance,* May 1979, pp. 291–306.

Olsen, Paul. "Sources of Process Innovation in the Textile Industry." Ph.D. dissertation, Graduate School of Business Administration, Harvard University, 1974.

Reich, Robert B. *The Next American Frontier.* New York: Times Books, 1983.

Schumpeter, Joseph A. *The Theory of Economic Development.* New York: Oxford University Press, 1961.

Science Indicators—1980. Report of the National Science Foundation. Washington, D.C.: U.S. Government Printing Office, March 31, 1981.

Suzuki, Ryohei. "Worldwide Expansion of U.S. Exports—A Japanese View." *Sloan Management Review,* Spring 1979, pp. 67–70.

Thurow, Lester. "A Productivity Disaster and a Savings Solution." *Boston Globe,* January 27, 1981, p. 52.

Von Hippel, Eric. "The Dominant Role of Users in the Scientific Instrument Innovation Process." Sloan School of Management, Massachusetts Institute of Technology, Working Paper 75-764. 1975.

The Concept of Manufacturing Strategy

Intensified competition in a number of global manufacturing industries recently has triggered renewed interest in the manufacturing function and the contribution it can make to a company's overall competitive success. There has been a growing recognition that manufacturing can be a formidable competitive weapon if equipped and managed properly, and that a key to doing that is the development of a coherent manufacturing strategy.

Most managers believe they have a fairly good idea of what a *business strategy* consists of, and they are generally familiar with the basic issues and concerns associated with the terms *marketing strategy* and *financial strategy*. But the fact that there is such a thing as a *manufacturing strategy*, beyond simply "doing whatever is required in order to carry out our other strategies" or pursuing "improved efficiency," comes as a surprise to many people, even those within the manufacturing function. The continual pressure for quick decisions tends to stifle strategic thinking and impels manufacturing managers to adopt stopgap measures that are drawn from a variety of concepts, techniques, and approaches. As a result, these measures are likely to lack clear purpose and lead to inconsistent results. Moreover, their selection and implementation are often disjointed and only indirectly linked to broader issues of general management concern.

The purpose of this chapter is twofold. In the first portion, we present a conceptual framework that we have found useful in thinking about how manufacturing capabilities can be used to achieve a competitive advantage. We begin by reviewing the link between a firm's overall *business philosophy* and its *competitive strategy,* and then describe the relationship between its competitive strategy and its *manufacturing* (functional) *strategy.* Next we discuss the kinds of decisions that are involved in implementing a manufacturing strategy.

Finally, we consider alternative approaches to defining and developing a "corporate manufacturing strategy" and recommend one that we have found particularly useful.

In the second portion of the chapter we describe some of the different ways a firm might pursue a competitive advantage and indicate where and how its manufacturing function can make an important contribution to creating that advantage. We also discuss the links between manufacturing strategy and what we refer to as a firm's enduring characteristics—the basic attitudes and preferences that shape the way it manages itself and competes in the marketplace. We end by outlining the remaining chapters in this book and describing how they fit into the framework we construct in this chapter.

2-1 COMPANY PHILOSOPHY AND MANUFACTURING STRATEGY

For reasons we explain shortly, the formulation and implementation of an effective manufacturing strategy normally takes several years, requires the support and coordinated efforts of many people throughout an organization, and once in place is difficult to change. Therefore, it is essential that such a strategy be based on a set of organizational values and preferences that are expected to endure for a long time, and that are widely shared. Perhaps this explains why the companies that have built the most formidable manufacturing organizations and are most adept at translating their manufacturing capabilities into competitive success—in short, the companies that have developed and implemented the most effective manufacturing strategies—are those that are characterized by a strongly held set of values and beliefs: a "philosophy of doing business."

We define a company philosophy as *the set of guiding principles, driving forces, and ingrained attitudes that help communicate goals, plans, and policies to all employees and that are reinforced through conscious and subconscious behavior at all levels of the organization.** Such a philosophy ties people together and gives meaning and purpose to their everyday working lives. When an organization comes under attack, or finds its environment changing rapidly, a consistent set of values enables people at all levels to contribute usefully, even though independently, to its overall objectives.

A "set of common values" is *not* a strategy but it can have similar impact, in that a set of shared objectives also serves to guide decisions and efforts throughout an organization. It encourages certain modes of behavior within

---

* During the early 1980s, the concept of a "corporate culture" gained widespread attention. Generally, culture has been used to describe the rules, norms, and expectations of an organization with regard to the behavior of its members. Such behavior, in turn, reflects the basic values, principles, and philosophies shared by the organization. In our discussions we do not separate such aspects of behavior from the philosophy and values behind them.

the organization and suggests how that organization ought to behave toward its own people, its customers, its suppliers, and the community it serves.

A number of highly successful U.S. firms (see Peters and Waterman, 1982) have developed very explicit, well-thought-out philosophies that help communicate what is and is not important to the firm and, more significantly, what is and what is not "right." For example, there have traditionally been three tenets of IBM's company philosophy: (1) respect for the dignity of the individual, (2) first-rate customer service, and (3) excellence. Hewlett-Packard's philosophy encompasses both business practice and people management:

1. Company-related philosophies

   Pay as you go (no long-term borrowing)
   Market expansion and leadership based on new product contributions
   Customer satisfaction second to none
   Honesty and integrity in all matters

2. People related philosophies

   Belief in our people
   Emphasis on working together and sharing rewards (teamwork/partnership)
   A superior working environment

These and other companies, such as Timken and S. C. Johnson, believe that their philosophies are so powerful and important that they take precedence over, and serve to screen, all strategic plans and decisions. In particular, they feel their philosophy should infuse all their product/market strategies.

Whether stated explicitly or only implied, such a philosophy can have a profound impact on an organization. It serves as an umbrella over the various corporate, business, and functional strategies adopted by different groups within the company. It not only establishes the context within which day-to-day operating decisions are made but also sets bounds on the strategic options available to the firm. Further, an organization's philosophy guides it in making tradeoffs not only among competing performance measures (such as flexibility, delivery, cost, and quality) but also between short-term and long-term goals. Finally, the degree to which a philosophy is able to achieve consistency among diverse activities tends to be proportional to its coherence and the extent to which that philosophy is shared throughout the organization.

It is not uncommon in firms that have developed strong philosophies to find that the allegiance of managers and workers to their company supersedes their allegiance to their professions. Employees tend to use a common vocabulary, and a set of common examples (a sort of folklore) guides their behavior. They pride themselves on the "company way" of doing things and are embued with a sense of tradition and continuity. Former employees retain a strong sense of pride in and loyalty to the company and feel a common bond with other "alumni."

As will be described later in this chapter, a manufacturing strategy consists of a pattern of decisions affecting the key elements of a manufacturing system. Because the choices that constitute this pattern are affected by, and should be reflective of, the company's philosophy, making fundamental changes in a manufacturing strategy requires careful attention to its potential interaction with that philosophy (both implied and explicit) and the associated driving forces within the organization. Moreover, companies do themselves a disservice if they fail to exploit the contribution that the manufacturing organization can make as an integrating, coordinating, and communicating force. If managed properly, the manufacturing function can play a unique role in helping to define, support, and enhance the philosophy *and* competitive success of the business, operating in concert with all its functions. This is the theme of this chapter—in fact, this entire book.

2-2 CHARACTERISTICS OF A STRATEGY

The word "strategy" (derived from the Greek military term *strategos,* meaning, literally, "the general's art") has been used so extensively in the past decade that it has lost much of its unique meaning when applied to the practice of management. Most definitions of strategy, however, include such elements as establishing purpose, setting direction, developing plans, taking major actions, and securing a distinctive advantage. (See, for example, Christensen et al., 1982, p. 93.) At least five important characteristics are common to the use of the term in business:

1. **Time horizon.** Generally, the word strategy is used to describe activities that involve an extended time horizon, both with regard to the time it takes to carry out such activities and the time it takes to observe their impact.
2. **Impact.** Although the consequences of pursuing a given strategy may not become apparent for a long time, their eventual impact will be significant.
3. **Concentration of effort.** An effective strategy usually requires concentrating one's activity, effort, or attention on a fairly narrow range of pursuits. Focusing on these chosen activities implicitly reduces the resources available for other activities.
4. **Pattern of decisions.** Although some companies need to make only a few major decisions in order to implement their chosen strategy, most strategies require that a series of certain types of decision be made over time. These decisions must be supportive of one another, in that they follow a consistent pattern.

5. **Pervasiveness.** A strategy embraces a wide spectrum of activities ranging from resource allocation processes to day-to-day operations. In addition, the need for consistency over time in these activities requires that all levels of an organization act, almost instinctively, in ways that reinforce the strategy.

Because the word *strategy* is used in a variety of settings and has such a range of definitions, it is useful to identify and contrast different types of management-related strategies. As outlined in Figure 2-1, business organizations, especially those structured around functionally organized business units, develop and pursue strategies at three levels. At the highest level, *corporate strategy* specifies two areas of overall interest to the corporation: the definition of the businesses in which the corporation will participate (and, by omission, those in which it will *not* participate), and the acquisition and allocation of key corporate resources to each of those businesses.

The definition of the businesses in which a corporation will engage can be based on any of several dimensions. For example, some corporations refer to themselves as steel companies, others as glass companies, and still others as aluminum companies. All such companies tend to focus their activities around a particular material and its associated production processes. Others, such as consumer products firms, use a market segment or group of consumers to guide their selection of activities to engage in. We expand on this topic in Section 2-5.1.

Figure 2-1   Levels of strategy. First level might also refer to the group or sector level in a large, diversified organization. Second level usually refers to a division or strategic business unit (SBU)

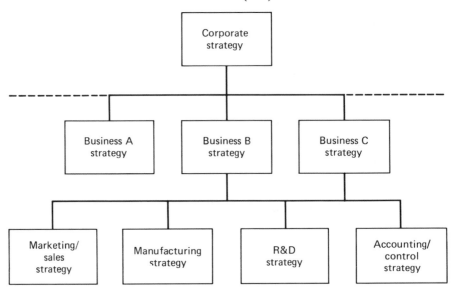

The second element of corporate strategy—the acquisition and deployment of resources—is usually dominated by a strong finance staff at the corporate level. This group typically is given primary responsibility for acquiring financial resources and, through a capital budgeting system, allocating them to various aspects of the firm's businesses. Human resources are just as important, of course, and many firms recently have begun strengthening their corporate-level personnel activities in the hope that their acquisition and deployment of valuable human resources can become as sophisticated and well integrated as their management of capital.

The second major level of strategy identified in Figure 2-1 is that associated with a strategic business unit (SBU; or strategic planning unit, SPU), which is usually a subsidiary, division, or product line within the firm. As noted in Chapter 1, many U.S. corporations have moved to an organizational structure that is composed of a number of relatively autonomous SBUs, each with its own business strategy. A *business strategy* specifies (1) the scope of that business, in a way that links the strategy of the business to that of the corporation as a whole, and (2) the basis on which that business unit will achieve and maintain a competitive advantage.

Specifying the scope of a business requires a statement of the product/market/service subsegments to be addressed. Such a statement is necessary not only to prevent direct competition among the firm's business units (several of which may operate within the same industry, such as "consumer products"), but also to focus the efforts of each unit on activities that are likely to enhance its competitive position in that business. A given SBU might achieve a defensible competitive advantage using one of a variety of approaches, including such generic ones as "low cost/high volume," "product innovation and unique features," or "customized service in selected niches." To be effective, such an advantage must be sustainable using the unit's own resources, take into account competitors' strategies, and fit the customer segments being pursued.

The third level is comprised of *functional strategies.* Once a business unit has developed its business strategy, each functional area must develop strategies that support this strategy. As illustrated in Figure 2-1, Business B might have four such functional strategies: a marketing/sales strategy, a manufacturing strategy, a research and development strategy, and a financial/control strategy. In another business unit different functions might be involved, such as distribution, field maintenance, or quality assurance.

To be effective, each functional strategy must support, through a specific and consistent pattern of decisions, the competitive advantage being sought by the business strategy. For example, decisions in such areas as pricing, packaging, distribution, and field service—all subparts of the marketing functional strategy—would be very different if the desired competitive advantage were high volume/low cost rather than, say, unique features/customized service. Similarly, such research and development decisions as the selection of technologies to be pursued, whether to be a technological leader or follower, and whether to emphasize basic research or developmental engineering/manufacturability of designs constitute subparts of the R&D functional strategy. It cannot be overemphasized that it is the *pattern of decisions* actually made, and the degree to which that pattern supports the business strategy, that constitutes a function's strategy, not what is said or written in annual reports or planning documents.*

An important aspect of functional strategy that is often overlooked is the difference between horizontal and vertical activities. Briefly, vertical activities are those that relate a single function to the business-level strategy or relate a subfunction to the overall functional-level strategy. These are more easily tackled, by academics as well as practitioners, because they follow classic hierarchical organizational relationships, as seen from the perspectives of both the manager and the technical specialist. Horizontal activities are those that cut across multiple functions at fairly low levels. Examples are quality improvement, product development/manufacturing startup, and large-scale engineering projects. These require much more coordination and consistency among functions than do vertical activities and should also be addressed when different functional groups formulate their strategies.

2-3 DEFINING MANUFACTURING'S STRUCTURE, INFRASTRUCTURE, AND STRATEGY

As implied by the preceding discussion of different kinds of strategies, an effective manufacturing operation is not necessarily one that promises the maximum efficiency or engineering perfection, but rather one that fits the needs of the business—that strives for consistency between its capabilities and policies and the competitive advantage being sought. Translating the business strategy into an appropriate collection of bricks and mortar, equipment, people, and procedures requires resources, time, and management perseverance to ensure literally hundreds of manufacturing decisions, large and small, are mutually supportive.

Because of the diversity of manufacturing decisions that must be made over time, an organizing framework that groups them into categories is useful both in identifying and in planning a firm's manufacturing strategy. A framework that we have found particularly helpful in working with a variety of firms uses eight major categories, as summarized in Table 2-1.

It is the collective pattern of these decisions that determines the *strategic capabilities* of a manufacturing organization. Like any piece of machinery, a

---

* Some writers and managers distinguish between an "enunciated" (or planned) strategy and an "implemented" strategy. We do not make that distinction because it suggests that developing a strategy and then implementing it are somehow separable. As will become apparent in subsequent chapters, we think the development of a manufacturing strategy is an interactive process involving planning and execution at various levels and in a variety of areas. In the end, it is the pattern of decisions actually pursued that determines the firm's manufacturing capabilities.

Table 2-1
Manufacturing Strategy Decision Categories

Capacity—amount, timing, type
Facilities—size, location, specialization
Technology—equipment, automation, linkages
Vertical Integration—direction, extent, balance
Workforce—skill level, wage policies, employment security
Quality—defect prevention, monitoring, intervention
Production planning/materials control—sourcing policies, centralization,
  decision rules
Organization—structure, control/reward systems, role of staff groups

manufacturing organization is able to do certain things easily and well, and other things only with difficulty—if at all. These inherent strengths and weaknesses are the direct result of the pattern of decisions pursued by manufacturing management, just as the capabilities and limitations of an airplane are the consequence of the pattern of decisions its designers and producers made.

The first four decision categories in Table 2-1 are typically viewed as *"structural"* in nature because of their long-term impact, the difficulty of reversing or undoing them once they are in place, and the fact that a substantial capital investment is required to alter or extend them. This latter aspect has led many organizations to rely on their capital budgeting process as the primary mechanism for reviewing and screening these structural manufacturing decisions.

The last four decision categories generally are considered more "tactical" in nature because they encompass myriad ongoing decisions; they are linked with specific operating aspects of the business; and they generally do not require highly visible capital investments. We include these *infrastructure* categories in Table 2-1, however, because we have found that their cumulative impact can be just as difficult and costly to change (if not more so) as those belonging to the first four categories.

Some of the important subareas within each of these categories are also listed in Table 2-1. For example, the *technology* category includes decisions regarding the technology that is incorporated in specific pieces of manufacturing equipment, the degree of automation in the production and material-handling processes, and the connections between different production stages.

These eight decision categories are closely interrelated. A factory's total annual capacity depends on whether its production rate is maintained at about the same level over time or changed frequently. Similarly, workforce policies interact with location and production process choices, and purchasing policies interact with vertical integration choices. Decisions regarding organizational design also are highly dependent on vertical integration decisions, as well as on the company's decisions regarding how various plants are located, specialized, and interconnected.

Over time, management must make decisions in all these categories, each of which presents a variety of choices and can have a major impact on the manufacturing function's ability to implement and support the organization's business strategy. For example, although an assembly line is highly interdependent and inflexible, it generally promises lower costs and higher predictability than a loosely coupled batch-flow operation or a job shop (see Chapter 6). Similarly, a company that tries to adjust production rates so as to "chase demand" generally has higher production costs and poorer quality than one that tries to maintain more level production and absorb demand fluctuations through inventories.

Only infrequently will an organization make a basic change in any one of these categories (this being almost the definition of a "structural" decision), but, depending on the industry and the firm, it probably will make at least one major decision that falls into one of these categories during the course of any year. It is critical that these decisions, made throughout the organization and at all levels, be consistent with the decisions made at other points in time and within other categories, and that their cumulative result over time is the desired manufacturing structure and infrastructure. Otherwise, unintended drifting will take place. *It is this pattern of structural and infrastructural decisions that constitutes the "manufacturing strategy" of a business unit.* More formally, a manufacturing strategy consists of a sequence of decisions that, over time, enables a business unit to achieve a desired manufacturing structure, infrastructure, and set of specific capabilities.

As the competitive strategy of an SBU evolves, change usually becomes necessary in *all* of these decision categories if consistency is to be preserved. Again and again we have found that the root cause of a "manufacturing crisis" has been that a business's manufacturing policies and people—workers, supervisors, and managers—have become incompatible with its facilities and technology choices, or that both have become incompatible with its competitive needs. Even more subtly, facilities may still be consistent with policies, but the manufacturing organization that attempts to coordinate them may no longer be doing its job effectively. The manufacturing organization is crucial, because it is the glue that keeps manufacturing priorities in place and welds the manufacturing structure and infrastructure into a competitive weapon.

Defining manufacturing strategy in terms of a pattern of decisions suggests criteria for evaluating the appropriateness of a given manufacturing strategy. These criteria generally fall into one of two groups, as indicated in Table 2-2. The first group concerns various types of consistency: one manufacturing strategy is considered "better" than another to the degree that it displays more *internal* consistency (within the manufacturing function and across functions in the business unit) and/or *external* consistency (between the manufacturing function and the environment of the business unit). The other group of criteria concerns the degree to which the manufacturing strategy augments the external competitiveness of the business, that is, enhances the competitive advantage it is seeking.

Table 2-2

Criteria for Evaluating a Manufacturing Strategy

Consistency (*internal and external*)

Between the manufacturing strategy and the overall business strategy

Between the manufacturing strategy and the other functional strategies within the business

Among the decision categories that make up the manufacturing strategy

Between the manufacturing strategy and the business environment (resources available, competitive behavior, governmental restraints, etc.)

Contribution (*to competitive advantage*)

Making tradeoffs explicit, enabling manufacturing to set priorities that enhance the competitive advantage

Directing attention to opportunities that complement the business strategy

Promoting clarity regarding the manufacturing strategy throughout the business unit so its potential can be fully realized

Providing the manufacturing capabilities that will be required by the business in the future

Later chapters provide more information about how one identifies and evaluates a manufacturing strategy, but three things are important to keep in mind at this point.

1. A manufacturing strategy is determined by the pattern of the decisions actually made (that is, by what managers do), not by what the business says its manufacturing strategy is.

2. The more consistent those decisions are, and the extent to which they support the SBU's desired competitive advantage (business strategy), the more effective the manufacturing strategy is likely to be.

3. Although individual decisions are usually driven by, and in support of, specific products, markets, or technologies, the primary function of a manufacturing strategy is to guide the business in putting together the *set of manufacturing capabilities that will enable it to pursue its chosen competitive strategy over the long term.*

Being able to move from the level of specific decisions to developing general capabilities—and back again—is central to developing and implementing an effective manufacturing strategy.

2-4 THE CONCEPT OF A CORPORATE MANUFACTURING STRATEGY

Given the notion that a manufacturing strategy must be tailored to the needs of a specific business, what value is there (positive or negative) in carrying our conceptualization one step higher—to the level of a *corporate* manufacturing strategy for a multibusiness firm? Using the preceding definitions of different levels of strategy, and the eight major decision categories (Table 2-2) that collectively determine a manufacturing strategy, we shall consider three definitions of a corporate manufacturing strategy and the implications of each.

The first maintains that a corporate manufacturing strategy exists only if each business that the company is engaged in adopts the *same* (or very similar) manufacturing strategy. Most references to "corporate manufacturing strategy" seem to imply this definition. However, some reflection on Figure 2-1 and Table 2-1 suggests that such a definition is not particularly useful. Since each business has unique aspects, and therefore a unique business strategy, a common manufacturing strategy is unlikely to be appropriate. Even in firms in which several businesses employ similar business strategies (or seek similar competitive advantages), usually they are sufficiently different that they require somewhat different manufacturing strategies.

A second, and we think more useful, definition of corporate manufacturing strategy can be stated using Table 2-3. In one sense, this second definition simply clarifies and corrects the first, but it does so in a manner consistent with the levels of strategy identified in Figure 2-1. In Table 2-3, each business unit is permitted to have its own manufacturing strategy, as indicated by the different symbols (000000, //////, and ++++++) that are found within the eight major decision categories under each of the three business units (A, B, and C).

Each SBU within the corporation may pursue similar policies within certain subcategories, even though its complete manufacturing strategy is unique. If so, it may be possible to identify a few corporate-wide policies, regarding certain types of manufacturing decisions, that are common across all (or most) of the businesses in which the company engages. In Table 2-3 these are indicated by the symbol ××××××. The column on the far right contains examples of such common policies for a hypothetical corporation. For example, a firm might specify certain size and location characteristics for its individual manufacturing facilities, or certain personnel policies, independent of the particular business or division involved. In fact, many of these common policies are likely to arise out of the philosophy and values that the corporation shares with all its business units.

The corporate manufacturing strategy under this definition consists of those subparts of each of the eight decision categories that are governed by common policies across all the firm's businesses. The choice of the decisions to be held constant in this manner can vary significantly for different companies. In some corporations, for example, decisions regarding workforce policies may be left entirely to the individual business unit. In others a strong corporate culture may dictate that a common set of workforce policies be applied to all business units, whereas quality decisions may be left entirely to individual divisions.

Determining which decisions should be held constant for a given firm can be a difficult problem, because it involves tradeoffs between *ease of control* and *focus.* Some people believe that all subelements should be adapted to local circumstances; this, of course, thwarts attempts to identify the commonalities (and develop associated controls) that could be the basis of a corporate manufacturing strategy. Most companies, however, lean in the opposite direction: they require too much commonality.

A third definition is sometimes implied in discussions of "corporate manufacturing strategy." It simply identifies those areas where a corporate-wide perspective, and focused efforts, would be preferable to letting each business unit develop its own manufacturing policies. In essence, this simply raises division-level issues to the corporate level for analysis and solution. For instance, when the U.S. Occupational Safety and Health Act (OSHA) was first passed, a number of companies established a corporate-level position to monitor adherence to the Act because few of their operating units had enough experience (or motivation) to do so properly. Later many of those efforts were decentralized and eventually became embedded in the manufacturing strategy adopted by each individual business unit.

Another area where it is often useful to adopt a corporate-wide perspective is in basic R&D, particularly that relating to manufacturing processes. A company may decide that it will need a certain manufacturing capability in the future, even though none of its business units has an immediate need for it. Therefore it may choose to develop an in-house capability in that technology so it will be available when needed. For some period of time that capability would be found only at the corporate level, although subsequently it would show up in one or more of the business units.

This third definition of corporate manufacturing strategy is very consistent with that outlined in Table 2-3. For this reason it can be considered simply an extension of the second definition, which is the one we prefer.

2-5   SEEKING COMPETITIVE ADVANTAGE THROUGH A MANUFACTURING STRATEGY

The theme of this book is that, if the manufacturing function assembles and aligns its resources through a cohesive strategy, it can play a major role in helping a business attain a desired competitive advantage. The notion that manufacturing can be a competitive weapon, rather than just a collection of rather ponderous resources and constraints, is not new, although its practice is not very widespread. As is discussed in detail in Chapter 14, most manufacturing-based businesses simply seek to minimize the negative impact that manufacturing can have. Even in many well-managed firms, manufacturing plays an essentially *neutral* role, reflecting the view that marketing, sales, and R&D provide better bases for achieving a competitive advantage.

To understand the potential contribution that the manufacturing function can make in strengthening a firm's competitive position, it is useful to look

Table 2-3
The Concept of a Corporate Manufacturing Strategy

Dimensions of a Manufacturing Strategy	Individual Business Strategies			Examples of Generic (Corporate-Wide) Policies and Guidelines
	Business A[a]	Business B[a]	Business C[a]	
Capacity[b]	×××××× 000000 000000 000000	×××××× ///// ///// /////	×××××× ++++++ ++++++ ++++++	A common set of criteria to be used in developing/presenting an investment proposal Policies for the economic or competitive conditions required to plan/start/postpone capacity changes
Facilities[b]	×××××× ×××××× ×××××× 000000 000000	×××××× ×××××× ×××××× ///// /////	×××××× ×××××× ×××××× ++++++ ++++++	Parameters governing the size and location of individual facilities Guidelines for permanent reductions in capacity at mature facilities
Technology[b]	×××××× 000000 000000 000000 000000	×××××× ///// ///// ///// /////	×××××× ++++++ ++++++ ++++++ ++++++	Policies for the organization and layout of production processes Criteria for equipment selection and the levels of automation to be pursued
Vertical Integration[b]	×××××× 000000 000000	×××××× ///// /////	×××××× ++++++ ++++++	Policies for make/buy analysis and changes in backward integration Rules for establishing internal transfer prices
Work force[b]	×××××× ×××××× ×××××× 000000	×××××× ×××××× ×××××× /////	×××××× ×××××× ×××××× ++++++	Establishment of benefit packages and pay scales Policies on unionization, hiring, promotion, and employment stability

36

Quality[b]	×××××× ×××××× ××××××	Standardized reports, reporting relationships and job definitions
	×××××× ×××××× ××××××	
	000000 ////// ++++++	Guidelines on performance measures such as the cost of quality, field failures, and expected quality levels
	000000 ////// ++++++	
Production planning/ Materials control[b]	×××××× ×××××× ××××××	Parameters for manufacturing system specifications and hardware approval
	×××××× ×××××× ××××××	
	×××××× ×××××× ××××××	Rules for measuring and evaluating inventory performance
	000000 ////// ++++++	
	000000 ////// ++++++	
Organization[b]	×××××× ×××××× ××××××	Definitions for job classifications and direct/indirect staffing levels
	000000 ////// ++++++	
	000000 ////// ++++++	Policies regarding manufacturing engineering support levels and use of outside services

[a] Each column represents the manufacturing strategy (pattern of manufacturing decisions) that complements a specific business strategy.

[b] Each row represents behavior, practices, and policies in that decision category that are consistent across businesses (indicated by ×××××), and those not consistent across all businesses.

more closely at the relationship between manufacturing strategy and business strategy, and how the attitudes and preferences that underlie a business strategy also shape its manufacturing strategy. Identifying such preferences, which relate to specific aspects of the "company philosophy" we discussed earlier, can assist a business unit in setting priorities, making necessary tradeoffs, and developing more effective functional strategies. In this section, four general types of preferences—dominant orientation, pattern of diversification, attitude toward growth, and choice of competitive priorities—are described and their implications for manufacturing strategy discussed.

2-5.1   The Dominant Orientation of the Business Unit

Some companies have a strong market orientation. They consider their primary expertise to be the ability to understand and respond effectively to the needs of a particular market or consumer group. In exploiting this market knowledge, they use a variety of products, materials, and technologies. Gillette and Procter & Gamble come to mind. Other companies have a material, or product, orientation. They develop multiple uses for their product or material and follow those uses into a variety of markets. Corning Glass, Goodyear, DuPont, and Shell Oil are examples of companies with such a dominant orientation. Still other companies and businesses are technology oriented (most electronics and pharmaceutical companies fall into this class), and tend to follow the lead of their technological expertise into various materials and markets.

In essence, such companies believe that by confining themselves to activities that allow their various business units to exploit similar capabilities, they can do much better than if they tried to pursue a full range of business strategies in a very diverse set of business activities. A company that defines itself in this way often finds it very difficult to venture outside its dominant orientation. An example is provided by Texas Instruments' decision, in the early 1970s, to produce consumer products such as electronic calculators, digital watches, and home computers. Although TI may continue in some of these consumer markets, its announcement in mid-1981 that it was abandoning the digital watch market, followed by a similar announcement two years later concerning home computers (its explanation in each case was that this would allow it to devote more resources to its primary business, integrated circuits) illustrates how difficult even a "natural" diversification move can be for such a company.

Since most dominant orientations incorporate implicit, if not explicit, judgments as to the relative importance of various functions and their roles in achieving a competitive advantage, they establish strong mind-sets within an organization as to the role that manufacturing should play in its competitive strategy. Those mind-sets are very real constraints. If they are negative or neutral, they must be identified and addressed if manufacturing is to make a significant positive contribution to the company's competitive success.

2-5.2   The Pattern of Diversification

A second, and related, preference is the pattern of diversification a company follows. Diversification can be accomplished in several ways: (1) product diversification within a given market; (2) market diversification (geographic or consumer group) with a given product line; (3) process, or vertical, diversification (increasing the span of the process so as to gain more control over vendors or customers) with a given mix of products and markets; and (4) unrelated (horizontal) diversification, as exemplified by conglomerates. These patterns of diversification are closely interrelated with a company's dominant orientation. They also reflect the company's preference to concentrate on a relatively narrow set of activities, products, or markets rather than spread itself broadly over many.

Generally speaking, the greater the variety in a company's businesses, the more likely it is that there will be variety in the business strategies pursued and thus in the manufacturing strategies adopted. Unfortunately, our observations suggest that the greater the variety of manufacturing strategies, the less likely it is that senior-level managers will develop a detailed understanding of manufacturing's potential contribution. This is due both to the fact that there are not enough common threads for them to exploit from their position and because they are unlikely to be familiar with all the technologies involved.

2-5.3   The Attitude Toward Growth

The role and importance of growth is a third factor influencing the competitive role of manufacturing. For some companies, growth represents an *input* to the company's or business unit's planning process; for others it is an *output*. Every company continually confronts a variety of growth opportunities. Its decision to accept some types and to reject others signals, in a fundamental way, the kind of company it prefers to be. Some companies, for example, in their concentration on a particular market, geographic area, or material, accept the growth permitted by that market or area or material. Other companies, however, are managed so that a certain rate of growth is required if they are to function properly.

Within companies that require a certain rate of growth, two different approaches for transmitting that orientation to individual business units can be observed. Under one approach the corporation requires each business unit to meet that growth rate. Under the other, each business unit is assigned a mission within the "corporate portfolio" that encourages it to pursue a specified rate of growth (as well as other dimensions of expected performance).

The firm's attitude toward growth has a powerful influence on its attitude toward manufacturing as a competitive weapon. In businesses in which high growth is considered essential, the primary task assigned manufacturing is often simply to keep up with that growth—"get the product out the door!" This need tends to take precedence over establishing a competitive advantage on other dimensions of manufacturing effectiveness. Divisions or businesses in which growth is not the primary motivating factor, on the other hand, are more likely to assign a larger and richer strategic role to manufacturing.

2-5.4 The Choice of Competitive Priorities

Another set of enduring preferences—that act, in a sense, to integrate and summarize the others—is embodied in the way a company chooses to compete in the marketplace and the types of markets it pursues. In its simplest form, a company's competitive posture indicates whether it prefers to seek high profit margins (and low volumes) or high volumes and low margins. Some companies, for example, consistently seek out high-volume products, even when this decision subjects them to severe cost-reduction pressure or low margins. This sort of competitive preference often is pervasive throughout a company; that is, most of its business units adopt a similar competitive posture.

Price (and therefore cost) is the most familiar competitive dimension, but it is not the only basis on which a business can compete. A business can configure its competitive strategy around several different modes of competition, and the clearer the priorities placed on these modes, the greater the role that manufacturing can play in supporting that strategy.

In some businesses the basis of competitive advantage is superior *quality*, achieved either by providing higher product reliability or performance in a standard product (for example, Mercedes-Benz) or by manufacturing a product with features or capabilities that are unavailable in competing products. The cost of providing higher quality, as defined this way, must be balanced against the market's willingness to pay for it, of course. The nature of this balance has powerful implications for the role of manufacturing in the business.

Another competitive dimension that some businesses use to differentiate themselves in the marketplace is *dependability*. Although the products of such firms may be priced higher than the products of others, and they may not offer the highest performance or the latest technology, they do work as specified, they are delivered on time, and the company stands ready to mobilize its resources instantly to ensure that any failures are corrected immediately. IBM, Caterpillar Tractor, and Sysco are often cited as examples of companies whose business strategies emphasize such "peace of mind."

Still another important basis for competitive advantage is *flexibility*. There are at least two important types of flexibility: product flexibility and volume flexibility. A business that competes on the basis of product flexibility emphasizes its ability to handle difficult, nonstandard orders and to take the lead in new product introduction. Smaller companies often make this their primary basis of competitive advantage. Other businesses compete through volume flexibility, emphasizing their ability to accelerate or decelerate production very quickly and juggle orders so as to meet demands for unusually rapid delivery. Successful companies in highly cyclical industries, like housing or furniture, often make volume flexibility a primary priority.

Within a given industry different companies (or business units) give different emphases to each of these four competitive dimensions: price, quality, dependability, and flexibility. It is difficult (if not impossible), and potentially dangerous, for a company to try to compete by offering superior performance along *all* of these dimensions simultaneously, since it will probably end up second best on each dimension to some other company that devotes more of its resources to developing that competitive advantage. Instead, a business must attach clear priorities to each dimension, and these priorities will determine how that business positions itself relative to its competitors. Specifying and clarifying these priorities is the first step in formulating manufacturing's role in the business, since the acid test of whether a business has a strategy is whether it displays a consistent set of preferences through the pattern of decisions it makes over time.

2-6 MANUFACTURING'S ROLE AS A COMPETITIVE WEAPON

In the context of this web of preferences, attitudes, and competitive priorities, the task for manufacturing is to structure and manage itself so as to mesh with, reinforce, and enhance its SBU's competitive strategy. Manufacturing should be capable of helping the business do the things it considers essential without wasting resources in lower-priority pursuits, because if resources are diverted to low-priority tasks, some of the activities that are really important simply will not get done. Understanding the company's biases and preferences, and their implications for manufacturing/decision patterns, is a prerequisite to realizing the full potential of a manufacturing organization.

Up to this point we have concentrated on what a manufacturing strategy is and how it can support a given business strategy. We now want to challenge the idea that the role of the manufacturing function is simply to assist in implementing the strategy that others have developed. We argue throughout this book that manufacturing should take a more proactive role in defining the competitive advantage that is to be pursued. It must communicate clearly to top management the constraints it operates under, the capabilities it can exploit, and the options available to it. And it must seek collaborative relationships with other functions. In fact, manufacturing cannot become a significant competitive weapon unless it takes this kind of active role. While Chapter 14 explores the mechanisms and procedures that can be used to accomplish this, and gives specific examples of companies that have adopted this kind of proactive approach for manufacturing, we close this section with a few points to think about.

Common sense suggests that manufacturing should play an equal role with other functions in defining the competitive strategy for the business. That is, top management should consult manufacturing to get its perspective on the major issues facing the business, the strategies being proposed by other functional heads, and the options open to manufacturing. If such an approach is to work, the status and credibility of the firm's manufacturing managers must be made equal to those of other functional managers. This may require changes in how potential manufacturing managers are selected and trained, the career paths they follow, and the way their performance is measured and evaluated. Helpful though such actions might be, unfortunately, they will not be truly successful unless the equality of manufacturing becomes embedded in the "culture" of the organization.

If manufacturing's role in the firm is made credible by its culture, moreover, the firm is less likely to experience the type of disaster that can occur when manufacturing falls out of step with the other functions. It helps managers make the appropriate tradeoffs between short-run and long-run interests and provides a mechanism for viewing decisions that are often regarded as merely tactical (workforce, quality, production planning/materials, etc.) in their strategic context.

The firm's philosophy (and derived culture) specifies the kind of organization it wishes to be, how it is viewed by competitors, stockholders, employees, and the public, and the common values these groups share. The implications of this are particularly important for manufacturing, because a philosophy is effective only to the extent that it is widely shared by the people in the organization, and the majority of a company's people usually are members of its manufacturing organization. Recognizing that the manufacturing organization is the major "keeper" of the company's philosophy is an important step in expanding the contribution that manufacturing can make.

Finally, strategy development should be an ongoing interactive process, with inputs and perspectives contributed by all functions, rather than a single, all-encompassing (and inevitably dated and incomplete) statement at a given point in time. It is easier for manufacturing to play an active, rather than reactive, role in companies that encourage creativity and consistency across functions and over time.

2-7   A LOOK AHEAD

The next several chapters of this book address the major decision categories outlined in Table 2-1, with particular emphasis on what we call the structural elements: capacity, facilities, technology, and vertical integration. In Chapter 3 we examine issues relating to the firm's total manufacturing capacity: how much is enough in a given situation, when should capacity be added (or reduced), and how much should be added at one time. Some companies seem to equate "manufacturing strategy" with "capacity strategy." As indicated in Table 2-1 (and as we demonstrate in subsequent chapters), although it is an important component of a manufacturing strategy, developing a reasoned approach to capacity management is just the first step.

In Chapters 4 and 5 we discuss how this total production capacity should be divided up and assigned to specific facilities. Chapter 4 concentrates on where these facilities should be located and how they can be specialized (focused) around different pieces of the total task of production. We also discuss what a "facilities strategy" consists of (and how it is different from a "capacity strategy") and describe different approaches that companies have taken in developing their facilities strategies. We end with a discussion of the notion of a "focused facility" and present some of the emerging evidence that suggests the potential value of focus.

To implement its chosen capacity and facilities strategies, a company must make a series of consistent facilities decisions over a long period of time. Moreover, these decisions are likely to be made by different people in different locations and at different levels in the organization. To enforce consistency in these decisions, it is not enough to have enunciated a strategy and communicated it broadly. A company must also put into place a set of policies and procedures—particularly a capital budgeting system—that encourages decisions that are consistent with the strategy and discourages those that are inconsistent. This is the subject of Chapter 5.

In Chapters 6 and 7 we turn to the third item in Table 2-1: process technology. We begin by looking at how a company's process technology affects and is viewed by people at different levels of the organization. We show how these different perspectives fit together and argue that a firm's manufacturing strategy is likely to be emasculated if it is based on an understanding of technology that is too narrow and mechanistic. This often occurs when technology decisions are addressed only from a top-management perspective, particularly if this group is dominated by managers who suffer from "technology aversion."

In Chapter 7 we describe how a firm's choice of process technology interacts with its product line structure and marketing strategy, and how this interaction can lead to either a competitive advantage or competitive vulnerability. Using the framework provided by the "product/process matrix," we emphasize again the centrality of a firm's technology decisions to its overall competitive strategy and provide examples of the traps it can fall into if it lacks this understanding.

In Chapter 8 we begin to pull the threads of the previous four chapters together, by showing how capacity/facilities decisions can combine with technology decisions to produce a predictable pattern of improvement in a firm's manufacturing effectiveness. The concept of the "experience curve" provides the organizing framework for this discussion, and it enables us to describe how the issues covered in Chapters 3 through 7 can be translated into a long-term cost improvement program. We end with a discussion of some of the implications of experience curve theory for business/corporate strategy. The roots they share illustrate again how a firm's manufacturing strategy can inform and interact with its competitive strategy.

In Chapter 9 we move to the fourth item in Table 2-1, the firm's vertical integration and sourcing strategy. We discuss how, and in what direction, its decisions regarding the span and balance of its operations are likely to affect its competitive effectiveness. This impact is poorly understood by too many managers, who tend to regard vertical integration decisions in "make versus buy" terms and therefore allow their decision processes to be dominated by financial considerations. We end by discussing some of the alternatives to vertical integration that occupy the long grey area between "make" and "buy."

In Chapter 10 we culminate the discussion of the previous nine chapters by describing how a firm can manage the evolution over time of its manufacturing technology and structure, which include capacity, facilities, process technology, and sourcing decisions. In addition, we return to the product/process framework described in Chapter 7 and show how a firm's choice of a path through this matrix reflects different competitive strategies and leads to different kinds of competitive advantage. This framework also provides new insights into the nature of the experience curve, as well as into the complex interactions that occur between the various components of a manufacturing strategy. We end by discussing the kinds of problems that are typically encountered when managing major process transitions, and the organizational attitudes and capabilities that are called for in developing a firm's manufacturing structure and technology into a strategic resource.

In Chapters 11 through 13 we turn our attention from the different ingredients of a manufacturing strategy, and how they can be combined and shaped over time, to descriptions of the different ways that these issues are dealt with in leading manufacturing companies in Germany (Chapter 11) and Japan (Chapter 12). Although companies in these two countries tend to base their approaches to manufacturing on different philosophies of management, and emphasize different activities and performance criteria, they have much in common. We discuss these commonalities, as well as the differences in their approaches, in Chapter 13. The principles that guide the behavior of these companies, despite their somewhat old-fashioned aura, are deeply held and produce consistent and effective decisions. Their example provides compelling evidence as to how a well-equipped and well-managed manufacturing function can make a powerful contribution to a company's competitive success.

Chapter 14, the conclusion to this book, provides an opportunity to review and distill some of the ideas we have covered and to think about the issues that remain. We emphasize the importance of the role that infrastructure—people, policies, and procedures (the last four items in Table 2-1)—plays in successful manufacturing organizations and describe the long process that is involved in building a company's capabilities to the point where it can truly compete through manufacturing.

SELECTED REFERENCES

Andrews, K. R. *The Concept of Corporate Strategy,* rev. ed. Homewood, IL: Dow Jones-Irwin, 1980.

Christensen, C. Roland, Kenneth R. Andrews, Joseph L. Bowers, Richard G. Hamermesh, and Michael E. Porter. *Business Policy,* 5th ed. Homewood, IL: Richard D. Irwin, 1982

Grant, J. H., and W. R. King. *The Logic of Strategic Planning.* Boston: Little, Brown, 1982.

Hofer, Charles W., and Dan Schendel. *Strategy Formulation: Analytical Concepts.* St. Paul: West Publishing Co., 1978.

Pascale, Richard T., and Anthony G. Athos. *The Art of Japanese Management.* New York: Simon & Schuster, 1981.

Peters, Thomas J. "Putting Excellence into Management." *Business Week,* July 21, 1980, pp. 196–205.

Peters, Thomas J., and Robert H. Waterman, Jr. *In Search of Excellence.* New York: Harper & Row, 1982.

Porter, Michael E. *Competitive Strategy.* New York: Free Press, 1980.

Skinner, Wickham. *Manufacturing in the Corporate Strategy.* New York: John Wiley & Sons, 1978.

Wheelwright, Steven C. "Japan—Where Operations Really Are Strategic." *Harvard Business Review,* July–August 1981, pp. 67–74.

Wheelwright, Steven C. "Reflecting Corporate Strategy in Manufacturing Decisions." *Business Horizons,* February 1978, pp. 57–66.

Long-Term Capacity Strategies

3-1 OVERVIEW: STRATEGIES VERSUS DECISIONS

It is important to understand the critical difference between a capacity *decision,* which would be triggered by a capital authorization request for an expansion of capacity, and a capacity *strategy,* which would place each capacity decision in the context of a longer-term sequence of such decisions. While much of the literature on capacity planning looks at it in the context of a specific decision facing an organization, we take the longer-term perspective first. Then we consider specific decisions as they define and implement the organization's chosen strategy.

A capacity strategy is based on a series of assumptions and predictions about long-term market, technology, and competitive behavior. These include:

1. The predicted growth and variability of primary demand.
2. The costs of building and operating different sized plants.
3. The rate and direction of technological evolution.
4. The likely behavior of competitors.
5. The anticipated impact of international competitors, markets, and sources of supply.

A capacity strategy is a major element of a firm's manufacturing strategy. As such, it embodies the corporate/business philosophies, behavioral preferences, and driving forces that we described in Chapter 2. At the same time, it should reinforce the other strategies and objectives adopted by the firm.

As emphasized in our discussion of the concept of manufacturing strategy in Chapter 2, it is the sequence of specific capacity decisions over time that determines what an organization's long-term capacity strategy actually is. Production capacity can be changed in a variety of ways, and it is sometimes difficult even to define or measure capacity. Is it physical space, equipment, output rates, human resource capabilities, materials, or all of these? For this reason, a capacity strategy does not consist simply of a line drawn on a graph to indicate the total production capacity that will be needed at different dates in the future. It requires a statement of how much of what kinds of capacity are to be provided in conjunction with a specific scenario describing the likely evolution of the firm's environment over time.

Although each of a firm's manufacturing capabilities establishes limits on its overall capacity, in a given situation one or two key resources are likely to be most critical. At that particular time the availabilities of those resources will represent the most appropriate means for measuring the firm's capacity. Thus in one situation physical space may be most appropriate, in others it may be equipment hours or workforce levels. Whichever measure is used, we assume in the remainder of this discussion that it is a surrogate for all of the resources required for the firm to meet its desired production levels.

Even if a firm's long-term capacity strategy is not spelled out explicitly, the pattern of the firm's decisions over time often reflects the existence of such a strategy. For example, the firm may attempt to stay well ahead of demand in adding capacity, or it may prefer to lag behind. Such behavior reflects one important aspect of a capacity strategy: *when* capacity is to be added or reduced. But the answers to a number of related questions—such as what will serve to signal the need for a change in capacity, the sizing of such changes, and the relationship of these aggregate capacity decisions to specific facilities decisions—help define the capacity strategy and affect its overall effectiveness.

This chapter introduces a set of concepts and techniques that are useful both in formulating a capacity strategy and in guiding the individual decisions required to implement it. Section 3-2 discusses some of the basic issues that relate capacity to expected demand. The concept of a "capacity cushion" is defined, and we suggest some guidelines for choosing the size of the cushion that is appropriate for a given situation.

The notion of a capacity cushion is a useful way to approach the development of a long-term capacity strategy. Maintaining such a cushion at the desired level is extremely difficult, however, because demand is continually changing. Moreover, for a variety of economic and technical reasons it is usually necessary to add or subtract capacity in "chunks." While Section 3-2 focuses on the timing of capacity changes, Section 3-3 deals with issues related to the size of these new chunks of capacity. In the appendix to this chapter we use a simple mathematical model to illustrate how one could go about determining the optimal size for each chunk of capacity to be added. Although the assumptions upon which these calculations are based are perhaps too simplified to be applied directly to most real-life decisions of this type, they make it possible to address the important issues in a systematic manner and provide useful insights regarding key relationships.

One of the most important of these relationships is that between the cost of a unit of output and the total capacity of the facility producing that unit. The concept of "economies of scale" plays such a critical role in the analysis of capacity decisions—as well as in many other types of decisions discussed throughout this book—that it is covered in some detail in Section 3-3. We also discuss the lesser known, but equally important, topic of "diseconomies of scale."

Unlike the more quantitative approaches of Sections 3-2 and 3-3, Section 3-4 describes several different philosophies that can be adopted when approaching a series of capacity decisions (that is, in pursuing a capacity strategy). This section concludes with a look at some of the opportunities for integrating the business unit's capacity strategy with its overall business strategy.

3-2 THE TIMING OF CAPACITY INCREMENTS— THE CAPACITY CUSHION

At the most basic level, a capacity strategy proposes what the company's posture should be regarding the amount and timing of capacity changes in relation to demand changes. Three options, shown in Figure 3-1, illustrate the range of possibilities available when demand is expected to grow steadily.

Policy A: Try Not to Run Short

This policy implies that the company should build and maintain extra capacity (analogous to a safety stock in inventory management) so that the likelihood of running short is *less* than the likelihood of having excess capacity. The greater the capacity provided, the smaller the likelihood of running short.

Such a policy requires the creation of a "capacity cushion"—an amount of capacity in excess of expected demand. For example, if the expected monthly demand on a facility is $500,000 worth of goods, and it can produce as much as $550,000, it has a 10 percent capacity cushion. A 10 percent capacity cushion can be turned around and viewed as a "90 percent capacity utilization."* Unused capacity generally is expensive. Why, then, might a company want to consider having such a capacity cushion?

One reason a company might be willing to incur this added cost is that such a cushion would make it possible to respond to *unexpected* demand surges, like those that come from sudden large orders placed by existing customers, or first orders from new customers. In addition, it would provide the capability of faster delivery without the expense of overtime and the disrup-

---

* More precisely, a 10 percent capacity cushion corresponds to a 91 percent capacity utilization, since

$$\text{capacity utilization} = \frac{\text{capacity required}}{\text{capacity provided}} = \frac{x}{(1.00 + 0.10)\,x} = 91 \text{ percent}$$

Figure 3-1 Alternative capacity expansion strategies

Policy A: Capacity leads demand

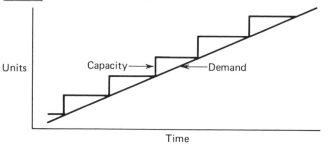

Policy B: Capacity in approximate equilibrium with demand

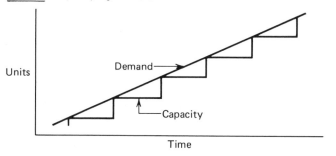

Policy C: Capacity lags demand

tions resulting from the need to reschedule production or upset deliveries to other customers. In a growing market, it also may enable a firm to attract the business of new customers who are not getting the service they think appropriate, because their suppliers (your competitors) are capacity constrained—that is, do not have the capacity cushion that you have. Finally, it can enable a firm, in a growing market, to take market share from competitors who are concerned more with their short-term profitability and return on investment than with their long-term market position.

Policy B: Build to the Forecast

This policy implies that over time the company will attempt to match, as nearly as possible, its production capacity to the anticipated demand.

If, for example, a firm's current capacity were expected to be fully utilized in three years, and if the lead time to build a new plant were two years, then the firm might delay building the new plant for about a year. If demand grew more rapidly than forecast, or if the construction period were longer than expected, the company would find that demand had outstripped its capacity and it would lose potential sales if it did not react by expanding the capacity of existing facilities (through overtime, weekend shifts, etc.), or by subcontracting the deficit to outside companies. On the other hand, if demand fell short of expectations, the company might find itself stretching construction lead times to minimize surplus capacity. However, on average, it would prefer to have "about the right amount of capacity"—the likelihood of an excess being about the same as the likelihood of a shortfall.

Policy C: Maximize Capacity Utilization

This policy implies that the company will build a *negative* cushion into the capacity plan, so that the likelihood of running short is greater than the likelihood of having excess capacity.

This policy is sometimes referred to as a "conservative" approach in that it requires less investment than would be required to provide a positive capacity cushion. It assures the firm of high capacity utilization and therefore provides a higher average rate of return on manufacturing investment than would be possible with a lower utilization rate. In addition, when new capacity is added, it tends to be fully utilized almost immediately. On the other hand, it may also lead to a slow deterioration in a firm's market position. For this reason, such a policy is not conservative in the sense of being low risk. It simply substitutes one type of risk (losing potential sales) for another (having underutilized facilities).

3-2.1 Alternative Types of Capacity Cushion

Up to this point we have used the term "capacity" to mean *production* capacity, but if we think of capacity in its most basic sense—*the ability of a business to meet market demands*—it is apparent that there are actually several ways that this capacity can be provided. These vary along a number of important dimensions, including the speed of response, cost, flexibility, and risk of obsolescence.

One obvious way to meet demand is by carrying inventories, either of finished goods or of parts and components that can be assembled quickly into finished goods. This approach provides the quickest response to a demand surge, but it is often the most risky. It requires that the company know exactly what products will be demanded and in what quantities. If its forecasts are wrong, then the firm not only may not have enough of some products, but also may find itself stocked with a large inventory of obsolete products.

The more familiar view of capacity is that associated with various production resources: floor space, equipment, people, and systems. This kind of capacity cannot provide the same speed of response as inventories, but it is more general: the specific mix and volumes of products demanded can be produced within the company's normal lead time. Instead of incurring the risk of obsolete inventory, the company will incur the cost of unused capital resources which have a smaller risk of obsolescence. To use a gambling term, one is "betting on the come."

It is possible, of course, to provide only a partial capacity cushion—of plant and equipment, say, but not of people. Then, if demand materializes, one will have to use overtime or hire additional people. The tradeoff is between the speed of response and the investment required (just as in deciding whether to hold inventories or provide additional production capacity).

A third step, one that would imply a still slower response time but even less committed investment and the least risk of production inefficiency or product obsolescence, would be a capacity cushion in the form of cash that is specifically earmarked for plant and equipment expansion. If this cash is kept in a specific account, and the decision procedures for using it are set up in advance, when demand grows to the point where additional capacity is called for, it will not be necessary to go through the full capital appropriations process in order to authorize its construction. Holding capacity in this form slows the response time considerably, to a matter of months or years instead of weeks, but it does speed up the process of channeling the firm's resources to meeting the needs of existing and potential customers.

The final, and least effective, form of capacity cushion is simply to have a general-purpose cash cushion. In a firm with such a cash cushion, a request for additional plant or equipment must compete with other corporate needs, including the general need to "hold a cash reserve for contingencies." Getting through the process of authorizing the use of these funds for plant and equipment may add several months to the process, but at least the money is available—a resource that one's competitors might not have.

A good example of the various kinds of capacity cushion that a firm might consider is the situation faced by Litton's Microwave Oven Division in 1973. [See "Atherton Division of Litton Industries," Harvard Case Services, 9-673-114.] Keeping in mind the uncertainties associated with a product in the early stages of its life cycle, as well as its prospects for substantial growth, this firm contemplated a wide range of capacity options. The five major options were: (1) stick with its existing production capacity for another 6–12 months (and let its capacity cushion erode as demand expanded), (2) build inventory and work overtime in order to meet unexpected demand surges, (3) add a second shift at an existing facility, (4) add plant and equipment at the existing facility, and (5) build a new facility. Factors considered by management in deciding among these options included the anticipated strength of consumer spending, the time to get capital requests approved by corporate management, the economics of each option, and the likely moves of competitors.

What is best for any organization—where in the series of tradeoffs between speed of response, efficiency, flexibility, and risk it should position itself—depends very much on the circumstances. In a growing market there is usually relatively little long-term risk associated with having more production capacity than is absolutely necessary to meet expected demand, because almost certainly the company will need that extra capacity within a year or so. If it expects continuing market growth, the firm simply would be adding capacity a few months before it is absolutely required. Although this might penalize its short-term ROI, it might enable the firm to attract some new customers from capacity-constrained competitors. In a stagnant or declining market, the penalty associated with making a mistake is much greater, of course.

3-2.2 Determining the Appropriate Capacity Cushion

From this point on we will confine our analysis to production capacity alone, although the same general approach would apply to other types of capacity cushions as well. The decision as to how much of a production capacity cushion to provide (if any) generally is based on a comparison of the relative costs of having more capacity than is needed (the cost of unused plant and equipment and underutilized human resources) with the costs of not having enough (the cost of overtime, subcontracting, and lost profits).

In its simplest form, the size of a firm's capacity cushion should reflect the magnitude of the ratio

$$\frac{C_s - C_x}{C_s} \tag{3-1}$$

where C_s represents the opportunity loss per unit of not having enough capacity (s = short), together with any penalties (such as overtime premiums) associated with not being able to meet demand during a given time period, and C_x represents the annualized cost (during the same time period) of having an unneeded unit of capacity (x = excess). In general, if this ratio is greater than 0.5, more capacity than the median forecast of demand should be provided; if it is less than 0.5, a "negative cushion" is called for. Therefore, highly capital-intensive industries (C_x large) will tend toward small or even negative capacity cushions (and high average utilization rates), while low capital-intensive, high-profit margin (C_x small, C_s large) industries will tend toward large capacity cushions and lower utilization rates.

For example, if it costs $1 per year (in interest costs, maintenance, fixed operating costs, etc.) for each additional unit of annual production capacity (C_x = 1), and if the lost profit margin and penalty costs associated with not being able to satisfy demand out of the firm's own production facility at its normal operating rate is $3 per unit ($C_s$ = 3), then the value of the ratio is (3 − 1)/3 = 0.67. This indicates the need for a small positive cushion.* If C_s were equal to $2, on the other hand, the ratio would equal 0.5, so capacity should be just

---

* More precisely, the total production capacity available should be large enough that there is a two-thirds probability of being able to satisfy the demand during the year.

large enough that there is a 50 percent likelihood of being able to satisfy total demand during the year. That is, the company should "build to the forecast"—no cushion.

This approach clearly takes a very short-term, simplistic point of view. Building a plant is a long-term proposition, and generally plant capacity cannot be increased one unit at a time. Nor is it easy to obtain accurate values for the cost parameters required to perform such a calculation. For example, the "annualized cost" of a unit of "excess capacity," C_x, is a convenient fiction: the cost of a unit of capacity usually depends on how many units are added at one time (see Section 3-3) and changes over time as the plant ages, the product mix is altered, and the production technology is modified. Similarly, the "shortage cost" per unit, C_s, may include such difficult-to-evaluate components as the *future* lost profits from customers that turn to competitors' products because you have insufficient capacity to meet their needs, and the long-term costs associated with a reputation as an "unreliable supplier."

At a basic conceptual level, however, this ratio captures the kind of tradeoff that managers must take into account as they grapple with the question "How much capacity is enough?" The situation faced by Zenith Radio Corporation in mid-1966, when it had to decide how much additional capacity to build for assembling color television sets, is representative. [See the case "Zenith Radio Corporation (AR)," Harvard Case Services, 9-674-026.] Industry sales had doubled each year for the previous three years; by 1966 they were in excess of 5 million units annually. Zenith had been able to maintain a market share of about 20 percent during this period, but by mid-1966 its assembly capacity of approximately 1 million units per year (4,000 per day) was stretched to the limit. Industry demand was expected to increase to between 7 million and 10 million sets per year within two years. The factory selling price for each set was about $370, and its contribution margin was roughly 25 percent, or $90. (Zenith's after-tax profit was about 7 percent of sales at that time.)

One of the proposals for additional capacity considered by Zenith would have provided a total of 7,300 sets per day (roughly 1.8 million per year). This proposal would have expanded two existing plants and added a new plant whose capacity would be 2,100 sets per day. Building this new plant would have required an investment of about $6 million.

One might begin the evaluation of this proposal by examining the costs and benefits of providing capacity for an additional 1,000 sets per day (250,000 per year). Since television assembly at that time was relatively labor intensive and exhibited few economies of scale, we will assume that building a new plant 50 percent larger than the one proposed would have cost about 50 percent, or $3 million, more. On the other hand, if all these additional sets had been sold in any given year, Zenith's sales would have increased by about $92.5 million ($370 × 250,000). Its profit after tax would therefore have risen by about $6.475 million (and as much as $12 million in the unlikely event that none of its fixed costs increased). Therefore, if the additional capacity had been built and all of it had been used to meet customer demand, the payback for the incremental investment would have been less than one-half year (based on profit after tax).

Even if only half of this additional capacity had been used, the payback would have been less than one year. With such an analysis in the back of its mind, Zenith management decided to build a larger plant.

Although the case does not provide the kind of detailed information needed to calculate the values of C_x and C_s precisely, rough values can be estimated as follows:

C_x = \$450,000 (\$3 million for 1,000 sets per day, at an annual interest and amortization cost—in 1966—of 15 percent)

C_s = \$7,000,000 (profit after tax associated with sales of an additional 1,000 sets per day)

The ratio from Equation 3-1, therefore, is

$$\frac{7,000,000 - 450,000}{7,000,000} = 0.936$$

This suggests that, on the basis of economic considerations alone (and some very rough calculations), Zenith should have provided enough production capacity to achieve a probability of over 90 percent of meeting 1968 demand. Although the data in the case are somewhat vague, this implies an assembly capacity of somewhere between 2.2 and 2.5 million sets per year (or 8,800 to 10,000 sets per day). As noted earlier, in a situation like Zenith's, where demand is growing rapidly, building a sizable capacity cushion is much less risky than it would be in a slow growth or cyclical demand environment.

3-3 THE SIZING OF CAPACITY INCREMENTS—SCALE CONSIDERATIONS

Closely tied to the question of how much capacity to provide to reach a desired production goal are issues relating to the size of the increments of capacity to be added at various points in time. The costs of acquiring and operating a production facility are usually affected by its size, or "scale." Although it is generally accepted that a new facility (increment of capacity) that is twice as large as another will often not cost twice as much to build or operate, it is necessary to be more precise when making an actual decision to add capacity. This section discusses the underlying causes of scale economies—both positive and negative—and examines their relationship to such concepts as a plant's "optimal" and "minimum economic" size.

3-3.1 Economies of Scale

The observation that a production facility's total manufacturing costs generally increase at a slower rate than its production volume has led to the concept of "production economies of scale." This concept often is used—sometimes without careful analysis—as a justification for adding products to an existing plant or building a new plant that is bigger than currently needed. Although the concept is based on plentiful evidence of actual cost behavior, so many different phenomena are encompassed by the term that confusion often arises as to what it really means in a specific situation. Moreover, different forms of scale economies (*and* diseconomies) affect not only capacity decisions but also many of the other types of decisions addressed in this book.

Economies of scale can arise for a variety of reasons because they derive from many different components of total cost. Therefore, unless the logical connection between the scale economies observed in a given situation and the circumstances and actions that apparently caused them is carefully identified, inaccurate forecasts of future costs can result. Perhaps the easiest and most logical way to sort out the various causal factors that underlie such economies is according to time period.

Short-Term Economies of Scale

In the very short term, most of the time-dependent costs in a plant are relatively independent of the actual production volume. Hence they are called "period" costs or, unfortunately, "fixed" costs. We say "unfortunately" because the term "fixed costs" is often misconstrued to an even greater extent than is the term "economies of scale"; all costs are variable over the long run and are fixed only to the extent that decisions to change them require time to take effect. In a situation where many of the costs associated with production are difficult to change quickly (the wages of salaried workers, depreciation and insurance costs on plant and equipment, property taxes, interest costs on borrowed capital, and in many settings, even the cost of direct labor), increasing the volume of production will not cause total costs to increase proportionally.

The major increase in total cost will come from the "variable" or "direct" costs of production, such as those associated with material and energy usage, wear-dependent machine costs, and, sometimes, direct labor costs. Therefore, the total cost per unit of production will decrease as total production increases:

$$\frac{\text{fixed costs} + \text{variable costs}}{\text{total production}} = \frac{\text{fixed costs}}{\text{total production}} + \text{variable cost/unit} \quad (3\text{-}2)$$

This effect is sometimes referred to as "spreading the overhead costs."

This type of scale economy is closely linked to the firm's capacity strategy because of the impact of factory utilization rates on operating costs (and therefore on profits). Figure 3-2 shows the impact of such short-term economies, arising out of fluctuations in capacity utilization, on one chemical plant's total unit costs.*

* In keeping with the terminology used in discussing learning curves (see Chapter 8), we find it convenient to measure scale economies in terms of the percentage of cost reduction associated with each doubling of volume. Thus a scale economies ratio of 68 percent would

Figure 3-2   Analysis of capacity utilization scale economies for a chemical plant
(monthly unit costs—logarithmic scales)

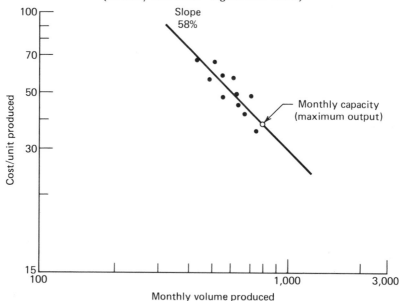

The reason we call this a short-term effect is that over time most of these fixed costs can be changed: salaried personnel can be added or reduced, investment in inventories or equipment can be increased or decreased, and whole areas of plants can be added or shut down. Also, as plants reach their capacity limits, new production capacity must be added. Since increments are usually added in sizable chunks, the operation shifts rather quickly from a situation in which it is operating at full utilization to one where it is underutilized. Therefore, this type of scale economy, although real, can be transitory. In order to achieve economies that are more lasting, changes must be made in the way the existing process is managed.

Intermediate-Term Economies of Scale

Over an intermediate time period the firm can exploit increased production volume to reduce costs in several related ways. One is to increase production run lengths, thereby reducing the number of changeovers that must be made to satisfy a given volume of sales. Therefore, the average cost per unit behaves like the average cost in equation (3-2):

$$\text{average cost} = \frac{\text{changeover cost}}{\begin{array}{c}(\text{number of units} \\ \text{per production run})\end{array}} + \text{running cost/unit} \qquad (3\text{--}3)$$

imply that unit costs would drop to 68 percent of their former value with each doubling of production volume.

The extent of these economies depends on the magnitude of the cost of changeovers, which include such components as:

1. The actual cost of changing over the equipment to a different product (for example, resetting guides, fixtures, dies, and instruction modules, and perhaps adjusting and cleaning internal parts).
2. "Run-in" and "run-out" costs (the cost of excess scrap and reduced labor efficiency at the beginning and end of production runs).
3. The cost of lost production (when equipment is operating near full capacity, the time lost during changeovers may result in lost sales or lead to overtime and other costs to compensate for this lost production).

It is possible to increase production run lengths without changing the total production level, of course. However, two factors usually make this undesirable. First, increasing the run length in the absence of a compensating increase in the demand rate will tend to increase the firm's finished-goods inventory, requiring additional capital and storage facilities, and increasing the risk of obsolescence. Second, for a given level of total demand, as the average production lot size increases, the time between runs also increases. In the presence of an uncertain demand rate this increases the likelihood that the firm's finished-goods inventory will become unbalanced. Such imbalance could be costly in terms of increased backorder costs, emergency production runs, and lost sales.

Another way that increased production volume can be translated into lower costs in the intermediate term is by dedicating resources (equipment and people) to certain products or tasks. This can lead to fewer changeovers and make it possible to use lesser-skilled (and lower-paid) operators as well, since the skills required to make changeovers, produce a variety of products, or participate in the introduction of an entirely new product no longer would be required. In addition, dedicating equipment and people to the production of a single product makes it possible to tailor tools, jigs, fixtures, and materials-handling equipment to the specific requirements of that product and thus reduce cycle times, material waste, maintenance, and so forth.

One other way that scale economies can be exploited in the intermediate term is by employing equipment that is specially designed to produce a given product. When a product's production volume exceeds a certain level, it no longer makes sense to use smaller, general-purpose machines in its production. The use of high-volume, customized machines often reduces total costs. For example, the amount of operator time per unit produced can usually be reduced substantially.

Figure 3-3 depicts two alternative approaches to achieving intermediate economies of scale for the chemical plant described in Figure 3-2: by using a series of general-purpose lines, or by using a series of more specialized lines (the unit costs are hypothetical). It should be noted that the risks associated with dedicated, more specialized (and therefore less flexible) lines would have to be weighed against their intermediate-term cost advantages.

Figure 3-3   Intermediate-term scale economies for a chemical plant
(logarithmic scales)

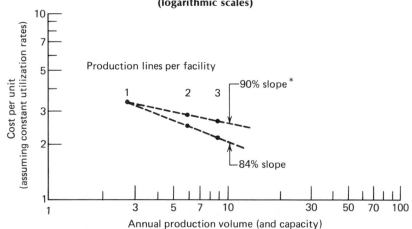

* The 90 percent slope indicates scale economies from multiple lines of a given size (with no change in product assignments); the 84 percent slope reflects scale economies from more dedicated and specialized multiple lines of that given size.

Long-Term Economies of Scale

When engineers and economists refer to scale economies, they usually mean long-term economies. These can be broken into two subcategories: static and dynamic.

The term "static economies of scale" refers to the economies that arise from using one large machine rather than a number of smaller ones to produce a product. This often results in savings because the production capacity of much equipment is roughly proportional to its interior *volume*, whereas its cost is more closely related to the equipment's *surface area* (which is where the materials—cement, steel, and glass—and labor hours are concentrated). Since the volume of a geometric body increases faster than its surface area, both the construction costs and operating costs generally follow a curve* of the form where

$$C(V) = KV^k \qquad (3\text{-}4)$$

where $C(V)$ = the cost associated with a capacity increment of size V
K = a constant scale factor
k = a number between 0 and 1 that defines the "degree" of scale economies

* In practice, this curve is seldom as smooth as this equation would indicate. Only increments of certain sizes may be technologically feasible or available from equipment suppliers. So the actual curve often contains scallops, blank areas, and step changes. It should also be noted that when $k = 1$, there are no economies of scale; if V doubles, so does $C(V)$. As k gets smaller, the economies of scale become more pronounced. In practice, k is almost always between 0.6 and 1.0.

Consider, as an example, the cost of making a steel can. If the ratio of its length to its diameter is kept constant, its volume (V units) will increase with the cube of its radius, while its outside surface area will increase only with the square of its radius. Its cost equation therefore is

$$C(V) = KV^{2/3} \tag{3-5}$$

This example is not as simplistic as it might appear at first glance. Most production units that process liquids (including molten metals) are basically cylinders—large steel cans. Thus it is not surprising that the cost of chemical reactors, iron-making blast furnaces, oil refineries, and ocean freighters all increase roughly according to the two-thirds power of their capacities. For such cost functions, a doubling of capacity causes costs to increase about 60 percent,* which has led such industries to adopt a rule of thumb known as "the six-tenths rule" when estimating the costs of different-sized capacity increments.

Other factors also underlie construction economies of scale. Some of them are analogous to the concept of "spreading the fixed costs" that we discussed earlier. For example, certain startup costs are often not directly proportional to the size of the facility: one must employ the services of architects, engineers, and lawyers no matter what sized unit is being considered, and their fees are sometimes surprisingly independent of the size of the unit. Similarly, the cost of environmental impact statements, negotiations with zoning boards, and governmental agencies often increases less rapidly than unit size.

The cost per unit of operating such a facility, moreover, can be affected by technological opportunities. More sophisticated measuring instruments, auxiliary equipment, and control devices all become economical at higher volumes. They often make it possible to reduce labor costs, increase output yield, and improve product quality.

Sometimes, building a larger facility permits one to adopt an entirely different technology—one that might function ineffectively or be uneconomic at low volumes. These technology-related savings, resulting from using a large production unit rather than a combination of smaller ones, complement those that are a function of simple geometry. Both types are generally classified as "static economies" because they are embodied in the choice of the equipment itself, not in the skills that are gained in using the equipment to manufacture products. Figure 3-4 indicates for a chemical plant how such static long-term economies might contrast with intermediate-term economies.

The term "dynamic economies of scale," on the other hand, refers to the improvement in marginal cost per unit, *at some given scale*, that results from

* This follows from the fact that when a production facility's capacity is doubled, its cost will be proportional to $2^{2/3} = 1.6$, or 60 percent more than the cost of only half as much capacity. Note that, using the terminology of Figures 3-2 and 3-3, this corresponds to a scale slope of $1.6/2 = 0.8$, that is, each doubling of capacity is accompanied by a reduction in unit cost to 80 percent of its former value.

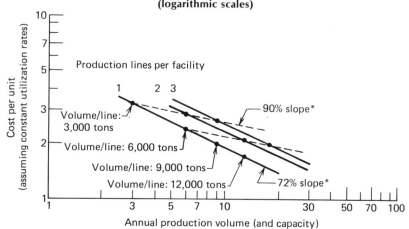

Figure 3-4   Long-term scale economies due to size and technology (logarithmic scales)

* The 90 percent slope was achieved by using multiple lines of a given size (same process); the 72 percent slope was achieved by using longer, larger lines.

the skills and experience in using the equipment that is accumulated by the organization. It recognizes that the equipment manufacturers (who, in effect, transmit processing technology between firms) do not determine entirely the production cost of the companies that buy their equipment. Constant advances in processing technology accrue from myriad minor improvements in equipment, labor capabilities, management methods, product changes, and so forth, as well as through formal R&D programs. Long-term economies of scale, therefore, arise from "learning by doing" (we return to this topic in Chapter 8) as well as from equipment geometry and technology.

Both static and dynamic economies of scale are illustrated in Figure 3-5, which depicts the marginal costs of production for two competitors. Each is investing in a new production unit (for making, say, precision mechanical components for the same product market). The first is just entering the business. For different capital investment levels it may acquire any one of four technologies; their marginal cost relationships are specified by curves C_1 through C_4. The second is an existing large producer that will apply its acquired experience, labor resources, management skills, and understanding of processing methods to the new equipment that replaces its old equipment. It may be able to realize marginal costs as specified by the lower dotted curve, C'_4, at approximately the same investment level and with basically the same technology as that used by the new entrant.

If both firms make investments at scale "4," the newly entering firm will realize *static* scale economies of *s* dollars per unit by purchasing the largest production facility rather than the smallest one. The established firm, however, will be able to realize an *additional d* dollars per unit as a result of the dynamic economies that accrue from its greater experience and accumulated knowledge.

Figure 3-5   Static and dynamic economies of scale for a precision parts plant

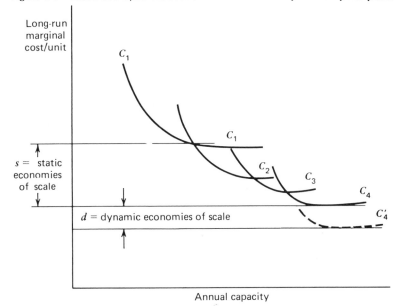

Dynamic economies occur when the most effective technology is not obtainable from equipment suppliers alone, or from engineers who work simply on the *design* of equipment. For example, in one study, Stobaugh and Townsend (1975) attempted to separate the contribution of static and dynamic scale economies, among other factors, to the patterns of price reductions in 82 petrochemical products. Although their analysis is not conclusive, it suggests that the cost reductions (over a five-year planning horizon) resulting from dynamic scale economies exceed those resulting from increased static scale economies by a two-to-one factor. Price reductions attributed to greater product standardization alone roughly equaled those from static scale economies, even with near-commodity items like petrochemicals. For complex products at an early stage of their life cycle, an even larger contribution from dynamic economies and product standardization would be expected. Similarly, in a study of the U.S. semiconductor industry, Tilton (1971) concluded that the most successful competitive strategies were those based on dynamic rather than static scale economies.

3-3.2   Diseconomies of Scale

As Keynes observed (and, probably, many others before him), "There is no such thing as a free lunch." So it is with economies of scale. Increasing the scale of production can enable a firm to reduce certain costs, but it can also cause other costs to increase. These "diseconomies of scale" fall into four main categories.

Distribution Diseconomies

As a manufacturing plant gets bigger, it usually has to ship its output over a larger geographic area. Moreover, if the density of its customers decreases rapidly as one moves away from the plant, the distribution costs required to supply an expanding region will probably increase much faster than the sales volume. Even in cases where the company does not incur the transportation costs directly, it may have to pay "freight equalization charges" to prevent competitors nearer the customer from gaining a cost advantage. The result is that the company's *total delivered cost* per unit may decrease up to a certain volume level (because of production economies of scale), and then begin to increase beyond that level (because of distribution diseconomies).

Therefore, in situations where the transportation cost per unit is very high in comparison with its sales price (examples include bricks, cement, and manufactured housing), companies may be constrained to a rather small geographic market area. On the other hand, they may also be almost invulnerable to the attacks of competitors who are located outside their "home market." Should a new competitor choose to locate a new plant in this home market, and there are pronounced economies of scale in construction or operations, the costs (and even the prices) of the two competitors may be higher than those of the original producer when it was alone in serving the market. This is because each of them would now operate at a lower, and less efficient, volume than did the former company by itself.

The same type of distribution diseconomy of scale may affect the demand for a firm's products in situations where the response time to customer requests for service or assistance is an important marketing advantage. For a given geographic area in which customers are located with a constant density, it can be shown that the average distance between a plant (or service center) and a customer is inversely proportional to the square root of the number of plants in the area:*

$$\text{average distance} = k \left(\frac{\text{area served}}{\text{number of plants}} \right)^{1/2}$$

Therefore, too few large plants may both increase the transportation costs associated with servicing distant customers and reduce the firm's total sales because of its customers' preference for the better service provided by a competitor's nearby plant.

Diseconomies of Bureaucratization

As the scale of a production unit increases, so does the workforce required to operate it. The larger the workforce, the more supervisors, coordinators, and managers are required. Since managers usually feel that the number of people

---

* This formula has also been used to determine the optimum number of firehouses or schools in an urban environment. (See Kolesar and Blum, 1973.)

reporting to them ought to be less than some maximum number (generally 8 to 12), organizations tend to grow like pyramids: as the base of the pyramid (representing the number of workers) grows, so does the number of layers of managers—each of whom probably requires at least one support person (a secretary, assistant, etc.). As the number of layers in the management hierarchy grows, communication and coordination becomes more difficult, so additional support personnel are required. For example, whereas a 200-person workforce would normally have at most three organizational levels above the worker, a 2,000-person workforce typically has four or five levels.

The results are predictable: management costs increase; the organization's response time (both to external forces and internal crises) deteriorates; and the workers on the plant floor—the base upon which the pyramid rests— lose their sense of identity and personal loyalty, both to each other and to the firm as a whole. It becomes increasingly likely that some of the information that filters up or down through the organization will get lost or distorted. Worse, first-level supervisors (on whom the workers depend for direction and support) may lose some of their decision-making authority and credibility if they are constrained by incorrect or incomplete information.

Another danger arises when the workforce in a plant becomes too big in relation to the population in its immediate area. As a community becomes more and more dependent on a single plant or company, it tends to become more concerned with its activities. Often this growing sense of dependence can lead to increased surveillance of plant activities by community leaders, followed by attempts to become more involved in internal decisions. Eventually this process can lead to open hostility. As a result, many companies put a "cap" on the number of people that can be employed at one of their plants—limiting it, say, to 3–4 percent of the working population within a 20-mile commuting distance. (See Schmenner, 1982, pp. 10–11.)

The result of all these factors is that large plants are more likely to attract successful unionization efforts (which has the effect of adding another bureaucracy to the organization), as well as increased public scrutiny. There is some evidence that the frequency of labor disputes also goes up. For example, Prais (1973) reported that less than 10 percent of the plants in the United Kingdom employing fewer than 400 workers experienced strikes during 1971–1973, while more than 50 percent of the plants employing more than 5,000 workers experienced strikes during that same period. (See also Shorey, 1975.)

Diseconomies of Confusion

Although related to the problems of bureaucratization, the diseconomies that fall into this category arise from a different phenomenon: the impact of increasing the number of products, processes, and specialists in a given plant as it grows in size. Combining dissimilar activities does not reduce complexity; it merely covers them with a common roof. Unless this complexity is managed carefully, the organization can begin to work at cross-purposes and, sometimes, to dissolve into chaos.

Our observation of many factories suggests that the number of people whose role is primarily one of coordination across functional or department boundaries tends to increase more than proportionally with the number of separately managed units (departments, functions, process stages, etc.) in a plant. This phenomenon is analogous to one often observed in large networks (railroads, truck lines, time-sharing computer systems, etc.), where the "supervisory costs" (those associated with supervising the operations of each unit) increase in rough proportion to the number of units, but the "coordination costs" (associated with coordinating the operations of different units) increase with the number of *links* between units.

For example, a network with four units (shipping terminals, product lines, process stages, etc.) has six links between them. If another unit is added to the network, the number of links goes up to 10. In other words, its supervisory costs will increase by 25 percent, but its coordinating costs will increase by 67 percent. Going to six units increases the number of links to 15.* These and related issues are discussed further in Chapter 4 where we address the topic of facilities focus.

Diseconomies of Vulnerability to Risk

The more resources that a firm places in a plant, the more dependent it becomes on that plant's successful operation. Should the plant be struck by a natural disaster (flood, fire, hurricane, earthquake, etc.) or a human one (strike, accident, mismanagement), the performance of the company as a whole will be seriously impaired. To reduce their vulnerability to the kind of risks that are associated with putting "too many eggs in one basket," companies often prefer to allocate the production of certain critical products or components into two or more separate locations.

In summary, diseconomies of scale are just as real and important as economies of scale, even though they have not received equal attention in the economic literature. The management literature, on the other hand, is increasingly reflecting the recognition that small companies and plants often outperform their larger counterparts in the same industry. Even today, however, too many companies seem to regard diseconomies of scale as the result of a set of factors that "good" managers should somehow be able to overcome.

3-3.3   Optimal Economic Size

The foregoing discussion of the economies and diseconomies of scale leads naturally to the notion of an "optimal plant size." The basic concept is straightforward: As the size of a production unit increases, it can exploit more and more scale economies, but it also becomes increasingly subject to diseconomies. Management's task is to select the size that makes it possible to manufacture its products at a low total delivered cost, or the one that promises the

---

* In general, the number of links between *n* nodes in a network is equal to ½ n (n - 1).

highest total profits (which sometimes leads to a different answer), and at the same time is compatible with the company's values and attitudes regarding competitive priorities, desirable working environments, and risks of various types.

Identifying this optimal size involves, at best, a rough approximation in practice, and it is usually based more on "gut feeling" than on factual data. Determining the best size for a facility is difficult both because it is hard to distinguish the impact of "bad management" from "wrong size," and because it depends on a number of situational factors, such as the facility's age and its general environment—labor, government, market, competition, technology— all of which change over time.

In spite of these measurement difficulties, management behavior in a number of industries appears to reflect a belief that there is an optimal economic size for a facility. (See Schmenner, 1982.) Most are stated in terms of ceilings on the maximum sales revenue to be generated, the number of workers employed, or the floor space to be provided. Schmenner found that stated employment ceilings ranged from about 300 (for firms in highly competitive, labor-intensive industries like apparel, shoes, and metalworking) to 6,000 (firms in capital- or technology-intensive industries like transportation equipment and electronics). A few industries, like aerospace, appeared to have no ceilings at all.

Schmenner also found that as an industry matures, firms tend to use smaller facilities than they operated when they were growing rapidly; some even dismantle facilities considered excessively large. The reasons managers gave for preferring smaller facilities included:

1. The confusion and complexity of larger plants.
2. The difficulty of maintaining control over larger facilities.
   Management philosophy regarding motivation and incentives.
   The maximum number of management layers desired at one site.
   The desire to avoid unionization.
3. A concern about becoming too dominant in the local community.

All of these reasons relate directly to factors identified previously and reflect management's need to balance the economies and diseconomies of scale.

The concept of "minimum economic size" is also useful in capacity planning and follows naturally from the previous discussion. Simply stated, it is the smallest production unit that is competitively and operationally viable. Clearly, the minimum economic size depends on the industry's technology, the market served, the nature of competition, and several other factors. Schematically, it can be depicted as in Figure 3-6.

From Figure 3-6 it can be seen that strong economies of scale (indicated by the curvature of the total cost curve) occur up to point *A*. Therefore the average cost per unit decreases rapidly up to that point. Between points *A* and *B*

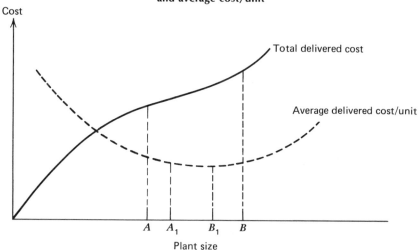

Figure 3-6   Conceptual presentation of total delivered cost
and average cost/unit

the total cost curve flattens out, indicating that the increase in the total delivered cost is approximately proportional to the increase in plant size over that range. The average cost per unit, therefore, varies only slightly between A and B. Beyond point B the total cost curve shows a reverse curvature, indicating that diseconomies of scale outweigh economies of scale; as a result, the average cost per unit increases for plant sizes beyond that point.

Building a plant bigger than size A leads to some cost improvements but not compelling ones; any plant size in the range from A to B can be thought of as cost-competitive, or "economic." Looking only at this cost curve, Plant A can be thought of as the "minimum economic size," but other considerations may affect this selection. For example, only plants larger than size A_1 may be viable for technological or organizational reasons, equipment may come only in certain sizes, or the cost of certain overhead functions necessitates production volumes above a certain level. Therefore, point A_1 might be the minimum *feasible* economic size in this industry. (Note that Plant Size B_1 would be the *optimal* economic size that we discussed earlier.)

It should be reemphasized that the minimum economic size is a somewhat elusive concept, because there are no clear breaks in the curve depicted in Figure 3-6. Nor, as discussed in later chapters, do all firms compete solely on the basis of price (and therefore delivered cost). Hence the size of the "minimum economic plant" is a matter of judgment that depends very much on the individual company and its competitive strategy, just as the "optimal" plant size does.

As an illustration of some of the points made in this section, studies of plant sizes in the same industry (see Bain, 1966, and Scherer et al., 1975) have shown that the median-sized plant varies widely among different countries and is often substantially *smaller* than the theoretical "minimum economic plant."

These studies also suggest that the average plant size tends to increase as the size of the total market in a given country increases, whereas the kinds of technological and economic considerations that tend to permeate discussion of economies of scale are largely independent of market size. These results do not imply that business managers are not "rational" as much as they suggest that in their decision-making they take more factors into consideration than do economists.

3-4 DEVELOPING A CAPACITY STRATEGY

If strong scale economies exist, it clearly does not make sense for a firm to try to match the growth in demand for its product with a series of small capacity additions. Capacity should be added in chunks. The question is, how big should these chunks be, and when should they be added?* To address the question of the size and timing of the capacity chunks to be added, we return to the three types of strategies depicted in Figure 3-1, and begin by assuming that the company never wants to run short of capacity. Moreover, the company can bring new capacity on-line at the moment that it runs out.

In our earlier discussion of the amount of capacity cushion that a company should seek to maintain over time, it was assumed that it was possible to keep this cushion within acceptable limits by careful choice of capacity increments. If scale economies make it advisable to add capacity in rather large chunks (compared with existing capacity), however, it may not be possible to fine-tune this capacity cushion as suggested by the simple ratio (Equation 3-1) developed in Section 3-2.

Under such circumstances, a sequence like that depicted in Figure 3-7 provides a more appropriate framework for thinking about this problem. If we assume that demand is growing at a rate of G units per year, and that the company is adding capacity in chunks of V units every T years, the company's capacity cushion will be very large immediately after a new increment has been added (at time t_1, for example), so it would be almost impossible for the company to run short during this period. However, the probability of running short approaches 100 percent as time t_2 approaches. The question is, how much of an expected deficit (D) should the company plan for toward the end of this period—just before a new increment is added?

The basic tradeoffs that must be made involve, first, the reduced cost per unit from building a larger chunk of capacity; second, the cost of underutilized facilities until demand grows to the point where this additional capacity will be needed; and third, the penalty associated with being short of capacity during

---

* In practice, this issue is complicated by a number of related issues having to do with whether the capacity increment is being added to an existing plant or is in a separate location. There also may be organizational complications associated with putting it in place and managing it effectively. The sizes of the increments may be restricted to what equipment suppliers are able to provide, and sometimes to what the firm can afford at a given time.

Figure 3-7   Capacity expansion strategy over two cycles

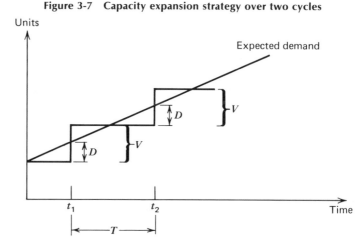

some significant part of the firm's capacity replenishment cycle. Therefore, a firm that overbuilds will be paying both capital (interest) charges for some amount of unused capacity and the costs of maintaining it so that it can be used when it is needed, but it will operate a lower-cost facility and avoid the cost of shortages.

Two other factors must be considered in today's environment. First, during the 1970s, equipment costs generally experienced a higher rate of inflation than did the costs of the goods they produced. Therefore, the interest cost should be adjusted to reflect the "real" interest rate for the money invested in an increment of capacity—the actual interest cost less the anticipated inflation rate in construction costs.

Second, building capacity before it is needed increases the risk of technological obsolescence. In many industries, major technological advances occur with shocking suddenness. Although this is particularly true of industries that depend heavily on electronics or computer technology, no industry is immune to such disruption. The technology of plate glass production, for example, was completely overturned in the late 1950s when the float glass process was introduced by Pilkington Glass, Ltd., a relatively small English firm. And the newspaper industry, whose technology had been relatively stable for more than 200 years (since Gutenberg, according to some industry observers), experienced a series of profound technological changes between 1960 and 1980 that made much of its traditional production equipment and skills obsolete.

Assuming that such adjustments can be made properly, and that future costs and demand growth are roughly predictable, it is possible to estimate the net cash flows that will result each year from adding capacity increments of any given size in such a way that the firm keeps roughly abreast of a specified pattern of growth in demand. Then some approach, such as discounted present value (to be discussed in Chapter 5, particularly Appendix A), can be used to aggregate these net cash flows. This provides a means for evaluating the financial impact of any given sequence of capacity increments and demand growth rates. If rather restrictive assumptions are made about the demand pattern and costs, the discounted present value of certain simple capacity strategies can be obtained directly through mathematical manipulation, as described in the appendix to this chapter.

Given the complexities and uncertainties associated with estimating costs and demand growth in practice, it is usually unrealistic to try to develop a capacity expansion plan simply by minimizing a single summary measure, as described above. It is more useful to concentrate on developing a conceptual framework that will guide one in the right direction when confronting various alternatives for expanding capacity. The remainder of this chapter seeks to provide such guidance.

3-5 FOUR APPROACHES TO CAPACITY EXPANSION

The foregoing discussion has sought to separate the capacity expansion decision into its two basic components: (1) the general relationship between capacity and demand and (2) the amount of capacity to be added at a given time, and to provide some insight into the circumstances that might lead companies to make different choices in different situations. In doing this we employed some simple models to evaluate the impact of different capacity strategies. Those models, unfortunately, require an unrealistic ability to forecast the evolution of costs and demand, and usually hold all but a few factors constant so as to simplify the analysis. Since most business managers are not blessed with such prescience, they are generally forced to fall back on more intuitive approaches for making capacity decisions. In practice, most of these approaches are based on one of four different policies of capacity expansion.

1. *Don't Build Additional Capacity Until the Need for It Develops* (Policy A in Figure 3-1). Usually, the need for additional capacity is greatest during periods of rapid demand growth, such as at the peak of a business cycle. Firms that adopt this approach, therefore, often find themselves motivated to expand their capacity at about the same time as several of their competitors. These simultaneous decisions to expand not only can drive up construction costs for everybody but can lead to a sudden large increase in industry capacity (often at about the time the industry growth rate slackens). Bloated capacity, coupled with shrinking growth, then increases the competitive pressure on everyone in the industry. To avoid such boom and bust cycles, some companies adopt an alternative approach.

2. *Outguess the Market by Following a Countercyclical Strategy.* This strategy dictates that a firm add capacity at a lower point in the business cycle, when the firm (as well as its competitors) still has excess capacity. This course of action can result in reduced construction costs for the maverick firm, but it is obviously riskier. The manager who recommends building a plant at such a time is in a very vulnerable position. He or she becomes, in effect, a "soothsayer"--and subject to all the slings and arrows of that calling. Therefore, some companies adopt a third approach, which represents a modified version of the second.

3. *Buy for the Long Haul* (usually Policy B or C in Figure 3-1). This is analogous, in a sense, to "dollar averaging" in the stock market. It is based on the idea that only a genius or a fool tries to outguess the market on a continual basis, and that it takes only one mistake to have your classification downgraded. Instead, if a firm's management believes in the necessity of maintaining or increasing its market position in the industry over the long haul, it should simply decide how much capacity will be needed at some comfortably distant point in the future and base its decisions regarding the size and time-spacing of capacity additions around this goal.

Strategies 2 and 3 both represent attempts to chart a capacity expansion course that may be out of step with the moves of competitors. This can be a risky course, particularly if the firm is relatively small and the industry is dominated by a few giants. If the firm "guesses right" by building capacity at the right time, and the industry leaders guess wrong, then the small firm may reap substantial rewards—temporarily at least. But if the firm guesses wrong and the leaders guess right, the firm's competitive position may be seriously undermined. Depending on management's aversion to risks of this sort, a fourth expansion strategy is sometimes chosen.

4. *Follow the Leader(s).* This strategy is: "Build when they build." If they are right, you benefit, too. If they (and you) are wrong together, then neither you nor they will gain any competitive advantage. If the leaders do exercise some control over the industry, they may be able to respond to their misfortune by raising prices when industry capacity is tight, or by not dropping them when excess industry capacity is available; then your firm will be able to hide under this price umbrella.

The behavior of the smaller oil companies and independent oil tanker chartering companies in the early 1970s appears to reflect this fourth strategy: the oil giants were buying new oil tankers, so everybody else did, too. Unfortunately, the Arab–Israeli war in late 1973 was followed by rapid increases in the price of crude oil. Attempts to conserve oil and economic slowdowns followed in most of the major oil-consuming nations. Hundreds of only slightly used supertankers anchored in secluded bays and fjords around the world during the late 1970s offered mute testimony that following the leaders does not always pay off.*

---

* As an aside, it can be noted that both strategies 1 and 4 can cause several companies in an industry to make similar capacity expansion moves at about the same time. A cynical outsider (an antitrust lawyer, say) might claim that this is evidence of collusion. It is usually nothing of the sort—any more than a long line waiting to buy tickets for a hit musical represents collusion. But how can one prove that one *isn't* colluding? The usual prescription is lots of other lawyers, time, and money!

3-5.1 Integrating the Firm's Capacity Strategy with Its Business Strategy

Most of the discussion of capacity strategy thus far made two implicit but critical assumptions: (1) a capacity strategy deals with *expansion,* and (2) that expansion occurs as a *reaction* to increased demand. Although such assumptions provide a useful starting point for capacity analysis, they are too narrow to deal adequately with management's responsibilities in this field. Situations in which a contraction in demand requires a rationalization of capacity is dealt with explicitly in Chapters 4 and 5. In this section we discuss the possibility of *proactive* capacity changes that can influence the demand for the firm's products and therefore support its business strategy, as opposed to *reactive* changes that simply respond to forecasted demand.

Capacity expansion can be used aggressively as a strategic weapon. For example, a capacity increase may cause demand to increase faster than it would otherwise (on the assumption that "supply creates its own demand"), or it may make competitors hesitate to add capacity themselves. If the selected business strategy is to "invest and grow" by increasing volume and reducing costs, aggressive capacity expansions can play an important preemptive role. (See Porter, 1980.)

When a company adds to its production capacity by building a new facility, it also adds to the total capacity in the industry. As we have seen, if construction costs are subject to strong economies of scale, each capacity increment should be a large one. Smaller competitors may become uneasy about adding to their own capacity after such a large increment has come onstream, particularly if adding capacity is expensive. They may fear that too much capacity will lead to price wars and other forms of cutthroat competition. Therefore, by following such a preemptive strategy, a large and financially strong company may be able to discourage its competitors from adding to their capacity as fast as it does. Therefore, the firm can meet its own capacity needs and, at the same time, force its competitors to alter their plans. Over time, as the less aggressive competitors' share of industry capacity shrinks and the average age of their facilities rises above that of more aggressive competitors, they may be driven slowly out of the market—leaving their former customers to the victors.

Although such firms may feel that their reluctance to add capacity is logical (and can probably justify it with analyses showing that such capacity additions would not meet some desired return on investment), a series of such apparently logical steps will lead almost inevitably to disaster. Such a scenario is particularly poignant because many U.S. industries seem to be captives of this sort of logic. As a result, they are steadily being displaced in the international marketplace by foreign competitors who are willing to invest at a faster rate.

A good illustration of the opposite behavior—the planned use of capacity expansion to deter competitors—is provided by Texas Instruments' moves to enter or expand its position in various markets for electronic components. TI's announcements of price cuts and added capacity almost always precede other strategic moves aimed at increasing its market share and establishing a dominant position in a business.

Another illustration is provided by Georgia-Pacific's 1980 announcement (to the pulp and paper specialty chemical industry) of its new tall oil plant and the firm's intention to build volume quickly. GP revealed its plan during a presentation at the industry association's annual meeting, purportedly for the purpose of informing others about the technology installed in its new plant. However, to outside observers, the message was clear: "We are just completing a major facility, which has significant scale economies. It is up to date, and we are willing to take the steps necessary (including cutting prices) to fill it up. Therefore, the best thing for competitors to do is to give up a little business and make it easier on everyone." On the basis of comments from several of those attending this meeting, it appeared that GP's past behavior made such a message very credible.

Location decisions also can help support business objectives. For example, building a new factory in a geographical area where one has not previously had any production capability not only enables a company to service the existing demand for its products in that area but also brings it closer to existing and potential customers. Its workers and managers become neighbors of these customers, and their proximity encourages relationships that may prove stronger than those established by more distant competitors. In effect, the company becomes an "insider" in its new economic and social community and accrues all the advantages of that position.

Competing on the basis of low cost (or preemptive market moves) is not the only way a firm's capacity strategy can complement its business strategy. At Trus Joist Corporation, a manufacturer of roof and floor support systems for the construction market, management has pursued a policy of maintaining capacity 20 percent in excess of *projected peak seasonal demand*. (See the case study, "Trus Joist Corporation," Harvard Case Services 9-675-207.) With its competitive emphasis on quality and fast delivery of a customized product, this capacity strategy has enabled the firm to guarantee delivery within three weeks of order receipt, even in peak periods when its competitors traditionally had to lengthen their delivery times. To make such a capacity cushion economically feasible, management has pursued several complementary moves in product design, facilities development, and production technology. The company's approach has been to determine what was required to implement its chosen strategy, rather than taking conventional industry plant size economics as "given" or simply following industry practice when making capacity decisions.

There are, of course, limits to the aggressive use of capacity in business strategy. A variety of industries have found themselves so overbuilt that literally years were required before their members could regain some semblance of profitability. The PVC (polyvinyl chloride) industry in the early 1980s provides one such example. Aggressive capacity strategies on the part of the four leading competitors, combined with significant scale economies and a slowing of market growth (even a temporary decline), resulted in industry average capacity utilization rates of 50–60 percent—well below breakeven levels. Recognizing the causes of overbuilding can help avoid such problems in planning one's capacity strategy. Those identified by Porter (1980) are summarized in Table 3-1.

This chapter provides an overview of some of the concepts that are useful in developing and planning a capacity strategy: a series of capacity decisions that form a coherent pattern. Implementing such a capacity strategy requires the development of (1) strategies for specific facilities, and (2) procedures to

Table 3-1
Causes of Overbuilding Manufacturing Capacity

Technological Factors

Adding capacity in large increments
Economies of scale
Long lead times in adding capacity
Minimum efficient scale increasing over time
Changes in production technology

Structural Factors

Significant exit barriers
Motivation from suppliers
Building credibility with customers
Integrated competitors
Effect of capacity share on market share
Effect of age and type of capacity on demand

Competitive Factors

Large number of firms
Lack of credible market leaders
Entry of new competitors
Advantages of being an early mover

Information Flow Factors

Inflation of future expectations
Divergent assumptions or perceptions
Breakdown of market signaling
Structural change
Financial community pressures

Managerial Factors

Management background and industry experience
Attitude toward different types of risk

Governmental Factors

Perverse tax incentives
Desire for indigenous industry
Pressures to increase or maintain employment

Source. Adapted from Porter, 1980, pp. 324–339.

ensure that decisions affecting specific facilities support the desired pattern. These topics are covered in Chapters 4 and 5.

SELECTED REFERENCES

Bain, Joe S. *International Differences in Industrial Structure.* New Haven: Yale University Press, 1966.

Erlinkotter, Donald. *Preinvestment Planning for Capacity Expansion: A Multilocation Dynamic Model,* Ph.D. dissertation. Ann Arbor, MI: University Microfilms International, 1970.

Freidenfelds, John. *Capacity Expansion.* New York: Elsevier–North Holland, 1981.

Kolesar, P. and E. Blum, "Square Root Laws for Fire Engine Response Distances." *Management Science,* Vol. 19, No. 12, August 1973.

Manne, Alan S. *Investments for Capacity Expansion.* London: George Allen and Unwin, 1967.

Morris, William T. *A Capacity Decision System.* Homewood, IL: Richard D. Irwin, 1967.

Porter, Michael E. *Competitive Strategy.* New York: Free Press, 1980.

Prais, S. J. "The Strike Proneness of Large Plants in Britain." *Journal of the Royal Statistical Society (A),* Vol. 141, Part 3, 1973, pp. 368–384.

Scherer, F. M., Alan Beckenstein, Erich Kaufer, R. Dennis Murphy, and Francine Bougeon-Maassen. *The Economics of Multiplant Operation.* Cambridge, MA: Harvard University Press, 1975.

Schmenner, Roger W. *Making Business Location Decisions.* Englewood Cliffs, NJ: Prentice-Hall, 1982.

Schmenner, Roger W. "Before You Build a Big Factory." *Harvard Business Review,* July–August 1976, pp. 77–81.

Shorey, John. "The Size of the Work Unit and Strike Incidence." *Journal of Industrial Economy,* Vol. 23, No. 3, 1975, pp. 175–188.

Stobaugh, Robert B., and Phillip L. Townsend. "Price Forecasting and Strategic Planning: The Case of Petrochemicals." *Journal of Marketing Research,* February 1975, pp. 19–29.

Tilton, John E. *International Diffusion of Technology: The Case of Semiconductors.* Washington, DC: Brookings Institution, 1971.

Waddell, Robert M., Philip M. Ritz, John D. Norton, and Marshall K. Wood. *Capacity Expansion Planning Factors in Manufacturing Industries.* Washington, DC: National Planning Association, 1966.

Wein, Harold H., and V. P. Sreedharan. *The Optimal Staging and Phasing of Multiproduct Capacity.* East Lansing: Michigan State University, 1968.

Weiss, L. W. "Optimal Plant Size and Extent of Suboptimal Capacity," in *Essays on Industrial Organization in Honor of Joe S. Bain,* R. T. Masson and P. D. Quall, eds. Cambridge, MA: Ballinger, 1975.

Appendix. Calculating the Discounted Present Value of Given Capacity Strategies in a Growing Market Under Specified Demand and Cost Assumptions

3A-1 ASSUMING NO SHORTFALL IN CAPACITY IS PERMITTED

If we assume that demand is growing by G units each year, then it can be shown that the discounted cost* of building capacity increments of size V at every point in time where demand outstrips existing capacity (Policy A in Figure 3-1) is given by

$$\text{TDC } (V,G,i) = \frac{C(V)}{1 - e^{-iV/G}} \tag{3A-1}$$

where TDC (V,G,i), the total discounted cost of this strategy, is a function of V (volume), G (annual growth in units), and i:

$C (V) =$ cost of a unit of capacity of size V; and
$i =$ annual cost per dollar of unutilized facilities (including the cost of interest, maintenance, insurance and obsolescence, but deducting the rate of inflation)

Under this growth assumption the time between successive additions of capacity will always be the same: $T = V/G$.

On the other hand, if demand is predicted to grow at a constant *percentage* rate, g, each year (rather than a constant *amount,* as before) and we continue to add capacity at constant time intervals, the size of successive capacity increments will have to increase steadily as the unit growth per year increases. The formula for the discounted cost of following this strategy of adding a capacity increment every T years is

$$TDC (T,g,i,d_0) = \frac{C [V(T)]}{1 - e^{-(i-kg) T}} \tag{3A-2}$$

---

* A brief discussion of the rationale for using their discounted present value as a summary measure for a series of cash flows stretching off into the future is provided in Chapter 5. This appendix is intended for readers who have some technical training in that and other quantitative techniques. Further information about the calculations on this and the next several pages is contained in Manne (1967). See particularly Chapters 2, 9, and 10.

where $T =$ time between capacity additions
  $g =$ percentage growth in demand each year
  $i =$ net annual cost of underutilized facilities (as on page 75)
  $d_0 =$ demand at the beginning of time period T_0
  $V(T) =$ increase in demand experienced between time T_0, and when the
      next increment is needed:

$$V(T) = d_0\, e^{gT} \tag{3A-3}$$

One can then substitute possible values of V into either of these equations and determine the value that minimizes the long-run discounted cost of this kind of capacity strategy.

If the construction cost has the form described in Equation 3-4, $C(V) = KV^k$, the optimal capacity increment can be calculated directly by solving for T in the following equations: (a) arithmetic demand growth:*

$$(e^{it} - 1) = iT/K$$

or (b) geometric demand growth:

$$[e^{(i - kg)T} - 1] = \frac{(i - kg)}{kg}[1 - e^{-gt}]$$

and then using the value to solve for V, either using $V = GT$ (if growth is linear), or $V = d_0 e^{gT}$ (if growth is exponential).

Example

The calculations of TDC for various values of V, when d is growing by a constant amount each year, and assuming

$$i = 15\%$$
$$g = 3,000 \text{ units per year}$$

and

$$C(V) = 0.00335\, V^{0.7}$$

in millions of dollars (e.g., a plant having annual capacity of 12,000 tons costs $2.4 million), are as follows:

V	$C(V)$ ($ in millions)	$1 - e^{-iV/G}$	$TDC\,(V,G,i)$ ($ in millions)
10,000	$2.114	0.39347	$5.372
12,000	2.401	0.45119	5.323
14,000	2.675	0.50342	5.314
16,000	2.937	0.55067	5.334
18,000	3.190	0.59343	5.375

* This is obtained by expressing Equation 3A-1 in terms of $T = V/G$, differentiating with respect to T, and solving for the value of T at which the derivative is equal to zero.

The optimal value of V is about 13,500 tons, or roughly 4.5 year's worth of demand growth.

3A-2 MINIMUM COST CAPACITY STRATEGIES WHEN SHORTFALLS ARE PERMITTED

Assuming that the company never runs short of capacity in a growing environment is generally unrealistic. This section of the appendix, therefore, focuses on the analysis of capacity strategies of the type depicted in Figure 3-7.

It can be shown (see Manne, 1967, Chapter 10) that if there is a positive penalty cost (C_P) attached to every unit that is demanded but cannot be supplied, if the cost of an increment of capacity V is given by $C(V) = KV^k$, and if demand is growing at a constant *amount* per year, G, then the optimal amount of the expected deficit, D, right before a new increment of capacity becomes available is proportional to the ratio (i/C_P): the time value of money tied up in unused facilities divided by the penalty cost per unit. Unfortunately, the effect of the value of C_P on both D and the size of the increment V that should be added is extremely complicated. About the best that can be said is that both V and D should *increase* as the penalty cost decreases. If C_P is *very* large, however, it will not be advisable for the company *ever* to run short of capacity. Therefore, $D = 0$ and the problem reduces to one we discussed earlier (see Figure 3-1, Policy A).

The reason that V increases as C_P gets smaller becomes clear when one remembers that D, the amount of the shortage right before a new capacity increment becomes available, also increases as C_P gets smaller (because the ratio i/C_P gets larger). Therefore, when a new capacity increment is added, it will quickly become fully utilized because of the pent-up (or redirected) demand represented by D. Since each new increment is soon operating at capacity, less penalty is attached to building a larger increment and reaping the benefits of construction and operating economies of scale. If *no* penalty is attached to not meeting demand (that is, it can be deferred indefinitely without cost), the company will *never* build any capacity and the shortage D will increase as demand increases. An example can help illustrate these points.

Using the same assumptions given in the example in the first section of this appendix—growth in demand of $G = 3,000$ tons per year, an annual cost of underutilized facilities of $i = 15\%$, an economies of scale exponent of $k = 0.7$, and a plant of size 12,000 tons costing \$2.4 million—then the following values can be shown to be approximately optimal:

Penalty Cost per Ton Short (C_p)	Optimal Capacity Increment (V)	Expected Shortage Just Before Next Increment (D)
$10,000	13,500	0
200	16,000	2,900
100	19,500	6,700
50	30,000	18,000
25	83,000	73,400

It can be shown also that rather large changes in these optimal values have relatively little impact on the total discounted cost function—doubling (or halving) the V values given above, for example, causes total discounted costs to increase by less than 8 percent.

Again, the nature of the assumptions involved should be stressed—particularly that demand is growing at a constant, known amount each year, and that the penalty cost is a constant value per unit short, no matter how long the undercapacity situation exists or how much undercapacity is involved. Seldom, of course, can one compress all the implications of not being able to meet demand out of one's own facilities into a simple "penalty cost per unit." Customers may decide to take their business elsewhere, to "more reliable suppliers" or "suppliers who are willing to grow with us"; subcontractors may be encouraged to enter the business themselves; and competitors may mistake your "rationality" for weakness and be emboldened to attack your markets. Therefore, while interesting and suggestive, this analytical formulation of the problem and the insights one can gain from it are probably too simplified to be applied directly to an actual capacity decision. This approach, however, does allow us to better understand and approximate the various tradeoffs that must be taken into account when making such decisions, and to examine their interaction in a systematic way.

4

Facilities Strategy

The distinction between a capacity *strategy* and a capacity *decision* was stressed in Chapter 3, where a capacity strategy was defined as a pattern of time-sequenced capacity decisions. In this chapter, we deal with two topics that are closely intertwined with such a capacity strategy: overall facilities strategy and individual facility decisions. The framework we use to relate capacity decisions to facilities decisions incorporates four different levels: (1) manufacturing strategy (at the highest level), (2) capacity strategy, (3) facilities strategy, and (4) facilities decisions as the operational mechanism by which capacity and facilities strategies are integrated and pursued.

In practice, firms often, over an extended period of time, make a series of facilities decisions that do not appear to be guided by any facilities strategy, or even any apparent capacity strategy. They usually exhibit such behavior when their management is in a reactive mode—that is, responding to events as they unfold. Therefore, when specific facility decisions arise they become the natural focus of attention. In such organizations these decisions are typically viewed as more concrete (and usually more urgent) than such abstract activities as strategy formulation. Unless all four levels are addressed explicitly, however, a firm is likely to make facilities decisions that are inappropriate, in the sense that they result in a set of facilities that are incapable of meeting the firm's long-term needs.

This chapter is divided into four main sections. The first focuses on the plant network—a group of two or more plants—and describes several approaches that can help managers develop a facilities strategy for such networks. These approaches are rooted in analyses of physical capacity, geography, functional needs/corporate philosophy, and product-market/process focus, respectively. Characteristics of the settings in which each approach is particularly useful are also described.

The second section deals with the facilities strategy for an individual plant. It reviews the typical life cycle of a manufacturing facility, describes some of the basic strategic decisions associated with various stages of that life cycle, and finally explains how a firm can use the concept of "charters" or "missions" to establish performance guidelines for a facility at a given time.

The section concludes with a discussion of the "plant-within-a-plant" concept, which represents a natural extension of the facility focus concept at the sub-plant level.

The third section addresses facilities strategy as it relates to the long-term evolution of an industry. The notion of an industry life cycle is used as a framework, and the combined effect of slowing growth, increasing scale economies, and stagnating productivity are explored. The concept of a "U-shaped" cost curve, as it relates to such industry evolution, is discussed.

The fourth section deals with the development of an integrated facilities strategy. This requires creating organizational processes that ensure that the basic elements of a facilities strategy—decisions related to the size, location, and specialization of one or more facilities—are addressed systematically on an ongoing basis, and are responsive to the evolution of the organization, its strategies, and its environment.

The concept of a "focused facility," which cuts across many of the topics in this chapter, is covered in the appendix to this chapter. That discussion includes a definition of facilities focus and empirical evidence on the nature of its impact at four levels—industry, multiple plants, a single plant over time, and multiple production lines within a plant. Suggestions for identifying the areas where such benefits are most likely to be observed are also presented. Procedures for planning and making individual capacity and facilities decisions are the subject of Chapter 5.

4-1 STRATEGY FOR MULTIPLANT FACILITIES

For all but the smallest of manufacturing concerns, a facilities strategy must deal with multiple facilities and address such issues as the assignment of specific products, processes, customers, and markets to individual facilities. We discuss four approaches that represent different perspectives on the analysis and planning of multiple facilities. Each handles different issues with varying degrees of effectiveness, and their combination covers the full range of concerns that management must address. For each approach, the driving forces that lead a firm to favor one choice over another range from the economics of the technology, to the evolution of the firm and its product lines, to its organizational structure and general philosophy of management. In light of this discussion, managers should be able to identify the key issues and concerns in their own setting and choose the combination of these four approaches that will make it possible to deal with them effectively.

4-1.1 Physical Facilities Analysis

Instead of seeking to create a comprehensive set of manufacturing capabilities, this approach is limited to providing sufficient floor space so that a firm's employees can meet the requirements imposed by its long-term aggregate sales plan. It is based on estimates of certain critical ratios (such as the number of square feet of floor space per employee, sales per employee, and sales per square foot) that can be used to forecast the physical space (and, by implication, production capacity) that will be needed at some point in the future.

The roughest form of this kind of analysis uses historical values for these ratios as a means for converting future sales projections into aggregate square footage and employment requirements. Refined versions of this approach may track the trends in these critical ratios, break sales-to-standard labor hours down into individual labor categories (rather than simply using the total number of employees), break down total floor space by specific usage requirements (for example, high bay or low bay, or warehouse versus production space), and consider the impact of alternative product–plant combinations on space requirements. For one heavy equipment manufacturer that used this approach, Table 4-1 contains summary forecasts of the standard labor hours required by each of its product lines, for each of four possible approaches to assigning products to plants over a five-year planning period. Similarly, Table 4-2 summarizes the projected workforce and space requirements, over a 20-year time horizon, for an electronics firm that followed a similar approach.

The physical space approach to multiplant facilities planning is often observed in high-growth companies where the department or group responsible for providing facilities has difficulty obtaining accurate projections of specific needs. Such people often must contend with two- to four-year lead times for adding capacity (including the time required for property acquisition), while making irreversible decisions without much guidance from their marketing and manufacturing counterparts. Perhaps the best approach in such situations is to estimate aggregate needs and provide sufficient amounts of different types of facilities at the right times, but leave it to those directly involved to determine later just what should go into each facility. Such an approach may also be appropriate when a firm simply wants a ballpark estimate of the space and personnel requirements that would be required to support different marketing projections.

Another situation where such an approach to facilities planning might be appropriate is when a company has established clear guidelines for all its facilities. An excellent example is the Hewlett-Packard Company, of whom it has been said "if you've seen one of HP's facilities, you've seen them all." In fact, HP's facility in Penang, Malaysia looks exactly like its California facilities, including the rolling hills and landscaping around the plant. HP management has decided that all its manufacturing facilities should be similar, and facilities planning is done at the corporate level. Using key ratios and sales projections is a very simple but practical way to facilitate this approach.

Some additional rules of thumb usually are needed to make this approach operational. Often these involve statements as to the optimal facility size; these might relate to sales dollars per year, square feet of floor space, number of people, or even the number of acres desired per site. In the early stages of developing a facilities planning process, these rules are likely to be based on the

Table 4-1
Heavy Equipment Manufacturer—Standard Hours
Required for Future Capacity
(standard hours in thousands)

Product–Plant Alternatives	1979	1980	1981	1982	1983
Base: Expand Present Facilities					
Cedar Rapids, crawlers	619	686	707	796	863
Cedar Rapids, excavators	357	407	456	493	546
	976	1093	1163	1289	1409
Add domestic LS3400	0	0	124	145	145
	976	1093	1287	1434	1554
Add tower cranes	51	61	70	82	90
	1027	1154	1357	1516	1644
Bowling Green, trucks	344	340	403	434	478
	1371	1494	1760	1950	2122
1. New Large Cable Crane Facility					
Cedar Rapids, crawlers	449	498	514	578	627
Cedar Rapids, excavators	357	407	456	493	546
	806	905	970	1071	1173
Add domestic LS3400	0	0	124	145	145
	806	905	1094	1216	1318
Separate large cranes	170	188	193	218	246
Add tower cranes	51	61	70	82	90
	221	249	263	300	326
Bowling Green, Trucks	344	340	403	434	478
	1371	1494	1760	1950	2122
2. New Excavator Facility					
Cedar Rapids, crawlers	619	686	707	796	863
Add Tower cranes	51	61	70	82	90
	670	747	777	878	953
Separate excavators	357	407	456	493	546
Add LS3400	0	0	124	145	145
	357	407	580	638	691
Bowling Green, trucks	344	340	403	434	478
	1371	1494	1760	1950	2122
3. Product Switch					
Cedar Rapids, crawlers	619	686	707	796	863
Cedar Rapids, trucks	344	340	403	434	478
	963	1026	1110	1230	1341
Add tower cranes	51	61	70	82	90
	1014	1087	1180	1312	1431
Bowling Green, excavators	357	407	456	493	546
Add LS3400	0	0	124	145	145
	357	407	580	638	691
	1371	1494	1760	1950	2122

Source. "FMC-Cable Crane and Excavator Division (B)," Harvard Case Services, 9-679-147.

Note. Nominal capacity in 1979 was 440 for Bowling Green and 1,300 for Cedar Rapids—a total of 1700.

Table 4-2

Electronics Firm—Twenty-Year Growth of Manufacturing Requirements

Organizational Unit	Manufacturing Employment (Number of Sites)[a]				
	1980	1985	1990	1995	2000
Division A	5,900 (3)	9,200 (5)	17,700 (9)	30,600 (16)	50,300 (26)
Division B	1,800 (1)	3,200 (2)	6,800 (4)	11,800 (6)	18,600 (10)
Division C	1,000 (1)	1,500 (1)	2,500 (2)	3,900 (2)	5,600 (3)
Division D	10,500 (6)	14,000 (7)	14,000 (7)	14,000 (7)	14,000 (7)
Totals	19,200 (11)	27,900 (15)	41,000 (22)	60,200 (31)	88,400 (46)

[a] Assumes 2,000 employees maximum per site of 20 acres.

example set by other leading companies who are considered to have good manufacturing operations. Or they may represent reactions to past mistakes—downsizing future facilities, for example, because an existing facility has been found to be too large. As their planning processes becomes more sophisticated, firms usually move toward one of the three approaches outlined next.

4-1.2 Geographical Network Analysis

This approach to developing a multiplant facilities strategy is often observed when transportation costs constitute a significant portion of the total delivered cost of a company's products, or in market environments where proximity to customers and markets is a key source of competitive advantage. The former category includes basic materials (for example, steel, aluminum, cement, and glass) and bulky or heavy commodity-type products (such as plastic or cast iron pipe). The second category includes industries that offer customized products and are subject to relatively low production scale economies (for example, packaging materials and job shop printing). It is also seen in firms whose customer service capabilities are linked to their manufacturing facilities and constitute a major portion of their value added (for example, architect-specified building products and field-installed, specialty industrial products). While the basic framework for this approach was developed primarily for the first category (significant transportation costs), the same general concept and procedures are applicable to the second.

The approach combines a geographical analysis of customer density (or demand by region), with analyses of production economies of scale, overhead cost structures, and transportation economics. It seeks to determine the best set (number and size) of facilities and the territory to be served by each. A good illustration of this approach comes from the fiberglass insulation industry, where there are three major competitors: Owens-Corning Fiberglas (OCF), Johns Manville (JM), and Certainteed/Saint Gobain (CT). As illustrated in Figure 4-1, each of these firms has six to eight manufacturing facilities serving very similar geographical territories.

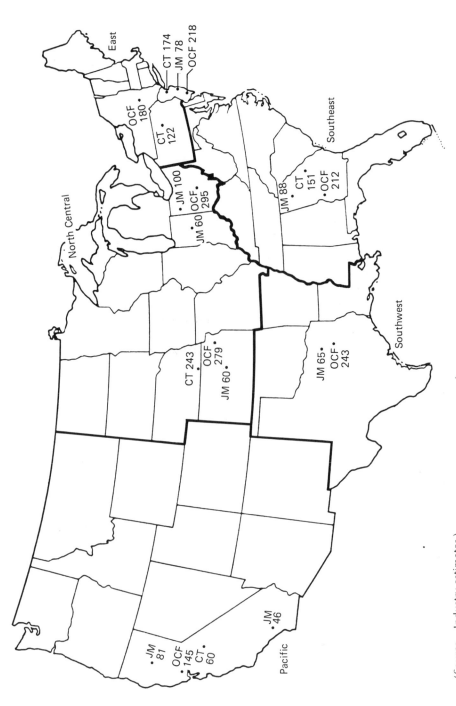

Figure 4-1   Geographical location of fiberglass insulation capacity (1979)

East

CT 174
JM 78
OCF 218

OCF 180

CT 122

Southeast

North Central

JM 100

OCF 295

JM 60

JM 88

CT 151

OCF 212

CT 243

OCF 279

JM 60

Southwest

JM 65

OCF 243

JM 46

JM 81

OCF 145

CT 60

Pacific

(Source.   Industry estimates.)

Note.   Numbers beside company initials indicate annual plant capacity.

84

A glance at the plant locations in Figure 4-1 suggests that all three firms have used the same approach in designing their facilities network, although those familiar with the industry would recognize other important factors as well. OCF, the original firm in the industry (it still has more than 50 percent of the market for fiberglass insulation), based its plant strategy on this geographic approach, since distribution costs for fiberglass insulation constitute 10 to 20 percent of total delivered cost. As others entered the market, they found that they had to compete on a delivered price basis with OCF, and this would be possible only if they located their plants near those previously established by OCF.

Implementing this approach requires that one understand the relationships between production costs (which are driven by production technology), logistics costs, market evolution, and the bases of long-term competitive success. While inventories are only one component of total logistics cost, in many networks they are very important. For example, the "square root law," which asserts that the total inventory in a system is proportional to the square root of the number of locations at which a product is stocked, is observed in many warehouse networks. (See Maister, 1977.)

Karnani (1983) has used a set of assumptions about the mathematical form of both production and transportation costs to show that in an optimally sized plant the ratio of transportation costs to production costs does not depend on the plant's cost structure or the demand density. Instead, it depends only on the parameters that measure various economies of scale effects. Karnani showed that as production scale economies increase, the optimal plant size increases (so that the production cost per unit decreases), and the trading area of the facility expands since the firm can trade off lower production costs against somewhat higher transportation costs. Similarly, an increase in transportation economies of scale (with respect to volume or distance) also causes the optimal plant size to increase. Karnani goes on to assert that a ratio involving only parameters of these two types of scale economies can be used both as a rough indication of whether existing facilities are of the appropriate size, and in guiding the planning for future facilities.

While transportation and production cost tradeoffs are clearly the key issue in the short term, over the longer term the other two issues—the pattern of market development and the basis of competition—gain in relative importance and further complicate this approach to facilities planning. To illustrate, consider a hypothetical company that services a market in a rectangular geographic area like that shown in Figure 4-2.

If only one plant is needed to service total demand (which would be likely in the early phase of the market's development), then the best (that is, least-cost) location for this plant would be the point at which the total cost of raw material transportation, production, and distribution to customers is minimized—at point A, say. On the other hand, if the company expects the market ultimately to develop to the point where three equal-sized plants would be needed to service it, then these three plants should be located at points B, C,

Figure 4-2   Plant location alternatives with market development

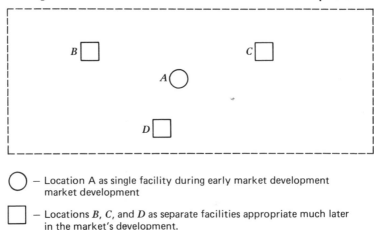

◯ — Location A as single facility during early market development
market development

▢ — Locations *B*, *C*, and *D* as separate facilities appropriate much later
in the market's development.

and *D*. Thus, while *A* may be the best location for a single plant, it may be a very poor location around which to build a multiplant network.

Developing a facilities network that will meet a firm's long-term needs often, therefore, requires that individual decisions be based more on judgment than on hard data. For example, a firm facing a situation like that shown in Figure 4-2 might proceed in one of two directions:

1. Establish an appropriately sized plant in a core market area, and expand it incrementally as the market grows until it gets "too big." At that point, consider adding other plants to the network.
2. Establish "beachhead" plants at all critical locations before expanding any one of them.

Although the first approach promises greater economies of scale and fewer co-ordination problems for top management, it allows competitors to become en-trenched in areas outside the original "core" location and complicates the later relocation of production. If plant location is an important competitive weapon, it may be very difficult for the firm to enter other regions in response to market growth or shifts, because competitors are well established there already.

The second strategy, which is analogous to the way a spider builds its web, reduces the risk of being blocked out of certain markets but may compel a young organization to construct and coordinate a complex plant network, often at a higher initial cost. In addition, it requires the availability, or the develop-ment, of production technologies that are efficient at low volumes. If such technologies can be developed, the second strategy becomes much more viable and may enable the firm to preempt its competitors in the long term while achieving satisfactory returns in the intermediate term.

The Trus Joist Company, the manufacturer of customized roof and floor support systems described in Chapter 3, provides a good example. It faced competition both from a number of small firms, who were unable to exploit scale economies but had many local service outlets (both wholesalers and distributors), and from a few large firms who had large-scale facilities. In order to be able to compete with both types of firms, Trus Joist developed manufacturing processes that were efficient at low volumes. This enabled it to construct a network of more than a dozen plants throughout the United States before its total corporate sales had reached $100 million. Each plant was designed to be profitable at a relatively low production volume, and its sale force was able to exploit these "local" sources of production, which enabled the company to provide improved service and fast delivery. Trus Joist's strategy has proven very successful. As its sales grew, however, emphasis shifted to identifying larger-scale production processes that promised lower manufacturing costs, so as to better serve the much larger market for the company's products.

4-1.3 Functional Needs and Corporate Philosophy Analysis

This approach combines many of the elements of the two outlined above, and firms often turn to it after relying on one of the others. It is a more comprehensive and integrated approach in that it takes into account the full range of factors that comprise a multiplant facilities strategy. Rather than basing facilities expansion plans on forecasts of floor space requirements, or informal rules about the maximum number of employees that are permitted at one site, this approach looks at facilities in terms of their basic characteristics. It seeks a configuration of facilities that best incorporates these characteristics within the framework established by corporate philosophy and organizational preferences.

In the electronics industry, for example, one can identify three basic types of manufacturing facilities: technical development/prototype manufacturing, component manufacturing, and assembly/test. The differences between these basic types lead naturally to the idea of splitting total production into three separate plants: a parent (or mother) plant, a components plant, and an assembly plant. Some characteristics of each of these generic types of facilities are shown in Figure 4-3. A "campus" made up of several buildings at a single site is one way to combine such a mixture of facilities.

In high growth/high technology companies, the rate of product evolution is such that a given facility may produce several generations of a product (many of which were not even conceived when the facility was established). Therefore, what is important over the long term are *generic* capabilities, not an ability to produce a specific product. In addition, the technological orientation of these firms usually leads them to have a preponderance of engineers and salaried employees; transfers of such people between facilities are easier if they convey a consistent image and are embedded in similar physical environments.

Some firms, such as Hewlett-Packard and Tektronix, have developed

Figure 4-3   Multiple plant modules for electronics firm's facilities strategy

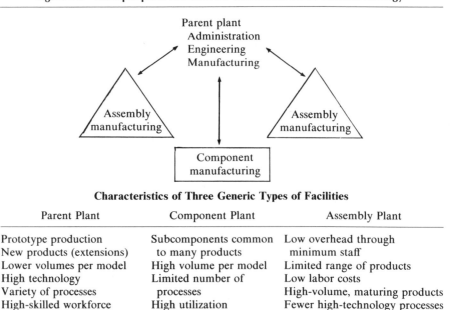

Characteristics of Three Generic Types of Facilities

Parent Plant	Component Plant	Assembly Plant
Prototype production	Subcomponents common	Low overhead through
New products (extensions)	to many products	minimum staff
Lower volumes per model	High volume per model	Limited range of products
High technology	Limited number of	Low labor costs
Variety of processes	processes	High-volume, maturing products
High-skilled workforce	High utilization	Fewer high-technology processes
Good technical support staff	More capital-intensive	

clear statements regarding the desired locational characteristics and internal configuration of their facilities. Other electronics firms, such as ROLM and Tandem (who only recently have reached a size that requires multiple plant locations), seem to be adopting similar models. The way the elements of this approach are defined, and specific decisions made, can be illustrated using the approach adopted by these firms.

They look for sites that have many of the same characteristics as their original headquarters location: good weather, a growing population, an attractive community environment for professional engineers, and sufficient size that a major plant complex would employ no more than 3 or 4 percent of the population within a 20-mile radius. Firms starting out in the San Francisco–San Jose, California area seem to feel that locations such as Portland or Corvallis (Oregon), Vancouver (Washington), Colorado Springs (Colorado), and Austin (Texas) meet these guidelines.

The campuses they develop often follow a hub-and-spoke layout, with the parent plant (the technical support center) forming the hub and the components manufacturing and assembly/test buildings representing the spokes.*

---

* A number of multisite manufacturers use a variation of this hub-and-spoke concept, dispersing facilities over several locations rather than at a single campus. For example, in many medium-sized electronic firms the original site (San Francisco–San Jose area) retains the role of parent plant to two types of spoke locations: assembly plants in "equivalent," but somewhat lower-cost, locations (Oregon, Colorado, etc.), and component plants near critical resources (particularly low-cost labor).

The criteria used in defining each type of facility might include minimum acreage requirements (for example, 100 acres for a component manufacturing facility, 90 acres for an assembly facility, and 70 acres for a parent facility), pleasant physical surroundings (typically, rolling hills and trees) that present a low profile to the adjacent community, and easy access by automobile for employees so that commuting is not onerous.

Many firms using this approach not only have a model of what a complete set of facilities (campus) should look like when it is fully developed, but also follow a prespecified sequence of steps when building a new complex. Phase 1 is usually the development of the parent facility, which includes some manufacturing and a significant amount of engineering support (as might be required for a new product line). Phase 2 might be the addition of a satellite assembly operation (with lower overhead and labor rates) to produce some of the higher-volume, more standardized products. Phase 3 might be the development of a component operation (for example, printed circuit-board production) to reduce the cost of an important process step or to separate special technical requirements from more general-purpose assembly requirements. Phase 4 might be the development of one or two additional satellite assembly operations, each concentrating on a different subpart of the product line.

Hewlett-Packard's Santa Rosa, California complex is an example of such a facility. It consists of six major modules, each of which is a separate division. Each involves some component manufacturing and some parent-type operations but is concerned primarily with assembly and testing. Each is limited to a maximum of 1,000 to 2,000 employees. Tektronix's guidelines, as implied by their behavior in the early 1980s, suggest a complete campus (based on a hub-and-spoke arrangement) consisting of no more than 15,000 employees and a maximum of 4,000 at any one site. Individual buildings at a site appear to have a maximum of 400 to 500 employees.

The facilities strategies used by both HP and Tektronix reflect top-management decisions regarding the maximum size for an operating unit and the appropriate number of people to be employed at a given division or site. When a plant complex approaches the maximum size permitted by the corporation, organizational steps are taken to facilitate the eventual split-off of some part of the product line or market being served. This newly separated organization can then become a separate entity with its own group of manufacturing facilities.

Several aspects of this approach make it attractive. First, and perhaps foremost, it is based on a systematic framework for facilities planning that meets the long-term functional needs of the organization while requiring a minimum amount of detail concerning specific products and markets. Second, it reflects the company's philosophy and culture, as well as its competitive strategy. Thus it provides facilities that are appealing to those within the organization. Third, it recognizes the potential benefits of customizing different facilities to meet the needs of different markets or process technologies.

While the transportation network approach seeks to focus facilities around the needs of a particular geographic region or market, it normally does not take into account the differences in facilities necessitated by the various production stages involved in producing a product or those associated with different product lines. An approach based directly on corporate philosophy or workforce environment issues can incorporate these differences but often does so at the expense of geographic fit. The notion of "focused facilities" attempts to include both considerations and has strong intuitive appeal to managers, both because of its implications for management control and because of its proven potential for achieving a competitive advantage. This is the subject of the next section.

4-1.4   Product/Market-Process Focus Analysis

This approach is a natural extension of the one just described. It expands the generic, function-based definitions of different types of plants to include much more specific product, market, and process characteristics. Multiplant facilities planning is viewed as the development of a set of facilities that will provide the specific manufacturing capabilities required by the firm's products, markets, and production processes over the long term. Because of its specificity, this approach tends to be most applicable to more stable product/market environments, such as industrial components, heavy equipment, automobiles, electrical equipment, and metal-forming companies. Even in such stable industries, however, most facilities last for several product generations, so that the match between needs and capabilities requires periodic adjustment.

Its comprehensiveness and its dependence on systematic long-range planning make this approach an unlikely one for most manufacturing firms to use at the outset of their facilities planning efforts. A more likely choice would be one based on the ad hoc needs of specific product or market segments, a transportation network approach, or one aimed simply at correcting problems encountered at existing facilities (for example, moving to a new plant when an older one becomes noncompetitive).

The philosophical basis of this approach is the concept of facilities focus: that narrowing the range of demands placed on a manufacturing facility will lead to better performance because management attention can be concentrated on a few key tasks and priorities. Possible dimensions for focusing individual facilities include: the markets served, the production volumes of different products, the degree of product customization required, and the nature of the process technology employed (separating component manufacturing from assembly manufacturing is of this type). Some arguments for and against different approaches to focus are listed in Table 4-3. What makes the focus concept so powerful—and demanding—as a framework for multifacilities strategy development is that it can incorporate the specific demands on and capabilities of each facility.

Although the concept of focused facilities was proposed more than a decade ago (see Skinner, 1974), only in the past few years have data been gathered that enable the development of quantitative assessments of its impact. The

Table 4-3
Advantages and Disadvantages of Alternative Approaches to Focusing Facilities

Advantages	Disadvantages
Volume Split (high volume vs. low volume)	
Exploits economies of scale, where appropriate	Duplication of production processes, overhead, and inventories
Permits focusing on either cost effectiveness or production flexibility	Low volume plants can become orphans if not monitored carefully
Encourages customized development of production and management systems for products at different stages of their life style	
Product/Market Split	
Very responsive to market/customer needs and priorities	Duplication of resources across several facilities
Facilitates new product introduction	Product transfers become awkward
Permits specialization by market segment	Tendency to become unfocused as market shifts (high and low volume products produced in same plant)
Simplifies product cost estimation	Load imbalances develop as different markets grow at different rates
	Less emphasis on, and concentration of, technical skills in market-dominated environments
Process Split	
Concentrates technological expertise	Impedes radical changes in products or processes
Less duplication of equipment for producing common parts	Slows organization's response to totally new product/market requirements
Easier to balance loads among plants and keep utilization high	Longer cycle times and large pipeline inventories
Can develop customized process control systems	Higher cost of coordination
Encourages standardization	

appendix to this chapter summarizes some recent empirical findings, offers tentative explanations for the observed benefits, and suggests guidelines for implementing a focus-based multiplant strategy.

Because this approach to developing a multiplant facilities strategy is situation-specific, it is best described through an example. In the early 1970s, the Motor Division of the Reliance Electric Corporation began to develop a new facilities strategy. [See "Reliance Electric Motor Division (B)," Harvard Case Services, 9-678-191.] Reliance management's first step was to take inventory of its existing facilities and identify the set of capabilities each provided. The information they obtained (see Figure 4-4a) was backed by a detailed analysis of the production processes found at each facility and the range of products and markets served by each.* This enabled the Motor Division to compare each plant's manufacturing processes with the requirements of the product/markets it served. (This general framework is developed further in Chapter 7.)

A complementary analysis, performed by Reliance's management, is shown in Figure 4-4b. It involved looking at the profitability of individual segments of the division's product line and highlighting the products that were above or below average in profitability. Associating each of these product line segments with specific manufacturing facilities indicated the contribution of each facility (positive or negative) to the division's overall profitability.

After analyzing the data in Figure 4-4, Reliance's management concluded that improving the facilities used to produce certain products would lift the profitability of the whole product line. The addition of the Athens plant in the early 1970s corroborated this idea: while very narrowly focused, and running at lower capacity utilization than the other three plants, it had been extremely successful. When this conclusion was coupled with the division's long-range plans, which called for significant increases in production volume over a ten-year period, it was decided that the right facilities strategy would not only enable Reliance to meet expected demand, but would make a significant improvement in its overall profitability as well.

Using this framework, Reliance managers developed a long-term facilities strategy. First, they ascertained the optimal size of a plant for their motor business. Using the Athens plant as a guide, they defined "optimal" as $35 million annual net sales billed, two-shift capacity, and 400 hourly workers. Next, after comparing the company's long-term capacity requirements with this choice of plant size, they developed a proposal for a coordinated set of seven focused plants, as shown in Figure 4-5a. The configuration of each facility was dictated by the production volumes required by various subsegments of the product line, the range of motor sizes that could be manufactured with a single set of equipment, and the potential profitability of different production processes.

As Figure 4-5 shows, Reliance's plan included three new facilities (Gainesville, Plant 6, and Plant 7), together with a refocusing (that is, a narrowing of the product market requirements and process capabilities) of its existing plants. The anticipated impact of these actions is shown in Figure 4-5b. As a result of this analysis, the division's proposal to corporate management was for not just a single new plant but for three new plants to be built over a seven-year period. Concluding that this facilities strategy made sense, corporate management authorized the first phase: construction of the Gainesville plant.

A major strength of this approach to multiplant facilities planning is that it provides a basis for developing customized strategies for individual facilities.

---

* The Athens plant shown in Figure 4-4 was not built until 1970; it was designed to produce a specific product line taken from the Ashtabula plant.

Figure 4-4   Reliance Electric Motor Division facilities planning

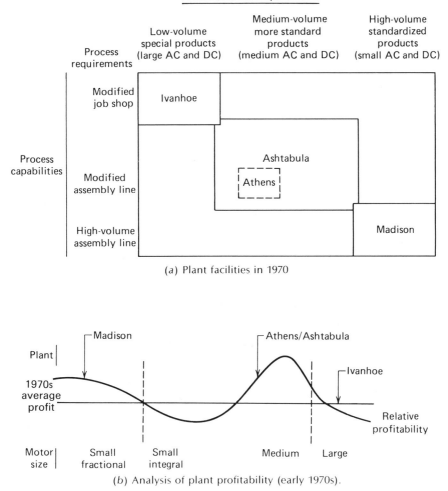

(a) Plant facilities in 1970

(b) Analysis of plant profitability (early 1970s).

(*Source.* "Reliance Electric Motor Division (B)," Harvard Case Services, 9-678-191.)

This is illustrated in Figure 4-6, where the four plants operated by the Lynchburg Foundry Corporation in the mid-1970s are positioned (the framework is similar to that used by Reliance Electric's Motor Division, but is applied to the foundry and castings business). This type of analysis helped Lynchburg Foundry identify the best way to add a new facility to its existing operations. Figure 4-6 indicates a major gap between Plants 2 and 3. (Plant 2 was a relatively large castings plant making low-volume items, and Plant 3 was a small castings plant making high-volume items for the automobile industry.) Lynchburg reasoned that with existing facilities near capacity and optimally sized, further growth in its full line of castings would require a new facility.

Figure 4-5   Reliance Electric Motor Division 1984 facilities

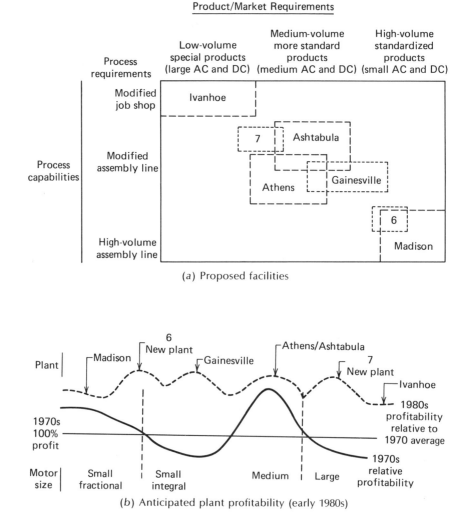

(a) Proposed facilities

(b) Anticipated plant profitability (early 1980s)

(*Source.* "Reliance Electric Motor Division (B)," Harvard Case Services, 9-678-191.)

An examination of the company's product/markets and production processes identified a major opportunity in the area indicated by a question mark in Figure 4-6: providing medium-sized, higher-volume castings to heavy equipment manufacturers. Because the plant was intended to service customers like Caterpillar Tractor, the facility was designed to meet Caterpillar's specific requirements. Caterpillar was not asked to guarantee the plant's success; it simply was asked to describe what capabilities would best meet its needs. Lynchburg assumed that if it designed its new facility around those requirements, Caterpillar would find it to be the most appropriate foundry in the world for

Figure 4-6   Facilities focus and multiplant strategies at Lynchburg Foundry Corporation

Production Process Characteristics	Product-Market Characteristics			
	Low-volume special products	Low-volume multiple products	Few major products, higher volume	High-volume standardized products
Jumbled flow (Job shop)	Plant 1			
Disconnected line flow (batch)		Plant 2		
			?	
Connected line flow (assembly line)			Plant 3	Plant 4

supplying any new order for castings. This approach (1) provided Lynchburg with a long-range plan for facilities that were individually focused, and (2) linked this new facility to a viable, long-term market, one it felt was particularly attractive.*

Given this background, let us summarize the characteristics that make this approach so attractive for developing a multiplant facilities strategy. First, it meets specific short-term needs, but within a long-term perspective. Thus it becomes easy to translate a general facilities strategy into one in which each facility is provided with a clear statement about the role it is expected to play, and how it will be evaluated. A major difficulty of most traditional approaches is that after a firm puts together a set of facilities, it still faces fundamental decisions regarding which products and markets should be served by each facility and what adaptations should be made to facilitate those assignments.

Second, this approach provides a long-term road map for the entire organization—general managers and functional specialists alike. It links organizational capabilities and needs with facilities development, and ensures that both conform to the chosen manufacturing strategy. For example, the long-term facilities strategy developed in the mid-1970s by FMC's Cable, Crane and Excavator Division—to provide a separate plant for each of the division's four major products (see Table 4-1)—not only helped its manufacturing organization to achieve better focus, but also guided the restructuring of the whole organization to better serve those four major product areas. [See "FMC-Cable Crane and Excavator Division (B)," Harvard Case Services, 9-679-147.]

* This foundry, built in the late 1970s, was referred to within Lynchburg as its "focused foundry." It has been very successful, both in attracting the general class of customers for which it was designed and in building a solid base of Caterpillar work.

Finally, as it did at Reliance Electric's Motor Division, this approach can turn the development of a facilities strategy into a proactive process, involving other functions and management levels. It creates and capitalizes on opportunities, rather than simply reacting to the changing requirements for existing products and markets.

4-2 INDIVIDUAL FACILITY STRATEGIES

A facilities strategy should contain not only an overall plan for a set of plants but also a plan for each individual facility within the multifacility network. This section addresses a number of important topics involved in developing such plans. First we discuss the life cycle of a manufacturing facility, breaking it down into four stages. Recognizing that most facilities pass through these stages can help a firm ensure that each facility achieves its maximum contribution during each stage. Moreover, since actions taken during early stages restrict what can and cannot be done during later stages, the long-term viability of an individual facility can be enhanced or jeopardized by decisions made long before.

Following naturally from this discussion of stages is the concept of a charter, or mission, for a facility. Such a charter changes as the facility evolves along its life cycle to reflect its changing role in the overall organization. The second part of this section, therefore, describes such plant charters.

Up to this point we have used the concept of "focus" primarily to help conceptualize the role and configuration of individual facilities within a plant network, but the same basic idea can be applied *within* a single facility. The idea of a "plant within a plant," the subject of the third part of this section, is one way to achieve focused areas within a single facility.

4-2.1 The Stages of a Manufacturing Facility's Life Cycle

A facility's life cycle can be divided into four major stages: initial planning and start-up, incremental expansion, maturation and reinvestment, and finally, renewal or shutdown. The first stage is the one most closely related to the preceding section on multiplant facilities strategy, since most new facilities are constructed either in the expectation of growth or a major improvement in profitability. Understanding the original motivation for building a plant can become important later on, because it contains implications about the proposals that will (or will not) arise naturally when modifications to that facility are planned. In addition, it helps one better understand the strengths and weaknesses of the planning process that led to this first stage.

Typically, a new facility is expected to be up and running quickly, so that it can meet the firm's immediate needs and provide a solid base on which to expand and become increasingly profitable. Schmenner (1982) has suggested some of the issues that ought to be addressed during this design phase. These include:

1. The definition of the products to be manufactured and their desired output levels.
2. The plant's capacity and technological capabilities.
3. The specific process technology to be used and the work flow pattern to be followed within the plant.
4. The number of workers and the mix of their skills.
5. The recruiting, training, and other human resource policies to be adopted in the pursuit of workforce goals.
6. The production scheduling and control systems to be employed.
7. The interrelationships between this facility and other facilities, as well as with suppliers, the distribution system, and ultimate customers.
8. The overhead functions and support staff to be provided—both those contained within the facility and those "borrowed" from outside sources.
9. A provision for the subsequent expansion and development of the facility and its human resources.
10. The capabilities and tasks that will *not* be required of the plant (at least during early stages).
11. The events that would cause a change in the basic plan for the facility.

The more thought that goes into these issues, the greater the likelihood that the plant's first stage will be successful. A healthy sense of organizational limitations is also helpful: trying to do too many things that are new (for example, new products, new processes, new materials, and new customers) or trying to move too quickly (in adding employees, equipment, customers, or building volume) at this stage can be disastrous. Good project management is critical in avoiding these pitfalls.

The second major stage in a facility's life cycle is that of incremental expansion and investment. Once a plant is established and has become viable economically, it embarks on a period of increasing utilization and sequential expansion. Significant improvements in financial performance are likely to occur; in fact, this is often a facility's most profitable period.

Self-discipline and a long-term perspective are particularly important during this stage, as one must guard against three tendencies, each of which can spell disaster in later stages. The first tendency is to add tasks and responsibilities that do not match the long-term capabilities desired for the facility. When a plant is successful, the firm's sales organization tends to put more products into it; customers want to be served by it; and its managers, riding the crest of success, want to take on additional responsibilities. Specific guidelines are needed to counter these seductive pressures to unfocus the facility. One effective mechanism for establishing such guidelines and instilling self-discipline is to develop explicit plant charters, to be discussed in the next section.

A second major tendency in this second stage, as the facility begins to generate sizable cash flows, is to restrict the search for additional investments to projects that promise to raise the overall capacity and profitability of the plant. Preoccupied with incremental expansion, management may neglect the need for continually renewing the facility. If, under the pressure of growth, it fails to invest sufficiently in upgrading existing product lines, worker skills, and operating systems, management may discover that sections of the facility are slowly becoming obsolete and deteriorating into "problem areas." If unsolved, such operating problems can spread, leading eventually to the curtailment of further investment and a search for other facilities where new products and additional production volume can be placed.

The third tendency to be guarded against is overexpanding. Even when an appropriate focus is pursued, and the facility is maintained and continually improved, its capacity may be expanded beyond what is later considered to be the optimal size. Two characteristics increase this pressure to keep expanding: (1) it is almost always cheaper and faster to expand an existing facility than it is to build a new one, and (2) it is usually easier to measure the economies of scale than its diseconomies.

In Chapter 5 we describe some procedures for counteracting these three tendencies, so that the incremental expansion stage can become a solid base for long-term viability.

The third stage is marked by slowing growth as the facility matures. Growth may stop entirely if management decides that further expansion of the facility would push it beyond its optimal size. Just as the physical plant (equipment and buildings) matures during this stage, so do other key dimensions: the workforce (since fewer new workers are being added at the bottom, and turnover is generally less at more senior levels), the production processes (particularly if new investment is directed toward new products and new technologies at the expense of maintaining existing products and processes), and the products and markets themselves. Of course, not all of these factors mature, or stop growing, at the same time, which further complicates facility management and development.

A key question during this stage is whether certain products should be moved out of the maturing facility to another facility. Unless the facility can continue to increase its output without expanding its floorspace or workforce, or the demand for its products stops growing, such moves are almost inevitable. If procedures for renewing the plant's capabilities have not been initiated during the preceding stage, the product lines promising the greatest future growth (and those with the strongest advocates elsewhere in the organization) are likely to be moved. Moving these product lines out leaves the less profitable lines in the older facility, further compounding its problems.

Management must recognize the subtle but inevitable changes that occur in a facility over time, and pursue activities that enable it to retain a viable cost structure based on appropriate task assignments and products. Thus a combination of decisions designed to foster investment, to enhance worker capabilities and motivation, to clarify the allocation of costs, and to prevent the incremental liquidation of important assets is needed.

The final stage of the facility's life cycle is up to management. It can be a period of renewal (a continuation of the third stage), during which the facility continues to adapt to evolutions in its products, markets, production processes, and other basic capabilities, *or* it can degenerate into a downward spiral that ends in the shutdown of the facility.

When a facility reaches this final stage, management finds itself facing one of three possible futures. The first, which requires preplanning in each of the preceding three stages, is that of continuing self-sustaining, incremental renewal. A comprehensive overall plan for the continuing development of the whole facilities network, as discussed in Section 4-1, together with effective decision-making procedures (the topic of the next chapter), is essential if this is to occur.

Second, if preceding stages have not laid the groundwork for ongoing, incremental renewal, at some point management will have to decide whether to overhaul the facility thoroughly in an attempt to move it back to an earlier stage in its life cycle or to let its performance continue to erode. Overhauling a facility can take several years and require major changes in the products and markets served, massive investments in new equipment and process modernization, and other potentially risky changes. Such attempts to overhaul facilities seldom are successful.

Third, shutting down or selling a facility is clear admission by management that it has failed to develop a viable long-term asset, and that it is unwilling to make the investment necessary to turn it into one. We want to stress that these problems are rooted in decisions made during preceding stages. Such an outcome, therefore, is an indictment of those earlier decisions, an awkward fact in organizations where the people who made those decisions have risen to top-management positions—sometimes on the basis of the short-term returns that accrued from ignoring the facility's need for ongoing renewal.

A recent study by Schmenner (1982) gives some indication of what happens to facilities that are not renewed continuously. In his survey of 175 facilities that eventually were closed, Schmenner found that 12 percent were overhauled and relocated to a new site, 24 percent were sold (the product/market organization was often sold along with the plant), and the remaining 64 percent were closed. These facilities' products and markets were absorbed into other facilities owned by the organization or subcontracted to outside facilities.

Management's goal should be to manage the first two stages of a facility's life cycle in such a way that the third stage can become self-sustaining, so that no plants will have to be closed (see Bluestone and Harrison, 1982). This presupposes effective decision processes that recognize this long-term goal, as well as overall capacity and facilities strategies that can guide its execution.

4-2.2 Plant Charters

As suggested in the preceding section, directing a facility through the various stages of its life cycle requires that it retain an appropriate focus and build essential capabilities. Developing a "plant charter" is one effective means of doing this. A charter is simply a statement of what is expected from a plant, and the capabilities is should have; equally important, it should include an indication of what the plant will *not* do. Table 4-4 summarizes the guidelines developed by one firm to tell its plant managers what a "complete" plant charter should include.

The basic purpose of a plant charter is to provide guidance to those whose actions can affect the plant's focus and development. Some companies have found it useful to involve nonmanufacturing as well as manufacturing groups in defining such charters. One format for summarizing a given facility's characteristics is shown in Table 4-5. The Materials Used column, for example, is of interest primarily to those involved in design and procurement; the Production Processes column to manufacturing engineers and equipment purchas-

Table 4-4

Sample Facility Charter Statement

Products and Volumes (by item or product group)
  Volume capabilities
  Rank order of priorities required

What Must the Plant Do Well? (mission statement)
  Key leverage points and critical competitive factors
  General scenario for expansion/development (facility life cycle)

Process Capabilities and Capacities
  Capabilities by type of production process
  Capacities
  Changes over time

Development Directions
  Plant and equipment
  Production planning and control
  Labor and staffing
  Engineering
  Organization and management

Specific Objectives (by product and year)
  Unit costs
  Service level
  Capacity utilization
  Scrap loss
  Inventory investment
  Cost structure

Table 4-5
Primary Dimensions for Plant Charters

Materials Used	Production Processes	Products Produced	Customers/Markets Served
Volume	Flexibility	Number SKU's	Seasonality/cycles
Sources	Throughout time	Size and shape	Geographical loca-
Specifications	Cost structure	Run length	tion
Availability	Scale economies	Annual volumes	Size of firm com-
Transportation	Learning curves	Setups	petitors
Location	Automation	Weight	Delivery require-
Handling	Yield	Quality	ments (lead times,
Cost	Skills required	Components	order size, order
Preprocessing	Equipment types	Materials	frequency)
Lead times	Job categories	Features	Field service needs
	Separable departments	Standardization	To order/to stock
	Value added	Product life cycle	Purchase decision
	Support staff		Price sensitivity
			Life cycle stage
			Distribution chan-
			nel
			Product function

ers; and the Products Produced column to R&D personnel, particularly those involved in new product planning and product line management. Finally, the Customers/Markets Served column can guide the sales organization in determining which product/market activities best match the plant's capabilities.

Table 4-6 attempts to redefine the measures in Table 4-5 in terms appropriate to the facilities of one organization, the Lynchburg Foundry Corporation. It describes the characteristics and charters of each of Lynchburg's four industrial castings plants. These charters were developed primarily to provide the sales force and its estimating department with guidelines for determining which jobs (and customers) to assign to which plant. As a consequence of the development of Table 4-6, the company determined that several products had been misassigned and transferred them to more appropriate facilities. The company also discovered that several others did not fit *any* of its plants, and over an extended period of time these were transferred to the foundries of other firms, where the fit was better. This freed capacity that Lynchburg could put to better use.

Defining plant charters can be an effective way to implement a program of focusing facilities and to ensure that people making decisions throughout the organization do not inadvertently undermine its manufacturing strategy. Plant

Table 4-6

Job Criteria Guidelines for Achieving Focus—Lynchburg Foundry Corporation

Item	Plant 3 Archer Creek	Plant 2	Plant 1	Plant 5 (New)
Amount of pattern change	1 Shift, limited number of jobs	1 shift	See molds below	4 per 8 hours maximum
Knock-out criteria	Easy, no cut-off or sledge	No real constraints	No constraints	No constraints
Minimum run	1 Shift (8 × 300 molds)	1 Shift / 200 Molds/hutch / 100 Molds/twin	100 Molds/shipment on loops 2 & 3. 25 molds per shipment on slinger	2 Hours or 50 molds
Type of quality	Automotive	Auto to caterpillar	Caterpillar	Caterpillar
Weight constraint	Max. 35–40 cstg., 170 mold	1 to 100 cstg., 275 max. pour weight	800 cstg., ductile max.—1000 cstg., gray max.	250–1500 cstg., 1000 max. duct., 1500 max. gray
"Fragilability"	No fragile parts due to anchor conveyor	No restriction	N/A	N/A
Iron types	Ductile, no special alloys	25/40 Gray irons alloys—all commercial ductile	25/40 Gray—all commercial ductile	All gray & ductile grades
Handling requirements	No special handling	Can special handle	1000 Restriction	2000 Limit
Space requirements	Can't overload cores	Minimum space—tight shift	Flast/mold fit	Cored
Core/mold load	Minimum cored work	200 Twin / 250 Hutch	24 x 36 to 52 x 60. 12/12, 40 x 40, 22/16; core/no core balance	No-bake / Shell oil sand
Cleaning requirements	Minimum of intricate jobs	All types expect small intricate passages	Unlimited	No restrictions
Heat treat	No new heat treat	No restrictions	No restrictions	No liquid Quench
Chills	No chill jobs desired	OK, but not desirable	No restrictions	No restrictions
Mix flexibility	Keep to minimum	Maximum mix flexibility	50/50 Gray/ductile loop balance	80% Ductile no blocks

Notes. Plant 4 is a pipe plant that does not make any of the products made by Plants 1, 2, 3, and 5. Plant 5 is the "focused foundry" concentrating on Caterpillar type work.

charters that explicitly allow for differences among facilities help tailor organizational expectations (and performance measurement) to reflect those differences. We return to this topic in Chapter 14.

4-2.3   Within-Facility Focus—The "Plant-Within-a-Plant"

Once a plant's overall charter has been defined, it may be advisable to break it into subparts that relate to individual departments or work centers. The same concept of focus that can help a firm divide responsibilities and capabilities among multiple plants can be used within a single facility. Carried to its extreme, it can lead to the creation of "plants-within-a-plant": physically separating various parts of the facility and dedicating portions of the workforce to each subunit. Or the boundaries may be less tangible, appearing only as a redirection of organizational relationships. The greater the separation between subunits, the easier it is for each to configure itself to meet the specific needs of its assigned tasks. Open communication and cooperation among those working in different subunits, however, may be hampered by such separation.

One approach is to focus subunits within a plant around portions of the product line. Figure 4-7 summarizes how this approach was applied to the assembly of an industrial product. (See Chapter 7 for an explanation of the framework depicted at the top of this figure.) This facility was split into five major subunits and each was assigned a set of products having specific requirements (as indicated in the lower portion of Figure 4-7). Each subunit was given its own production line and its own dedicated hourly workers and support staff personnel. Each had its own production and materials control person, its own maintenance engineer, and an appropriate number of quality inspectors and hourly workers.

4-3   THE IMPACT OF THE INDUSTRY LIFE CYCLE ON FACILITIES STRATEGY

In this section we address some of the implications of an industry's maturation. Leone and Meyer (1980) have suggested that firms relate their facilities plans to the "industry life cycle" using the "U-shaped cost curve" concept. In Figure 4-8 the vertical axis represents the *current-dollar* cost per unit of new capacity, and the horizontal axis represents time (the industry life cycle).

Leone and Meyer argue that during the early phases of its development an industry typically experiences declining costs (in current dollars) per unit of new capacity. The marginal cost of each additional unit is less than the average cost per unit during this period, and therefore the average cost declines. Since pricing is usually based on average costs, any additional output that is sold swells profits and increases a firm's incentive to expand capacity further.

On the basis of an analysis of several major industries (including electric

Figure 4-7 Within-plant focus of an industrial products assembly facility

Process Structure	Product Structure			
	Low-volume/ low standardization, one-of-a-kind	Low- to medium-volume/ multiple products	High- to medium-volume/ few major products	High-volume/ high standardization commodity products
Jumbled flow job shop	1			
Disconnected line flow		2		
Connected line flow			3	
Assembly line				4
Automated assembly				5

Product/Market/Process Characteristics of Subunits

Group 1	Group 2	Group 3	Group 4	Group 5
High quality Extra flexibility Design Volume— low Process High cost General purpose	High quality Flexibility Volume Design High cost General purpose	High quality Flexibility Volume Design Process Medium cost General purpose	Competitive cost—not greater than 20 percent Medium flexibility Medium EOQ Minimum vertical integration Minimum automation Dependability	Competitive cost-low cost Dependability High standardization Inflexible—volume, design, process Long production runs Vertical integration Automated assembly

utilities, paper, and steel), Leone and Meyer identified a list of "tendencies" generally associated with capacity decisions in industries that find themselves on the left-hand side, or declining cost portion, of the U-shaped curve. While Leone and Meyer warn that there are no hard and fast rules, they observe that, in general, companies tend to:

1. Build large-scale facilities.
2. Build new "green field" plants.

3. Lead demand growth with preemptive capacity additions.
4. Exploit economies of scale and compete on the basis of price.
5. Locate in areas of growing demand and less-developed countries.
6. Exploit operating leverage by choosing capital-intensive technologies.
7. Utilize debt to finance new facilities.
8. Forecast demand using relatively simple trend projection methods.
9. Expand by building new capacity rather than by expanding existing facilities.

If industry growth and technological progress begin to slow during a period of price inflation, the rate at which new capacity leads to lower costs may be more than offset by the inflation rate; that is, the marginal cost curve may begin to increase. When this happens, the firm's marginal cost may come to exceed its average cost, and then its average cost will increase. If pricing continues to be based on average cost, incremental volume actually reduces profitability and weakens the incentive to expand. In industries that are able to base the prices of their products on their marginal cost, windfall profits will accrue to the firms with older facilities.

Leone and Meyer identify a number of "tendencies"—once again not following any hard and fast rules—that can be observed in these situations:

1. Building small-scale facilities.
2. Renovating existing facilities.
3. Making more frequent capacity additions to better track (or even lag) demand.
4. Competing on the basis of service, quality, and other dimensions rather than on low cost (and the economies of high-volume operations).
5. Locating in developed countries with existing markets.
6. Choosing less capital-intensive technologies.
7. Forecasting demand using sophisticated analytical methods in order to minimize unused capacity.
8. Expanding by acquiring existing capacity in the industry.

The U.S. electric utility industry illustrates the impact of the development of this U-shaped cost pattern on capacity and facilities decisions. Before the early 1970s, this industry was clearly on the left-hand side of the curve. The construction cost per unit of new capacity, in current dollars, was declining because of both static and dynamic economies of scale. New facilities' operating cost per unit also was lower than that of existing capacity. This meant that the marginal cost of generating additional electricity was lower than the average cost, and both the marginal and average costs were falling over time. Because regulatory agencies allowed the pricing of electric power to be based on aver-

Figure 4-8   U-shaped cost development pattern.

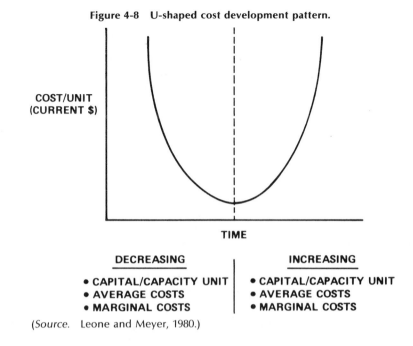

COST/UNIT
(CURRENT $)

TIME

DECREASING	INCREASING
• CAPITAL/CAPACITY UNIT	• CAPITAL/CAPACITY UNIT
• AVERAGE COSTS	• AVERAGE COSTS
• MARGINAL COSTS	• MARGINAL COSTS

(*Source.*   Leone and Meyer, 1980.)

age cost, it was extremely attractive for utilities to add new capacity and to encourage growth in the demand for electricity through reduced rates. Moreover, the time interval that elapsed between the time they reduced their average cost and electric rates were lowered (the so-called regulatory lag) tended to work in favor of the utilities, since their profit margins would increase temporarily. This increased profit could be used to increase capacity and lower operating costs still further.

In the late 1960s and early 1970s, however, the electric utility industry entered the right-hand side of the U-shaped cost curve. This shift was not recognized immediately by the industry. New capacity began to have higher construction and operating costs per unit than did most older capacity. Marginal costs and average costs both increased, but marginal costs rose faster than average costs. Since utility rates were still based on average costs, companies soon found that the full cost of electricity produced in new facilities often exceeded the price they could charge customers. As a result, they became increasingly reluctant to add capacity, their profit margins and return on assets declined, and they shifted from trying to increase demand to trying to limit it. The regulatory lags in rate adjustments became a tremendous burden, as utilities' marginal costs exceeded the average costs on which the rates had been based.

Many factors contribute to the existence of such U-shaped cost patterns: economies of scale, the rates of market growth and technological change, resource depletion, and general price inflation. Moreover, it is often difficult to identify the exact location of an industry (much less an individual firm) on such a curve at any point in time. Still, this is a useful concept to keep in mind when developing a facilities strategy.

4-4 DEVELOPING AN INTEGRATED FACILITIES STRATEGY

As described in Chapter 2, a facilities strategy requires choices regarding the size, location, and specialization of individual facilities, and an understanding of the interaction of these decisions. Many of the issues related to these three elements have been described both in Chapter 3 and in previous sections of this chapter, but a few deserve additional comment.

With regard to size, three important concepts have been defined. First is the notion of *minimum* economic size. This, together with an understanding of the pressures and expectations associated with the start-up stage of an individual facility's life cycle, helps one to specify what the initial scope of a new facility should be. Second is the notion of *maximum* economic size: the point at which diseconomies of scale more than offset economies. Somewhere between these two values lies the *optimal* plant size. Although the optimal size of a given plant is usually difficult to identify precisely, the notion of determining the general parameters of such an optimally sized facility and using them to guide the development of one's facilities strategy is a useful one. The number of employees, the number of levels of management, the characteristics of the technology employed, and the company's philosophy regarding organizational structure are all important determinants of this optimal plant size.

We have not addressed the second major element, facility location, in the same depth. Several excellent references, such as Schmenner (1982), explore these issues thoroughly, so we confine ourselves to a couple of comments.

The story is told of the executive who went to three different consultants, asking each how they helped companies choose a location for a new facility. Each consultant had his own approach. The first sought to develop a set of criteria that captured all of the important characteristics of various locations. These criteria were then assigned priorities and used to screen prospective sites to identify the best possible option. The second consultant used an elaborate computer simulation model, which combined the important economic variables relating to site selection with the company's marketing forecasts, to predict the consequences of different location choices under each of several scenarios.

The third consultant took a very simple approach. He asked the decision maker one question: "Where do you want to live?" While tongue in cheek, this story captures some of the disparity between the tremendous detail that can be developed as part of a location study and the subjective nature of the decision process often found in practice. Which approach a firm chooses is not a function of its overall sophistication. We know of some very sophisticated electronics companies, for example, who have adopted a variant of the third approach. They ask, "Where would our employees want to live?" (In many cases, those are also nice places for top executives to visit!)

Managers seeking to identify the factors most important to their business may refer to criteria such as those summarized by Schmenner (1982):

1. Access to markets/distribution centers.
2. Access to suppliers and resources.
3. Community and government aspects.
4. Competitive considerations.
5. Environmental considerations.
6. Interaction with the rest of the corporation.
7. Labor.
8. Site attractiveness.
9. Taxes and financing.
10. Transportation.
11. Utilities and services.

Each of these criteria may be more or less important depending on the specific situation. Moreover, in most cases the location chosen is far less important than the way the facility is managed once it is in place.

The third major element of a facilities strategy is specialization. The concept of focus is a powerful one, and most manufacturing organizations could benefit by giving it more attention. At least six ways of focusing plants are commonly observed in practice: market focus, product focus, volume focus, process focus, product/market focus, and geographical focus. Determining which (or which combination) of these is most appropriate for one's own organization is central to the development of a facilities strategy. This topic is explored further in the appendix to this chapter and by Schmenner (1979).

Simply choosing which type of focus to adopt is not enough. To insure that the focus chosen is adhered to over time, management should carefully monitor developments in each facility; plants seem to gravitate away from focus just as thermodynamic systems gravitate toward maximum entropy. Developing plant charters and utilizing the plant-within-a-plant notion are two ways to add discipline and commitment to the focus concept.

Important as it is to deal with these three elements in developing an integrated facilities strategy, we emphasize again that strategies are the manifestation of a pattern of decisions over a long period of time. Therefore, simply making isolated decisions "correctly" is not enough. One must work to develop decision-making *procedures* that will reinforce the chosen strategy throughout the organization, and win top-management approval for decisions that are crucial to its successful implementation. We expand on these issues in Chapter 5.

We close this chapter on facilities strategy with two major recommendations. The first is that a facilities strategy should be regarded as a proactive element of the overall manufacturing strategy, rather than a reactive one. That is, rather than waiting until the growth in one's market makes it imperative to add additional capacity, or the increasing unprofitability of an existing facility requires a major change in technology or organization, firms should think of their facilities decisions as some of their most powerful levers for achieving their long-term objectives. Hopefully, some of the frameworks and approaches outlined in this chapter will aid in doing that.

The second recommendation is to beware of the following kinds of often-observed practices: concentrating on individual decisions rather than on an overall strategy, viewing capacity simply in terms of production volume rather than as a set of specific manufacturing capabilities, directing resources exclusively to building new facilities rather than to upgrading the capabilities of existing facilities, and allowing the many status quo–enforcing mechanisms at work within any organization to impede attempts to improve continually one's facilities and procedures over time.

Pitfalls

SELECTED REFERENCES

Bluestone, Barry, and Bennett Harrison. *The Deindustrialization of America.* New York: Basic Books, 1982.

deVoto, Bernard (Ed.). *The Portable Mark Twain.* New York: Viking Press, 1946, p. 560.

Hayes, Robert H., and Roger W. Schmenner. "How Should You Organize Manufacturing?" *Harvard Business Review,* January–February 1979, pp. 105–118.

Karnani, Aneel. "The Tradeoff Between Production and Transportation Cost in Determining Optimal Plant Size." *Strategic Management Journal,* Vol. 4, January–March 1983, pp. 45–54.

Leone, Robert A., and John R. Meyer. "Capacity Strategies for the 1980s." *Harvard Business Review,* November–December 1980, pp. 133–140.

Maister, David H. "Centralization of Inventories and the Square Root Law." *International Journal of Production Distribution,* Vol. 6, 1977, pp. 124–134.

Rutenberg, David P. "Multinational Plant Location." In *Multinational Management.* Boston: Little, Brown, 1982, Chapter 9.

Schmenner, Roger W. "Every Factory Has a Life Cycle." *Harvard Business Review,* March–April 1983, pp. 121–129.

Schmenner, Roger W. *Making Business Location Decisions.* Englewood Cliffs, NJ: Prentice-Hall, 1982.

Schmenner, Roger W. "Look Beyond the Obvious in Plant Location." *Harvard Business Review,* January–February 1979.

Skinner, Wickham. "The Focused Factory." *Harvard Business Review,* May–June 1974.

Wheelwright, Steven C. (Ed.). *Capacity Planning and Facilities Choice.* Division of Research, Graduate School of Business Administration, Harvard University.

Appendix.   Empirical Evidence Regarding Facilities Focus

The assumption that underlies the notion of facilities focus is that a factory or, for that matter, any organizational entity will perform better when assigned a narrower, more clearly defined set of tasks than it would when required to perform a broader, more nebulous set of tasks. As outlined by Skinner (1974), this concept recognizes that within any manufacturing facility managers are continually forced to make tradeoffs among competing objectives and reflects the belief that those tradeoffs will be made more consistently and in the appropriate direction if only a few specific requirements are placed on the facility. Mark Twain's Pudd'nhead Wilson put it somewhat more colorfully: "Behold the fool saith, 'Put not all thine eggs in the one basket'—which is but a manner of saying, 'Scatter your money and attention'; but the wise man saith, 'Put all your eggs in one basket and—WATCH THAT BASKET' " (deVoto, 1946).

Focusing a facility is one approach to reducing the diseconomies of scale discussed in Chapter 3. Moreover, a growing body of empirical evidence is helping to clarify the potential value of such focus.

4A-1   THE IMPACT OF FOCUS

The focus concept can be examined at four different organizational levels. At the highest level—an entire corporation—some of the benefits of focus can be seen by comparing several firms in a single industry. Figure 4-9a shows the operating margin and total 1977 sales for each of 11 companies (identified as A through I) producing a certain basic metal. As we discuss in Chapter 8, an experience curve analysis would suggest that as size increases, the operating margins in such a commodity-based business should also increase. While this seems to be the case generally, the straight line drawn through the data in Figure 4-9a is not a good fit to the individual observations.

A better explanation of these different profitability levels is provided by the degree of focus that each company has been able to achieve. One way of measuring focus in this industry is to count the number of product lines (or families; examples include sheets, tubes, and bars) produced—the fewer the product lines, the more focused the company. There are six major product lines.

Figure 4-9b graphs the operating margins of the same 11 companies against the number of product lines produced. The group of companies G through I are the narrow product-line firms, each producing only one or two major types of products. The group of firms A through E are the broad product-line firms, each producing five or six major types of products. Because of the significant transportation costs in this industry, the larger firms have con-

Figure 4-9 The impact of focus on companies in one industry

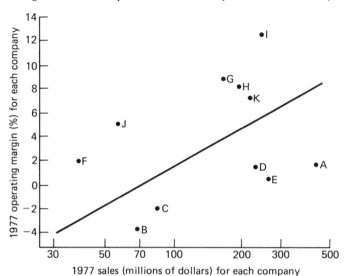

(a) Profitability as a function of size

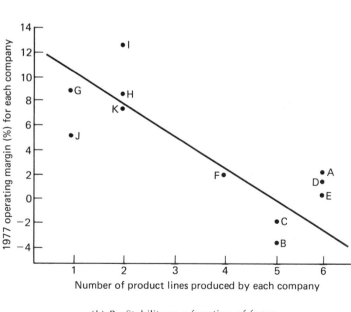

(b) Profitability as a function of focus
(product lines produced)

(*Source.* Boston Consulting Group, unpublished data. Used by permission.)

structed multiple plants, each serving a separate geographical territory, and all of the product lines produced by the company are generally made in each plant. Thus the broad product-line companies also have the less focused facilities.

Combining the information in Figure 4-9*b* with that in Figure 4-9*a* suggests that there are two groups of companies in the industry, one falling along a higher profitability line (Companies F–I) than the other (Companies A–E). It is evident that, while size is important to profitability, focus—as measured by the number of product lines produced in each facility—is even more important. Thus a highly focused firm like J, with less than $70 million in annual sales volume, can be as profitable (on a percentage basis) as a less focused firm with sales of $300 million or more.

A second level at which focus has an impact is across several plants in the same company, as shown by the data in Table 4-7. These data summarize 1979 plant profitability and other operating measures for a company operating seven regional plants scattered across the United States. Note that Plants A and B have almost twice the operating margin of Plants F and G. In addition, as shown by the table's bottom line, Plants A, B, and F are all roughly equivalent in size, while Plants D and G are almost twice as large. Although this process-intensive firm had long considered scale to be the major determinant of overall profitability, Table 4-7 does not support such a conclusion.

These seven facilities also can be compared by looking at their effectiveness at producing the firm's largest selling product (Product X). The second line in Table 4-7 indicates that Product X's profit margin surpasses the average margin at each plant, but that its relative profitability across the seven facilities follows the same pattern as overall operating margin. (The next to the last line in the table indicates the percentage of the total facility's output that is represented by Product X.)

This company decided that the differences in the profitabilities of its

Table 4-7
1979 Facilities Focus and Plant Profitability for a Process-Intensive Firm

	Plants						
	A	B	C	D	E	F	G
Gross operating margin (percent)	39.3	36.6	31.4	29.4	29.4	20.3	20.2
Product margin (percent)	49.1	41.4	39.6	41.0	42.3	34.2	36.7
Total number of products	10	5	17	19	20	19	31
Total number of divisions served	4	2	5	6	6	5	7
Percent of product to own division	95	96	70	50	50	45	30
Percent of Product X to total output	30	48	30	20	19	20	11
Volume index	56	44	59	100	51	59	99

plants were best explained by the degree of focus each was able to achieve. Three different measures of focus—(1) the total number of products produced in each facility, (2) the total number of divisions served (all these plants serve their own division as well as at least one other division in the corporation), and (3) the percentage of the plant output that goes to its own divisions—are shown in Table 4-7. The percentage of production going to the facility's own division was selected by this company as the best measure of focus, since it had chosen to organize into separate divisions because it felt it important to concentrate on the specific requirements of different customer groups. Thus the higher the percentage of a plant's output sold to other divisions, the greater the pressure on the plant to respond to the needs of those other divisions (and their customers), as opposed to the needs of its own division.

A third level at which the impact of facilities focus can be examined is illustrated in Figure 4-10. For a single firm with a single plant, this figure summarizes the impact *over time* of narrowing the product line and thereby increasing the plant's focus. As shown at the bottom of Figure 4-10, over a five-year period the number of major products produced at this facility went from 20 down to six. Its standard cost per unit (in constant dollars) decreased 23 percent with each doubling in the *average volume per model.* This decrease was attributable partly to increasing capacity utilization over this period. Other evidence collected by the firm, however, confirmed the conclusion that the narrowing and focusing of the product line was the most significant factor behind the reduction in costs. In fact, as its product line narrowed, the plant's attainable capacity actually increased by about 20 percent.

When this firm tracked its overhead costs per unit versus the *number of models produced,* it found a similar pattern. Finally, a single overhead item, inventory, was studied by comparing physical inventory turns to volume per model. It, too, followed a pattern similar to those for standard cost per unit and overhead cost per unit.

A fourth level at which the impact of focus might be considered is that of the individual production line within a facility. Depending on the detail and accuracy of a firm's cost accounting system, the relationship between overall performance and production line focus may be difficult to capture. However, the approach taken by one European packaged goods manufacturer is shown in Figure 4-11. This firm identified nine production lines (not all in the same facility), each of which performed comparable operations and tasks. It used line utilization as a surrogate for overall profitability. Focus was measured by the number of package sizes produced on a line.

As indicated in Figure 4-11, this firm found that its utilization rates dropped from the 90–100 percent range when a production line concentrated on a single package size, to about 35 percent when as many as seven package sizes were being run on a production line. While some falloff in line utilization would be expected with such variety, this firm had anticipated (before gathering the data) that utilization rates might fall from the mid-90s to only the mid-70s for this range of package sizes. The firm also examined its manufacturing overhead rates (per unit and as a percentage of total costs) and found

Figure 4-10   Impact of product line focus on standard cost

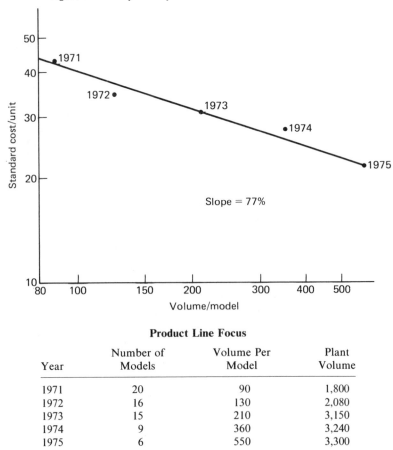

Product Line Focus

Year	Number of Models	Volume Per Model	Plant Volume
1971	20	90	1,800
1972	16	130	2,080
1973	15	210	3,150
1974	9	360	3,240
1975	6	550	3,300

(*Source.* Boston Consulting Group, unpublished data. Used by permission.)

that in those facilities with focused production lines, overhead rates were one-third to one-half what they were in plants with less focused production lines.

   Although the four examples cited above come from different industries and provide data at different levels of aggregation, the conclusions are consistent. Focusing manufacturing operations can have significant benefits; indeed, it may be one of the most important factors affecting the overall performance of a production facility. Some of the reasons behind this impact are examined below.

4A-2   IDENTIFYING THE SOURCES OF FOCUS BENEFITS

Most internal accounting systems require that many costs be averaged across products, product lines, and production processes, so it is difficult to identify

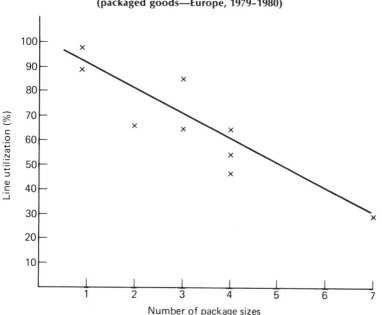

Figure 4-11   Measuring the impact of production line focus
(packaged goods—Europe, 1979-1980)

clearly the impact of focus on costs. However, a major study conducted by one firm examined the differences in both direct and overhead cost categories for two separate plants that produced machined components. One facility, Plant I, produced components for 125 models or products, whereas the other, Plant II, produced components for only 30 models or products. Plant II was somewhat less than half the size of Plant I. As shown in Figure 4-12, total costs per equivalent component (as measured along the vertical axis) were significantly lower in Plant II, the more narrowly focused facility. Most of this cost difference came from overhead categories rather than from direct costs.

A more detailed comparison of the benefits of focus is presented in Table 4-8. This table compares the performance of an American firm making heavy construction equipment in two different facilities with that of a more focused Japanese competitor operating a single facility. As indicated, both of the American firm's plants are roughly the same size (in terms of output) as the Japanese plant. However, the Japanese plant outperformed the American plants in each of the three cost categories indicated. For example, the American competitor's older facility, Plant A, required almost twice the labor hours of its newer facility, Plant B, which, in turn, required almost two-and-a-half times as much labor as the Japanese plant.

The Japanese plant and a "more competitive American plant" can be compared by referring to the first and the last columns in Table 4-8. This comparison adds another perspective to the benefits of focus. As discussed in Chapter 12, leading Japanese manufacturers work tenaciously to reduce in-process inventories, production cycle times, and set-up times as a means for cutting

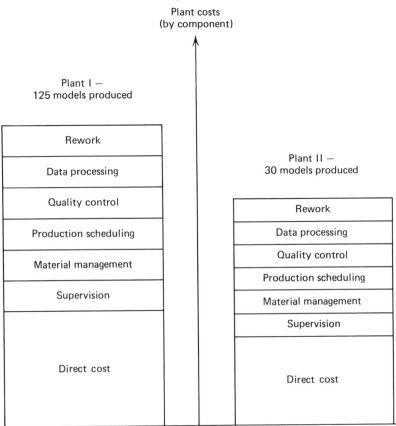

Figure 4-12   Facilities focus and plant overhead—machine component manufacturer

(*Source.*   Booz Allen & Hamilton. Used by permission.)

their indirect and overhead costs. The final column in Table 4-8 assumes that the American company's newer plant has the potential, through increased focus, to cut its set-up times by four-fifths and its work-in-process inventory by one-half. The combined effect of those two actions would cut Plant B's labor costs roughly in half and bring them much closer to those of the Japanese competitor's plant. This and other evidence suggests that overhead costs are much more dependent on the variety of products and processes in a facility than on its size (scale) or other variables.

Table 4-9 summarizes the benefits of focus gained by the firm whose seven plants were compared in Table 4-7. This company carried out a detailed analysis of the differences among its plants in an attempt to identify the sources of these benefits. It found that they could be grouped into four categories: process technology benefits, product technology benefits, asset utilization benefits, and market responsiveness (or competitiveness) benefits.

Table 4-8

**Productivity Comparison of
Japanese and American Construction Equipment Competitors
(indexed to the Japanese competitor)**

	Japanese Competitor	American Competitor		
		Plant A	Plant B	Plant[a] B'
Units/day	100	105	86	86
Labor/unit/day				
Direct	79	146	121	79
Indirect	17	221	96	47
Salaried and other	4	67	25	18
Total	100	434	242	144

Source.   Boston Consulting Group, 1982.
[a]Assumes five times faster setups and half the work-in-process inventory.

Although the research into the impact of facilities focus is still in its early stages, the data gathered so far suggest that the concept deserves additional study and that manufacturing managers should reconsider their facilities and capacity strategies in the light of the provocative evidence that is accumulating about it.

Table 4-9

Sources of Focus Benefits (same firm as Table 4-7)

Process Technology[a]
  Fine tuning
  Cost control
  Incremental improvements
Product Technology[a]
  Adapt to fit process
  Adapt to fit market
  Modify to solve secondary manufacturing problems
Asset Utilization
  Working capital control
  Fixed plant and equipment
  Worker specialization and attention
Market Responsiveness
  Close functional ties
  Narrower market requirements

[a] Improvements in design, decision making, and execution.

Implementing Facilities Planning Processes

5-1 OVERVIEW

The preceding two chapters concentrate on the *content* of capacity and facilities strategies. Underlying those discussions is the notion that changing a firm's strategy entails more than changing one or more individual decisions; it must change the *pattern* of those decisions over time. To achieve such a pattern change, a company usually has to alter its decision-making *processes* or procedures. This chapter, therefore, is addressed entirely to managerial procedures that can be used in facilities planning and decision making. There are at least three reasons for giving this topic so much attention.

First, because capacity and facilities proposals generally involve substantial investment, firms usually require that they be subjected to a number of tests and evaluation techniques that are primarily financial in nature. Learning to use such techniques skillfully and wisely not only enhances the likelihood that the appropriate decisions will be made, but also provides expertise that can be transferred readily to the evaluation of other structural decisions—such as the equipment and process technology decisions that we begin discussing in the next chapter.

Second, most corporations have a fairly well-developed capital allocation (budgeting) procedure that their manufacturing organizations must follow when requesting funds for facilities improvements. Developing skill in shepherding proposals through the corporate labyrinth is essential if the manufacturing function is to assemble the resources that will allow it to secure a competitive advantage.

Third, a number of difficult-to-quantify, nonfinancial issues permeate virtually all aspects of manufacturing strategy. One of the best ways to educate the rest of the organization about these issues is by systematically addressing them in the context of a series of facilities decisions.

Before outlining this chapter, we briefly describe what we have found to be the typical scenario followed by U.S. companies when evaluating major facilities projects. As summarized in Table 5-1, it is narrow in scope, limits attention to traditional alternatives, deals only with a single facility and a specific problem(s), and is dominated by financial considerations. As a consequence, it tends to omit or undervalue long-term competitive issues; the series of decisions that it produces sometimes never quite fit together; and truly innovative proposals are generated and considered only in response to unusual pressure, at which point it is often almost impossible to do much more than simply "manage the damage." Eventually its continuing use almost inevitably leads to gaps and weaknesses in the manufacturing organization's strategic capabilities.

The purpose of this chapter is to suggest procedures and activities that can help organizations avoid these types of problems, and to encourage the formulation and execution of coherent capacity and facilities strategies. In Section 5-2 we address such issues as who should be assigned to the project team entrusted with the generation and evaluation of a proposal, how they should proceed, and some techniques they might find useful in fulfilling their mission. Specific ideas are presented for staffing and organizing the project team, selecting and utilizing financial evaluation techniques, and directing and integrating the team's individual steps. Section 5-3 and Appendix A to this chapter describe the mechanics of some of the more popular approaches used in evaluating the financial impact of such proposals. In Section 5-4, we report on some of the procedures that companies have found helpful in making deci-

Table 5-1
Typical Scenario for a Major Capacity/Facilities Investment Project

1. The project is formulated as a "capital investment proposal," usually involving a single facility.
2. The purpose of the proposal is to recommend an investment in facilities that will meet the needs of a specific product and market.
3. To simplify analysis and evaluation, the project is evaluated as if it would not have any impact on existing facilities.
4. The proposal is generally triggered either by growth in demand or unsatisfactory performance in an existing facility (typically attributed to structural inadequacies in that facility).
5. A team of managers and specialists is given responsibility for defining and evaluating various options for overcoming these deficiencies; it is expected to recommend one of these alternatives and guide it through the capital approval process.
6. Early on, key senior managers are interviewed to ensure that their assessments and suggestions are considered, but the bulk of the project team's efforts are devoted to performing financial analyses of the most preferred alternative(s), to ensure that it meets stated investment hurdles and can withstand the scrutiny of the corporate financial staff when the final proposal is submitted to top management.
7. The alternative recommended tends to fit the pattern of past recommendations (unless key managers have changed) and primarily addresses the specific near-term problem.

sions and developing plans that are consistent with their capacity and facilities strategies. This section also outlines management's role in developing an effective facilities planning process and getting it started.

5-2   DIRECTING THE CAPACITY AND FACILITIES PLANNING PROCESS

Managing the capacity/facilities planning process within a firm requires attention to three basic considerations. The first is organizational: who will participate in the preparation of specific plans and project recommendations. This involves determining the level in the organization at which such planning will be undertaken, as well as the number and qualifications of the individuals on the project team. The second has to do with problem definition: what will (and will not) be considered as inputs and options. This entails defining the scope of the project, the motivation for it, and the orientation to be taken by the project team. The third concerns the tools to be supplied: what procedures will be followed in generating and evaluating alternatives, and in selecting the alternative to recommend to top management. Each of these issues is discussed in this section.

5-2.1   Organizational Aspects

Schmenner's study (1982) of the plant location decisions made by *Fortune* 500 firms identified seven organizational approaches that were used in capacity and facilities planning. The primary dimension along which these approaches varied was that of centralization versus decentralization. At one extreme, some evaluations were conducted entirely within a centralized corporate function; at the other were evaluations performed at a division or business unit level with no significant corporate input. Table 5-2 summarizes these approaches and the characteristics of the firms that use them.

Centralized Large Group Corporate Study

This approach is particularly common in large, integrated, process-intensive firms such as those involved in basic metals, forest products, and chemicals. In such firms, most projects are initiated by senior corporate management. Management initiatives are frequently prompted by business plans that indicate capacity shortfalls, or reports of a facilities problem in one of its divisions. Each project normally is handled by corporate staff specialists who have ongoing responsibility for capacity and facilities planning. The task of the division concerned is to gather the necessary data rather than trying to "sell" its proposal to corporate officers. The magnitude of these decisions—often entire plant complexes are involved—tends to increase the appropriateness of a highly centralized large group study.

Table 5-2

Characteristics of Seven Organizational Approaches to Capacity and Facilities Planning

Centralized ←——————————————————————————→ Decentralized

Centralized Large-Group Study	Central Staff-Controlled Study	Division-Controlled Study	Division-Only Study
Composed of a variety of staff specialists	Operating division initiates request, but corporate staff directs study	Division-initiated and led	Division-initiated and led
Process initiated by upper-level corporate management	Division often retains veto power	Must meet some important corporate hurdles along the way	Plant manager often taken from project team
Capacity and facilities choices viewed as key strategic decisions	Led by experienced staff member—often from manufacturing services or real estate	Possible check of content of final plans (not just financial returns) by corporate staff executive	More "selling" and "lobbying" required to get top management approval
			Frequently use outside location consultants

Centralized Small-Group Study	Central Staff-Led Study	Division-Led Study
Often CEO-initiated and led	Operating division initiates, corporate staff guides study process	Division initiates, leads, and prepares capital appropriation request
Capacity and facilities planning viewed as key strategic concern	Corporate staff helps division select option and obtain final approval	Corporate staff has one or more team members
Frequently tied to redirection or pursuit of specific strategy		Corporate expertise used as input for specialized data (e.g., locations or environmental or legal)

Centralized Small Group Study

This second form of the centralized group study differs considerably from the large-group approach just outlined. It is likely to be found in a setting where the CEO considers himself or herself to be the chief strategist for the firm and views capacity and facilities planning as the primary means for carrying out this strategy. This approach is also frequently used by highly centralized companies that are run by CEOs who have come up through the ranks; agricultural equipment manufacturers often fit this mold. In the centralized small group study, facilities planning tends to be conducted in a somewhat ad hoc manner, and it is likely to be intertwined with corporate decisions regarding the businesses that it wants to emphasize or deemphasize. The study group itself might consist of the CEO (as project leader), together with a few long-term staff members who have worked closely with the CEO in the past.

Division-Only Study

At the other extreme of the centralization/decentralization continuum is the approach often followed in diversified multidivisional firms. In such division-only studies, the capacity/facilities planning activity is initiated by the division itself. The extent to which it is based on a formal business plan is seldom very visible to top management; therefore approval of individual proposals often requires considerable "selling." Overseeing this process—which often dictates that key people sign off on the proposal before it reaches the board of directors—is the responsibility of division managers. They have wide latitude in managing the project team's generation and evaluation of proposals, as long as it is submitted for final approval according to corporate specifications.

The study team charged with developing the proposal for a specific project often ends up coordinating its implementation after approval; in fact, the manager for a new plant is sometimes selected from the team. As a result, the proposal is often identified with one individual, whose track record inevitably becomes an important consideration in the project's final evaluation. Since most divisions build new facilities, or make major modification in existing ones, only infrequently, it is not unusual for such a study team to seek the assistance of consulting companies that specialize in facilities and location decisions.

Staff-Controlled Study

Unlike the two previously described organizational approaches, this and the three remaining approaches require that the study team obtain inputs from both the corporate staff and the division. In the central staff-controlled study, the operating division typically initiates the request for a project but the corporate staff maintains control over its evaluation, either through its assignments of team members or by virtue of its experience and "objectivity." While the division generally retains veto power over the staff's recommendations, most of the actual analysis is performed by the central staff, which is generally led by

an experienced executive from the corporate manufacturing, financial, or construction departments.

Staff-Led Study

This approach gives the division more influence than it has in the staff-
controlled study, but the project is still dominated by the central staff. The division generally initiates the study proposal, but once senior management gives
the go-ahead, the corporate staff takes over, using the division's representatives
on the team to gather data and help delineate alternatives. After several alternatives have been generated, the central staff helps the division select the most
appropriate one (or the one most likely to get corporate approval). The staff
also assists in formulating the proposal so that it contains the information, and
follows the format, required to get it through the company's capital budgeting
process.

Division-Led Study

Here the division takes primary responsibility for initiating and leading the
study, as well as for the preparation of any capital appropriation requests
associated with the final recommendation. However, corporate management
usually seeks to impose some consistency on the procedures used by the divisions, often by requiring that one or more corporate staff personnel be included
in each project team. Corporate expertise tends to be concentrated in such specialized areas as location planning, meeting government requirements or environmental restrictions, and technological evaluation and forecasting.

Division-Controlled Study

Like the previous approach, this structure gives the division full responsibility
to initiate, evaluate, choose, and champion individual capacity and facilities
projects. This approach is often used when projects occur infrequently, involve
considerable informal communication and agreement, and depend more on the
performance records of the managers involved than on "objective" (quantitative) analyses. What is different between the division-*led* study and the divi-
sion-*controlled* study is the specification of certain key hurdles that the division
must surmount if it is to earn corporate approval for its recommendation. Such
hurdles might include illustrating that the proposed new facility is really
needed by the entire corporation, that its design meets corporate guidelines,
and that its expected returns exceed minimum corporate standards.

Some of the characteristics that influence companies in choosing among
these very different approaches can be inferred from looking at the companies
that have adopted each of them, as reported by Schmenner (Table 5-3). As
might be expected, capital-intensive industries tend to adopt the centralized,
large-group study approach. Firms whose divisions are highly interdependent,
require special coordination, or are particularly concerned that facilities be
used efficiently, also tend toward corporate staff domination of such projects.
Division-dominated projects, on the other hand, are more likely to be found in

Table 5-3

Companies Representative of Different Organization Approaches to Capacity and Facilities Planning

Increasing Staff Domination ← → Increasing Division Domination

Centralized	Staff controlled	Staff led	Division led	Division controlled	Division-only study
Centralized large-group study	Westinghouse (1 other company)	United Technologies (1 other company)	Whittaker (2 other companies)	Levi Strauss	Beatrice Foods
Alcoa			American Standard	Pet	Black and Decker
Anheuser Busch	Burroughs (some projects)	FMC	Burlington Industries	TRW	Brown Group
Cities Service	Company Z	General Foods	Crown Zellerbach (small projects)	Union Camp (small projects)	Company X
Company W	Oxford Industries	Honeywell	Dart Industries		Dart Industries
Crown Zellerbach (large projects)	Reliance Electric	Ralston Purina	Del Monte		Perkin Elmer
U.S. Steel		Texas Instruments (sometimes)	Diamond Shamrock		RCA
(2 other companies)			Du Pont		(1 other company)
			IBM		
Centralized small-group study			Indian Head		
Agrico Chemical Group (of the Williams Companies)			Inland Steel		
Cluett, Peabody			Lockheed		
Company Y			Martin Marietta		
Gold Kist			Motorola		
Land O'Lakes			Phillips Petroleum		
Texas Instruments (sometimes)			Pillsbury		
(1 other company)			Rockwell International		
			Simmons USA		
			Union Camp (large projects)		
			Union Carbide		
			Burroughs (some projects)		

conglomerates or large diversified companies with fewer interconnections between divisions.

Some companies use different approaches depending on the type of project in question. For example, large new plant complexes (or the "campuses" described in Chapter 4) may be under the jurisdiction of corporate staff-dominated teams, while the smaller satellite facilities that were part of the original master plan for the complex are left to the division.

One of Schmenner's more interesting overall findings is that over the past few decades there has been a gradual shift from division-dominated to corporate staff-dominated approaches. Schmenner concludes that this movement reflects the increasing complexity of facility and location decisions, as well as the difficulty of controlling a network of geographically dispersed operations. This trend, in turn, has led large firms to adopt more formal (and more thorough) approaches to capacity/facilities planning than used to be the case. Some of the mechanisms such firms employ to help guide individual projects are described in the next section.

5-2.2 Managing Capacity/Facilities Planning Projects

Given the nature and importance of capacity/facilities decisions, it is not surprising that most firms approach them individually and sequentially—by formulating a series of discrete projects that can be analyzed, evaluated, and implemented as needs and opportunities arise. Such a project-by-project approach makes efficient use of both staff specialists and line managers and reduces the likelihood that important details will be overlooked.

Before looking at the sequence of steps that firms typically follow when managing this process, it is useful to consider the motivations that usually impel firms to initiate such activities. Increasing demand is the most common motive; companies are generally reluctant to forgo opportunities to grow with their markets, and thus a projected increase in demand almost invariably triggers a capacity review and the development of proposals for meeting any projected shortfall. In fact, the procedures that most firms follow in evaluating various proposals appear to assume implicitly that their primary goal is to provide increased capacity. Other motivations for reviewing capacity needs can be equally, if not more, important in certain cases, however.

A reduction in demand, for example, may also trigger a capacity review. It does not usually bring the same degree of pressure to bear on the organization as does an increase in demand, because the firm as a whole may still be growing and thus can shift products from more crowded facilities to underutilized ones. But when facilities are highly specialized, or inappropriate for various reasons, firms may be forced to consider the closing or sale of a plant. The question is, "Which plant?" Generally this decision cannot be made on a decentralized basis or according to a democratic process.

Three other reasons for conducting a capacity or facilities review are observed occasionally. One is a major technological change. Such changes may encourage, even force, a plant to make a transition from one stage to the next in its development (as described in Section 4-2), and require replacing or upgrading a substantial amount of the plant's equipment. If a firm understands the plant's evolving needs as it matures, it can usually address such decisions using the project management approaches outlined in this section. But if it lacks this perspective and is caught by surprise, a major change in technology may lead to the precipitous closing of one facility and the starting up of another.

Facilities investment may also be motivated by events in the firm's external environment, such as government legislation or major changes in competition. The pollution control legislation of the 1970s, for example, initiated numerous projects for altering production processes. Many of these had little effect on capacity or competitive effectiveness, however, because they were viewed only in negative terms and not combined with other effectiveness-enhancing facility modifications.

An even more compelling motivation—but, unfortunately, one observed only infrequently in practice—is the opportunity to make a significant improvement in the firm's competitive position, often through a linked sequence of facilities projects. Under the careful and consistent guidance of senior management, capacity and facilities planning procedures can be made more and more proactive, as discussed in Section 5-4.

The remainder of this section examines the eight steps commonly found in capacity and facilities planning procedures; these are summarized in Table 5-4. We describe each step's basic purpose, the issues raised in carrying it out, and the approaches that are typically followed in dealing with these issues.

Step 1.   Audit and Evaluate Existing Capacity and Facilities

The major objective of this step is to define appropriate measures of the capacity of individual facilities, as well as of the business as a whole. Such measures must take into account the cost structures and performance characteristics of the technologies employed in these facilities. The companies that stumble over this step typically do so because they define capacity too narrowly.

Although the term "capacity" is used at various levels of management as though it represented a precise and measurable quantity, identifying the capac-

---

Table 5-4

**Capacity and Facilities Planning Projects:
Eight-Step Procedure**

1. Audit and evaluate existing capacity and facilities.
2. Forecast capacity/facilities requirements.
3. Define alternatives for meeting requirements.
4. Perform financial analyses of each alternative.
5. Assess key qualitative issues for each alternative.
6. Select the alternative to be pursued.
7. Implement the chosen alternative.
8. Audit and review actual results.

ity of a facility (or set of facilities) for operating purposes can be extremely difficult. At least eight important aspects of capacity should be considered.

1. *Capacity depends on the interaction of various resource constraints.* While usually defined as the maximum output rate that is achievable during a given time frame, that rate represents the combined result of a variety of resources (equipment, labor availability, storage space, etc.), any one of which can be the limiting factor or "bottleneck." A facility's capacity, therefore, can fluctuate rapidly as one bottleneck is supplanted by another. Managers sometimes prefer some capacity measures (such as floor space or machine hours) over others because they are easier to measure, it takes longer to change them, or because of biases in accounting procedures that expense some factors of production (labor and materials) but capitalize others (physical plant and equipment).

2. *Capacity is mix dependent,* because different products can consume different amounts of the various factors of production. Expressing capacity in terms of such aggregate measures as sales dollars or "equivalent units" may avoid this complication if product mix changes are small, but major swings in the mix can cause such measures to give misleading signals.

3. *Capacity is technologically based,* since the manufacturing technology used by a firm places important limits on its overall capacity and the efficiency with which various resources are consumed. Therefore, an estimate of capacity necessarily implies some assumption about the process technology employed.

4. *Capacity is dynamic,* in that as a manufacturing facility gains experience in producing something, and discovers and removes successive bottlenecks, its total capacity tends to expand with time, even without major new investments.

5. *Capacity is location specific.* Even though a firm's aggregate capacity is the sum of the capacities of each of its facilities, it is sometimes not possible to allocate an increase in overall demand to an underutilized plant. As discussed in Chapter 3, transportation costs may make it unprofitable for plants in some locations to service certain customers or regions, and competitive factors may require proximity to customers. Excess labor or materials in the wrong location are seldom any more helpful than excess machinery and floor space.

6. *Capacity may not be sustainable.* Even within a single facility there is usually considerable uncertainty as to the meaning of the capacity measure that is used in planning production. When stated as so many units per time period, for example, it may mean the average sustainable output over a month, the maximum achievable output for a shorter period of time, or the best performance actually achieved in the past.

7. *Capacity depends on management policies.* Managers operate production facilities using policies that affect the number of hours worked per week (through the amount of overtime and the number of shifts), the degree of production smoothing, and the amount of capacity cushion that is considered appropriate—all of which directly affect the facility's capacity.

8. *Capacity is storable.* As a result, it is often difficult to determine how much of a facility's total output was generated by its innate production capabilities, and how much resulted from reducing various in-process inventories. Maintaining excess equipment (to allow regular maintenance) or excess labor (to fill in for missing employees) represents other forms of stored capacity. A capacity measure that reflects the use of such cushions may not be sustainable for extended periods.

Unfortunately, Step 1 is passed over rather quickly in most firms, and only one or two fairly narrow measures of existing capacity (and other capabilities) are used. While this may facilitate the movement of a proposal through subsequent steps, it often severely limits the range of alternatives considered in Step 3 and may lead to less creative solutions to particular facilities problems.

Step 2.   Forecast Capacity/Facilities Requirements

If Step 1 has been carried out comprehensively, it provides a framework for the analysis that is required for this step. In fact, the two steps are sometimes done in parallel. Step 2 involves forecasting future requirements by technology, product/market, and geographic area. In forecasting these requirements one should include external (competitive) as well as internal factors, and use different approaches so as to cross-check the estimates that result. As part of this analysis it is also useful to develop a forecast of the cost structure that is likely to be required in order for the firm to be competitive at some future date.

Before this can be done, one must get agreement on the time horizon that is appropriate for the capacity planning process. Firms typically base their time horizon on the lead time required to implement the project, plus the number of years that are expected to elapse before it achieves desired profit levels. Industry norms also can serve as a guideline, but it is important to avoid being constrained by past practice and to consider alternative—usually longer—horizons. This may encourage the firm to consider a *sequence* of decisions, within the context of the facility's entire life cycle, rather than just the specific proposal under review.

In the late 1960s, for example, the Carborundum Corporation found itself with a choice between making a small incremental expansion at an existing site or building a large new plant in a different region of the country. [See "Carborundum, Inc.," Harvard Case Services, 9-672-131.] Looking at the sequence of expansions that might follow the initial one proved very useful in deciding which initial action would be most appropriate. (Malpas, 1983, in fact, advocates taking "the plant after next" explicitly into consideration when evaluating a proposal for a new plant.)

One should also attempt to relate this long-term capacity plan to other plans that have shorter duration. Figure 5-1 suggests one approach for doing this. It breaks capacity planning into four different time frames: long-range planning (more than one year), annual planning, short-term scheduling (up to three months), and, finally, dispatching (generally less than one month). The level of the managers involved differs for each time horizon, as shown at the left in Figure 5-1. While top management is likely to be directly concerned with long-range capacity planning (the topic of both this chapter and the preceding one), plant and shop floor managers typically handle job order scheduling and dispatching. Annual capacity planning (often referred to as aggregate planning or master scheduling) usually involves senior manufacturing managers and their functional counterparts in marketing, engineering, and development.

Notice that each segment of capacity planning in Figure 5-1 is naturally linked to those segments having longer- and shorter-term duration. For example, the annual capacity plan constitutes one portion of the long-range capacity plan, but it also establishes the framework within which schedules are developed and modified as the firm proceeds through the year. Capacity planning for the shorter time horizons also involves some interaction among functions, but those tend to be at lower levels than in the case of annual or longer-range capacity plans.

Using the time horizon to divide capacity planning into manageable subsegments makes it easier to identify the types of decisions required for each major factor of production, as shown in Table 5-5. This highlights the need to view capacity not just as floor space or capital equipment, but also in terms of human resources and materials. Most long-term capacity/facilities planning procedures, unfortunately, deal only with plant and equipment decisions—the upper left-hand corner of Table 5-5—which implies that they are the most critical decisions. Our own view is that the human resource and logistics issues are

Figure 5-1 Capacity planning and the time horizon in operations

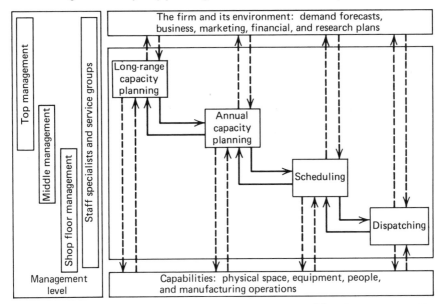

(*Source.* Adapted from "Note on Capacity Management," Harvard Case Services, 9-674-081.)

Table 5-5

Capacity Planning Decisions by Time Horizon

Capacity-Determining Decisions	Types of Decisions—By Time Horizon			
	Long-Range Capacity Planning	Annual Capacity Planning	Scheduling	Dispatching
Acquiring and deploying physical space and capital equipment	Selection of capabilities Location decisions Timing decisions Amount Capital spending	Minor changes Subcontracting Product mix	Allocation of facilities to products in specific time periods	
Acquiring and deploying human resources	Hiring and layoff policies Skill requirements Timing Quantity Training and development	Number of shifts Overtime Hire–fire Line balancing	Overtime Allocation of labor to products (jobs) in specific time periods	Rescheduling, expediting, and detailed coordination of all three factors of production
Acquiring and deploying materials	Material requirements Long-term contracts Vendor selection Warehouse requirements Timing Quantity	Short-term purchase commitments Shipping schedules Inventory planning	Ordering materials Marshalling materials Inventory control Allocation of materials	

Source. Adapted from "Note on Capacity Management" Harvard Case Services, 9-674-081.

at least as important, because they provide many of the crucial linkages between strategy and tactics.

Step 3. Define Alternatives for Meeting Requirements

In spite of the obvious need to consider a variety of alternative approaches to meeting projected facilities requirements, many firms react to a projected shortfall in demand, as identified in Steps 1 and 2, by thinking simply in terms of expanding existing production capabilities: another machine, another shift, or another plant. Planning systems that respond to such shortfalls by occasionally triggering a comprehensive review of the available alternatives, however, are much more likely to generate proposals that have the potential to make a significant improvement in a company's competitive position.

An example of one company's assessment of the alternatives available to it is contained in Table 5-6. Four different alternatives are presented (C1–C4). Although other possible options undoubtedly existed, this list is richer than that typically generated. Contrast it, for example, with that developed by a well-known pharmaceutical company. Impelled by rapidly increasing prices of petroleum-based purchased materials in the mid-1970s, it decided that it should begin manufacturing certain chemicals that it was buying currently from outside suppliers. Unfortunately, the only alternatives it considered were either to build a new plant or to buy a used one. Subsequent events suggested that it might have been wiser to consider *other* ways for solving the problems it faced: rapidly increasing materials costs and occasional interruptions in supplies. As suggested in Chapter 9, a joint venture arrangement, a long-term purchase contract, or even increasing raw material inventories, were other options worth considering.

One reason firms tend to consider only obvious expansion options is that they wait too long before deciding to act. This places the team responsible for proposing a solution under tremendous time pressure. Unless it can come up with a quick alternative, it is likely to restrict its attention to the proposals already favored by certain key people within the organization. The team soon realizes that building "more of the same" is always faster than doing a comprehensive review and, perhaps, developing an entirely new approach.

A lack of creativity during this step is also to be expected if the team is composed entirely of long-time employees who are intimately familiar with the organization's historical practice regarding such decisions. Such people tend to recommend a continuation of those previous approaches. The Zenith Radio Corporation nearly fell into this trap in the mid-1960s when it asked its recently retired vice president of manufacturing (who had done an outstanding job for many years) to prepare a capacity and facilities expansion proposal. Not surprisingly, his proposal was completely consistent with Zenith's historical pattern of expansion, despite evidence of impending major changes in the color TV market. Zenith had to bring in an outside consultant in order to develop the "new approach" that it subsequently adopted.

Adopting a longer time horizon often encourages a study group to expand the alternatives considered. It also makes it possible to consider changing

Table 5-6

One Company's Approach to a Major Capacity and Facilities Planning Project

Assignment

In-depth analysis of all major options for meeting the division's capacity requirements for next 5 or more years, followed by preparation of capital request for management selected option.

Timing

Project team to complete analysis of alternatives in four months, and preparation of capital request for selected option by the end of month 5.

Project Team Staff

Senior division industrial engineer (team leader)
Staff analyst from corporate planning
Division industrial engineers (up to four, as needed)

Location

Industrial engineering offices at division headquarters

Plan Outline

A. Determine manufacturing requirements
   1. Obtain sales forecasts from marketing—pessimistic, most likely, optimistic—covering five years.
   2. Obtain from marketing a prediction of business conditions for subsequent 10-year period.
   3. Establish whether or not it is likely we will attempt to build domestically the small end of the product line. Preliminary cost estimates for these units are now being analyzed.
B. Measure requirements
   1. Convert forecasts into direct labor hours and adjust for performance.
   2. Separate above into requirements for:
      a. Product line A
      b. Product line B
      c. Product line C
      d. Product line D
   3. Group requirements for various alternative plans.
C. Prepare alternative plans
   1. Product line as is at Plant 1 and product line as is at Plant 2
   2. Provide new facility for Product C
   3. Transfer manufacturing of Product line C to Plant 2; transfer Product line B to Plant 1
   4. Provide a new facility for Product line D
   Note: Analysis of each alternate plan is to include:
      1. Floor space requirements
      2. Direct labor requirements
      3. Assessment of learning curves
      4. Capital equipment requirements
      5. Schedule for transfer of work (if required)
      6. Provisions for future expansion
      7. Profitability index

Table 5-6 (*continued*)

D. Decision making
    1. Evaluate alternatives
    2. Decide on best alternative(s)
    3. Make recommendation(s) to management
    4. Obtain management approval
E. Prepare capital authorization request(s)

---

the focus of certain facilities. Creative approaches to facilities focus can also be encouraged by asking managers to think in terms of the set of facilities that would be desirable at some comfortably distant time in the future, and how each should be focused. This allows one to evaluate alternative expansion proposals in the context of where the firm would like to "end up" after several years.

Imposing certain constraints can sometimes motivate the consideration of alternatives that otherwise might not be defined. Specifying a facility's maximum size in advance, for example, makes it easier to identify the number of facilities that will eventually be needed to supply a given market, and encourages thinking about the sequence in which they might be added.

Step 4. Perform Financial Analyses of Each Alternative

Once the options are clearly defined, they must be evaluated along financial and other quantitative dimensions. The next section of this chapter outlines a number of techniques—payback, accounting rate of return, discounted cash flow, and internal rate of return—that can be used in this evaluation. Each alternative considered should be evaluated using a common set of assumptions. It is often useful, therefore, to develop a computerized financial model for evaluating similar proposals; this can also aid in estimating the sensitivity of important financial summary measures to changes in key assumptions.

Before evaluating various options, one must decide how they will be compared. Any project can be made to look attractive if it is compared against something sufficiently unattractive. Since the whole purpose of a financial evaluation is to determine the relative attractiveness of various increases in investment, the most appropriate place to begin is to identify the best possible course of action that uses the minimum amount of additional resources; this becomes the "base case." Notice that this base case may involve substantial changes in operations; it does not mean doing nothing. (Most projects, particularly those that support expansion and growth, look excellent when compared with doing nothing!) With such a base established, each option can be compared in terms of the cash flows and benefits that represent changes from that base.

Step 5. Assess Key Qualitative Issues for Each Alternative

In this important step, one reviews the qualitative factors that are relevant to each alternative. These might include factors that one cannot quantify without access to data that are unavailable, as well as those for which no good quanti-

Table 5-7

Qualitative Factors Considered by FMC Project Team

1. Learning costs associated with each capacity and facilities option. These costs represent startup learning required for a facility to reach its anticipated stable rate of productivity. (In 1978 dollars, these costs had totaled $15.17 million for the Bowling Green plant from 1974–1978, the first five years of that plant's existence.)
2. Costs associated with the impact of potential strikes on each option. Assessments were obtained on the number of strikes over a 10-year period and their average duration. These were combined with engineering estimates of the costs of a strike of different lengths under each option.
3. Costs resulting from a failure to develop the capabilities assumed in the financial analysis of each option. This was measured in relationship to long-term productivity levels at a plant. For example, for 1978, Cedar Rapids' productivity was 74.2 percent and Bowling Green's was 63.5 percent. Originally, Bowling Green had been expected to achieve 73 percent productivity, but current expectations were that it would level off at 70 percent, resulting in 3 percent productivity never being achieved.
4. Market share loss due to quality/reliability problems of each option. These losses were assumed to affect only the first five years of each option and reflected the increased chances of quality and reliability problems associated with options other than expanding in place.
5. Costs associated with diseconomies of scale (the large-plant syndrome). These costs would occur if Cedar Rapids were expanded, since it was already considered larger than optimum.
6. Sales loss due to start-up problems. Some sales would be lost in the first year if time schedules slipped or orders couldn't be filled on time.
7. The ability of more narrowly focused (dedicated) facilities and organizational units to increase market share. With increased focus, it was felt that long-term market shares could be improved over what would otherwise be the case.

Source. "FMC (B)," Harvard Case Services, 9-679-147.

tative measures exist, such as short-term versus long-term considerations, the ease of implementation and operation, and the fit with the firm's competitive environment and business strategy.

An approach for dealing with those qualitative factors that represent major uncertainties is illustrated by the approach followed by FMC (See Section 4-1.4). After developing a facilities plan in 1975 and then observing subsequent events, the company incorporated several new qualitative concerns into its evaluation of a similar plan five years later. Various managers were asked individually to make assessments of the possible outcomes for several different courses of action, and these assessments were combined to develop consensus measures of their financial impact. Table 5-7 summarizes the seven areas examined by the company's project team.

Step 6. Select the Alternative to Be Pursued

Deciding which of the alternative proposals should be recommended is not enough; one must also decide how to guide the chosen proposal through the approval process (that is, the capital budgeting procedure). The composition of the project team plays an important role in insuring that all important factors are taken into account and analyzed objectively. We are familiar with one company where the project team was composed entirely of engineering and production managers. There was a conspicuous absence of representatives from human resources/labor relations, marketing, or international operations, even though the proposal involved supplying overseas divisions as well as domestic ones. The alternative recommended by this project team was later described as "what one might expect when engineers talk to engineers." During its implementation, several major stumbling blocks were identified that could be attributed directly to perspectives that were missing in the original project team. Eventually these problems torpedoed the project.

As suggested in Section 5-2.1, the organizational level that is assigned responsibility for a given project will have a major impact on how alternatives are evaluated and presented for approval. The composition of the project team aids in defining and evaluating alternatives; it also affects the political process through which the project's approval is achieved and the degree to which various constituencies within the firm support its implementation. If the project team includes a wide range of perspectives, it is more likely to develop flexible approaches for each situation than to apply a standard procedure that may overlook important factors. Some companies assign two different teams to the same project, so as to introduce an element of competition into the development of alternatives and to create an incentive for thoroughly investigating common alternatives. A similar approach is often used in R&D project management; in fact, much of the literature describing parallel R&D projects can be applied to capacity/facilities projects.

If a project is largely division-initiated and directed, it must finally be "sold" to corporate management. Understanding the realities (and biases) of the corporate approval processes can help division managers ensure that the project they back can surmount the procedural hurdles of higher corporate levels. Depending on the corporate mechanisms used to verify proposed projects, at least three different approaches are available for getting a division's recommendations approved. One is to use a demonstrably "objective" approach based, say, on a particular *technique*. One company's team, for example, developed an elaborate decision tree that showed how different sales levels would affect the profitability of each of the alternatives they were considering. This proved to be a persuasive mechanism for getting their recommendation approved.

The Reliance Electric Motor Division (see Section 4-1.4) followed a second approach: it emphasized the *strategic logic* of its long-term capacity and facilities plan. While the usual financial analysis was conducted by the corporate staff, it was understood to be largely a formality and was confined simply to double-checking the calculations carried out by the project team.

A third approach is to perform an exhaustive *financial analysis.* In many diversified companies, the role of the corporate staff is largely confined to financial evaluation. Therefore, a thorough analysis of the financial implications of the recommended alternative at the division level is essential. But division management must also make sure that it has evaluated the strategic and qualitative factors properly, even if that is not what finally "sells" the project to corporate management.

The basic rule to follow in selecting which of these approaches to adopt is the old lawyer's dictum: "When you have the law on your side, argue the law. When you have the facts on your side, argue the facts. And if you don't have either, wave your arms and raise your voice!"

Step 7.   Implement the Chosen Alternative

Once an alternative has been recommended and approved, two other important issues must be addressed. The first has to do with the performance measures that will be used to monitor the project's implementation. When a major expansion or modification of an existing facility is involved, it might be necessary to redefine the facility's charter before developing such measures. Not only should time-related and budget-related milestones be established, but it is also important to review periodically the basic capabilities being provided and the sources of competitive advantage being sought.

The second issue revolves around identifying those actions and resources that will have the greatest impact on the overall success of the project. The firm must make certain that these resources are provided and applied in a timely and effective manner. In the case of one oilfield equipment manufacturer, for example, this involved identifying the major tasks required to support a sequence of capacity/facilities decisions over a five-year period, estimating the skills that would be required at each step along the way, and developing a plan for obtaining those skills and capabilities, either internally or from outside sources. This analysis led it to develop an extensive PERT chart and appoint a full-time project manager to assure that each of the critical tasks (as well as the overall project) was progressing as planned.

Step 8.   Audit and Review Actual Results

Most organizations do not audit results in any systematic fashion. Such an audit can serve a very useful purpose, however, in that it provides feedback for improving the procedures the firm uses to develop future capacity and facilities plans. The results of a major facilities investment need to be reviewed both against the milestones that were proposed in its implementation plan and against the problems that triggered it. In one industrial products firm, the audit review process included a requirement that a second approval be obtained for any capital that was not spent during the year for which it was authorized. This helped insure both that expenditures were not being postponed just in the interest of boosting short-term profits, and that the conditions that originally justified the expenditure still existed when it was actually made.

The few firms that we have observed carrying out this kind of audit and review have found that it is most beneficial when it is not simply a financial review, but also checks whether the completed project is supporting the firm's strategic objectives as it was intended to do. Such reviews also help maintain the integrity of the analysis going into such projects. Moreover, they serve to police the proposals submitted to the capital budgeting process, ensuring that capital has been spent on what was approved.

5-3 THE FINANCIAL ANALYSIS OF PROPOSED FACILITIES INVESTMENTS

The success of a manufacturing organization is largely measured by the effectiveness with which it utilizes the various kinds of assets entrusted to it: facilities, technologies, and skills. The lifetimes, degrees of liquidity, rates of obsolescence, and riskiness of these assets vary according to their form, scale, and location. Moreover, they tend to be highly immobile once in place. While it is possible to sell buildings and move equipment, at a price, it can be extraordinarily difficult to move the people whose skills are necessary to make such plant and equipment productive. Finally, the choices made at one point in time affect not only current operations, but also the environment within which future decisions will be made. Hence changes and additions to manufacturing assets have to be made carefully and patiently, step by step, over a long period of time.

Given the magnitude of these assets in most manufacturing-based enterprises, it is not surprising that senior managers scrutinize all requests for major additional investments. A formal capital budgeting and performance review system is usually set up to review such requests. Unfortunately, these systems are so effective that sometimes they become the primary means by which the firm's manufacturing function is "managed." We return to this topic in Chapter 6.

When such financially dominated firms go about developing a facilities plan, much of the manufacturing manager's time is devoted to preparing investment authorization requests that follow a prespecified format and provide evidence that the proposed investment will surpass the firm's stated financial objectives. This usually requires considerable care—and often some imagination as well. This section provides an overall framework for thinking about alternative methods for evaluating a proposed investment, and describes some specific techniques that are commonly used. The appendices to this chapter illustrate the basic mechanics of these techniques and the extent to which some of their key results are comparable.

Throughout this discussion, although we continually emphasize the necessity of maintaining a long-term perspective when developing and evaluating major investments in the manufacturing function, it is important to keep in mind that it is often difficult to maintain such a perspective in the face of short-term needs and opportunities, career aspirations, and organizational politics. Therefore, toughness, persuasiveness, and commitment are probably more important to a manufacturing manager's success than knowledge of the latest financial technique. However, these techniques must be thoroughly understood in order to defend one's proposals before those who understand only numbers. If a proposed investment does not meet the firm's stated financial goals, the amount of persuasion required to get it accepted, in preference to other proposals that apparently do, rises by several orders of magnitude.

5-3.1   A Framework for Assessing the Financial Attractiveness of Proposed Investments

Before examining specific techniques for financial analysis, it is useful to consider a framework for organizing the options available. Most business organizations—in fact, most people—have three major concerns in mind when they contemplate a proposed investment:

1.   Security—How safe is my money? How soon will I be able to get it back?
2.   Recompense—How much more will I get back than I invested?
3.   Predictability—How sure am I about the anticipated returns from this investment?

Since the security and the predictability criteria both embody concerns about the riskiness of an investment, they are sometimes lumped together into a single criterion. However, it is useful to separate them since they describe two different kinds of risk. The predictability of an investment refers to its internal uncertainty (such as the amount of the investment required, its returns, their timing, and the project's lifetime). Security is more concerned with uncertainties external to the investment that might, for example, cause one to want to discontinue the project and invest in something else if unanticipated problems or opportunities present themselves. Thus it is related to the desire for liquidity, with "wanting your money back in your own hands, than knowing exactly what the investment's returns will be.

Senior financial managers often express concern about a fourth aspect of a proposed capital investment: the "smoothness" of its cash flow characteristics over time. A major part of their job is ensuring that the firm has sufficient funds on hand each year to meet its annual capital charges (both interest on debt and stockholder dividends), to finance the investments that it is likely to want to make, and to meet unexpected demands for cash. Large investments whose returns are highly variable from year to year (even if relatively predictable) can complicate this task considerably.

Many managers also seem to believe that stockholders prefer smooth earnings growth over time (and hence smooth dividend growth) rather than erratic patterns. The belief in this supposed preference is almost as strong as the evidence various researchers have collected that indicates that stockholders do not appear to have any such preference—or if they do, it does not appear to affect significantly the prices they are willing to pay for a firm's common stock.

The main beneficiaries of such smoothness are undoubtedly corporate managers, who are thereby spared the intense scrutiny (and possible criticism) of the external financial community that is triggered by reductions in the profitability of the activities for which they are responsible.

5-3.2 Measures of Security

The most commonly used measure of the security of a proposed investment is its *payback*—the length of time between the initial investment and the point when the organization gets its money back. The approaches used to estimate payback range from simply dividing the initial investment by its average annual cash flow to calculating the time at which the cumulative cash flow becomes positive. (See Appendix 5A.)

Many companies require that a proposed investment meet a given payback criterion before they look at any other measures of its attractiveness. This hurdle may be rather arbitrary, reflecting the firm's capital constraints or the degree of risk to which it is willing to expose itself. It may depend on the type of investment being considered, and tends to vary by industry, reflecting some implicit estimate of the rate of technological or market change expected there.

In the semiconductor industry, for example, most companies require paybacks of less than two years on new investments. This reflects both the rapidity of product and process obsolescence in that industry and the shortage of capital—resulting from high growth rates and heavy reliance on internal financing—that is typical of semiconductor companies. The dependence on internally generated funds, in turn, often stems from the reluctance of outsiders to lend money to firms that are exposed to such risk, and from the unwillingness of the semiconductor firms themselves to take on the burden of large interest charges, given their volatile earnings prospects.

5-3.3 Measures of Recompense

Assuming that the project's payback is acceptable, most firms next want a measure of its *expected earnings generation ability:* How much more will it get back from the project than it invested in it? Several measures of recompense are used in practice; three are described below:

$$\frac{\text{average annual profit after tax}}{\text{average beginning-of-year investment (book value)}} \qquad \text{(A)}$$

$$\frac{\text{average annual net cash flow}}{\text{initial investment}} \qquad \text{(B)}$$

$$\frac{\text{total cash inflow over the project's life}}{\text{initial investment} \times \text{life of the project}} \qquad \text{(C)}$$

Approach A attempts to duplicate the "book return on investment" (ROI), which is the usual accounting measure of a company's total earnings generating ability. Approach B is an "improvement" used by some companies to reflect the actual cash flow, including depreciation, arising from the investment. Since using book value in the denominator would, in effect, double-count the impact of depreciation, the entire initial investment is used. Approach C is simply a different version of calculation B to drive home the point that we get the same result whether we think in terms of an annual *average* rate of return or a *total* return over the lifetime of the investment.

Both approaches A and B are easy to calculate and, for lifetimes in the range of 5–15 years, they usually lead to similar values. They tend to diverge more and more, however, as the investment lifetime increases; as demonstrated in Appendix 5B, for very long-lived investments method A will lead to ROI estimates that are about twice those of method B.

Both approaches suffer from two flaws. First, they are based on average (or total) cash flows and do not take into account the *timing* of these cash flows. Most companies, like individuals, would prefer to receive cash sooner than later.

The second flaw is more subtle. It would be convenient to be able to argue that payback and return on investment are reciprocal concepts—that the first measures the *quickness* of return without taking into account the *total* return, while the second measures the total return without taking into account its quickness. If this were true, one could recommend an investment analysis based on both measures—one focusing on the security criterion and one on the recompense criterion. Unfortunately, although there is some truth in this assertion (particularly if the investment's cash flows vary considerably from year to year), the world is not always that simple.

The great majority of the investments one sees in practice are similar to the example used in Appendix 5A and involve an initial cash outflow followed by a sequence of inflows. In this situation the return on investment, as calculated using approach B, is essentially the inverse of the payback period calculated earlier. In other words, these two calculations are simply variations of the same calculation. Using numbers drawn from Appendix 5A:

$$\text{payback} = \frac{\text{investment}}{\text{annual return}} = \frac{800}{185.5} = 4.3 \text{ years}$$

and

$$\text{return on investment} = \frac{\text{annual return}}{\text{investment}} = \frac{185.5}{800} = 23.2 \text{ percent} = \frac{1}{4.3}$$

This reciprocal relationship does not hold exactly in practice because actual cash flows in the project's early years may not equal the average over its whole life; the cash outflows associated with the investment itself may be separated from the cash outflows resulting from its implementation; and different approaches may be used for calculating depreciation and incorporating it into the calculation.

5-3.4 Recompense—The Discounted Cash Flow Approach

The way to resolve these two criticisms, both in theory and, increasingly, in practice, is to take into account explicitly the "time value of money" for the firm considering the investment, that is, its preference for receiving a dollar in Year 1 rather than in Year 2, say. The value of such an acceleration in receipts depends primarily on what the firm can do with this extra dollar during that year.

If, for example, the firm is able to invest any spare funds in other investments that promise on average a 12 percent return on investment (with roughly the same degree of risk), then a dollar received now is equivalent to $1.12 received a year from now, $1.2544 = (1.12) × (1.12) received two years from now, and so on. Alternatively, $0.737 (1/1.2544) received now is equivalent to $1.00 received in two years. These equivalences assume that every unused dollar can be invested in these "other investments," and that no other factors would cause the company to prefer one year over another.

Following this approach one can discount the cash flows, whether positive or negative, that a proposed investment is expected to generate at any point in the future back to their "equivalent" present value. One then subtracts the value of the proposed investment (or its present value, if this investment takes place over several years) from the sum of these present values to obtain the *net present value* (NPV) of the investment. This measure becomes a means of comparing alternative investment proposals. Further details about this approach are provided in Appendix 5A.

Recompense—The Internal Rate of Return

Because the present value is measured in monetary units (for example, dollars), it does not provide a good measure of the *efficiency* of invested capital, that is, how "profitable" the investment is *per dollar invested.* Therefore, it is difficult to compare projects requiring different amounts of initial investment. One measure of efficiency that is sometimes used is the ratio (net present value)/(initial investment), which attempts to translate the NPV figure into a per-dollar basis. Some firms refer to this as a "profitability index."

Another common measure is the "internal rate of return" (sometimes called the "internal yield"), which is defined as the discount rate that causes the project's net present value to equal zero (see Appendix 5A). This rate is equivalent to the "yield to maturity" of a bond.

Although both net present value and internal rate of return allow one to take the time value of money into account when comparing different investments, neither provides a theoretically correct measure of the efficiency of the capital invested, and neither can be used reliably to indicate which subset from among a group of proposed projects will yield the highest total present value to the firm if there is a constraint on the investment funds available. Nor are the two measures internally consistent: it is entirely possible that one proposed investment has a *higher* present value (and a higher present value per dollar invested) than another, using a given opportunity rate, but has a *lower* internal rate of return.

Another problem that arises when trying to compare a series of investments is that the "book return on assets" described earlier, whether calculated using expression A or B, can be quite different from the internal rate of return. This disparity is distressing because the book ROI (analogous to a firm's average return on assets) usually is calculated periodically as part of its accounting/reporting and control process. Hence a project's observed ROA (or the ROA of a group of assets all of which were recommended on the basis of a net present value or an internal rate of return criterion) may bear little resemblance to the measures used when deciding to adopt that project. That is, the project's promised internal rate of return will be one number, but the return on assets used to measure its ongoing performance may be some very different number—even though all cash flows turned out to be exactly as predicted. We discuss this issue in greater detail in Appendix 5B.

Finally, a number of academics and business practitioners (among them Hayes and Garvin, 1982; Mechlin and Berg, 1980; Myers, 1983; Malpas, 1983) have expressed concern about the overreliance on any approach that is based on systematically discounting the future when choosing among alternative investments. The kinds of shortcoming they describe include:

1. Companies tend to pick hurdle/interest rates that are too high (and therefore overdiscount future cash flows), both in comparison with their historical returns on investment and with the actual rates of deterioration of their existing investment base.

2. In most cases the implicit assumption is made that investment decisions are reversible: if not pursued today an investment can always be pursued tomorrow (whereas delaying certain kinds of investments may lead a company into a position of strategic vulnerability from which it can be very difficult to extract itself).

3. Such approaches tend to understate the value of investments that have high "option content" (such as when the experience gained as a result of an investment may lead to opportunities, foreseen or unforeseen when the investment was made, to invest in more profitable activities in the future); investments in capital equipment embracing new technology, R&D, process improvement, and human skill development all fall into this category.

4. They also encourage the evaluation of investments on a project-by-project basis, rather than taking into account their interrelationships or the strategic competitive implications of making—or not making—certain investments.

5. The apparent objectivity and mathematical logic of such approaches can delude managers into thinking that they are being precise and objective when, in fact, the results obtained are based largely on a number of assumptions and estimates that were arrived at very subjectively.

5-3.5   Financial Measures of Predictability

The third dimension of concern with regard to a proposed investment is the predictability of its returns, which is an attempt to measure how sure the organization is about these anticipated returns. Thus, such uncertainties as the amount of investment required, the project's annual returns, the timing of certain major external events, and the project's useful life all fall into this category. While a variety of approaches are sometimes used to measure the predictability of a proposed investment, we examine only three. The first tries to evaluate directly the *knowable* uncertainty associated with the investment. The second alters the capital budgeting and financial review process itself in an attempt to reflect the firm's attitudes toward different kinds of risks. The third introduces inflation into the calculation and describes ways to evaluate its impact on the attractiveness of proposed investments.

Predictability—Explicit Measurement of Uncertainty

A number of approaches for identifying and measuring the uncertainty associated with a proposed capital investment have been advocated and tested. Most begin with the computation of one or more measures of security and recompense, as described earlier, based on the expected values of the different variables defining the project (investments, cash flows, rate of obsolescence, etc.). If those expected values lead to acceptable summary measures, then an attempt is made to assess the investment's overall predictability.

The simplest way to do this is to conduct a "sensitivity analysis" of each of the principal variables: each variable is changed by some amount (plus or minus 20 percent, say, or plus or minus the amount whose probability of being exceeded in each direction is 10 percent), and the impact of these changes on the project's payback, present value, and other measures is observed. For those factors identified as having the greatest impact, one can experiment with other variable values in an attempt to determine how big a change is required in order to cause the summary measures to take values outside an acceptable range.

A more formal way to measure the uncertainty/predictability of a proposed investment is to assess subjectively the probability distributions of all the key variables, and use these probability distributions to determine (usually through Monte Carlo Simulation) the resulting profitability distribution of the overall measure. This approach is commonly called "risk analysis" (see Hertz, 1964, 1968; Hayes, 1975). While much has been written about it, few companies today use it, largely because of the problems involved in assessing all the required probability distributions—particularly those describing the interaction of two or more variables. An increasing number of companies, however, have adopted an intermediate step in which three levels for each variable are

assessed ("optimistic," "most likely," and "pessimistic," say) and used to estimate the likely range of each summary measure.

Predictability—Adjusting the Financial Review Procedures

In the attempt to incorporate the impact of a project's uncertainty into their
evaluations, companies sometimes modify their capital budgeting and financial
review procedures in one of two ways. One is to require that different types of
projects meet different hurdle rates. Up until now we have assumed that all
projects must surpass a single hurdle rate—the same book return on investment
or internal rate of return, say. It can be argued, however, that different types of
investment projects have different levels of risk or importance to the firm, and
therefore the same benchmark rate of return should not be used for all of them.
The multiple hurdle rates used by one company are summarized in Table 5-8.

Using different hurdle rates for different types of investments has the effect of channeling an increased percentage of the firm's investable funds into
certain types of activities and away from others. Hence apparently innocuous
changes in hurdle rates can have important long-term effects on a firm's competitive position. There is increasing evidence, for example, that since the mid-
1960s U.S. firms have increased their hurdle rates for investments designed to
reduce manufacturing costs. If so, it provides another explanation for the decline in the rate of productivity growth in the United States during the 1970s.

The existence of multiple hurdle rates may also provide an explanation
for a common complaint of business managers: "Why is our return on assets
only 10 percent when all our new projects over the past several years have
promised at least a 20 percent return?" Other than the previously mentioned
disparity between the value of the internal yield that is projected for an investment and the ROA that is actually observed, it may reflect the fact that an increasing proportion of the firm's investment capital is being directed toward
preserving or replacing existing facilities—which in many companies need
show only a small return on investment—rather than into investments in new
products or processes that must surpass a higher rate of return.

Another modification that is often made in financial review procedures is
to require that higher levels of management be involved in the review process
as the amount of money at stake increases. In the case of very large investments, the board of directors usually is involved.

Predictability—The Impact of Inflation

These paragraphs differ from the preceding ones in that, instead of describing a
technique for incorporating the impact of uncertainty on a proposed project,
we deal here with one of the major sources of such uncertainty in the recent
past: inflation. The pervasive impact of inflation on all three of our measures—
security, recompense, and predictability—is such that we feel obligated to address it directly, if only briefly.

For the past two decades—when much of modern financial theory was
being developed and the most popular financial textbooks were being written—the financial evaluation procedures that most firms used either excluded

Table 5-8
Illustration of Multiple Hurdle Rates

| Purpose of Investment | Examples | Affected by Proposed Investment | | | | |
		Cost	Volume	Tech-nology	Business Risk	Hurdle Rate
Maintain existing business	Replace/re-build exist-ing facility	NC[a]	NC[a]	NC[a]	NC[a]	None
	Meet gov-ernment re-quirements for environ-ment, safety, health, and so on					
Reduce costs/im-prove pro-cess	Rationalize process	Decrease	NC[a]	Small change	Small increase	15 percent
	New equip-ment to re-place labor or improve quality of product					
Maintain process/in-crease vol-ume	Plant ex-pansion, equipment purchase, increase in-ventory	Decrease	Increase	NC[a]	Small increase	15 percent
New prod-uct or pro-cess		—	—	—	Increase	25 percent

[a] NC = No change.

completely the impact of inflation or afforded it minor importance. Both were reasonable approaches in the United States and other developed countries until the early 1970s. Since that time, however, inflation rates of 5 to 15 percent have become commonplace in the United States, Western Europe, and the Far East. Many economists believe that such rates will continue into the foreseeable future. Business executives have found themselves under increasing pressure (with little prior preparation) to understand and deal with a phenomenon whose influence is pervasive and pernicious.

Initial attempts to incorporate inflation's impact were naively simplistic, usually proposing only that the costs and revenues associated with an investment be "adjusted for inflation" (by multiplying them by an estimated rate of inflation) before calculating their discounted present value or internal rate of return. Scaling up both costs and revenues by the same ratio to reflect inflation usually makes proposed investments appear more attractive, since this causes their profit margins to be scaled up as well. The truth is much more complex. Inflation causes a variety of changes in the values of different variables associated with an investment project. These changes take place over different periods of time and are affected by the nature of the investment project.

First, costs tend to increase. This, after all, is the operative definition of inflation. Usually material costs increase first and then, after some lag, labor and overhead costs increase.

Second, over a period of time the company raises the prices of its products. The time it takes to restore its previous profit margin depends on how fast the impact of rising costs gets translated into profit declines, the competitive situation, and the extent to which the government seeks to control prices.

Third, as the company's sales grow (in monetary value, not in unit volume), its working capital requirements increase. Accounts receivable tend to increase with sales revenue, while accounts payable increase with material costs, cash balances increase with labor rates and accounts payable, and inventories increase with the cost of goods sold—a combination of both material costs and labor costs. Therefore, even though the company's investment in fixed assets is unaffected until they are replaced with new assets, its total assets must increase.

Fourth, again over time, the cost of capital rises. Potential purchasers of both debt and equity demand higher rates of return to compensate for the loss of their money's purchasing power.

Fifth, after a period of time the company will either expand production capacity or replace old equipment. At this point, it is affected by the inflation rate prevailing in the capital equipment industry.

Sixth, under the impact of higher interest rates (and associated pressures for higher dividend payments) and the need for new higher-priced equipment, firms begin increasing the percentage of debt in their capital structure.

In short, inflation has a number of complex, interacting, and partially compensating effects that are difficult to capture realistically within most companies' procedures for evaluating proposed manufacturing investment. In many cases it is possible to model these effects, and test their impact on a proposed investment, through the use of a computer simulation. Our intent here, however, is simply to warn against the kind of simplistic assumptions and approaches that many firms follow.

5-4   INTEGRATING FACILITIES PLANS WITH LONG-TERM STRATEGIES

The preceding sections of this chapter deal with a number of the specific tasks that should be addressed in the course of an effective facilities planning process. These range from organizing the project team to selecting specific techniques for evaluating the financial impact of various proposals. While each of these tasks is important, it is even more critical that the process as a whole be managed so as to achieve the desired end. We conclude this chapter with a broad, evolutionary perspective on the role of facilities planning in a company and some examples of firms that have been able to make substantial improvements in their facilities planning processes.

5-4.1   Selecting the Facilities Planning Process to Aim For

At the outset of this chapter, Table 5-1 summarized the typical scenario that companies follow when faced with a major capacity/facilities investment project, and we commented on some of its weaknesses. We contrast that now with the scenario we have seen in a handful of firms who have adopted a more effective facilities planning process—one that led to the formulation, acceptance, and execution of decisions that reinforced their capacity/facilities strategies. This scenario, summarized in Table 5-9, differs in three significant respects from the traditional scenario of Table 5-1:

Table 5-9
Strategy-Driven Capacity/Facilities Decision Processes

1. Individual projects are related directly to the major elements of the firm's competitive environment.
2. Alternatives are defined creatively, and represent a broad variety of options compared with past practice, both that of the firm and that of the industry.
3. Individual projects explicitly address issues of size, location, and the specialization of individual facilities, as well as the timing and amount of capacity to be added.
4. A facility investment is evaluated in terms of its impact not only on the performance of any new or modified facility, but also on the overall performance of the firm's other facilities.
5. Specific recommendations fit into the context of an overall pattern of decisions, although they may also reflect directional changes that are supportive of the business's long-term competitive strategy.
6. Projects arise not just in response to immediate growth needs or poor performance in specific facilities, but are proactive and opportunity-oriented, addressing the full set of manufacturing capabilities needed to support the desired competitive advantage.
7. Recognizing that facilities last over several product/market generations, decision-making procedures are used that take into account the future transitions and roles likely to be required of specific facilities.

1. The most important distinction is in philosophy and task definition. Facilities are viewed as providing certain specific long-term capabilities that are desired by the firm, rather than simply production capacity for existing products in existing markets.
2. The breadth of issues addressed when making individual decisions is much

more comprehensive, and these decisions are integrated through a guiding strategy.

3. The decision-making procedures used place relatively less emphasis on financial analyses and more on qualitative factors, long-term effects, and the overall health of individual and combined facilities.

As an illustration of how such an overall process might look in practice, consider the approach followed by an agricultural equipment manufacturer whose annual sales were approximately $75 million. The administrative procedure this firm used for capacity/facilities planning projects is loosely structured and easily adapted to individual situations. Table 5-10 outlines the major steps in its approval process. A similar list would be developed for every project. In this company the manufacturing function is assigned responsibility for identifying the need for such a project, both because the company is organized functionally and because it is believed that the biggest impact of such projects would be on manufacturing.

In one case this firm recognized that an expansion of its production ca-

Table 5-10

Capacity Planning Approval Procedure—Agricultural Equipment Manufacturer

Manufacturing Identifies Opportunity
1. Vertical integration
2. Solve major supplier problem
3. Add needed physical space
4. Good financial return

Manufacturing and Marketing Prepare Project Proposal
1. Follow 8-step sequence
2. Emphasis on validating critical assumptions
    Suppliers' ability to react
    Forecast of volume requirements
    Labor and equipment requirements
    Resulting cost structure
3. Sensitivity analysis
4. Conclusions and recommendations

Audit and Validation by Finance
1. Project review and numerical evaluation
2. Comparison to alternative investment opportunities
3. Recommendations

Board Approval

Implementation
1. Project management
2. Audit of results by finance
3. Establishment of plant performance evaluation criteria

pacity was necessary to meet an expected increase in demand. Once this was recognized, manufacturing worked closely with marketing to prepare the project proposal. A project team consisting of the marketing vice president, the manufacturing vice president, the product manager responsible for the products in question, and an outside consultant was formed. (The consultant's role was to improve the procedures and frameworks used in evaluating alternative proposals and to develop an implementation plan.)

The proposal that was recommended eventually consisted of building a new facility, making parts in-house that had formerly been purchased, and moving some existing operations to more appropriate facilities. Thus this project became an opportunity to review and rationalize the company's three existing plants while adding a fourth.

In pursuing the sequence of activities outlined in Table 5-10, major emphasis was placed on validating critical assumptions. Given the infrequency of major capacity expansions at this firm, the project team concluded that it was important to double-check all information and analyses. Every attempt was made to insure that both top management and the Board would be receiving an option whose merits were based on data that were as accurate as possible.

In a further attempt to validate the project team's recommendations, top management had them reviewed by the finance staff. Anticipating this, as part of its approach the project team had developed a computer model that could evaluate a range of options and conduct a sensitivity analysis. While this detailed financial review took additional time—and caused some uneasiness among project team members—it also led to a broader base of support for the project during its implementation. Once the financial review was completed, a final package was put together for Board approval. Table 5-11 is the table of contents for that package.

Given the homework that had been done in advance, Board approval was fairly rapid and implementation was turned over to the vice president of manufacturing, who had played a central role throughout the project. Since the finance staff had carefully evaluated the project proposal, it was natural for top management to assign it responsibility for auditing the project's implementation in accordance with the detailed implementation plan included in the project proposal.

To facilitate this financial audit, criteria were specified for evaluating each plant's performance. These criteria were also used in establishing a charter for the new facility that would distinguish it from existing facilities in terms of its capabilities and performance expectations. This helped focus each facility's attention on specific activities that were critical to both its success and that of the entire plant network.

5-4.2 The Evolution of Facilities Planning Processes

Most firms do not reach the point of having an effective facilities planning process in one step. Each organization must develop an approach that encourages its managers to address major issues systematically, but without unnecessary

Table 5-11

**Table of Contents for Proposal Submitted for Board Approval
in an Agricultural Equipment Manufacturer**

    I. General Comments
   II. Present Situation
         Existing plant and warehouse capacity and facilities evaluation
         Evaluation of future requirements
  III. What We Are Proposing
         Products
         Location
         Physical facilities
         Advantages
         Risks
         Costs
   IV. Financial Analysis of the Proposal
    V. Sensitivity Analysis
   VI. Recommendations
  VII. Time Table and Implementation Plan
 VIII. Appendix
        1. Sales forecast
           a. Ten-year sales projections for major product lines
           b. Reconfirmation of the market structure
        2. Detailed cost studies by product
        3. Details of the sensitivity analysis
        4. Site information
        5. Labor requirements
           a. Direct and indirect labor calculations
           b. Wage survey
         6. Estimated machinery list
        7. Construction cost estimates
        8. Information about competitors
        9. Resources needed to support our strategies
      10. Financial measures
           Cash flow, payback, return on book value, net present value, internal
           rate of return
      11. Miscellaneous information
           Breakdown of start-up expenses
           Computer program for analysis and evaluation

---

self-imposed constraints, and that continually seeks improvement in the planning process. In guiding such an evolution, it is often helpful to recognize that companies frequently pass through predictable stages.

In the initial stage, facilities investment proposals are generated in response to specific ad hoc needs, such as changes in demand, competitive pressures, or government regulations.

Recognizing the shortcomings of this approach, some firms move to a second phase where capacity/facilities projects are placed under the jurisdiction of the firm's financial planning process. Since such projects almost always involve capital spending, the firm begins to use its well-established capital budgeting procedures to screen them. Control over the implementation of approved projects is then exercised through each division's annual budget. In this second phase, therefore, the facilities planning process is financially oriented and directed toward meeting the criteria the firm has established for allocating financial resources.

In the third phase, firms move beyond a strictly financial perspective. Facilities proposals are considered to be an integral part of the firm's annual long-range planning process because it is recognized that, in addition to requiring capital, they provide opportunities for reviewing the status of existing manufacturing capabilities, reassessing the trends in those capabilities, and identifying the product/market forces that are likely to exert pressure on manufacturing in the future. The firm's long-range plan now includes major sections dealing with such issues as the capacity and quality of manufacturing facilities, human resources (particularly specialized technical skills), the anticipated changes in processing technology, and the manufacturing strategies that major competitors are likely to adopt—as well as the capital investment required.

The fourth phase is that advocated in Table 5-9: the development of a capacity/facilities strategy that is an integral part of the firm's manufacturing strategy. The intent is to evaluate each facilities proposal in the context of the firm's overall competitive strategy. Thus, while the first phase concentrates on event-triggered projects, this fourth phase views capacity and facilities as proactive tools for achieving long-term goals. This, in turn, gives manufacturing management the opportunity to exercise a true leadership role in the company.

5-4.3   Integrating Facilities Decisions, Plans, and Strategies

Talking about good administrative practices and the characteristics desired of a planning process is one thing; identifying what should be done to get an organization moving in the right direction is often quite another. Three approaches that were successful in actual firms are described next.

The first illustration comes from an oilfield equipment manufacturer that, three years after building a new facility, had not yet achieved the performance goals upon which the approval of that proposal had been based. Owing in part to this failure, a division in this firm found itself in need of additional capacity in 1981. Having waited too long to develop a comprehensive plan, the division faced a situation that was almost identical to the one it faced three years earlier. Still in phase 1 (characterized by reactive, ad hoc capacity/facilities projects), this division's first reaction was to follow the same procedure it had used previously. However, the division president and manufacturing vice president together became convinced that a repetition of the previous outcome would be disastrous.

The resolve of these two key executives led to a dramatic move, initially to a phase 2 and then, by the time the project was completed, to a phase 3 approach. The need for such a shift clearly existed; it quickly became apparent, however, that the required organizational skills and procedures did not. Two types of consultants were hired to complement and educate the division's project team. One, a team from a large consulting firm that had extensive experience in helping firms develop manufacturing strategies, worked with the project team in outlining major project steps, developing analyses, and guiding implementation. These consultants contributed specific skills to carrying out the individual steps that the project team undertook. They also brought a broader, more comprehensive perspective to bear on the task of capacity/facilities planning.

The second consultant played much more of a management development and advisory role. He was hired by the two key executives to monitor the task force's progress, to help educate its members in the new skills required and the tasks to be performed, and to sit in on the consulting team's periodic progress reports so as to contribute another point of view on what had been accomplished and what was still to be done.

The result: What started out as the construction of another large facility—and a repetition of the mistakes of the previous facility decision—ended up as a comprehensive review of the division's manufacturing needs. The group's final report recommended a specific long-term capacity/facilities strategy which would lead eventually to six facilities (three existing and three new). It also proposed major modifications in the production technologies employed in each facility, as well as a major refocusing of the products and markets served by each. This set of recommendations covered a ten-year time horizon and contained a plan for correcting the problems in the existing facilities, including the one built three years earlier. While the entire project ended up taking nine months, rather than the three initially anticipated, the division's managers concluded that the resulting proposal was what was needed to move them significantly closer to their strategic objectives.

A second illustration comes from a major consumer products company that chose to take a very different approach. This firm's manufacturing vice president had concluded that, while it had been following a very consistent pattern of capacity/facilities decisions in the past, this same pattern would not be appropriate for the future. The historic pattern had been to expand the company's sole domestic facility whenever additional capacity was needed, because this was always easier, cheaper, and faster; moreover, it promised better financial results than building a new facility. The manufacturing vice president was not alone in feeling that the existing facility had probably reached its maximum viable size, and thus a change was needed.

He used two levers to initiate a change in the firm's previous pattern of decisions. One was simply to take advantage of an existing internal situation. Two years earlier the firm had experienced a major increase in its inventories, yet its delivery times were lengthening despite an increasingly delivery-sensitive market. In responding to that problem, the manufacturing vice president chose to make it visible throughout the organization. In addition, he emphasized the link between the inventory/delivery problem and the size of the existing facility. In fact, the period of time during which manufacturing resources and attention were brought to bear to solve this problem successfully became known as the "year of the whale." Everybody in the organization was familiar with that phrase and knew that it was related to the company's historical pattern of expanding in place.

The other lever used by the manufacturing vice president to focus attention on the problems arising out of the size of the existing facility derived from a recent management action. An apparently modest organizational change had been made which split the responsibility for manufacturing one of the firm's products from the responsibility for other products. This split in manufacturing responsibilities kept the product in the same plant, but it was intended to be a first step to what he hoped would be a complete locational split. The new organizational unit quickly developed a new approach for producing that product, and put together data showing that a new facility not only was desirable eventually but could perform effectively even at existing volumes.

The manufacturing vice president then went to work to condition his organization to propose and support additional changes. In an attempt to raise its awareness of the need for new approaches within the organization, he hired an outside consulting firm to do a facilities study. While the consulting firm probably viewed its assignment as the development of a long-term manufacturing strategy involving multiple facilities, the vice president of manufacturing saw its role primarily as one of making his organization aware that such alternatives did exist, that techniques and tools were available to define and evaluate them, that at least one viable facilities strategy could be developed by an outsider, and, therefore, that his own people should be able to do even better!

The third illustration is provided by the Motor Division at Reliance Electric, described in Chapter 4. The division's general manager, who had responsibility for all aspects of the division's business except sales (which were handled as a group-level activity), had made substantial improvements in the division's performance over the previous five years. That progress, however, had been based mainly on trimming product lines, introducing new products, and using existing assets more effectively. No attempt had been made to get corporate approval for major new investments in facilities, nor had any systematic effort been made to improve markedly the performance of individual facilities.

This division general manager decided that if continued improvements in this division's overall performance were to be achieved, they were likely to be linked directly to coordinated improvements in the performance of his manufacturing organization as a whole. His belief in this idea was supported by the fact that a recently constructed plant in the division was performing significantly better than the three older plants. Simple arithmetic suggested that if the division's average plant performed as well as the new plant, its overall performance would be improved significantly.

When the division found itself out of capacity for one of its key product lines, the general manager used that as the impetus for developing a comprehensive long-term capacity/facilities plan for raising average plant profitability. This was a move from phase 2 (the phase where most divisions in the corporation found themselves) to phase 4, and led to the development of an overall manufacturing strategy which served as a blueprint for a number of other decisions as well.

As with the two preceding examples, a single individual—in this case the division general manager—served as the agent of change. He developed a vision of what he thought the manufacturing strategy and its supporting capacity and facilities strategies should look like. He then put together a project team that could fill in the details of this vision and, in the process, develop its own strategic capabilities. He also served in an advisory role to keep the project team moving in the desired direction. By the time the team had completed its assignment, it had developed a recommendation for a specific series of capacity and facilities decisions, and a long-range plan for improving manufacturing's support of the division's overall strategy. This included new plant charters for each of the existing facilities.

Although the illustrations above are very different, they include some common elements. One, and probably most important, is the leadership role taken by one or more key managers. Perhaps equally important is that in each case the firm's project team was provided with the skills and capabilities required if significant improvements were to be made in the capacity/facilities planning process. Third, in each of these situations management recognized that its objective was not just to extrapolate from the past but to use a current project or decision as the first step toward a desired future. Fourth, these managers all involved the rest of their organizations in upgrading their capacity and facilities plans, which helped insure effective implementation once approved.

SELECTED REFERENCES

Bierman, Harold, Charles Bonini, and Warren Hausman. *Quantitative Analysis for Business Decisions,* 6th ed. Homewood, IL: Richard D. Irwin, 1980.

Brigham, Eugene F. "Hurdle Rates for Screening Capital Expenditure Proposals." *Financial Management,* Autumn 1975, pp. 18–26.

Ehrbar, A. F. "Unraveling the Mysteries of Corporate Profits." *Fortune,* August 27, 1979, pp. 90–96.

Francis, Richard L., and John A. White. *Facility Layout and Location: An Analytical Approach.* Englewood Cliffs, NJ: Prentice-Hall, 1974.

Hayes, Robert H. "Incorporating Risk Aversion into Risk Analysis." *Engineering Economist,* Vol. 20, No. 2, Winter 1975, pp. 99–122.

Hayes, Robert H., and William J. Abernathy. "Managing Our Way to Economic Decline." *Harvard Business Review,* July–August 1980, pp. 67–77.

Hayes, Robert H., and David Garvin. "The Discounting Concept and Industrial Disinvestment." Harvard Business School Case Services, 9-682-077, 1982.

Hayes, Robert H., and David Garvin. "Managing as if Tomorrow Mattered." *Harvard Business Review,* May–June 1982, pp. 70–79.

Hayes, Robert H., and Roger W. Schmenner. "How Should You Organize Manufacturing?" *Harvard Business Review,* January–February 1978, pp. 105–118.

Hertz, David B. "Investment Policies That Pay Off." *Harvard Business Review,* January–February 1968, 96–108.

Hertz, David B. "Risk Analysis in Capital Investment." *Harvard Business Review,* January–February 1964, pp. 95–106.

Hillier, Frederick S., and Gerald J. Lieberman. *Operations Research,* 3rd ed. Oakland, CA: Holden-Day, 1980.

Holloway, Charles. *Decision Making under Uncertainty.* Englewood Cliffs, NJ: Prentice-Hall, 1979.

Klammer, Thomas P. "Empirical Evidence on the Adoption of Sophisticated Capital Budgeting Techniques." *Journal of Business,* July 1972, pp. 387–397.

Makridakis, Spyros, Steven C. Wheelwright, and Victor E. McGee. *Forecasting: Methods and Applications,* 2nd ed. New York: John Wiley & Sons, 1983.

Malkiel, Burton G. "Productivity: The Problem Behind the Headlines." *Harvard Business Review,* May–June 1979, pp. 81–89.

Malpas, Robert. "The Plant After Next." *Harvard Business Review,* July–August 1983, pp. 122–130.

Maynard, H. B. *Handbook of Modern Manufacturing Management.* New York: McGraw-Hill, 1970.

Mechlin, George, and Daniel Berg. "Evaluating Research: ROI Is Not Enough." *Harvard Business Review,* September–October 1980, pp. 93–99.

Middleton, C. J. "How to Set Up a Project Organization." *Harvard Business Review,* March–April 1967, pp. 73–82.

Modigliani, Franco, and Richard A. Cohen. "Inflation, Rational Valuation, and the Market." *Financial Analysts Journal,* March–April 1979, pp. 24–44.

Myers, Stewart. "Finance Theory and Financial Strategy." *Interfaces,* Winter 1983.

Sasser, W. Earl. "Match Supply and Demand in Service Industries." *Harvard Business Review,* November–December 1976, pp. 133–140.

Schmenner, Roger W. *Making Business Location Decisions.* Englewood Cliffs, NJ: Prentice-Hall, 1982.

Skinner, Wickham. "Manufacturing—Missing Link in Corporate Strategy." *Harvard Business Review,* May–June 1969, pp. 136–145.

Stallworthy, E. A. *The Control of Investment in New Manufacturing Facilities.* Essex, England: Gower Press, 1973.

Wheelwright, Steven C. "Capacity Planning Forecasting Requirements," in *Handbook of Forecasting,* Spyros Makridakis and Steven C. Wheelwright, eds. New York: John Wiley & Sons, 1982, pp. 37–52.

Wheelwright, Steven C. *Capacity Planning and Facilities Choice.* Boston: Division of Research, Harvard Business School, 1979.

Wheelwright, Steven C., and Spyros Makridakis. *Forecasting Methods for Management.* 3rd ed. New York: John Wiley & Sons, 1980.

Wilkes, F. W. *Capital Budgeting Techniques.* New York: John Wiley & Sons, 1977.

Appendix 5A.   Techniques for the Financial Evaluation of Proposed Manufacturing Investments

Given the importance most firms place on the financial evaluation of proposed investments, it is essential that manufacturing managers seeking corporate approval of decisions they feel necessary know how to use the available techniques correctly and effectively. Using the framework of Section 5-2.3—Security, Recompense and Predictability—this appendix illustrates the mechanics of several of the most commonly used measures. Appendix B explains why individual measures may give conflicting (or not directly comparable) results.

To facilitate our exposition, we will work with a specific numerical example: a hypothetical proposal to automate partially a company's material

Table 5-12

Proposal to Automate Partially the Materials Transport System ($ in thousands)

End of Year	Equipment-Related Costs[a]	Depreciation[b]	Labor Savings[c]	Income Taxes on Savings[d]	Profit	After-Tax Cash Flow[e]
0	$ 800					
1	200	$ 100	$ 250	$ (26)	$ (24)	$ 76
2	—	100	300	104	96	196
3	—	100	325	117	108	208
4	—	100	350	130	120	220
5	—	100	350	130	120	220
6	50	100	350	104	96	196
7	50	100	350	104	96	196
8[f]	100	100	350	78	72	172
Totals	1,200	800	2625	741	684	1484
Averages		100	328.1	92.6	85.5	185.5

[a] Equipment cost consists of $800,000 in depreciable purchased equipment, plus $200,000 in installation and start-up costs which are expensed as incurred. After Year 5, increasing amounts will have to be spent in maintaining, refurbishing, and updating this equipment.
[b] Depreciation is calculated on a straight-line basis over an eight-year lifetime.
[c] Labor savings are reduced in the first year because of start-up and training problems. Thereafter they increase as projected production levels rise to the capacity limit in Year 4.
[d] Income taxes are calculated assuming a combination (federal plus state) income tax rate of 52%.
[e] Cash flow is equal to the actual cash transactions during the year: labor savings less equipment-related costs less income taxes. Therefore, in Year 1, the loss before tax is equal to labor savings less equipment installation costs less depreciation, or $50. This will reduce the taxes paid by the corporation by $26. Therefore the net cash flow after tax is $250 − 200 + 26 = $76.
[f] End of useful life occurs at the end of eight years; no salvage value or removal costs are assumed.

transport system. As outlined in Table 5-12, the costs and returns of this project can be summarized as follows:

1. An initial investment of $800,000 is required at the beginning of Year 1.
2. Labor savings (as outlined) will increase as the production volume increases during the first four years.
3. Labor savings are based on the assumption that the hourly labor rate will not change over the lifetime of the project.
4. The construction of a new plant in Year 5 will be necessary to handle further volume increases, but its costs and benefits are not part of this proposal.
5. The equipment will be scrapped and replaced with more modern equipment at the end of eight years. This follow-on project, however, is not considered part of this proposal.

This kind of proposal is one of the simplest that manufacturing firms must deal with because neither product characteristics, nor sales, nor costs in other departments (such as inventory or overhead costs) are expected to be affected.

Measures of Security

In its simplest form, the payback of this proposal is the initial investment divided by its average annual cash flow, or

$$\text{payback} = \frac{\$800,000}{\$185,500} = 4.3 \text{ years}$$

A more precise way to estimate the payback is to calculate the cumulative net cash flow of the project in each year of its life. As shown in Table 5-13, this cash position becomes positive in the fifth year.

Table 5-13
Net Cash Position Calculations for Material Transport
Automation Project (Table 5-12)

End of Year	Net Book Value Beginning of Year	After-Tax Cash Flow	Net (Cumulative) Cash Position— End of Year
0	—	—	(800)
1	800	76	(724)
2	700	196	(528)
3	600	208	(320)
4	500	220	(100)
5	400	220	120
6	300	196	316
7	200	196	512
8	100	172	684
Average	450	185.5	

Recompense—The Accounting Rate of Return

This measure can be calculated in a variety of ways. For example:

$$\frac{\text{average annual profit after tax}}{\begin{array}{c}\text{average beginning-of-year book}\\ \text{value of investment}\end{array}} = \frac{85.5}{450} = 19 \text{ percent} \tag{5A-1}$$

$$\frac{\text{average annual net cash flow}}{\text{initial total investment}} = \frac{(85.5 + 100 = 185.5)}{800} = 23.2 \text{ percent} \tag{5A-2}$$

$$\frac{\text{total cash inflow over life of project}}{\text{initial investment} \times \text{life of project}} = \frac{1484}{800 \times 8} \tag{5A-3}$$

$$= \frac{1.855}{8} = 23.2 \text{ percent}$$

None of these three approaches takes into account the timing of these projected cash flows. To see why this might be important, consider another proposed investment that requires the same initial outlay (investment) and generates the same annual after-tax cash flows, except that the cash flows for Years 1 and 8 are reversed: 172 in Year 1 and 76 in Year 8. The total cash flow would be the same for both investments, and therefore these three measures would all indicate that the alternative investment would be just as attractive as the initial one.

Most people, however, given the choice, would prefer the cash flow of 172 sooner (in Year 1) rather than later (in Year 8). One might argue that such a comparison could quickly be resolved by a common-sense inspection of the two proposals. But it is easy to generate other proposals whose superiority (or inferiority) to our example proposal is not easily resolved through the use of common sense. (Common sense is, after all, a somewhat slippery concept in that most people think they have it, but also believe that they are rather unique in this regard!)

Recompense—The Discounted Cash Flow Approach

Table 5-14 contains a discounted cash flow analysis of the automation proposal (Table 5-12) analyzed above. To simplify the calculations, we assume that the cash flows (savings) resulting from this project are received in a *lump sum at the end* of every year. If we needed to be more precise, we could make the assumption that all cash flows arrive halfway through the year, or even that they are spread uniformly throughout the year. Both of these approaches would necessitate the recalculation of the present-value factors used to discount these cash flows. Neither will be followed here, where our intent is simply to illustrate the technique. In fact, seldom will the selection of one of these "more realistic" assumptions have much impact on a decision of real strategic importance to a company—nor should it.

Table 5-14

Present-Value Calculations for Materials Transport Automation Project (Table 5-12)

End of Year	After-Tax Cash Flow	Present-Value Factor at 12 Percent	Present Value of Cash Flow	Cumulative Present Value
0	(800)	1.000	(800.0)	(800.0)
1	76	0.893	67.9	(732.1)
2	196	0.797	156.2	(575.9)
3	208	0.712	148.1	(427.8)
4	220	0.636	139.9	(287.9)
5	220	0.567	124.7	(163.2)
6	196	0.507	99.4	(63.8)
7	196	0.452	88.6	24.8
8	172	0.404	69.5	94.2

On the basis of the calculations in Table 5-14, our proposed investment shows a present value of $94.2 when the opportunity rate is 12 percent. It also shows a "discounted payback" (not against the original investment of $800, but against the value that this investment would grow to if invested at a 12 percent interest rate) in Year 7, rather than in Year 5 as before.

It is important to note that a present value that is negative does not imply that one has lost money by investing in the project; it may have a positive book return on investment. A negative present value merely indicates that it will not earn as much as would the same amount of money invested at the opportunity rate (12 percent in our example).

Table 5-15

Internal Yield of Materials Transport Automation Project (Table 5-12)

End of Year	After-Tax Cash Flow	Present-Value Factor at 15 Percent	Present Value of Cash Flow	Cumulative Present Value[a]
0	(800)	1.0000	(800.0)	(800.0)
1	76	0.8696	66.0	(734.0)
2	196	0.7561	148.1	(585.9)
3	208	0.6575	136.7	(449.2)
4	220	0.5718	125.7	(323.5)
5	220	0.4972	109.3	(214.2)
6	196	0.4323	84.6	(129.6)
7	196	0.3759	73.6	(56.0)
8	172	0.3269	56.2	(0.2) ≈ 0[b]

[a] Uses present-value factors accurate to seven digits, so may not give same product as (cash flow) × (four-digit present value factor).
[b] Approximately equal to zero.

Table 5-16
Internal Yield Calculations Based on Interest/Opportunity Loss

Year	Cash Balance Beginning of Year	Interest/Opportunity Loss on Cash Balance at 15 Percent	Cash Flow End of Year	Cost Balance End of Year
1	(800.0)	(120.0)	76	(844.0)
2	(844.0)	(126.6)	196	(774.6)
3	(774.6)	(116.2)	208	(682.8)
4	(682.8)	(102.5)	220	(565.3)
5	(565.3)	(84.8)	220	(430.1)
6	(430.1)	(64.6)	196	(298.7)
7	(298.7)	(44.9)	196	(147.6)
8	(147.6)	(22.2)	172	2.2 ~0

Recompense—The Internal Rate of Return

For our proposed partial automation project, the internal rate of return can be calculated as shown in Table 5-15, and is approximately 15 percent. The same fact is demonstrated in Table 5-16 in a slightly different way, to illustrate the implicit assumption contained in present-value calculations when the net cash balance in any period is negative. In effect, it is assumed that one "borrows" this amount from a lender who charges an interest rate equal to the opportunity rate.

Appendix 5B.   The Relationship Between the Accounting Rate of Return and the Internal Rate of Return

This appendix addresses a question of major concern when, as is often the case, a firm employs multiple financial measures. Why is book return on investment, as it is usually calculated for accounting purposes, often so different from internal rate of return (or internal yield), whose calculation is based on the time value of money to the firm? In answering this question, let us first determine under what circumstances the two procedures will lead to the same value.

Consider an investment of $1,000 that returns a gross profit before tax of $200 per year for 100 years before it is abandoned with no salvage value. Assuming that its annual depreciation is calculated on a straight-line basis over the 100-year period, the income tax paid each year will be (at a tax rate of 50 percent):

$$\text{TAX} = (\text{PBT} - \text{depreciation}) (50 \text{ percent})$$
$$= (200 - 10) (0.50) = 95$$

The project's profit after tax will therefore be $200 - 10 - 95 = 95$, and the project's cash flow will be:

$$\text{PBT} - \text{tax paid} = \text{PAT} + \text{depreciation}$$
$$= 200 - 95 = 95 + 10 = 105$$

The book ROA, following the approach of expression A (Section 5-3), therefore is

$$\frac{95}{(1/2)\,(1,000)} = 19 \text{ percent} = r_A$$

or, following expression B,

$$\frac{105}{1,000} = 10.5 \text{ percent} = r_B$$

The internal rate of return is the value of r (call it r^*) that causes the project's present value to equal 0:

$$\text{NPV} = -1000 + [\frac{105}{(1 + r^*)} + \frac{105}{(1 + r^*)^2} + \cdots \frac{105}{(1 + r^*)^{100}}] = 0$$

Since the term in brackets is equal to

$$\frac{105}{(1 + r^*)} [\frac{1 - 1/(1 + r^*)^{100}}{1 - 1/(1 + r^*)}] = \frac{105}{r^*} [1 - \frac{1}{(1 + r^*)^{100}}]$$

and $1/(1 + r^*)^{100}$ is essentially equal to zero for $r > 0.05$, then the internal yield satisfies

$$-1000 + \frac{105}{r^*} = 0$$

or $r^* = 105/1000 = 10.5$ percent. Therefore it is identical to r_B, the book ROI calculated using Expression B (Section 5-3).

The shorter the project's expected lifetime, the larger the depreciation and the smaller the profit after tax, so that when $n = 15$ years, both ways of calculating the book ROA yield the same value:

$$r_A = \frac{(200 - 1{,}000/15)(50 \text{ percent})}{1{,}000/2} = r_B \frac{200 - (200 - 1{,}000/15)(0.50)}{1{,}000}$$

$$= \frac{66.5}{500} \qquad\qquad = \frac{133}{1000} \qquad = 13.3 \text{ percent}$$

The internal rate of return, however, satisfies the relationship

$$-1000 + \frac{133}{r^*}[1 - \frac{1}{(1 + r^*)^{15}}] = 0,$$

which varies according to the value $[1/(1 + r)]^{15}$. For r^* in the vicinity of 10 percent $[1/(1 + r)]^{15}$ is approximately 24 percent, so the internal rate of return is about $(133)(1 - 0.24)/1{,}000 = 10.1$ percent.

Hence we can easily find values of n for which any two of the three measures are equal, but it is difficult to find situations in which they are all equal.

We can express the relationship between the three approaches somewhat more elegantly if we define the terms as follows:

$I =$ initial investment
$S =$ recoverable salvage value of I at the end of its useful life
$t =$ income tax rate
$PBT =$ annual (constant) profit before tax

The internal rate of return r^* can then be shown to satisfy the relationship

$$r^* = \frac{C(n)}{I} - (1 - \frac{S}{I})f(n,r^*) = r_B - (1 - \frac{S}{I})f(n,r^*)$$

where $C(n) = (1 - t) PBT + t(I/n)$, represents the investment's annual after-tax cash flow, and

$$f(n,r^*) = [r^*/(1 + r^*)^n - 1].$$

In words, the internal rate of return r^* is equal to the ratio of the annual cash flow to the initial investment (r_B, the accounting ROA calculated using expression B), less an amount determined by the percentage loss in value of the investment over its lifetime and the factor $f(n,r^*)$.

The interesting aspect of this calculation is that the function $f(n,r^*)$ is roughly proportional to $1/n$ [in that when n is fixed, $f(n,r^*)$ varies quite slowly with r^*, and it approaches 0 monotonically as n increases]. Therefore, r^* turns out to be equal to r_B less an amount that is roughly proportional to the investment's annual depreciation in percentage terms. For example, for $n = 15$, $f(n,r^*)$ is approximately equal to 0.033 for r^* in the vicinity of 0.10, so using our earlier example:

$$r^* = \frac{C(n)}{I} - (1.0)\, f(n,r^*) \sim \frac{133}{1000} - 0.033 \sim 10 \text{ percent}$$

which is approximately the same value we calculated above.

Not only does this approach show us roughly how far apart the internal rate of return r^* and r_B (the book ROI using expression B) will be, but since

$$r_B = \frac{C(n)}{I} = \frac{(\text{PAT} + I/n)}{I} = \frac{1}{2}\left[\frac{\text{PAT}}{1/2I}\right] + \frac{1}{n} = \frac{1}{2}r_A + \frac{1}{n}$$

we are also able to calculate easily the difference between r_A and r_B. Pulling these two relationships together:

$$r_A = 2(r_B - \frac{1}{n}) = 2[r^* + (1 - \frac{S}{I})\, f(n,r^*) - \frac{1}{n}].$$

Therefore, for n large and S small,

$$r_A \sim 2\, r_B \sim 2r^*.$$

Notice that if corporations did not have to pay taxes on income, so that the tax shield on depreciation did not affect the cash flow from the investment, then the internal rate of return would be equal to the book ROI (r_B, using expression B) less the value of $f(n,r^*)$. In this sense, $f(n,r^*)$ represents the *effective* amount of depreciation, in percentage terms, that should be deducted each year from the investment's apparent profit in order to match its book ROI with its actual internal rate of return.

Unfortunately, governments are unlikely to eliminate corporate income taxes or allow corporations to choose their own depreciation schedules. Therefore, companies are going to have to continue to be puzzled by the difference between the apparent performance (measured in terms of book return on assets) and the predicted return (measured by the internal rate of return) of the assets under their control.

The Technology
of Manufacturing
Processes

6-1   INTRODUCTION AND OVERVIEW

The word "technology" is probably as widely used as any in business today. However, its meanings vary tremendously in their scope, depth, and usefulness to managers. A review of some of the more common definitions, and the perceptions that the term brings to mind for various audiences, is a useful starting point for our discussion of manufacturing technology.

6-1.1   Three Perspectives on Manufacturing Technology

The analysts and statisticians who work in the financial community and for government organizations tend to adopt a macroeconomic perspective. They categorize technologies either by industry or the products produced (such as paper, computers, steel, petrochemicals, durable goods, and consumer products). While such categories may help one draw inferences about the manufacturing technologies commonly found in these industries, they are of little use to managers who face a specific technological decision in an individual firm.

Another outside group that concerns itself with manufacturing technology consists of equipment suppliers—whose product, in effect, is processing technology. The classifications used by this group range from very broad (for example, machine tool manufacturers, who provide manufacturing technology to a wide variety of industries) to very narrow (for example, manufacturers of marking machines that stamp identification codes on semiconductor packages). While such equipment manufacturers interact directly with individual firms, the definitions they use refer to specific kinds of equipment and seldom have broad relevance.

Our orientation in this and the succeeding four chapters is that of the manager within a manufacturing firm. For such a manager, the term "manufacturing process technology" has a variety of meanings. In general, we use it to refer to the collection of equipment, people, and procedures (systems) used to produce the firm's products and services. However, even this definition evokes very different perceptions, depending on the organizational level of the individual interpreting it. Figure 6-1 depicts the three major levels we examine in this chapter.

The lowest and most detailed level is that of the technical specialist, such as a process engineer or an industrial engineer. At this level, manufacturing technology primarily involves material conversion: the means by which equipment and labor make direct contact with materials to produce the desired product. Such conversion processes as machining, joining, finishing, and shaping are the focus of process engineers. Industrial engineers, on the other hand, tend to focus their attention on systems and procedures, such as physical layouts, material flows, and job design. Most firms also have other types of specialists who deal with various technical aspects of the process, but from somewhat different perspectives. Labor relations personnel, for example, concentrate on job definitions, pay schemes, and work rules; materials specialists concentrate on the procurement, storage, and flow of materials; and information specialists concentrate on the collection, processing, and transmission of data.

The second level in Figure 6-1 is that of the operations manager. This level includes manufacturing managers, plant managers, and operating department managers. Their perspective on manufacturing technology primarily reflects a concern with control: how to direct individual operations so that expectations (budgets and schedules) are met. Control is typically defined in terms of operating and coordinating the equipment and systems that were designed or selected by technical specialists (with the approval of these same operations managers).

The third organizational level is that of the senior general manager, as well as the top functional managers from such areas as marketing/sales, R&D, finance, and manufacturing. They seek to ensure that the process technology meets the requirements of the firm's customers and suppliers. Moreover, their attention is directed to the competitive implications of manufacturing process technology, in contrast to the operations managers' concern with control, and the technical specialists' preoccupation with technical issues.

To understand how a firm's choice of manufacturing technology may either augment or constrain its manufacturing strategy and competitive position, one must understand the concerns of all three management levels. Therefore, in this chapter we describe concepts that are useful to both technical specialists and operations managers and relate them directly to the needs of the general manager. Chapter 7 covers specific concepts and techniques that can help a general manager understand and work with process technology. Chapters 8, 9, and 10 then look at three key general management issues directly related to process technology: cost improvement, vertical integration, and the management of change in a process technology.

Figure 6-1   Organizational levels and perspectives on process technology

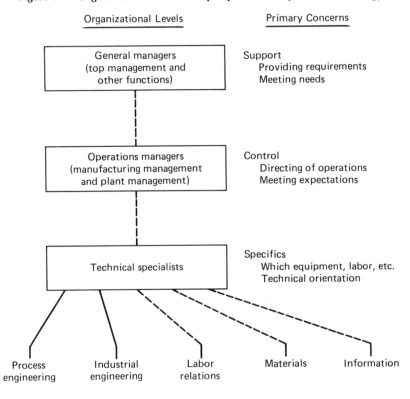

6-1.2   Chapter Overview

Most people view manufacturing technologies in very narrow terms. Engineers and other specialists, for example, tend to think in technical rather than operating terms. Although they willingly delve into the details of a given technology, they often ignore their control or competitive implications. Others (including some managers and too many students of management), on the other hand, display an unwillingness to master the details of a technology—a mode of behavior that has been characterized as "technology aversion"—because of their lack of technical education, experience, or motivation. Just as knowing one foreign language well seems to make it easier to learn others, knowing one technology well facilitates one's confidence and skill with others. If a manager lacks this kind of experience base, he or she may be hesitant and prone to error in selecting, integrating, and operating a particular process technology for a specific business purpose.

Our objective in this chapter is to provide an overview that will be helpful in understanding manufacturing technologies in a broad sense. Section 6-2 examines process technology from the technical specialist's perspective. Our intent is to provide the reader with an appreciation for the detailed information that must be dealt with by such specialists, the techniques and approaches they use, and how the decisions made at that level interact with those made at the operations manager level.

Section 6-3 focuses on the operations manager's perspective. We look at the key tasks, relating to process technology, that must be performed, the major concerns and issues that must be addressed, and some useful concepts and techniques for resolving them. Section 6-4, deals with the perspective of the general manager. We describe the attitude toward process technology that many general managers seem to have, and illustrate the kinds of problems it can lead to. Then we show how adopting a more strategic point of view can help a general manager evaluate and exploit the capabilities incorporated in a particular technology.

The final section deals with the notion of a "process technology strategy," which we embed in a discussion of two competing philosophies of technology management. This discussion serves as a basis for the following four chapters, which describe how a firm can develop and pursue an appropriate strategy for manufacturing technology.

6-2 PROCESS TECHNOLOGY—THE TECHNICAL SPECIALIST'S PERSPECTIVE

Process technology is typically regarded as the domain of two groups of technical specialists: process engineers* (who are responsible for equipment and its performance) and industrial engineers (who are responsible for worker job definitions and workflows). Both groups must deal with physical processes at a very detailed level. Although many readers may be familiar with the work of such specialists, we briefly describe the points of view they tend to adopt—and where they may have blind spots.

6-2.1 Process Engineering

Process (or equipment) engineers are called upon to deal with a variety of material conversion technologies that change the physical properties or appearance of materials, or combine them; Table 6-1 contains one possible classification of various process technologies. Their duties usually include selecting the process technology (as embodied in one or more pieces of equipment) to be used in obtaining a desired output. This choice is influenced by the materials used, the products made, and the competitive strategy being pursued. Firms that seldom need such process engineering skills, either because new types of equipment are added only infrequently or because only simple types of equipment (such as hand tools and basic fixtures) are used, may not maintain such

* Sometimes referred to as manufacturing process engineers or simply manufacturing engineers.

Table 6-1

Technical Classification of Manufacturing Processes

Processes for Changing Physical Properties

1.	Chemical reactions	4.	Hot working
2.	Refining/extraction	5.	Cold working
3.	Heat treatment	6.	Shot peening

Processes for Changing the Shape of Materials

1.	Casting	12.	Spinning
2.	Forging	13.	Stretch forming
3.	Extruding	14.	Roll forming
4.	Rolling	15.	Torch cutting
5.	Drawing	16.	Explosive forming
6.	Squeezing	17.	Electrohydraulic forming
7.	Crushing	18.	Magnetic forming
8.	Piercing	19.	Electroforming
9.	Swaging	20.	Powder metal forming
10.	Bending	21.	Plastics molding
11.	Shearing		

Processes for Machining Parts to a Fixed Dimension

Traditional chip removal processes

1.	Turning	7.	Sawing
2.	Planing	8.	Broaching
3.	Shaping	9.	Milling
4.	Drilling	10.	Grinding
5.	Boring	11.	Hobbing
6.	Reaming	12.	Routing

Nontraditional machining processes

1.	Ultrasonic	6.	Chem-milling
2.	Electrical discharge	7.	Abrasive jet cutting
3.	Electro-arc	8.	Electron beam machining
4.	Optical lasers		
5.	Electrochemical	9.	Plasma-arc machining

Processes for Obtaining a Surface Finish

1.	Polishing	7.	Superfinishing
2.	Abrasive belt grinding	8.	Metal spraying
3.	Barrel tumbling	9.	Inorganic coatings
4.	Electroplating	10.	Parkerizing
5.	Honing	11.	Anodizing
6.	Lapping	12.	Sheradizing

Processes for Joining Parts or Materials

1.	Welding	6.	Pressing
2.	Soldering	7.	Riveting
3.	Brazing	8.	Screw fastening
4.	Sintering	9.	Adhesive joining
5.	Plugging		

Source. Amstead et al., 1977.

skills within the organization. Instead, they are purchased "as needed" from engineering consulting firms or equipment suppliers.

In selecting from among alternative process technologies, a combination of materials science, mechanical, and economic analyses are used. The desired physical characteristics of the product also impose severe constraints on this selection, and it is often necessary to develop models and prototypes to insure that the process is capable of fulfilling its intended purpose.

6-2.2 Industrial Engineering

In cases where the equipment involved is fairly simple and straightforward, industrial engineers (I.E.s) may perform many of the process engineering functions just described. However, their primary concerns are with the tasks performed by individual workers and work stations, and the physical flows between work stations and materials storage areas. One way to grasp the nature of these activities is to examine the documents prepared in carrying them out.

For an individual product, an I.E. typically prepares assembly drawings and charts like those shown in Figure 6-2. These indicate the various components and subassemblies going into the product as well as the sequence that should be followed in combining them. The path of individual products through different work stations is specified using *routing sheets* (containing the operating steps and routing required for each part) and *process flow charts* (describing the desired sequence of specific tasks, inspections, movements, and storage operations). *Work-procedure guidelines* are developed using techniques associated with a branch of industrial engineering known as "methods engineering and time study." These guidelines define individual tasks and prescribe how they are to be performed at the assigned work station.

The industrial engineer is charged with ensuring the continual improvement of the firm's manufacturing processes through the development of methods improvements. Such improvements may include altering the product, the equipment, worker jobs, and the physical flows through the plant. Opportunities for process improvement usually fall into one or more of four categories: simplifying, eliminating, combining, or rearranging jobs.

While it may be possible to subcontract out some portions of the I.E.'s job (for example, developing the layout for a new production line or factory), manufacturing organizations tend to retain most of them in-house, particularly those skills that are called upon in day-to-day work. In fact, it is sometimes difficult to distinguish between the responsibilities of the industrial engineer and those of the line operating manager.

6-2.3 Other Technical Specialists

Three other categories of technical specialist, each playing a different role, are found increasingly in manufacturing firms. When these specialists are not available, their function is generally performed by line managers. Together

Figure 6-2   Engineering analysis of physical component relationships

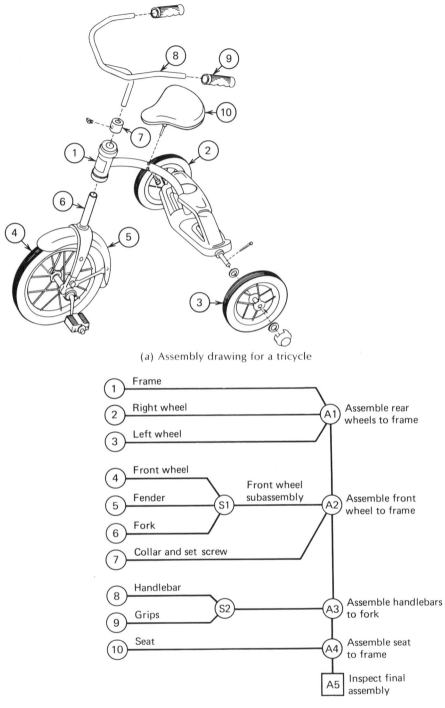

(a) Assembly drawing for a tricycle

(b) Tricycle assembly chart

(Source.   Schroeder, 1981. Used by permission.)

with industrial and process engineers, they constitute a critical part of the firm's manufacturing infrastructure (as described in Chapter 2).

What used to be called "personnel" or "labor relations" is now commonly termed *human resource management*. Industrial engineers sometimes perform this role, but they are usually more concerned with worker efficiency and equipment utilization. Human resource specialists, on the other hand, are more involved with such issues as the quality of work life, incentive systems, and employee benefits. In some organizations industrial engineering is assigned responsibility for dealing with the comfort and physical needs of the worker, while personnel/labor relations is entrusted with union negotiations and designing wage/benefit packages, and line operations managers are expected to deal with whatever is left over.

A second type of technical specialist found increasingly in manufacturing firms is the materials manager. Traditionally such functions as procurement, inventory management, and material flow and handling were performed by a combination of purchasing agents (who dealt with vendors), industrial engineers (who designed procedures), and operations managers (who managed within the constraints imposed by the procedures designed by industrial engineering and the materials provided by purchasing). Because of the increasing importance and interrelatedness of these tasks, the "materials specialist" is appearing in many organizations. In 1982, for example, the American Production and Inventory Control Society (APICS) had almost 50,000 members, most of whom classified themselves as materials specialists.

A third type of technical specialization is *information engineering*. As with the other two functions, historically this task was handled either by industrial engineers or operations managers as needed. More recently it has been performed within the materials function, which typically generates the bulk of the information needed for process management and is therefore a major user of the firm's computer system. However, by the late 1970s some firms had developed separate groups of technical specialists who were responsible for all the information systems required for managing their manufacturing process.

6-2.4   The Perspective of the Technical Specialist

Different types of technical specialists tend to share at least three important characteristics. The first relates to the allegiances of the people usually found in such technical specialties. As experts in a subset of the overall technology, they are more likely to identify themselves professionally with that subset than with the organization they work for. Many engineers who work in manufacturing, for example, regard their careers as being more closely tied to their specific engineering discipline than to their company or even their specific workgroup.

Second, such technical specialists usually spend their days fighting through a thicket of details and are under continual pressure to make myriad "little" decisions. While decisions that require large capital investments or major changes in operating procedures are likely to be sent up for review by higher-level managers, "operating" decisions seldom are subjected to such reviews. As long as those affected do not object, such decisions are made in the manner that the individual technical specialist feels is most appropriate. As a result, over time a firm's manufacturing organization can become, in effect, the prisoner of a series of decisions made almost autonomously by a variety of technical specialists in the normal course of doing their jobs. Each may appear to be small and nonstrategic in its impact, yet together they may require considerable amounts of information and have a significant impact on the firm's process technology.

A third characteristic, following naturally from the first two, arises out of the narrow, task-oriented perspective that is often adopted by these technical specialists. This perspective is the result of both training (combined with the personality characteristics that led them to seek such training) and job assignments that typically give them responsibility for only a small part of the total manufacturing system. The detailed and specific nature of such assignments makes it difficult to take a broader perspective. Thus the criteria used in data gathering and decision making tend to be dictated by the "standard approach" of the technical specialty one has adopted, rather than by the organization's objectives and long-range plans. Another contributing factor is the belief of many companies in the dictum that "engineers don't make good general managers," which prevents them from trying to develop the managerial capabilities and perspectives of their engineers. Such a belief is likely to become self-fulfilling. German and Japanese firms—as well as most U.S. high-tech firms—do not subscribe to such a belief, as is discussed in later chapters.

The operations manager must somehow interact with all these specialists, bringing them together when selecting or altering a process technology, managing an existing process so as to meet customer requirements, and coordinating its evolution over time. This is no easy task, as we will see.

6-3   PROCESS TECHNOLOGY—THE OPERATIONS MANAGER'S PERSPECTIVE

Just as technical specialists tend to have certain points of view about process technology, operations managers have their own biases. In part, these biases are a natural consequence of the fact that many operations managers are former technical specialists. People trained as industrial, process, or materials engineers tend to carry those professions' perspectives on process technology with them when they are promoted into operations manager positions, just as do those who came out of marketing or control. Thus operations managers often have to make a conscious effort to broaden their perspectives on process technology to include aspects that are more economic or commercial in nature.

The operations manager tends to view process technology simply as a means of meeting required output targets and performance goals. While these targets may be very specific and directly related to physical production, materials usage, equipment, and workers, the operations manager's concerns are fundamentally different from those of the technical specialist. Different concepts and techniques are needed for dealing with process technology at this level.

Table 6-2 contains a fairly comprehensive list of the issues that must be addressed by operations managers in dealing with a process technology. Issues are divided into three groups: (1) how the process technology works, (2) its economics, and (3) the key problems associated with managing it. Note that the first of these deals not only with technical characteristics but also with such operating considerations as flexibility, process balance, and tradeoffs. This table highlights the fact that both the physical and the informational aspects of the process must be dealt with. In fact, understanding information flows is often as important as understanding physical flows.

Table 6-2
The Operations Manager's Concerns Regarding Process Technology

How Does It Work (operating characteristics and constraints)

1. Inputs, outputs, and processing (cycle) time
2. Flow pattern (sequential and simultaneous)
3. Points where delays or accumulations (inventory) occur
4. Capacities and bottlenecks
5. Balance (fit) among the various process *resources*
   a. Human-time vs. machine-time
   b. Various skill levels required (e.g., unskilled vs. skilled, operating vs. maintenance people)
   c. Worker–supervisor ratios
   d. Operating times vs. set-up times vs. maintenance time
   e. Space requirements: workers, machines, and inventories
6. Balance between the various *stages* in the process (e.g., upstream and downstream processes)
   a. Raw material acquisition/preparation vs. use.
   b. Load/unload time vs. running time
   c. Making vs. testing/finishing
   d. Final product production vs. sales
7. Flexibility of process
   a. Time/cost of changeovers (including "learning" time)
   b. Flexibility of raw materials, machines, men, and products (both finished and in various stages of completion)
8. Trade-offs
   a. Set-up time vs. running time
   b. Inventory costs vs. operating costs
   c. Machine utilization vs. man utilization
   d. Machine utilization vs. inventory costs
   e. Monotony of job vs. ease and speed of training and changeovers
   f. Volume vs. tolerances/wastage
   g. Individual control vs. supervisor control vs. process control

Table 6-2 (*continued*)

---

9. What are the major uncertainties in the process? (Volume? Quality? Cost?)
10. What can go wrong? (What is most likely to go wrong and what is unlikely to go wrong?) What causes it to go wrong?
11. What happens when something goes wrong? How do you make it go right again?

What Are Its Economics?

1. Original costs vs. operating costs vs. "lifetime" costs
2. Lifetime (physical, economic, and technological) and payback characteristics
3. Costs vs. volume (breakeven analysis and economies of scale)
4. Cost breakdown by ingredients
    a. Materials
    b. Labor
    c. Supervision
    d. Inspection and testing
    e. Inventories
    f. Machines (operating costs and capital costs)
    g. Plant costs: space, logistics facilities, and support units
    h. Utilities
5. Cost of product changes

What Are the Key Operations/Manufacturing Problems Associated with It? (What must you be good at?)

1. Changes in volume?
2. Changes in products?
    a. Between products in a product line
    b. Between old and new products
3. Cost control? (Quality control? Inventory control?)
4. Work force management?
5. Planning, scheduling, and balancing (using scarce resources efficiently?)
6. Maintenance (and trouble-shooting?) Reacting quickly to disruptions?
7. Purchasing materials? Make/buy decisions?
8. Materials handling/transportation
9. Getting it out the door on time? Meeting specifications exactly?
10. Choosing the right technology at the right time?
11. Providing the appropriate capacity at the right time?
12. Location: close to material sources? Markets? Cheap labor? Cheap transportation?

6-3.1 Basic Process Analysis for Operations Managers

Faced with the need to coordinate and control a diverse set of operating procedures and resources, assembled in large part by a variety of technical specialists, the operations manager has to understand thoroughly the basic elements of the production technology and its operating characteristics. The development of a process flow diagram (in concept, much like the plant layout diagrams that industrial engineers prepare) can be a very useful tool for doing this. Figure 6-3 illustrates such a flow diagram for the production process of a cran-

Figure 6-3 Manufacturing process flow diagram—National Cranberry Cooperative

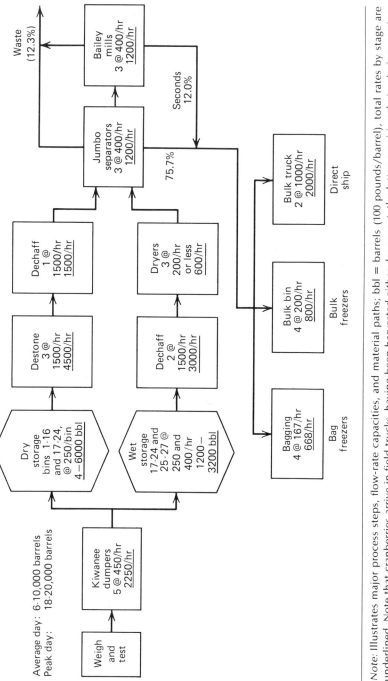

Note: Illustrates major process steps, flow-rate capacities, and material paths; bbl = barrels (100 pounds/barrel), total rates by stage are underlined. Note that cranberries arrive in field trucks, having been harvested either dry or wet, the latter requiring drying before sorting. (Source. "National Cranberry Cooperative," Harvard Case Services, 9-675-014.)

berry processing cooperative. [See "National Cranberry Cooperative," Harvard Case Services, 9-675-014.] The process begins with the weighing and testing of truckloads of cranberries; then the berries are separated from foreign materials (two paths are possible, depending on whether the berries were harvested wet or dry); they are divided according to quality; and then they are packed in one of three forms. Developing such a process flow diagram requires identifying key processing steps and inventory points and the dominant flow paths among them. Information about material flow rates and equipment capacity can also be added, as illustrated in Figure 6-3.

Developing a process flow diagram is usually straightforward, but it can be a useful exercise even for those familiar with a specific operation. It can help identify critical operations and aid in evaluating the impact of a change in one process step on others. As in the cranberry example, indicating the material conversion technologies (actual equipment) used and their maximum flow rates helps identify where coordination and control are likely to be particularly critical. Moreover, analyzing the balance of the production flow capacities at various steps of the process pinpoints bottlenecks and other opportunities for process improvement. Such analysis also can assist in planning workloads and production volumes, controlling process performance, and modifying its characteristics.

6-3.2   Generic Ways of Organizing Process Flows

Maintaining control over a process technology requires that the operations manager identify and carry out certain key tasks that depend on the basic workflow characteristics of the process. A useful way to get started in identifying what these tasks might be in a given situation is to divide all possible workflow patterns into five generic categories: project, job shop, batch, assembly line, and continuous flow. These categories range from general purpose, easily changed (fluid) process flow systems to specialized, highly interrelated (systemic) flow systems. After briefly describing each of these five categories, we look at other important ways to characterize processes.

Project

A project organization often is used by firms that produce a variety of customized products (such as buildings or prototype products) that requires the coordinated input of a variety of resources. Those who adopt such a project organization value its ability to produce a tailor-made product; they are willing to accept the higher costs (as compared with producing standardized products with a more specialized process) that result.

Standard procedures are seldom applicable in such a process, and it is often difficult to divide the total task into completely separable sets of responsibilities. Therefore, most important activities and resources—technical, managerial, direct labor, and so forth—have to be managed as a totality, acquiring and applying resources in a time-phased sequence so as to best achieve project goals. Scheduling the various tasks is sometimes facilitated by representing them in network form (such as critical path or PERT charts) to show the timing and interdependence relationships that must be satisfied if the planned outcome is to be achieved.

While each project generally results in a unique product, and therefore requires a unique set of activities and resources, it is possible for a company to build a business around providing the rather specialized management skills and resources needed for carrying out such projects. Thus some construction firms specialize in particularly large-scale projects; one of their competitive advantages is that they can manage such complicated jobs more effectively than less experienced firms.

Job Shop

A job shop process flow pattern generally is encountered when a firm produces small batches of a large number of different products, most of which require a different set or sequence of processing steps. Commercial printing firms, machine tool shops, and plants that make custom-designed printed circuit boards are all examples of such job shop technologies. While any single product (or "job") may use only a small part of the production system's skills and equipment, some processing steps may require such a large capital investment that one can justify incorporating them into the facility only if they can be used in the production of many products. Thus the flow pattern in a job shop may send different orders through a set of common operations and then forward them to other less standard tasks.

A job shop typically requires large amounts of in-process inventory, which often makes it difficult to know the precise location of a job at a specific time. As a result, the time it takes to complete the entire production process is usually much longer than the sum of the processing times for individual tasks. These characteristics make it important for a job shop to have a control system that tracks individual jobs, moves them to the next work center when they are ready, and provides information for estimating their completion times and costs.

Since most job shops are very flexible in terms of the products produced, flow paths followed, and resources used, it is usually difficult (and often misleading) to calculate their capacity; this will depend on the particular mix of orders being produced at a given time. From a customer's point of view, the products produced by a job shop generally can be produced faster and more economically than would be possible with a project organization.

Batch or Decoupled Line Flow Processes

A batch or decoupled line flow process is essentially a somewhat standardized job shop. Such a process is generally adopted when a business has developed a relatively stable line of products, each of which is produced in periodic batches—either to customer order or for inventory. Most of these products follow the same flow pattern within the factory. Items typically produced with such processes include specialty chemicals, heavy equipment, electronic devices, and metal castings. The volume per model of such products is not sufficient to justify specialized, dedicated equipment for any single class of product, yet it enables the business to use a process that is more specialized—and therefore less flexible—than a job shop.

While decoupled line flow processes have many similarities to job shops, they typically have less variety in the product flowpaths. As a result, the location of a specific job at a given time can be pinpointed more easily. In addition, the time to perform each production step tends to be shorter and more consistent across jobs because there is more similarity among the products being produced; set-up times (the time required for changeovers) are also more predictable, and usually less than is typical in a job shop. As a result, forecasting batch completion times is easier, production lead times are shorter, and work in process is less. Considerable variety is still possible in the products produced, however; therefore, flexible equipment and procedures and careful control over the work pace are still essential.

Assembly Line Processes

In this type of production technology the work stations are laid out in the sequence needed to produce a group of highly similar products. Examples include the assembly of automobiles, digital watches, and children's toys. The product passes through a series of steps at a prespecified and controlled rate. Individual operations are tightly specified, and failure to perform any one of them in the time allotted will slow down the whole line.

In many instances an assembly line is employed as the final step in a long series of production activities. For example, component parts may be made in a metalworking department (set up as a job shop); a variety of those components may be combined into subassemblies (set up as a decoupled flow process); and these subassemblies may be assembled and tested using an assembly line. Although many assembly lines are set up to produce only one product at a given time, it is sometimes possible to produce variations of a given product at the same time; this is commonly referred to as a "mixed model assembly line." For example, a General Motors' final assembly plant might produce a mid-sized Buick, followed by a mid-sized Pontiac, followed by a mid-sized Oldsmobile. Each will have different colors, engines, and options, yet all move down a single conveyorized assembly line according to a predetermined sequence.

Because an assembly line reduces the cycle time for each individual task but makes each worker dependent on the activities of the other workers on the line, one of the most critical responsibilities for the operations manager is to keep the line running smoothly. This requires precise planning as to the products to be made (and their sequence), the staging of components and other input materials, and the maintenance of the equipment so that the line will run without interruption. Materials planning and control are key management tasks.

The capacity of an assembly line is a function of the number of units produced per hour and the amount of time per week during which the line is running. It is not easy to change the production rate of such a line, since such changes generally require redefining and "rebalancing" the jobs to be performed by each worker. Hence assembly lines are rather inflexible. They can produce only a limited range of products, and even slight changes in product design may require that the line be shut down for days or weeks for retooling and rebalancing.

Continuous Flow Processes

This type of process technology organization occupies the most specialized end of the continuum. Oil refineries, high volume chemical plants, and food processing operations such as cereal plants or flour mills are examples of continuous processes. Like assembly lines, production takes place over a predetermined sequence of steps, but processing is almost totally automated and material flow is continuous rather than discrete. Equipment is designed and built for a particular flow rate and composition, and it can be extremely expensive to make any changes in the products produced or their rate of production.

Because continuous flow processes tend to be very capital intensive, one of management's primary tasks is to insure high equipment utilization rates. Maintaining equipment and providing the required amounts of input materials are critical. Whereas assembly lines usually require many input parts and materials, most continuous processes start with relatively few. Because of the substantial volumes and weights of these materials, however, the location of such facilities is important. Since continuous processes tend to run at high speeds, even a short period of off-spec operation is extremely expensive. Tight "real time" control is essential, both because of this and because the output of a continuous process often represents only one segment of a total production process. For example, a continuous process used to produce one material (a plastic resin, say) might be followed with processes that are more batch or job shop in nature, so as to convert the commodity-type output of the continuous process into specialized forms for individual customers.

6-3.3   Contrasting the Operating Characteristics of Different Production Process Technologies

The preceding paragraphs provide a general overview of the five major categories of process organizations. They outline a spectrum along which several operating characteristics vary. These characteristics can be grouped under four major headings—equipment and plant layout, workforce, material/information flows, and operating controls—and summarized for each of the five categories as in Table 6-3. It should be noted that three of these groupings are similar to the technical specialties described in the previous section, except that materials and information management have been combined, and industrial engineering has been separated into "equipment and plant layout" and "work-

Table 6-3

Characteristics of Major Categories of Production Processes

Characteristic	Project	Job Shop	Line Flow/Batch	Assembly Line	Continuous
Typical size of facility	Varies	Usually small	Moderate	Often Large	Large
Scale economies	Some, firm level	Some, firm level	Varies	Some, plant level	Large, plant level
Potential for learning improvements	Mostly confined to the individuals involved	Few, mainly in setups	Some	Moderate and continuous	Substantial and continuous
Equipment and Physical Layout Characteristics					
Process flow	No pattern	A few dominant flow patterns	One or two single dominant patterns	A rigid flow pattern	Clear and inflexible
Type of equipment	General purpose	Mostly general purpose, some specialization	Varies	Specialized, low and high technology	Specialized, high technology
Capital intensity	Generally very low	Low, as long as equipment utilization is high	Varies	Varies, moderate capital intensity	Capital intensive; equipment seldom idle
Definition of capacity	Fuzzy, usually expressed only in monetary terms	Fuzzy, in monetary terms only	Varies	Clear, in terms of output rates	Clear, expressed in physical terms
Additions to capacity	Incremental	Incremental over wide range	Varies	Incremental, but requires rebalancing	Some incremental, mostly in chunks
Bottlenecks	Continually shifting	Shifting frequently	Shifting often, but predictably	Generally known and stationary	Known and stationary
Speed of process ($/unit/time period)	Varies	Slow	Moderate	Fast	Very fast
Control over work pace	Worker	Worker and foreman	Worker, foreman, and production supervisor	Process design and management decisions	Equipment and process design

180

	Every job	Frequent	Some, not complex	Few and costly	Rare and very expensive
Set-ups	Every job	Frequent	Some, not complex	Few and costly	Rare and very expensive
Run lengths	Very short	Short	Moderate	Long	Very long
Process changes required by new products	Incremental	Often incremental	Often incremental	Incremental and radical	Often radical
Rate of change in process technology	Slow	Slow	Moderate	Moderate to high	Moderate to high
Direct Labor and Workforce Characteristics					
Labor content (value added)	High	Very high	Varies	Low	Very low
Job content (scope)	Large	Large	Moderate	Small	Varies
Worker skill level	High	High	Mixed	Low	Varies
Workforce payment	Hourly	Hourly or piece rate	Often piece rate	Hourly, often tied to percentage of standard	Hourly or salaried
Wage rate per hour	High	High	Moderate	Generally low	Varies
End-of-period push for output	Some	Much	Frequently occurs	Infrequent	None
Worker training requirements	Very high	High	Moderate	Low	Varies
Material and Information Control Characteristics					
Material requirements	Varies	Difficult to predict	More predictable	Predictable	Very predictable
Control over suppliers	Very low	Low	Moderate	High	Very high
Vertical integration	None	None	Very little	Some backward, often forward	Often backward and forward

Table 6-3 (continued)

Characteristic	Project	Job Shop	Line Flow/Batch	Assembly Line	Continuous
Inventories					
Raw material	None	Small	Moderate	Varies, frequent deliveries	Large, continuous deliveries
Work-in-process	Large	Large	Moderate	Small	Very small
Finished goods	None	Small or none	Varies	High	Very high
Responsibility for quality control	Direct labor, with management checks	Direct labor	Varies	Primarily QC specialists	Process control specialists
Production information requirements	Very high	High	Varies	Moderate	Low
Information systems	Elaborate for labor and management	Elaborate for labor and management	Elaborate, varies	Limited, mainly for management	Limited, mainly for management
Scheduling	Uncertain, frequent changes	Uncertain, frequent changes	Varies, frequent expediting	Process designed around fixed schedule	Inflexible, sequence often dictated by technology
Primary Operating Management Characteristics					
Staff needs	Coordination mainly	Coordination	Coordination	Process control and coordination	Process control
Importance of load forecasting	Little	Little	Some	High	High
Workforce management tasks	Training, assignment and motivation	Training, assignment, some motivation	Varies	Selection and attendance	Training and supervision
Response to business downturns	Layoff	Layoff	Layoff	Build inventory, then layoff	Cut prices, build inventory, then shut down
Challenges	Estimating, sequencing tasks, pacing	Estimating, labor utilization, fast response, debottlenecking	Designing procedures, balancing stages, responding to diverse needs	Productivity improvement, adjusting staffing levels, rebalancing when needed	Avoiding downtime, timing expansions, cost minimization

force" issues. Thus Table 6-3 simply delineates the operating responsibilities of managers having different technical specializations and shows the influence that the type of process organization has on each.

Starting with Equipment and Physical Layout Characteristics, it can be seen that such issues as facility size, capital requirements, set-ups, and run lengths change dramatically as one moves from the project end of the spectrum to the continuous flow end. Similarly, such Direct Labor and Workforce Characteristics as skill requirements, pay schemes, job content, and training also differ significantly by type of process organization. In the area of Material and Information Control, such aspects as supplier relations, scheduling systems, and inventory structure vary greatly.

The significant differences among these three groups of characteristics suggest that the operating managers of different types of process organization must have very different skills. This is highlighted in the final portion of Table 6-3 where it is indicated that staff and workforce needs, forecasting requirements, technical knowledge, and the typical response to business fluctuations all place very different demands on those who manage different types of production processes.

While it is important to understand that such differences exist, it is also necessary to recognize that constraints imposed by market conditions and equipment technology often dictate the dominant process organization found in a particular industry. In paper making, for example, paper machines operate continuously and tend to be organized as continuous flow processes, independent of the specific firm in question. In other industries, however, this may not be the case. In printing, by contrast, no single process organization dominates the others: the traditional commercial printer tends to use a job shop; book printers tend to use either a batch or an assembly line process; and newspapers tend to use a continuous process—going from a roll of paper at one end to bundled papers ready for delivery at the other end.

Because of the variety of options available to a firm, and the impact of each on a number of competitive dimensions, selecting the "right" process organization requires careful analysis. While the framework presented in this section can be useful in understanding the implications and limitations of various alternatives, other aspects are also important. Some of these other aspects are discussed in the next section. Selecting the appropriate process technology and organization (and their attendant characteristics) for a given situation is discussed in Chapter 7.

6-4 PROCESS TECHNOLOGY—THE GENERAL MANAGER'S PERSPECTIVE

General managers, including top management and the heads of a business unit's major functions, tend to view process technology from a very different perspective from those of technical specialists and operations managers. General managers are concerned with the extent to which a given process technology meets specific requirements: customers' needs, financial constraints, new product development cycles, and so forth. The firm's manufacturing system is viewed as just one of the means for achieving the overall goals of the organization, and therefore general managers seek to insure that it meshes with the requirements of other functions. This contrasts with the concern of lower level operations managers who seek congruence between the manufacturing function's overall mission and the activities of its various technical support groups.

We begin this section by describing two problems that arise frequently when general managers address issues involving process technology. This leads us to consider the perspective and approaches they tend to adopt when dealing with process-related decisions, and which often underlie the two problems just cited. Finally, we suggest the kind of changes in this perspective that will be necessary if these problems are to be alleviated.

6-4.1   Problems of "Imbalance" and "Bias" in the General Manager's Perspective on Process Technology

Many general managers think about process technologies too narrowly and superficially. Managers who have engineering or extensive experience in operations often think only in technical terms—like an industrial or process engineer—rather than in managerial terms. While they are not averse to getting into the details of their manufacturing technologies, their backgrounds may constrain their creativity when dealing with them at a managerial level.

Other managers (and students of management) who have little technical background may face the opposite problem: superficiality. A lack of technical or operations experience causes some managers to avoid getting into the process details that are central to the success of their business—a form of behavior that has been called "technology aversion." As we illustrate below, the kind of familiarity that is required is not simply the specification, in technical terms, of the means by which the technology converts inputs into outputs. What can and cannot be done technically also must be linked directly to managerial concerns and requirements.

The problems arising from too narrow a technical perspective can be illustrated by the case of a printing firm that recently sought to acquire a new printing press. Similar presses were offered by several suppliers; each of them possessed different features and capabilities. During the previous two years a certain brand of press had become particularly popular in the industry because of its excellent construction, the ease with which operators could run it, its manufacturer's reputation for service, and the variety and power of the technical features available as standard equipment.

When a salesman from this manufacturer visited the firm, he quickly learned that the president (and owner) considered his production process up to date, had a strong technical background himself, and felt that much of his company's past success was based on its process capabilities. After a series of discussions (with the salesman and other industry sources) concerning the technical aspects of the proposed new press, the president, more and more impressed with its apparent capabilities, decided to purchase it.

Unfortunately, soon after the press was installed, it was discovered that:

1. It would not run at its rated speed on the firm's primary type of work because this work was not the ideal size for that piece of equipment.

2. Set-ups took longer on the new press than on the firm's other six presses because of all the extra features, which required additional adjustments for each new job.

3. On the kind of work it did best, it did everything the equipment manufacturer promised. Unfortunately, on such work the company tended to be competing with other firms who used the same press; thus the firm had no competitive advantage on that work.

4. Because of its many features, more training (than was needed for other presses) was required before an operator reached the desired level of competence on the new press. The company found not only that it had to spend more on training, but also that operators demanded higher wages once they had been trained.

5. Since the new press required a greater investment than did simpler and older-technology presses, it had to be utilized more fully than some of the older equipment. It took a long period of time for the firm to make the necessary changes in its production scheduling and equipment loading rules.

Eventually it became apparent that this firm should have bought a more traditional piece of equipment, like some of its existing presses, instead of seeking to be at the forefront of press technology. Other presses would have been better suited to the requirements of the firm's type of work. Over the next several months the president learned that this kind of problem was typical in the printing industry, where many general managers and owners have technical backgrounds.

The other type of mistake is the complement to the one above: rather than getting too immersed in the details of a technology, some general managers avoid altogether—or delegate to others (who often have only a specialist's perspective)—important technical details. A simple example developed by Wickham Skinner (1978) involves the technology of cutting grass with a power lawnmower. The lawnmower was described to a prospective purchaser as follows: "It costs $188, has a gasoline engine, and cuts a 24-inch wide swath of grass. It is of high quality construction, and is made by a well-known manufacturer." After buying it, the technology-averse new owner took it home to try it out. He found that:

1. The cutting technology was based on a reel moving past a cutting bar, and therefore could not handle grass much higher than one-half the reel diame-

ter. It simply pushed forward and down the eight-inch-high crop of grass that had grown up during his annual summer vacation.

2. It was self-propelled, with no free-wheeling device, making it difficult for the operator to work close to and around his wife's formal flower gardens.

3. It took 30 minutes to change the cutting height, making it difficult for the operator to leave grass longer on hillsides (to cut down on erosion) than on flatter terrain.

4. It was not powerful enough to cut thick wet grass going uphill, yet half of the buyer's lawn was steeply sloping.

5. The reel-type cutting technology would not mulch leaves, which the prospective buyer hated to rake in the fall (and which a rotary mower might have handled).

6. The mower had a two-cycle engine, which meant that oil had to be mixed with the gasoline each time the tank was filled.

Given the requirements of this technologically averse buyer, it appears that an extra powerful four-cycle, rotary blade, self-propelled mower that offered easy handling for tight maneuvering and a simple height adjustment mechanism would have been much more appropriate. By confining his attention to the mower's basic function and cost, this buyer failed to provide for his lawn's specific technical needs. As a result, he made a poor decision.

Managers too often do the same thing. If they lack detailed knowledge about either the technical or the operating details of their process technologies, they tend to delegate to others decisions that they should make themselves. Moreover, as we see in Chapter 10, general managers' perceptions of the risks associated with a given technology may also be affected by their lack of detailed technical (or operating) understanding.

6-4.2 Defining Process Technology in Terms of a Set of Basic Capabilities and Limitations

When general managers are asked to state the criteria they use to evaluate manufacturing performance, they tend to describe not only the economics of the manufacturing process, but also its constraints, uncertainties, and skill requirements. Sometimes they include such noneconomic considerations as flexibility, quality, reliability, and timeliness. Table 6-4 provides one such list of manufacturing performance criteria. In essence, it combines the viewpoints of the technical specialist and the operating manager, as described earlier, and translates them into implications for higher level general managers.

The categories in this list are applicable to a wide variety of manufacturing process technologies. Moreover, they are described in a way that is compatible with the description of other business functions for which general managers accept decision-making responsibility. A process technology consists of more than just a group of workers, some equipment, and a physical setting; it

Table 6-4
Characterizing a Process Technology

Mechanics

How does the process work?
What *physically* happens, and what makes it happen?

Economics

How much does it cost—over the short term and over the long term?

Time Spans

How long does it take to set up?
How long does it take per unit, once set up?
How can one affect these?

Constraints

What can't be done?
What is very hard to do within an acceptable time/cost frame?

Uncertainties

What can go wrong?
What do people worry about?
What is predictable and what isn't?

Skills

What isn't done automatically?
What is it about the process itself—or managing the process—that takes a long time to
  learn?

Flexibility

How does the process react to changes?
Which changes are easy?
Which are not?

Reliability

What tolerances does the process meet?
How repeatable are those tolerances?

also includes the systems through which the process is managed. Together, these determine its responsiveness to changes in the requirements placed on it, and its ability to support overall business objectives. To manage it properly requires that one understand both its capabilities—the things it can do easily and well—and its limitations. Anybody who is trying to sell you a new piece of equipment (a snowmobile, say) will wax eloquent about all the things it can do. Before buying, be sure you understand all the things it *cannot* do!

One can go further and relate process capabilities directly to the four primary competitive dimensions described in Chapter 2: cost, flexibility, quality, and dependability. One company's attempt to do so is shown in Table 6-5. Cost/efficiency is affected by such things as productivity (of the workforce, capital equipment, and materials), capital utilization (as measured by the return on investment or the return on net assets), and the variable cost per unit. In some cases flexibility refers primarily to the ability to shift production from one product to another in the existing product line, to change the standard product mix, or to introduce new products. In other cases it relates to volume flexibility—the ability to react to unexpected surges or drop-offs in demand.

Measurements of quality can include product performance ratings, internal reject rates, rework costs, and product reliability as measured by field failures, customer returns, and warranty claims. They might also seek to capture the total cost of quality (that is, the cost of not "doing things right the first time") as defined by Crosby (1979). Finally, dependability covers such areas as the percentage of delivery promises actually met, the speed with which cus-

Table 6-5
One Company's View of the Way that Manufacturing Process Capabilities Reflect Priorities

Cost

This criterion refers to low total cost, including cost of the capital employed. This might imply minimum wages, particularly for hourly workers but also for supervisors. The amount of supervision would be determined by the need for cost minimization rather than the maintenance of quality or dependability levels. Capital equipment selection would be based on the need to produce at the lowest cost. Equipment would be replaced only when completely worn out and would likely be overhauled once or twice before actual replacement. Inventories would be maintained at the minimum level needed to avoid idle shop time, which takes precedence over customer service levels. Emphasis of this criterion maximizes return and minimizes investment.

Quality

This criterion focuses on maintaining high levels of quality, defined as significantly higher than competitive products and sufficiently high to support sales of the product even if its price is higher than competitors' prices.

Delivery Dependability

This refers primarily to meeting all delivery commitments for new orders and parts. It includes not only the capability to stock products, but also the ability to manufacture replacement parts quickly so that all delivery promises will be met.

Flexibility

Flexibility refers to the ability to make significant changes in manufacturing volumes and/or products. When given top priority, it entails high responsiveness to increases or decreases in customer demand in the short term (substantially less than one year). It also may be related to flexibility to changes in product designs, the acquisition of new product lines, and/or the significant modification of existing product lines.

tomer problems are solved, and the ability of both the product and its producer to meet their commitments to customers.

Stating process technology capabilities in terms of these four dimensions has an advantage in that marketing and manufacturing can use the same terms to describe their customers' needs. Thus, as is discussed in Chapter 7, these four dimensions can be used to link the capabilities provided by the process technology directly to the firm's product/market requirements.

6-4.3 The Traditional General Management View of Manufacturing Process Technology

The narrowness of general managers' typical perspective on process technology may well be the source of a number of the strategic problems surfacing in many U.S. manufacturing firms today. Its basic assumptions are summarized in Table 6-6. Understanding these assumptions, and the implied relationships contained in this "traditional, narrow/specific" perspective, makes it possible to think about the implications of an alternative approach—what we call a "broad capabilities" perspective.

1. *Narrowly Defined.* Viewing manufacturing process technology as largely technical and tactical in nature leads managers to delegate almost total responsibility for its maintenance and development to "experts." Equipment suppliers are expected to provide improvements in process technology (since they are the experts in the equipment technology), and plant management is expected to recommend the right equipment since they deal with its operating characteristics. Given this view, there is little need for general managers to be directly involved in such "technical" issues as the selection of new equipment

Table 6-6
General Management Assumptions and Views of Process Technology:
A Narrow Perspective

Narrowly defined: Technology is the realm of the technical specialist and/or the lower-level operating manager.

Separable: All outcomes can be foreseen, and assigned to specific investments; therefore individual projects can be evaluated one by one.

Product-specific: A technology has value only to the extent that it can produce or move specific products.

Capital-budget driven: All important issues and decisions can be addressed within the framework of the capital budgeting process.

The product of a few major breakthroughs: Significant competitive moves come from major, managed breakthroughs, not small incremental changes that are largely invisible to top management.

Technical-specialist dependent: Technical competence is neither required nor particularly useful to general management, in part because it encourages attention to technical detail rather than the big picture.

or the modification of an existing process, other than verifying and approving its financial characteristics.

2. *Separable.* This assumption flows naturally from "narrowly defined," and reflects the belief that manufacturing technology issues can be isolated both in time and by location, and therefore managed as a series of "projects." As a result, when general managers are asked to approve the recommendations of the project team, they assume implicitly that the project will not have a major impact on the existing process—or the way it evolves over time. A corollary to such a belief is that any process technology issue that *cannot* be separated out and analyzed as a "project" may safely be delegated to the manufacturing function to deal with without specific direction.

3. *Product-Specific.* Under this assumption, general management ties manufacturing technology decisions directly to specific products and markets. This ignores the fact that most technologies (processing equipment) remain in use over several product generations, and existing process technologies usually constitute the foundation for manufacturing the next generation of products, or expanding the existing product into other markets.

4. *Capital-Budget Driven.* This assumption, following naturally from the first three, leads general management to conclude that the capital budgeting process is the appropriate management mechanism for evaluating a manufacturing technology's major issues and decision requirements (involving narrowly defined, separable projects tied to specific product/market needs). Thus, whenever new capacity is under consideration, the reference point used is inevitably the existing technology. This implies that the incremental cost of a new manufacturing technology must be justified in the context of that existing product/market; as a result, the increased capabilities that come with it, and which may benefit future products, get little or no recognition. This assumption severely limits the number, timing, and types of new technology that are adopted (or even proposed).

A final aspect of this element of the traditional perspective is that the capital budgeting process is viewed as incorporating all of the technology's important risk/return tradeoffs. Moreover, the risks associated with a new process technology are often regarded as being additions to the risks associated with the old process technology. The risks associated with *not* moving to the new technology (the competitive problems that may be encountered if your competitors do, for example) are seldom factored in.

5. *Improvement Through Breakthroughs.* Given the separability of major manufacturing technology decisions, and top management's concern with the "big picture," there is an inherent bias against small incremental improvements. General management is encouraged to act as if most significant improvements in a process technology come from major breakthroughs. Further, they come from breakthroughs based on major investments of capital. However subtle, this attitude quickly becomes apparent to lower levels of management. In their view, since top management does not appear to be interested in (or encourage and reward) small incremental changes, such changes represent only risks, not opportunities, and therefore are to be avoided. If successful, they are not recognized as important; if unsuccessful, they may be significant in a negative way for the operating managers involved.

Unfortunately, an organization that is not motivated to pursue small incremental changes is unlikely to develop the knowledge base necessary to make major breakthroughs. Therefore, when a major breakthrough in manufacturing process technology does become possible, it is often subcontracted out to someone (such as an equipment supplier or engineering consultant) who "must know more about it than we do." We return to this issue in Chapters 10 and 13.

6. *Technical Knowledge Is the Domain of Specialists.* This final assumption is in large part the summation of the first five. Since the capital budgeting system can identify and handle all "important" manufacturing technology decisions, and specialists are available when "technical details" are dealt with, there is no need for general managers to understand either the technical (engineering) side of those technologies or their tactical (operating) side. Technical knowledge is therefore of little use to the general manager.

The combined effect of these traditional perspectives is to neutralize the potential competitive advantage of manufacturing technology. As long as all one's competitors behave in a similar way, and none seeks to gain a "first mover" advantage, this may be a defensible attitude. But even if no competitor adopts a different course, the resulting atrophy of organizational capabilities may be deleterious in ways that are subtle and hard to recognize before it is too late. Some examples will help to illustrate this.

One form of this behavior is displayed by several large American consumer products firms who appear to have accepted the six assumptions outlined above. The result has been a series of extremely conservative manufacturing decisions, including building large, general-purpose plants to house proven production technologies, and relying on external experts (usually equipment suppliers) to provide technical expertise. Their workforce's role has been viewed as neutral, at best, so the resolution of workforce issues is delegated to company-wide and industry-wide bargaining by a corporate labor relations staff.

To assure that "important" manufacturing technology issues get addressed, two very detailed control systems have been developed. One is a centralized cost accounting system, based on detailed criteria for evaluating individual operating units. This is believed to provide an early warning system for impending disaster (downside risks) or emerging opportunities (upside potential), which ensures that management is not surprised. The other is the capital budgeting system, in which any changes in process technology are treated as separate investment projects, given thorough analysis, and evaluated on the basis of their promised return on investment. These companies' financial conservatism has generally led to stagnation in their manufacturing technologies, which are changed only in response to the unequivocal needs of a specific new product or market.

A similar pattern of decision making is apparent in many producers of electronics equipment and instruments. These companies tend to use proven manufacturing technologies and to view manufacturing processes as competitively neutral. They are interested primarily in avoiding the downside risk of a manufacturing disaster. Extreme conservatism, as evidenced by the absence of a long-term program for improving and enhancing manufacturing technologies, is the result. We return to this topic in Chapter 14.

The slow rate at which several major new manufacturing technologies are being adopted today, despite their ready availability, also may be the result of these assumptions. These new technologies include manufacturing resources planning (an information-processing technology), robotics, flexible manufacturing systems (FMS), automated warehouses, and CAD/CAM. Each has been available, in increasing stages of development, for at least two decades; failures far outnumber successes in many firms where they have been tried, and their widespread adoption in the United States is still a long time away. Other countries, particularly Japan, have taken the lead in adopting some of these ideas.

The lack of progress in absorbing and adopting these new technologies is not surprising, since such adoption would require low-level initiative and high-level direction-setting actions, both supported by in-house knowledge. The traditional perspective, however, would support the adoption of these technologies only when the risks of doing so are perceived to be clearly less than the risks of sticking with the traditional technology. This will occur only when enough competitors (or a few particularly aggressive competitors) have made the changeover, thereby exerting increasing pressure on the more traditional firms to revise their assessment of the relative risks of retaining their existing processes.

6-4.4   An Expanded General Management View of Technology

In contrast to the traditional narrow perspective described above, a very different view of manufacturing technology is held by a handful of leading companies (see Table 6-7). This broader view incorporates alternative approaches to each of the six assumptions described in Table 6-6.

   1. *Broadly Defined.* The definition of process technology is expanded beyond technical, equipment-related considerations to include the implications for product design, material suppliers, manufacturing engineering, the workforce, and shop floor management. The information- and materials-flow linkages and controls that make up the manufacturing technology are also taken into consideration. Manufacturing technology is understood to be the total "system" of resources and organizational capabilities that are brought to bear to produce the firm's products and services.

   2. *Integrated.* Manufacturing technology, and its evolution, is an integrated activity that cuts across functional boundaries. Product designers, purchasing agents, operating personnel, and the field service organization all play

Table 6-7

General Management Assumptions and Views of Process Technology:
A Broad Perspective

Broadly defined: Process technology is defined in terms of flows, linkages, controls, and potential for improvement (suppliers, manufacturing engineers, and workers).

Integrated: Activities cut across functional boundaries and are continuous over time.

A set of general capabilities: These meet both the firm's current needs and its future product/market strategies.

The product of holistic decision-making processes: Includes a variety of subjective elements, non-financial as well as financial, long term as well as short term.

The result of organic improvement: Comes from relentless incremental efforts; the goal is a competitive advantage that is both continually increasing and difficult for competitors to imitate.

Dependent on technical generalists: Technical competence is viewed as essential to success, both for individual managers and the company as a whole.

an important role in developing the capabilities of an existing technology, and in helping design and introduce successor technologies. Perhaps equally important, since the technology is understood to encompass the full range of resources and activities required to manufacture the firm's products, the organization's know-how and procedures (software) are considered as essential a part of the technology as the equipment (hardware) itself. (We return to this issue in Chapter 14.)

3. *General Capabilities.* Manufacturing technology is viewed as a set of overall capabilities that are vital to the company's success. These capabilities are not limited to material handling and conversion, nor are they identified only with existing products. They are a valued source of future growth and competitive advantage, equal in importance to marketing and financial capabilities.

As an example, the Batesville Casket Company (a division of Hillenbrand Industries) has systematically developed a set of high-quality, cost-effective, metal working capabilities unique in the casket industry. These capabilities have enabled Batesville to enter a price segment not previously accessible to it. Its expansion into the luggage industry (through the acquisition of American Tourister) was based largely on the recognition that those same manufacturing capabilities could be a unique source of advantage in the luggage industry.

4. *Holistic Decision-Making Processes.* Closely tied to the third point is the understanding that capital budgeting techniques and a few financial measures cannot capture all the important issues and subtleties of manufacturing technology decisions. Planning and directing such activities require that the set of issues considered include such subjective, and often difficult to quantify, concerns as flexibility, consistency, quality of worklife, and adaptability to new products. Because manufacturing technology represents long-term capabilities and not just product-specific capacity, changes in a firm's technology have

strategic significance. Therefore, they are difficult to evaluate simply in terms of the usual financial measures, such as those described in Chapter 5.

5. *Organic Improvement.* A firm that adopts this perspective expects that improvement in manufacturing technology will come primarily from an accumulation of knowledge and relatively small changes, rather than from a few major technological breakthroughs. Such step-by-step progress is primarily dependent on the organization's internal capabilities; equipment suppliers and consulting engineers must be secondary contributors of ideas. While such internal expertise may be complemented by specialists outside the organization, the technology's basic capabilities must be sustained, renewed, and improved from within. Such Japanese firms as Toyota (autos), Matsushita-Reiki (refrigerators), and Sony (electronics) all attribute their technological progress to such a view. We expand on this point in Chapters 12 and 13.

6. *Technical Generalists.* Probably the most radical change in philosophy and perspective is represented by the sixth element: the view that it is essential for general managers to be competent in manufacturing technology, because it can be a major source of competitive advantage. It is not enough for top managers to understand the preceding five elements; they must also design and employ customized management systems that support and guide the development of the firm's manufacturing technology. Finally, by the example of their own involvement, they must establish the organization's norms for the types of technological risks and opportunities that are to be identified, accepted, and pursued.

An organization that adopts this expanded view of manufacturing technology (Table 6-7) will behave differently from one with the narrow view (Table 6-6) in at least three ways. The first concerns the firm's attitude toward progress in manufacturing technology, and how it prepares (or fails to prepare) for change. The second has to do with the kind of familiarity that its general managers have with manufacturing technology, how this familiarity affects their perceptions of its perceived risks and opportunities, and thus the types of activities they support. The third has to do with the way the firm assesses and develops its technological capabilities, and how these are translated into guidelines for technical specialists, operating (functional) managers, and general managers.

6-5 THE CONCEPT OF A PROCESS TECHNOLOGY STRATEGY

Like other elements of manufacturing strategy, a process technology strategy is defined as the pattern of decisions that determine the ultimate capabilities of the process. This chapter has identified some of those decisions and the organizational levels at which they arise—those related to technical specialties (equipment choices, industrial engineering priorities, workforce policies, and materials and information systems), those related to operations management (operating abilities and constraints, economics, and key problems/tasks), and those related to general competitive capabilities (cost, quality, product and service dependability, and flexibility). Simply reviewing these decisions may help a firm identify its past process technology strategy; more important, it can help its managers formulate a new strategy. This kind of strategic planning is the focus of the next four chapters.

But now, at least, we have some preliminary criteria for deciding whether a process technology strategy exists and how one might evaluate it. A good process technology strategy is characterized by at least three kinds of "fit." The first is internal to the manufacturing function: coordinating technical activities with operating policies. The second relates internal to external activities: meshing manufacturing capabilities with those of other functions and with the firm's overall competitive strategy. The third is consistency over time: ensuring that the firm's process technology evolves in a directed fashion, so that as technological capabilities are renewed and augmented, they reinforce and expand the firm's competitive position.

As a final note, it is now possible to comment on why the concept of process technology strategy is so hard to deal with in most firms. Essentially it is because of the breadth and depth of issues that must be considered and addressed. As is discussed in Chapter 10, developing a strategy requires that one manage not only the *content* of the decisions made, but also the *environment* within which those decisions are made—both management attitudes and administrative procedures.

SELECTED REFERENCES

Amstead, B. J., P. F. Ostwald, and M. L. Begeman. *Manufacturing Processes,* 7th ed. New York: John Wiley & Sons, 1977.

Chase, Richard B., and Nicholas J. Aquilano. *Production and Operations Management: A Life Cycle Approach,* 3rd Ed. Homewood, IL: Richard D. Irwin, 1981.

Crosby, Philip B. *Quality Is Free.* New York: McGraw-Hill, 1979.

Groover, Mikell P. *Automation, Production Systems, and Computer-Aided Manufacturing.* Englewood Cliffs, NJ: Prentice-Hall, 1980.

Hayes, Robert H., and William J. Abernathy. "Managing Our Way to Economic Decline." *Harvard Business Review,* July–August 1980, pp. 67–77.

Hayes, Robert H., and David A. Garvin. "Managing as if Tomorrow Mattered." *Harvard Business Review,* May–June 1982, pp. 70–79.

Marshall, Paul W., William J. Abernathy, Jeffrey G. Miller, Richard P. Olsen, Richard S. Rosenbloom, and D. Daryl Wyckoff. "Process Analysis." In *Operations Management.* Homewood, IL: Richard D. Irwin, 1975, pp. 4–19.

Miller, Jeffrey G. "National Cranberry Cooperative." Harvard Business School Case Services, 9-675-014, 1975.

Niebel, Benjamin W. *Motion and Time Study,* 6th ed. Homewood, IL: Richard D. Irwin, 1976.

Schmenner, Roger W. *Production/Operations Management: Concepts and Situations, 2nd ed.* Chicago: Science Research Associates, 1984.

Schonberger, Richard J. *Operations Management.* Plano, TX: Business Publications, 1984.

Schroeder, Roger C. *Operations Management: Decision Making in the Operations Function.* New York: McGraw-Hill, 1981.

Skinner, Wickham. *Manufacturing in the Corporate Strategy.* New York: John Wiley & Sons, 1978, esp. Chapter 7.

Wheelwright, Steven C. "Guiding Process Technology Improvements." Graduate School of Business, Stanford University, Working Paper, 1982.

Wheelwright, Steven C. "Reflecting Corporate Strategy in Manufacturing Decisions." *Business Horizons,* February 1978, pp. 57–66.

Wheelwright, Steven C. "Corning Glass–Erwin Automotive Plant." Harvard Business School Case Services, 9-675-152, 1975.

Matching Process Technology with Product/Market Requirements

7-1 INTRODUCTION AND OVERVIEW

In the preceding chapter, issues related to manufacturing process technology were examined from three organizational levels: the technical manufacturing specialist (such as a process or industrial engineer), the operations manager, and the general manager. This chapter expands upon the discussion of the general manager's concerns relating to process technology. However, rather than starting with a perspective from within the manufacturing function, we adopt that of the senior nonmanufacturing manager who wishes to assess the potential contribution that process technology can make to the overall business.

A basic schematic of a business's various functions, and their relationship to manufacturing, is presented in Figure 7-1. We deal in this chapter with the blocks labeled "Processes," "Products," and "Customers." That is, we want to concentrate on how the marketing and sales functions interact with the manufacturing function in the selection and development of process technology. We examine the relationship between the blocks labeled "Suppliers" and "Processes" in Chapter 9.

The primary interface between the manufacturing function and the customer was once the *sales force,* which placed orders directly with the factory and often was in personal contact with plant managers and others in the manufacturing organization. This interface was supervised by a general manager, who resolved major differences when they arose. With the increasing size and complexity of today's business organizations, such a structure often has proved

Figure 7-1   Manufacturing interfaces with other functions

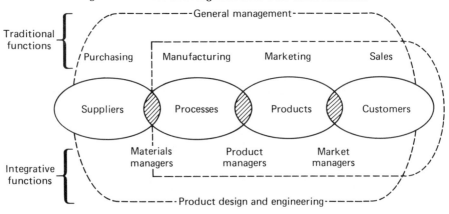

inadequate for integrating these two group's differing objectives. Consequently, in many firms the *marketing function* has grown to become the main link between its sales force and manufacturing organization. It is responsible for defining the firm's product strategy, selecting and positioning the products in the product line, and, frequently, transferring information from sales to manufacturing.

To assist in managing these interfaces, marketing managers have often found it useful to define positions such as "market managers" and "product managers." As suggested in Figure 7-1, these managers perform a coordinating function, representing not only the special interests of the two functions with which they work most closely, but also the concerns of general managers, product designers, and plant engineers. Such interface managers frequently alternate their attention between operating level issues (such as expediting a customer order through production) and general management level issues (such as assessing the effect of modifying a product on the process used to manufacture it).

But such organizational artifices, no matter how elaborate, are by themselves seldom capable of dealing adequately with all the possible linkages between manufacturing and the rest of the firm. An "informal organization"—a network of well-informed people who have developed good working relationships over a long period of time—is needed to handle all the contingencies that the formal organization inevitably neglects to provide for. And both the formal and informal organizations need a frame of reference, a common understanding of where the company is going.

The major purpose of this chapter is to describe some of the concepts and approaches that leading firms have found useful for integrating marketing/sales with manufacturing, and developing an effective set of manufacturing capabilities. Our premise is that for a company to develop a sustainable competitive edge, senior managers outside the manufacturing function need to have a broad understanding of the firm's process technology and how it interacts with other parts of the business. As we pointed out in Chapter 2, the extent to which manufacturing is able to make a contribution to a firm's competitive success depends importantly on the fit between the process technology chosen and the firm's overall competitive strategy.

The next section begins with an overview of a group of ideas deriving from the notion of life cycle analysis. Then we describe the complementary concepts of the product life cycle (which places changing demands on the manufacturing function) and the manufacturing process life cycle (which provides changing capabilities that can be exploited in the marketplace).

Next we discuss the interaction of process technology capabilities with various product/market needs, using a two-dimensional representation known as the "product/process matrix." After applying it to some practical situations, we examine a few of its limits. Two other forms of product/process interaction also are discussed. One deals with issues of innovation, based on some of the findings of Abernathy and Utterback (1975). The other describes an approach used by Abell (1980) to define customers and markets in a way that has implications for process technology.

Chapters 8 and 9 explore some of the specific process technology decisions that require the guidance of senior managers, and Chapter 10 discusses the overall task of managing major changes in process technology.

7-2   THE INTERFACE OF MANUFACTURING TECHNOLOGY WITH SALES AND MARKETING

Many managers, when asked about the relationship between the marketing and manufacturing functions in their companies, are likely to describe it as troubled and strained—or, at best, ambivalent. In one well-known article, Shapiro (1977) identified eight major areas in which problems tend to arise between these two functions. Shapiro's list of the typical views that marketing and manufacturing personnel have of each other is reproduced in Table 7-1. While this list focuses on a few, fairly specific kinds of interaction, it captures nicely the distinction between market needs and process technology capabilities. While not all of these eight problem areas relate directly to manufacturing technology, each has links with the definition of technology that we provide in Chapter 6.

In analyzing these eight problem areas, Shapiro focuses on such issues as evaluation and reward systems, inherent complexity, and differences in manager orientation/experience/"culture" as the basic causes of friction between marketing and manufacturing. While we tend to agree with much of his analysis, it is worth noting that similar differences tend to exist between any two of the functions in a business. However, our experience suggests that the marketing/manufacturing interface is the focal point of much more frequent and heated disagreement than occurs between other pairs of functions.

Dealing one-by-one with each of the problem areas in Table 7-1 is not by

Table 7-1

Functional Level Interactions of Marketing and Manufacturing

Problem Area	Typical Marketing Comment	Typical Manufacturing Comment
Capacity planning and long-range sales forecasting	Why don't we have enough capacity?	Why didn't we have accurate sales forecasts?
Production scheduling and short-range sales forecasting	We need faster response. Our lead times are ridiculous	We need realistic customer commitments and sales forecasts that don't change like wind direction
Delivery and physical distribution	Why don't we ever have the right merchandise in inventory?	We can't keep everything in inventory
Quality assurance	Why can't we have reasonable quality at reasonable cost?	Why must we always offer options that are too hard to manufacture and that offer little customer utility?
Breadth of product line	Our customers demand variety	The product line is too broad—all we get are short uneconomical runs
Cost control	Our costs are so high that we are not competitive in the marketplace	We can't provide fast delivery, broad variety, rapid response to change, and high quality at low cost
New product introduction	New products are our life blood	Unnecessary design changes are prohibitively expensive
Adjunct services such as spare parts inventory support, installation, and repair	Field service costs are too high	Products are being used in ways for which they weren't designed

Source. Shapiro, 1977.

200

itself likely to lead to a substantial increase in harmony between marketing and manufacturing. Instead, one needs to understand, in managerial terms, why that interface can so easily become a fault line in the firm—where the requirements that marketing places on manufacturing and the capabilities that the manufacturing process technology provides to marketing grind against each other, in opposite directions. One approach to developing that kind of understanding is based on an analysis of how product and process life cycles interact.

The regularity of the growth cycles of living organisms has long fascinated thoughtful observers, and invited a variety of attempts to apply the same principles—of a predictable sequence of rapid growth followed by maturation and decline—to companies and industries. The "product life cycle," for example, has been studied in a wide range of organizational settings, although there are sufficient questions (see, for example, Dhalla and Yuspeh, 1976) to raise doubts as to the universal application of the concept.

Irrespective of whether the product life cycle pattern is a general rule or holds only for isolated cases, it does provide general managers with a useful and provocative framework for thinking about the growth and development of a new product, a company, or an entire industry. However, one major shortcoming of this approach is that it focuses primarily on the marketing implications of the life cycle pattern, often to the exclusion of its manufacturing implications. In so doing it implies either that other aspects of the business and industry environment move in concert with the product life cycle, or that they are inconsequential. While such a view may help one reflect upon the kinds of changes that have occurred in different industries, an individual company or product line manager may find it too simplistic to be useful as a planning tool. In fact, the concept may even be misleading if it is used as the primary basis for strategic planning.

In attempting to relate the life cycle that governs products and markets to manufacturing technology, we begin by reviewing the way the life cycle is typically used in marketing analyses. Then we discuss an analogous concept called the manufacturing *process* life cycle. While the product life cycle describes how the growth and maturation of products and markets place changing demands on manufacturing, the process life cycle describes how the nature of and the capabilities provided by a process technology evolve through different stages.

7-2.1   Market Requirements and the Product Life Cycle

When marketers use this concept, they usually attempt to model a product's evolution over time by identifying a series of distinguishable stages that it passes through: introduction, rapid growth, competitive turbulence, maturation, and decline. Figure 7-2 describes the changes in strategic objectives, competition, product design, pricing, promoting, distribution, and informational requirements that are associated with each stage.

While the product life cycle is useful primarily in planning a firm's marketing strategy, one can also relate it indirectly to the firm's manufacturing

Figure 7-2   Dimensions of the product life cycle concept important to marketing

	Market development (introductory period for high learning products only)	Rapid growth (normal introductory pattern for a very low learning product)	Competitive turbulence	Saturation (maturity)	Decline
Strategy objective	Minimize learning requirements, locate and remedy offering defects quickly, develop widespread awareness of benefits, and gain trial by early adopters	To establish a strong brand market and distribution niche as quickly as possible	To maintain and strengthen the market niche achieved through dealer and consumer loyalty	To defend brand position against competing brands and product category against other potential products, through constant attention to product improvement opportunities and fresh promotional and distribution approaches	To milk the offering dry of all possible profit
Outlook for competition	None is likely to be attracted in the early, unprofitable stages	Early entrance of numerous aggressive emulators	Price and distribution squeezes on the industry, shaking out the weaker entrants	Competition stabilized. Few or no new entrants. Market shares relatively stable except when a brand gains substantial added perceived value through product improvement or price repositioning	Similar competition declining and dropping out because of decrease in consumer interest
Product design objective	Limited number of models with physical product and offering designs both focussed on minimizing learning requirements. Designs cost- and use-engineered to appeal to most receptive segment. Utmost attention to quality control and quick elimination of market-revealed defects in design	Modular design to facilitate flexible addition of variants to appeal to every new segment and new use system as fast as discovered	Intensified attention to product improvement, tightening up of line to eliminate unnecessary specialties with little market appeal	A constant alert for market pyramiding opportunities through either bold cost- and price-penetration of new markets or major product changes. Introduction of flanker products. Constant attention to possibilities for product improvement and cost cutting. Reexamination of necessity of design compromises	Constant pruning of line to eliminate any items not returning a direct profit
Pricing objective	To impose the minimum of value perception learning and to match the value reference perception of the most receptive segments. High trade discounts and sampling advisable	A price line for every taste, from low-end to premium models. Customary trade discounts. Aggressive promotional pricing, with prices cut as fast as costs decline due to accumulated production experience. Intensification of sampling	Increased attention to market-broadening and promotional pricing opportunities	Price repositioning whenever demand pattern and competitors' strategies permit. Defensive pricing to preserve product category franchise. Search for incremental pricing opportunities, including private label contracts, to boost volume and gain an experience advantage	Maintenance of profit level pricing with complete disregard of any effect on market share
Promotional guidelines Communications objectives	a) Create widespread awareness and understanding of offering benefits b) Gain trial by early adopters	Create and strengthen brand preference among trade and final users. Stimulate general trial	Maintain consumer franchise and strengthen dealer ties	Maintain consumer and trade loyalty, with strong emphasis on dealers and distributors. Promotion of greater use frequency	Phase out, keeping just enough to maintain profitable distribution
Most valuable media mix	In order of value: Publicity Personal sales Mass communications	Mass media Personal sales Sales promotions, including sampling Publicity	Mass media Dealer promotions Personal selling to dealers Sales promotions Publicity	Mass media Dealer-oriented promotions	Cut down all media to the bone—use no sales promotions of any kind
Distribution policy	Exclusive or selective, with distributor margins high enough to justify heavy promotional spending	Intensive and extensive, with dealer margins just high enough to keep them interested. Close attention to rapid resupply of distributor stocks and heavy inventories at all levels	Intensive and extensive, a strong emphasis on keeping dealer well supplied, but with minimum inventory costs	Intensive and extensive, with strong emphasis on keeping dealer well supplied, but at minimum inventory cost to him	Phase out outlets as they become marginal
Intelligence focus	To identify actual developing use-systems and to uncover any product weaknesses	Detailed attention to brand position, to gaps in model and market coverage, and to opportunities for market segmentation	Close attention to product improvement needs, to market-broadening chances, and to possible fresh promotion themes	Close analysis of competitors' strategies. Regular monitoring of trends in use patterns and possible product improvements. Sharp alert for potential new technological and new interproduct competition or other signs of beginning product decline	Information helping to identify the point at which the product should be phased out

(*Source.* Wasson, 1978. Used by permission.)

strategy. Figure 7-3 suggests the implications that different product life cycle stages have for four issues that are directly linked to manufacturing: production volume, product variety, industry structure, and the dominant form of competition. For example, manufacturing has a major stake in decisions that may affect such variables as product customization (versus standardization), volume per model, and the average time before obsolescence or replacement. Given this perspective, the product life cycle can be used to summarize the customer and product requirements that must be satisfied by the manufacturing function and its product technology.

A second aspect of the product life cycle that has a direct impact on manufacturing has to do with the nature of industry competition and the firm's

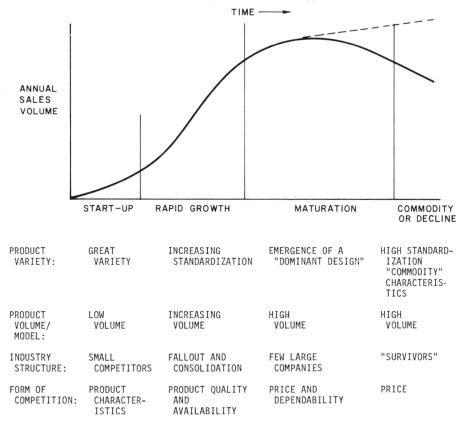

Figure 7-3   Characteristics of the product life cycle important to manufacturing process technology

	START–UP	RAPID GROWTH	MATURATION	COMMODITY OR DECLINE
PRODUCT VARIETY:	GREAT VARIETY	INCREASING STANDARDIZATION	EMERGENCE OF A "DOMINANT DESIGN"	HIGH STANDARD-IZATION "COMMODITY" CHARACTERIS-TICS
PRODUCT VOLUME/MODEL:	LOW VOLUME	INCREASING VOLUME	HIGH VOLUME	HIGH VOLUME
INDUSTRY STRUCTURE:	SMALL COMPETITORS	FALLOUT AND CONSOLIDATION	FEW LARGE COMPANIES	"SURVIVORS"
FORM OF COMPETITION:	PRODUCT CHARACTER-ISTICS	PRODUCT QUALITY AND AVAILABILITY	PRICE AND DEPENDABILITY	PRICE

major competitors. As suggested in Figure 7-3, the maturation of a market generally leads to fewer competitors, increasing industry concentration, and competition based more on price and delivery than on unique product features. As the competitive focus shifts during the different stages of the product life cycle, the requirements placed on manufacturing (in terms of cost, quality, flexibility, and delivery dependability) also shift.

A third aspect has to do with the nature of the product itself. The stage of the product life cycle affects the product's design stability, the length of the product development cycle, the frequency of engineering change orders, and the commonality of components—all of which have implications for the manufacturing process technology.

In short, the product life cycle concept provides a framework for thinking about both a product's evolution through time and the kind of market segments that are likely to develop at various points in time. It also highlights the need to change the priorities that govern manufacturing behavior as products and markets evolve. These priorities, in turn, have important repercussions for the process technology employed. As we see in Section 7-3, it is not always easy to determine when shifts take place in a product's position along its life cycle; trying to ascertain implications of such shifts for the manufacturing function (for example, adjusting the process technology so that its capabilities better meet market requirements) can be even more difficult.

7-2.2   Manufacturing Capabilities and the Process Life Cycle

While the life cycle concept has not been applied to manufacturing processes nearly as extensively as it has to product and market development, a number of authors have suggested that such cycles exist. As summarized in Table 7-2, Abernathy and Townsend (1975) have broken down the evolution of a production process into three major stages—early, middle, and mature. For each stage they describe six important characteristics that are of concern to manufacturing managers. Using technology that is analogous to that used in conjunction with the product life cycle, Table 7-2 suggests that a process life cycle begins with a "fluid" production process: one that is highly flexible but not very cost efficient. Then it proceeds toward increasing standardization, mechanization, and automation until it eventually becomes "systemic": very efficient, but much more capital-intensive, interrelated, and hence less flexible than the original "fluid" process (see Section 6-3).

The description of the process life cycle in Table 7-2 can be very useful in manufacturing planning and decision making, but it also can be used at a general management level to relate specific manufacturing capabilities to various stages of the process life cycle. For example, it can be used to predict how the product's manufacturing cost per unit is likely to change over time (Figure 7-4). While the stages through which the product technology passes do not necessarily match exactly those of the product life cycle, we attach the same names to them.

The first stage in the development of a process technology has the characteristics of a job shop. It is flexible (and therefore able to cope with low volumes) because it has few rigid interconnections; it is characterized by little automation or vertical integration. As the process matures, it passes through intermediate stages that may involve decoupled line flows (batch processes) and/or connected line flows (assembly lines). Eventually, the process technology may evolve into a continuous flow operation with high throughput volumes, low rates of process innovation, and less flexibility due to high levels of automation and vertical integration. A number of dimensions can be used to characterize these various stages. Four of these are of particular importance to manufacturing: process organization, throughput volume, rate of process innovation, and the levels of automation and vertical integration. These are summarized in Figure 7-4.

The concept of a process life cycle can be of great usefulness to general managers for two reasons. First, it conveys a sense of the capabilities provided by different stages of the process cycle, and second, it identifies the key tasks that must be carried out if those capabilities are to be provided. The stage of

Table 7-2

Dimensions of Process Technology Evolution Important to Manufacturing Management

Stage in the Productive Unit Life Cycle	Material and Parts—Inputs	Process Characteristics		Scale	Product	Modes of Process Change (in transition from one stage to the next)
		Technology	Labor			
I. Early	Raw materials and parts used as available from supplier Types and quality vary widely Limited influence over supplier	General-purpose equipment and tools used as available from industry Special adaptations to general-purpose machines are made by user (jigs, fixtures, etc.). Flow-through process needs careful management control	Most workers have a broad range of performance skills Considerable flexibility exists in type of tasks each worker can and must perform Labor organization (if any) is along craft or skill (trade unionism)	Capacity ill defined Greater volume achieved by paralleling existing processes Short-run economies of scale achieved through learning curve improvement of manual operations Few scale barriers to entry into industry segment	Great variety of products with different features and quality Frequent design change Market relatively insensitive to price and quality (imperfect market that is price inelastic)	Process rationalization Standardize tasks Develop even flow through all process steps Automate easy tasks Introduce systematic or mechanized materials handling Redesign product and process to automate difficult tasks ⇒

205

Table 7-2 (continued)

Dimensions of Process Technology Evolution Important to Manufacturing Management

Stage in the Productive Unit Life Cycle	Material and Parts—Inputs	Process Characteristics		Scale	Product	Modes of Process Change (in transition from one stage to the next)
		Technology	Labor			
II. Middle	Suppliers are strongly dependent Tailored material specifications imposed on supplier	Process automation is evident for some process tasks and systematized work flow Level of automation varies widely within process; islands of highly automated equipment are linked by manual operations Unique process equipment is designed for some tasks (often by outside firms)	Manual tasks are highly structured and standardized Labor is specialized with technical skills becoming more important Overhead labor functions such as maintenance scheduling and control are a significant cost	Capacity increased by equipment addition and advances to debottleneck particular operations Minimum size process necessary to compete in industry segment	Some segments of market sensitive to price and quality (encouraging standard products and scale economies) Significant volume achieved in some product lines	Systemic development Separate difficult-to-automate tasks from process or eliminate them Design products to have maximum common process elements Arrange administrative organization for congruence of control over process flow ⟹

206

III. Mature	Input's characteristics are optimized to process needs Supplier process integrated into overall process design Tasks that cannot be automated are segregated from process and are often subcontracted or performed by suppliers	Single units of equipment perform multiple process tasks and are integrated into automatic material handling equipment Formal systems engineering is required for process change Process equipment is designed as an integrated system, often by separate engineering groups or engineering companies Licensed technology may dominate, depending on the industry	Direct labor does monitoring and maintenance tasks Most important skills concern technical process equipment operation Labor classifications are rigid and are of primary concern to labor organization	Complete new facilities designed to achieve economies through spread costs Market growth and technological evolution pace scale increase Antitrust laws, logistics, or external factors eventually limit scale growth	Product variability is low and volume is high Standard products if price competition is prevalent or standard groups of products if product differentiation is prevalent Co- and by-products play greater role	Product and process realignment to meet changing markets and technological advances (may reset to earlier stage, 1 or 2 or stagnate during maturation)

Source. Abernathy and Townsend, 1975. Used by permission.

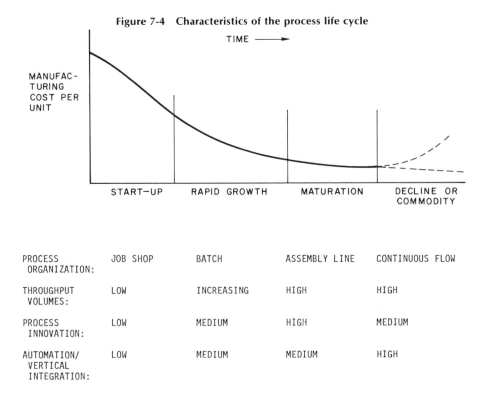

Figure 7-4   Characteristics of the process life cycle

PROCESS ORGANIZATION:	JOB SHOP	BATCH	ASSEMBLY LINE	CONTINUOUS FLOW
THROUGHPUT VOLUMES:	LOW	INCREASING	HIGH	HIGH
PROCESS INNOVATION:	LOW	MEDIUM	HIGH	MEDIUM
AUTOMATION/ VERTICAL INTEGRATION:	LOW	MEDIUM	MEDIUM	HIGH

the process life cycle in which a specific business finds itself at a given point in time is determined by decisions made both outside manufacturing (such as product line breadth, sales volume, and product design) and inside (equipment, materials flow, and information systems). Thus the evolution of a process technology can be viewed as a natural complement to the evolution of product technology; general managers should understand and work with both.

7-3   INTEGRATING PROCESS TECHNOLOGY CAPABILITIES AND PRODUCT/MARKET REQUIREMENTS THROUGH THE PRODUCT–PROCESS MATRIX

Figure 7-5 suggests one way in which the interaction of the product life cycle and the process life cycle can be represented. The rows in this matrix represent the major stages through which a production process tends to pass in going from the fluid form (top row) to the systemic form (botttom row). The columns represent product life cycle phases that progress from the great variety associated with the product's initial introduction (on the left) to the standardization associated with commodity products (on the right).

A company, a business unit within a diversified firm, or a product line can be characterized as occupying a particular region in this matrix, as deter-

Figure 7-5   Matching major stages of product and process life cycles—
the product-process matrix

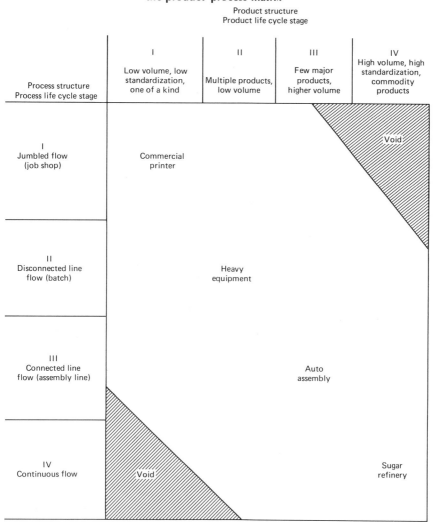

(*Source.* Hayes and Wheelwright, 1979a.)

mined by its stage in the product life cycle and its stage in the process life cycle. Some simple examples will illustrate this. Typical of a company positioned in the upper left-hand corner is a commercial printer. In such a firm each job is unique, and a jumbled flow or job-shop process (having the characteristics described in Chapter 6) is most effective in meeting product/market requirements. The market requires variety and relatively low volume per order, and competition consists of many firms offering a variety of product characteristics. A job shop process permits the economic production of relatively small lots, and requires great flexibility in workers and equipment.

Farther down the diagonal of this matrix, heavy equipment manufacturers usually choose a production technology characterized as a disconnected line flow (batch) process. This provides them with the capability to produce somewhat higher volumes, at somewhat lower unit costs, than would be possible with a job shop but retains considerable flexibility to produce a wide variety of products and customized features. The market, on the other hand, requires less variety than that served by the commercial printer, say, and may accept a basic catalog of models having a variety of options. Competition is likely to be among fewer competitors and is typically based on product quality, features, and availability.

Even farther down the diagonal are found producers of such products as automobiles or major home appliances. These companies generally choose to use a relatively mechanized and connected production process, such as a moving assembly line, that offers still lower unit costs but is much less flexible. The capabilities and constraints of this process fit with the market's requirements and competitive behavior.

Finally, down in the lower right-hand corner of the matrix are found such businesses as sugar or oil refining, where the product is essentially a commodity (in that price and delivery terms may vary slightly from competitor to competitor, but other product characteristics are essentially standard). The production process used is based on a continuous flow technology that makes possible low variable costs and high product consistency, at the expense of high fixed costs and low manufacturing flexibility. While such inflexibility and capital intensiveness would be a major disadvantage in businesses further up the matrix diagonal, the cost and delivery capabilities of continuous processes make them appropriate for the manufacture of such items as high-volume food products or chemicals.

The upper right-hand and lower left-hand corners of the matrix depicted in Figure 7-5 are empty. The upper right-hand corner characterizes a commodity product produced with a job shop process. This is simply uneconomical given a job shop's high variable costs. Rarely would a company knowingly locate itself in that sector because of the mismatch between market requirements and process capabilities. The lower left-hand corner represents a similar mismatch: the manufacture of very low volume products using a continuous, high fixed cost production process. Such a process is simply too inflexible to accommodate the changeovers required by a variety of unique product requirements.

7-3.1   Applications: Matching Products and Processes over Time

The examples cited above are the more common ones, involving "diagonal matches"—in which a certain kind of product structure (set of market characteristics) is paired with its "natural" process structure (set of manufacturing characteristics). However, a business may consciously seek a position away from the diagonal in order to differentiate itself from its competitors. Rolls-Royce Ltd., for example, still makes a very narrow line of motor cars using a process that is more like a job shop than an assembly line. On the other hand, a company that allows itself to drift away from the diagonal without understanding the likely implications of such a shift may end up with an unintended mismatch. This can spell significant trouble for the organization, as apparently occurred in the manufactured housing industry during the housing boom of the early 1970s, when several companies allowed (or encouraged) their manufacturing operations to become too capital intensive and configured around the needs of stable, high-volume production.

As a business moves farther away from the diagonal, it becomes increasingly dissimilar from its competitors. This may or may not make it more vulnerable to attack, depending on its success in achieving focus and exploiting the advantages of such a niche. It may also make it more difficult to coordinate its marketing and manufacturing functions, as the two areas confront increasingly different opportunities and pressures. Not infrequently companies find that, either inadvertently or by conscious choice, their positions on the matrix have become very dissimilar from those of their competitors, and drastic remedial action must be considered. This sometimes occurs, for example, when a domestic market is insulated from international competition for a long period of time, and then new international competitors suddenly enter that market with very different process technologies and/or product structures. It also occurs when small companies enter a relatively mature industry, and provides one explanation of both the strengths and weaknesses that are usually associated with their situation.

An example of two companies that chose very different approaches to matching their movements along these two dimensions with industry changes involves Zenith Radio Corporation and RCA in the mid-1960s, the high growth stage of the color TV industry's product life cycle. Zenith had traditionally followed a strategy of maintaining a high degree of flexibility in its manufacturing facilities. This would be characterized on the matrix as being somewhat above the diagonal. As described in Chapter 3, when planning additional capacity for color TV manufacturing in 1966 (on the basis of forecasts that industry sales would double over the next three years), Zenith chose to expand in a way that represented a clear move down the process dimension towards the matrix diagonal. It consolidated color TV assembly into two large plants, one of which was in a relatively low-cost labor area in the United States. While Zenith continued to have manufacturing facilities that were more flexible than those of other companies in its industry, this decision reflected corporate management's assessment of the need to stay within range of the rest of its competitors on the process dimension so that its excellent marketing strategy would not be constrained by significant manufacturing inefficiencies.

During this same period, RCA (which had traditionally chosen to lead the industry in adopting newer, more mechanized manufacturing technologies) was introducing highly automated and specialized equipment, such as transfer lines which automatically inserted electronic components into printed circuit boards. As the market evolved toward higher volumes and more standardized products, this represented a move down the process dimension to a position below the diagonal. This strategy backfired when the introduction of integrated circuits and totally solid-state designs obsoleted much of this automated equipment.

Six years after Zenith's 1966 realignment of its position on the process life cycle, it made another decision to keep all of its assembly of color TV sets in the United States rather than lose the flexibility and incur the cost of moving production to the Far East. This decision, in conjunction with others made during the mid-1970s, was called into question toward the end of that decade. Zenith again found itself too far above the diagonal in comparison with its large, primarily Japanese, competitors, most of whom had mechanized their production processes, positioned them in low-wage countries, and embarked on other cost-reduction programs typical of a position farther down and below the matrix diagonal. Zenith then decided to move most of its subassembly production to low wage locations outside the United States. These alternative competitive approaches can be depicted on the product–process matrix as shown in Figure 7-6.

Separating the major stages of the process life cycle from the stages of the product life cycle can be extremely helpful when general managers are grappling with the need to match process technology capabilities with product market requirements. Using this kind of two-dimensional representation encourages more creative thinking about organizational competences and the competitive role that various parts of the business can play. It can also lead to more informed predictions about the changes that are likely to occur in a particular industry, and to the development of a richer set of functional strategies for responding to such changes. Finally, it provides a natural way to bring manufacturing managers and marketing managers together so that they can relate their opportunities and decisions more effectively to overall business objectives. While this chapter deals primarily with the impact of process technology shifts within the product–process matrix, it also has implications for other aspects of manufacturing strategy, as we see in the next section.

7-3.2   Implications of Different Product–Process Choices

In this section we consider three issues that arise naturally when considering the interaction of product and process life cycles: (1) the concept of an organization's distinctive competence; (2) the management implications of selecting a particular product and process combination in light of competitors' selections; and (3) organizing different operating units so that they can specialize (focus) on separate portions of the total manufacturing task while still maintaining effective overall coordination.

The Concept of Distinctive Competence

Most companies like to think of themselves as being particularly good, relative to their competitors, in certain areas whereas they try to avoid head-to-head

Figure 7-6   Product-process matrix for U.S. color television (1960s to mid-1970s)

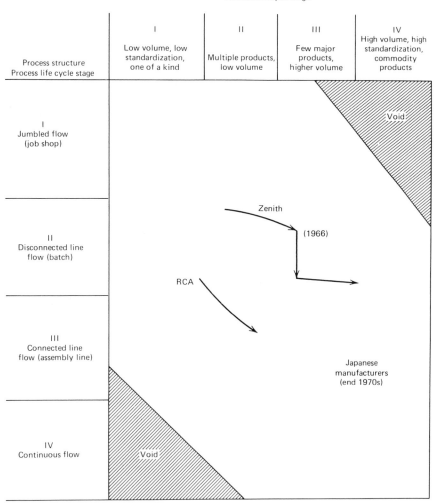

competition in other areas. Their objective is to guard this distinctive competence against outside attack or internal aimlessness and to exploit it wherever possible. Unfortunately, companies sometimes become preoccupied with the marketing aspects of their distinctive competence and lose sight of the nature of their competence in manufacturing. When this happens, the company's strategic thinking tends to be dominated by product, market, and product life cycle considerations. In effect, management concentrates its resources and planning efforts on a relatively narrow column of the matrix shown in Figure 7-5.

One of the advantages of a two-dimensional point of view is that it encourages a business unit to be more precise about what its distinctive competence really is, and to concentrate its attention on a restricted set of process technology alternatives as well as a restricted set of marketing and product alternatives. Real focus is achieved only when one's attention is concentrated on a "patch" in the matrix—implying a process focus as well as a product focus. As we argue in our discussion of facilities strategy in Chapter 4, narrowing the focus of a business unit's activities, and particularly its manufacturing activities, often can lead to substantial improvement in organizational performance. In fact, the notion of facilities focus discussed there relates both to the specific focus of a given physical facility and to the general focus of a firm's overall process technology capabilities.

Thinking about both process and product dimensions can even affect the way a company defines its "product." For example, the management of one specialized manufacturer of printed circuit boards initially assessed its position on the product–process matrix as being in the lower left-hand corner: producing a low-volume, one-of-a-kind product using a highly connected assembly line process. On further reflection, however, management decided that while the company did specialize in small production batches, the "product" it really was offering was a design capability for special-purpose circuit boards. In a sense it was mass producing designs rather than boards. Hence the company was not far off the diagonal after all. This reconceptualization of the company's distinctive competence was helpful when management began to consider a set of proposed investments which varied greatly in terms of their fit with the company's *actual* position on the matrix.

Not only can the use of a product–process matrix help make explicit a firm's (or business unit's) distinctive competence, it can also help it avoid the dangers of product or process proliferation. Introducing a new product or entering a new market, either in an attempt to increase the utilization of existing facilities or simply to take advantage of the apparent profitability of a customer request for a modified product, can lead to a continually expanding product line—in effect causing the business unit to move horizontally to the left on the matrix. Unfortunately this often sets in motion a scenario that is difficult for most firms to deal with, because both the production and marketing sides of the business tend to encounter problems (different but complementary) at the same time. Marketing is trying to adapt itself to new products (and, possibly, markets) for which its procedures are not adequately suited, while production is trying to adapt its processes to new products which put analogous strains on its operation.

This can lead to what has been described as the "creeping breakeven" phenomenon: in an effort to stimulate demand a company enters a new market or introduces a new product. While this move may be successful, the existing process technology is incapable of meeting this added scale and complexity without additional investment (more capacity, different equipment, or other changes). Success breeds failure. The increased investment causes the company's breakeven point to rise, offsetting the expected gains from the increased sales volume. This motivates the company to pursue additional markets and products so as to "break out of the box" in which it finds itself. Within the context of the product–process matrix, the business finds itself trying to move along one dimension while not adequately adjusting its position on the other. Eventually it is forced to move along that other dimension as well. If this represents an *expansion* of its process (for example, adding a job shop to what is essentially an assembly line process) rather than a *repositioning,* however, it tends to dilute the company's manufacturing focus, making it more and more difficult to match the success that other firms—who continue to focus on their distinctive competence—are able to achieve.

The packaging division of one major consumer products company provides an illustration of this syndrome. The sole reason for the division's existence in the corporation was to offer a low cost source of supply for a highly specialized packaging product. Being a profit center, this division realized that if it could pick up some less specialized, high-priced business from outside customers, it would be able to increase substantially its profitability. (At least that is what its cost accounting system indicated!) As the division moved in that direction, however, it encountered pressure from its new customers to change its process technology so that it could better meet their needs. As the division began to dilute the focus it had previously maintained, it experienced increasing friction with its original in-house customers.

This scenario is also observed when an industry leader finds its standardized product line being challenged by smaller firms who attempt to segment the mass market and target specialized forms of the product for different segments. Over time such competition may slowly erode the leading firm's market share to the point where its relatively high-volume, standardized process is no longer economical. In an attempt to counterattack, it may introduce specialized products of its own (in effect, moving to the left on the product dimension), only to find that its process technology cannot compete effectively with competitors who have focused their process technologies around the specific volume and product characteristics best suited to each segment of the market.

Management Implications of Different Product–Process Positioning Strategies

As firms alter their positions on the matrix by making different product and process choices, their competitive priorities and management tasks are profoundly affected. Looking at the process technology dimension, for example, we observe that the chief competitive advantage of a job shop process is its flexibility to both product and volume changes. As a firm moves toward more standardized process technologies, its distinguishing capabilities shift from flexibility and customization (product specialization) to product reliability, delivery predictability, and cost. A similar shift in competitive emphasis occurs as the firm moves along the product structure dimension. These movements and their associated priorities are illustrated in Figure 7-7 and described in more detail in Chapter 10. In general, a company that chooses a given process struc-

Figure 7-7 Competitive priorities and key tasks on the product–process matrix

Process Structure—Process Life Cycle Stage	Product Structure—Product Life Cycle Stage				Priorities	Key Manage Tasks
	I Low-volume/ low-stand-ardization, one of a kind	II Low-volume, multiple products	III Higher volume few major products	IV High-volume/ high-stand-ardization, commodity products		
I Jumbled flow (job shop)					Flexibility–quality Product customization Performance	Fast reactio Loading pla estimating pacity Estimating c and deliver times Breaking bo necks Order tracir and expedi
II Disconnected line flow (batch)						Systematizin diverse ele Developing standards a methods, i provement Balancing p cess stages
III Connected line flow (assembly line)						Managing l specialized complex o tions
						Meeting ma requireme Running eq ment at pe ficiency Timing exp sion and t nological change
IV Continuous flow					Dependability–cost	Raising req capital

Priorities	Flexibility–quality		Dependability–cost	
Dominant Competitive Mode	Custom de-sign General pur-pose High margins	Custom design Quality control Service High margins	Standar-dized design Volume manufac-turing Finished goods inventory Distribu-tion Backup suppliers	Vertical inte-gration Long runs Specialized equipment and processes Economies of scale Standardized material

216

ture can reinforce the characteristics of that structure by adopting the corresponding product structure.

For a given product structure, a company whose competitive strategy is based on offering customized products or features and rapid response to market shifts would tend to choose a much more flexible production technology than would a competitor that has the same product structure but follows a low-cost strategy. The former approach positions the company above the matrix diagonal; the latter positions it somewhere along or below the diagonal.

A company's location on the matrix also reflects what we referred to as its "dominant orientation" in Chapter 2. Most firms tend to be relatively aggressive along the dimension—product or process—where they feel most competent, and assume that the other dimension is a "given," in that it is determined by competitors and the general state of technological process in the industry. For example, a marketing-oriented company that is seeking to be responsive to the needs of a given market is more likely to emphasize flexibility and rapid delivery than is a more manufacturing-oriented company that seeks to mold the market to its own cost position or product specifications.

These two contrasting competitive approaches are illustrated in the electric motor industry by Reliance Electric and Emerson Electric. Reliance typically has chosen production processes that placed it above the diagonal for a given product and market, and it emphasizes product customization and performance. Emerson, on the other hand, has tended to position itself below the diagonal, emphasizing low-cost production. The majority of Reliance's products are in the upper left quadrant, while Emerson's products tend to be in the lower right quadrant. Even where the two companies' product lines overlap, Reliance is likely to look for the more customized applications, and to use a more fluid process to produce that product, while Emerson is likely to use a more standardized production process. Each company is continually seeking to develop a set of competitive skills in manufacturing and marketing that will make it more effective within its selected quadrant.

The decision to concentrate on the upper left versus the lower right quadrant has many additional implications for a business. A company that chooses to compete primarily in the upper left, for example, has to decide when to drop a product or abandon a market that appears to be progressing inexorably along its product life cycle toward maturity, while a company that chooses to compete in the lower right must decide when to enter that market. The latter company does not need to be as flexible as the company that positions itself in the upper left. Moreover, since product and market changes typically occur less frequently during the latter phases of the product life cycle, it has more room for error.

Organizing (Focusing) Operating Units to Encourage Specialization and Coordination

A company that takes into consideration the process dimension when formulating its competitive strategy can usually focus its operating units much more effectively on their individual tasks. For example, many companies face the problem of how to organize the production of spare parts for their primary products. As the sales volume of its primary products increases, the company tends to move down the matrix diagonal. The follow-on demand for spare parts for these products, however, may imply a combination of product and process structures much more toward the upper left-hand corner of the matrix. There are many more items to be manufactured, each in smaller volume, and the appropriate process tends to be more flexible than is the case for the primary products.

To accommodate the specific requirements of spare parts production, some companies develop a special manufacturing facility for them; others simply separate their production within the same facility. The least appropriate— and, unfortunately, most common—approach is to combine the production of spare parts with that of the basic product, which forces the manufacturing process to span a broad range of both product and process structures, reducing its effectiveness for both product categories.

The combined choice of product and process also determines the kind of manufacturing problems that are likely to be experienced. Some of the key tasks related to a particular process technology are indicated on the right-hand side of Figure 7-7. Recognizing the impact that the company's position on the matrix has on these important tasks often suggests changes in the policies and procedures used in managing the company's manufacturing function, particularly its manufacturing control system. The measurements used to monitor and evaluate manufacturing performance should also reflect the matrix position selected. Unfortunately, as Richardson and Gordon's survey (1980) of 15 manufacturing companies illustrates, most companies tend to use standardized measurement and control systems, no matter what their position on the matrix. Not only can designing more customized systems help a company avoid the loss of control over manufacturing that often results when its position on the matrix changes, it also suggests the changes in management skills, attitudes, and mindsets that may be needed.

While a fairly narrow focus may be required to succeed in any single product market, large companies generally produce multiple products for multiple markets. These products are often in different stages of their life cycles. Such companies can often benefit by separating their manufacturing facilities, and organizing each to meet the specific needs of different products.

In Chapter 4 we described one company that chose to separate its total manufacturing capabilities into a group of carefully specialized units: the Lynchburg Foundry Corporation. As outlined there, Lynchburg Foundry operates several different facilities, each representing a different position on the matrix. While each plant uses a somewhat different basic technology, they have many similarities. However, other elements of the manufacturing process used in each plant, such as the production layout, equipment, workforce organization, and control system, are very different. Lynchburg has chosen to design its facilities so that each meets the needs of a specific segment of the market.

This example of positioning individual manufacturing facilities (and their process technologies) to meet certain market segment requirements suggests another use for the matrix: identifying the suppliers who are most capable of meeting a company's needs. For example, high-volume automotive facilities need suppliers who can handle high-volume standardized products, whereas manufacturers of custom equipment who position themselves in the upper left quadrant are likely to be served much more effectively by suppliers who are also positioned in that quadrant.

On the other hand, companies that specialize their manufacturing units according to the needs of narrowly defined patches on the matrix may encounter problems integrating those units organizationally into a coordinated whole. Companies seem to be most successful when they organize their manufacturing function around either a product/market focus or a process focus, but not both. That is, individual operating units should either manage themselves relatively autonomously, responding directly to the needs of the particular markets they serve, or else they should be divided according to process stages (for example, fabrication, subassembly, and final assembly) and coordinated by a central staff (see Hayes and Schmenner, 1978).

Companies in the major materials industries—steel, oil, and paper, for example—provide classic examples of process-organized manufacturing operations. Most companies that broaden the span of their process through vertical integration tend to adopt such an organization, at least initially. By contrast, companies with a strong product/market orientation are usually unwilling to accept the organizational rigidity and lengthened response time that often accompany centralized coordination. For example, most companies in the packaging industry adopt such product/market-focused manufacturing organizations. They set up regional plants to serve geographical market areas in an attempt to reduce transportation costs and provide better response to customer needs.

Sometimes major competitive opportunities and entirely new market segments can be identified with the assistance of a product–process matrix. The restaurant industry, for example, has recently experienced major changes because it recognized such opportunities. As illustrated in Figure 7-8, the traditional short-order cafe uses a job shop process to produce low volumes of a wide variety of standard food items. The competitive emphasis of such local restaurants tends to be quick service and reasonable prices.

On the other hand, first-class restaurants almost invariably build their reputation by offering high-quality meals at high prices; service is slower but more elegant. Such restaurants are located in the extreme upper-left corner of the matrix. (In fact, it appears that some country restaurants in France are more properly located off the matrix—one sometimes gets the impression that the chef goes out and orders the raw materials for the meal after the customer places the order.)

In recent years, two new types of restaurants have made widespread gains in the marketplace by positioning themselves differently on the matrix. One of

Figure 7-8 Restaurant examples of product and process matching

Process Structure / Process Life Cycle Stage	Product Structure—Product Life Cycle Stage			
	I Low volume/low-standardization, one of a kind	II Low volume multiple products	III Higher volume few major products	IV High-volume high-standardization commodity products
I Jumbled flow (job shop)	Classic French restaurant			
	Traditional restaurant			
II Disconnected line flow (batch)		Short-order cafe		
III Connected line flow (assembly line)		Steak house		
			Burger King/ McDonald's	
IV Continuous flow				

these is the narrow-menu steak house, which concentrates on a single major type of food, offers a limited variety of side dishes, and employs a line flow production process. Several companies who were among the first to recognize the need for this type of service, and who tailored their skills and processes to meet the specific requirements of this market segment, have grown into substantial chains.

The so-called fast-food restaurants, like McDonald's, have positioned themselves even farther down the diagonal. They offer standardized products with few options and produce them in high volume with automated (or tightly controlled) processes. To ensure process standardization in such a service setting, McDonald's has designed its restaurants and chosen equipment in such a way that its site managers and workers are compelled to follow the intended production process.

But not all firms that attacked the fast-food market segment have followed the same philosophy and systems as McDonald's. Burger King, for example, has chosen to position itself in a slightly different location on the matrix, at least in the customers' eyes. As illustrated in Figure 7-8, Burger King has allowed customers a little more flexibility (they can select their own pickles, onions, catsup, and mustard), hoping to steal away from McDonald's those who prefer such "customization." While it may be hard to argue that offering customized condiments really represents a major difference in strategy, these two firms have also selected somewhat different production processes: Burger King "produces to order" (cooking hamburgers in response to individual orders), while McDonald's "produces to inventory."

Even in their advertising these two firms have sought to differentiate themselves. For example, McDonald's has used the phrase "We do it all for you." This really means "We run the production process the way it was set up to be run, and you don't have to worry about it (in fact, you can't interfere with it)." Burger King counters with "Have it *your* way." This suggests they will be responsive to individual customer requests, although they are constrained significantly by the narrow menu and standardized process they have adopted.

Like the U.S. auto companies, Burger King has adopted essentially the same position on the matrix as its major competitors, but it has sought to convince customers that they are actually farther to the left in their product structure. It has done this by offering options on items that have little effect on the production process but may affect customers' perceptions of the product and service being delivered (and perhaps the price they are willing to pay).

Offering customized products necessitates a close and effective interface between manufacturing and marketing. From a marketing point of view, almost all companies would prefer to offer broader product lines in order to match competitors' products. However, some manage such breadth much more effectively than do others. A firm that makes marketing decisions without taking manufacturing considerations into account may inadvertently cripple itself. For example, adding products whose market impact is marginal may seriously impair manufacturing effectiveness. In firms where marketing and manufacturing are closely coordinated, it is much more likely that the product options selected—like those at Burger King—will not detract from the firm's basic philosophy and matrix position.

As important as the marketing and manufacturing interface is in maintaining a desired position on the matrix, it is often no more critical than the interface between manufacturing and product engineering. When either engineering or manufacturing alters its basic strategy, the other must respond or the same types of mismatches that occur between manufacturing and marketing will occur. If communication across this interface is poor, engineering may design products that make it difficult, if not impossible, for manufacturing to employ the process technology it has chosen. In companies where the two functions cooperate closely and effectively, product design characteristics that are consistent with manufacturing capabilities are more likely.

7-3.3 Limits of the Product–Process Matrix Framework

Using the product–process matrix as a means for matching process technology and product line decisions has limitations, as does any theoretical construct. While these do not necessarily detract from the usefulness of the concept, it is important to keep in mind the fact that no single framework can ever handle all situations equally well. To suggest the nature of some of these limitations, we provide two illustrations in this section.

In this chapter we assume that the evolution of process technology along a process life cycle takes place through an ordered series of steps: standardization (of products, components, and equipment), rationalization (of flows, bottlenecks, and inventories), mechanization (of material conversion or handling steps, to replace labor), and, finally, automation (introduction of integrated systems that handle both material conversion and movement). This sequence is accompanied by increasing capital intensity, reduced process flexibility, and increased specificity to a narrower set of product and task requirements. Not all "progress" in process technology follows the same pattern, however.

For example, the recent development of flexible machining centers appears to offer firms both low cost and far greater flexibility for product changeovers than do older, less automated, and less capital-intensive processes. Similarly, some of the production practices adopted in Japan as part of "just-in-time" production and materials management systems require higher levels of equipment investment (together with lower machine utilization) but provide significantly increased production flexibility. Such improvements in production flexibility, in the absence of movement along the diagonal, might be thought of as a third dimension to the matrix. This dimension would represent increased overall effectiveness without a major change in the basic match between product life cycle and process life cycle. There are other approaches for handling changes in process technology that lead to improved performance without requiring compensating shifts in product/market offerings. The product–process matrix appears to be able to capture some of these, but not all; those other issues must be considered outside of the matrix.

A second example of the concept's limitations is when there is a breakdown in the assumption that a product's life cycle is equivalent to a market life cycle. While the two generally move in the same direction, they do not necessarily move at the same rate or to the same extent. The U.S. market for color television sets, for example, has clearly matured, yet numerous recent developments in product technology have caused the product life cycle to reverse direction—toward more variety and more options.

Another source of divergence between the product life cycle and the market life cycle occurs when the same product is sold into multiple markets. Again the color TV industry provides a good example. The personal computer and word processing markets, both of which were in the rapid growth stage of their life cycles in the early 1980s, utilize display devices that are similar in many respects to those found in TV receivers. Since they are often manufactured in the same facility, with the same production processes as TV displays, such products appear to be in the final stage of the product life cycle. Yet some of the products they go into are in the rapid growth stage. In a sense this limitation is simply the complement of one described earlier. In the case of flexible machining centers, a unidirectional process life cycle oversimplifies the realities of the situation, whereas in the case of display devices, a unidirectional product life cycle oversimplifies reality.

This latter difficulty also occurs when a market splits into price categories, and the products and customers in each major price segment follow separate product life cycles. In such a situation the low-end price segment may move very quickly to the final stage of the product life cycle, whereas higher price segments may never move beyond the middle stages. Many businesses appear to have these characteristics. For example, oscilloscopes, one of the most basic of electronic measuring devices, are positioned all along the matrix diagonal if the entire industry is lumped together. If split into two or three major price (and feature) segments, however, each can be represented by its own product–process matrix.

7-3.4 Integrating Product and Process Innovations

Shifts in position on the product–process matrix are often triggered by product or process innovations. Abernathy and Utterback (1975) have explored such innovations in some detail, and Figure 7-9 summarizes their research relating the rate of innovation along each dimension as the product life cycle evolves. Early in a product's life, great effort is expended on product design, and product innovation is rapid as competitors try to find a design that best fits the needs of potential users. Abernathy and Utterback refer to this early phase of product innovation as the search for a "dominant design"—a standardized product that can form the basis for rapid growth and market development. Ford's Model T car, the DC-3 airplane, the Xerox 914 copier, and the Kodak Instamatic camera are examples of such dominant designs.

According to Abernathy and Utterback, as the dominant design catches hold in the marketplace, cost reduction and process innovation geared primarily to lowering production costs, increasing yields, and building production

Figure 7-9   Patterns of product and process innovation

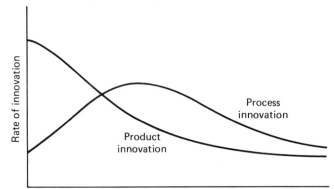

	Fluid Pattern	Transitional Pattern	Specific Pattern
Competitive emphases on	Functional product performance	Product variation	Cost reduction
Innovation stimulated by	Information on users' needs and users' technical inputs	Opportunities created by expanding internal technical capability	Pressure to reduce cost and improve quality
Predominant type of innovation	Frequent major changes in products	Major process changes required by rising volume	Incremental for product and process, with cumulative improvement in productivity and quality
Product line	Diverse, often including custom designs	Includes at least one product design stable enough to have significant production volume	Mostly undifferentiated standard products
Production processes	Flexible and inefficient major changes easily accommodated	Becoming more rigid with changes occurring in major steps	Efficient, capital-intensive, and rigid; cost of change is high
Equipment	General purpose, requiring highly skilled labor	Some subprocesses automated, creating "islands of automation"	Special purpose, mostly automatic with labor tasks mainly monitoring and control
Materials	Inputs are limited to generally available materials	Specialized materials may be demanded from some suppliers	Specialized materials will be demanded if they are not available, vertical integration will be extensive
Plants	Small-scale, located near user or source of technology	General purpose with specialized sections	Large-scale, highly specific to particular products
Organizational control	Informal and entrepreneurial	Through liaison relationships, project and task groups	Through emphasis on structure, goals, and rules

(*Source.* Abernathy and Utterback, 1975. Used by permission.)

volume begin to replace product innovation as the major focus of management attention. Product changes become less frequent and less radical, and process innovation begins to get more of the R&D budget. However, as investment in such activities moves the production technology closer to the continuous flow end of the process life cycle, both product and process become increasingly vulnerable to the introduction of a radically different new product (usually produced with a different process technology) that provides the same functions. Examples of this would be the replacement of mechanical calculators with electronic calculators, and the replacement of mechanical watches with electronic watches.

Achieving the appropriate balance between process innovation and product innovation is a critical management task. Some organizations simply focus their attention on a certain section of the process–product matrix, and concentrate their innovation efforts on one or the other of these two types of change. A classic example is Hewlett-Packard's instrument business, which has chosen to position itself in the upper left-hand quadrant of the product–process matrix. As most of its competitors have moved down the diagonal—where, according to Abernathy and Utterback, product innovation becomes less important and process innovation more important—HP has countered by introducing new product generations, and thereby moving back up to the left-hand corner. Thus it avoids the necessity to develop the organizational capabilities required for process innovation. In fact, many of HP's instrument businesses consider "innovation" to be synonymous with product innovation, and the manufacturing processes used are not changed unless required to do so by the next generation of product. When this happens, new processes are likely to be adapted, on an as-needed basis, from other industries where they are already well developed. Process and product transfer, not new process development or radical process innovation, becomes management's chief concern when contemplating changes in the manufacturing process.

A firm like Texas Instruments, on the other hand, has tended to concentrate its attention in the lower right-hand quadrant where process innovation tends to be more important than product innovation. TI often waits while others do much of the early product innovation (in the upper left-hand quadrant) until it identifies an appropriate entry point. After it enters, it uses its skills in process innovation to push rapidly down the matrix diagonal, displacing some of the product's original developers who neglected, either intentionally or unintentionally, to develop similar skills.

7-3.5 Product Technology Options and Manufacturing Process Technology

Up to this point we have assumed that there was a single dominant product technology, even when discussing product innovation. In some cases, however, companies have the choice of pursuing quite different product technologies, each of which may require a different process technology. One author who has explored some of the managerial issues associated with choosing among alternative product technologies is Abell (1980). In developing concepts for "defining one's business," he highlights three primary dimensions of concern to marketing managers: customer groups, customer functions, and alternative technologies. These dimensions and the way they might be used in developing alternative business definitions are illustrated in Figure 7-10.

Figure 7-10 A marketing definition of a business involving three dimensions

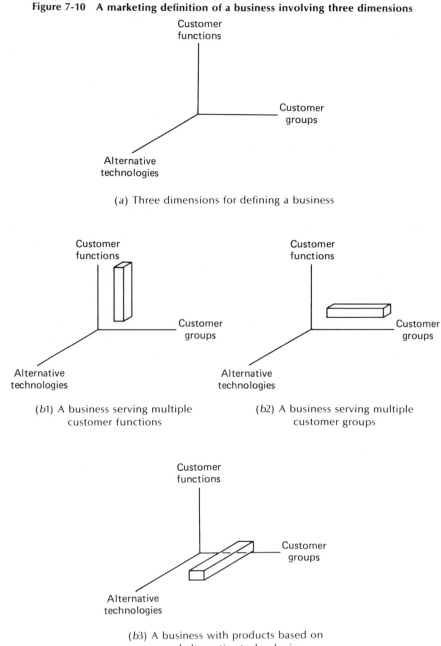

(*a*) Three dimensions for defining a business

(*b*1) A business serving multiple
customer functions

(*b*2) A business serving multiple
customer groups

(*b*3) A business with products based on
several alternative technologies

(*Source.* Abell, 1980. Used by permission.)

In Abell's terminology, firms (particularly their marketing functions) make decisions that define the range of their activities along each of three dimensions. (In a sense, he is splitting what we have called the product market dimension into three parts.) He uses the example of computerized tomography (CT) to illustrate the importance of looking at these dimensions separately. In the late 1970s four very different product technologies were available for diagnostic imaging: X-rays, computerized tomography (linking an X-ray machine to a computer), ultrasound, and nuclear. Each had been adopted as the primary product technology by at least one of the major competitors in the industry. Pfizer was pursuing computerized tomography, EMI and Ohio Nuclear were pursuing ultrasound, and GE was pursuing nuclear. Several other old-line equipment manufacturers were still heavily involved in traditional X-ray technology. In each firm, the selection of a particular product technology established different requirements for its process technology capabilities.

Refining the product market dimension, as suggested by Abell, can aid management's direction of process technology in three ways. First, by separating out the impact of product technology, its interaction with manufacturing technology can be addressed explicitly and systematically. Second, it highlights the need to coordinate and manage not only the manufacturing–marketing linkage, but also the manufacturing–product design and product design–marketing linkages. Third, the concept of focus is enriched by suggesting additional dimensions for specifying the degree of differentiation that a firm might pursue.

7-4 SUMMARY AND CONCLUSIONS

In this chapter we described and illustrated the use of a framework, the product–process matrix, that can help general managers link their company's process technology capabilities with product/market requirements. Other supporting concepts and techniques were also presented and outlined. Whatever techniques are used in a given situation, three major conclusions seem to emerge:

1. The development of a process technology strategy requires substantial general management inputs, not just functional expertise.

2. The integration of marketing and manufacturing is an iterative process. The firm must continually monitor market, product, manufacturing, and technological developments to insure that the desired match is pursued throughout the organization.

3. Designing a manufacturing process technology should not be an afterthought, a hurried response to market selection or product design. It must be configured around the needs of a particular product design and competitive strategy, while exploiting the availability of potentially applicable manufacturing technologies.

We pick up on these ideas in Chapter 10, where we discuss the management of changes in process technology.

SELECTED REFERENCES

Abell, Derek F. *Defining the Business: The Starting Point of Strategic Planning.* Englewood Cliffs, NJ: Prentice-Hall, 1980.

Abernathy, William J., and Phillip L. Townsend. "Technology, Productivity, and Process Change." *Technological Forecasting and Social Change,* 1975, Vol. 7, No. 4, pp. 379–396.

Abernathy, William J., and James Utterback. "Dynamic Model of Process and Product Innovation." *Omega,* Vol. 3, No. 6, 1975, pp. 639–657.

Blois, K. J. "Market Concentration—Challenge to Corporate Planning." *Long-Range Planning,* Vol. 13, August 1980, pp. 56–62.

Dhalla, N. K., and S. Yuspeh. "Forget the Product Life Cycle Concept." *Harvard Business Review,* January–February 1976, pp. 102–112.

Hayes, Robert H., and Roger W. Schmenner. "How Should You Organize Manufacturing?" *Harvard Business Review,* January–February 1978, pp. 105–118.

Hayes, Robert H., and Steven C. Wheelwright. "Link Manufacturing Process and Product Life Cycles." *Harvard Business Review,* January–February 1979, pp. 133–140.

Richardson, P. R., and Gordon, J. R. M. "Measuring Total Manufacturing Performance." *Sloan Management Review,* Winter 1980, pp. 47–58.

Shapiro, Benson P. "Can Marketing and Manufacturing Coexist?" *Harvard Business Review,* September–October 1977, pp. 104–114.

Wasson, Chester R. *Dynamic Competitive Strategy and Product Life Cycles.* Austin, TX: Austin Press, 1978.

Wells, Louis T., Jr. (ed.) *The Product Life Cycle in International Trade.* Cambridge, MA: Harvard University Press, 1972.

The Experience Curve

A FRAMEWORK FOR MANUFACTURING PERFORMANCE IMPROVEMENT

8-1   INTRODUCTION AND OVERVIEW

Changes in process technology are motivated by a variety of concerns, particularly those related to the cost of the product and the return on the assets invested. In this chapter we consider manufacturing cost dynamics (specifically, productivity improvement) within the framework of the learning curve, and its implications for both manufacturing strategy and business strategy.

The first systematic studies of the dynamic nature of manufacturing costs occurred in the 1920s (see Wright, 1936; Rohrbach, 1927). Analyses of airframe manufacturing for the Army Air Corps revealed significant opportunities for reducing the amount of labor required. The approach chosen—comparing direct labor hours required per unit of production to cumulative units produced—provided a relationship that was called first the "manufacturing progress function" and later the "learning curve." Subsequent studies over the past five decades have generally concluded that, for many products and industries, the direct labor per unit is a decreasing function of the cumulative number of units produced. When plotted on log-log paper, the data points tend to cluster around a straight line, suggesting that direct hours per unit can be approximated by some negative power of cumulative units.

Originally, learning curves only attempted to track and predict direct labor hours. More recently, the concept was broadened and the term "experience curve" was adopted. An experience curve relates *total* cost per unit (or, alternatively, value added per unit) to the cumulative number of units produced. As with a learning curve, an experience curve can often be approximated by a straight line when plotted on log-log paper. Both are examples of the dynamic economies of scale discussed in Chapter 3. We briefly discussed the relationship between static and dynamic economies of scale there, and we expand on that discussion in this chapter.

These concepts can be applied at a variety of organizational levels: individual worker, department within a factory, total factory, business (division), company, industry, and national economy. While the basic computational techniques used are analogous at each of these levels, collecting and interpreting actual data and determining their implications for management action can differ significantly depending on the level in question. It should be kept in mind, moreover, that an organization's experience curve is highly dependent on management behavior, and considerable judgment is required when applying such a curve to a specific situation. Although their mathematics may appear to be exact, their estimation is based on empirical data that are far from exact. Even the mathematics is suspect: it is not grounded on any natural laws and employs some very subjective assumptions.

The basic techniques for computing learning/experience curves are outlined in the next section, where we discuss the relationship between "learning" and "productivity growth." (The mathematics associated with the estimation and plotting of learning/experience curves is summarized in Appendix 8A.)

Section 8-3 contains several illustrations of actual learning/experience curves; these highlight some of the practical issues encountered when trying to calculate and apply the concept. In Section 8-4, we describe various actions that management can undertake to effect the rate at which cost improvements occur. A broad range of activities—from changing the way the workforce is organized, to technological innovation, to investment in new equipment—can combine to drive costs down.

In Section 8-5, some applications of learning/experience curves are examined at three levels. The first is that of the individual operation or business unit, and we describe how the experience curve can be used as a basis for developing a long-run cost reduction program. Most firms recognize the need for reducing costs (often this is stated in terms of a desired annual rate of productivity improvement), but they seldom know what rate of improvement is appropriate or how it can be achieved. As we will see, learning/experience curve theory can play a useful role in thinking about these issues.

At the second level we discuss how manufacturing strategy can be directly related to experience curve theory, and describe different strategies that businesses have adopted. (Appendix 8B shows how the strategy of an individual business can be tied to its overall corporate strategy using this concept.) At a third level, Section 8-5 looks at issues of industry and national productivity. Differences in the productivity growth rates of various manufacturing industries in different countries are interpreted using learning/experience curve concepts.

We conclude this chapter with some observations about both the usefulness and the limits of the learning/experience curve framework. These limits tend to be related more to market, environmental, and attitudinal constraints than physical or technological constraints. Moreover, managers often have to cut through organizational restrictions when attempting to coordinate the efforts of various corporate subgroups. This is particularly true in situations where one group (department, function, or division) is motivated to pursue systematic cost improvement, whereas others are motivated in different directions. Finally, we suggest that these concepts should be used only as a starting point, and as a complement to the other tools and techniques described in this book. We do not feel that all issues related to cost improvement can be answered within the learning curve framework, although we do think it is possible to gain useful insights when that framework is applied appropriately.

8-2 FUNDAMENTALS OF COST DYNAMICS

8-2.1 The Learning Curve

Whereas traditional models of productivity improvement typically assume that unit costs, or labor hours, can be reduced by a predictable percentage over a given *unit of time* (a year, say), the learning curve assumes a relationship between labor hours per unit and the *cumulative units* produced: hours per unit are reduced by a certain percentage each time cumulative volume doubles. Thus a 75 percent learning curve indicates that the labor hours required to produce the one-hundredth unit, say, will be 75 percent of those required to produce the fiftieth unit. Put another way, a 25 percent reduction in labor hours per unit occurs with each doubling of cumulative production volume.

For example, Table 8-1 presents one company's plan for producing a new product. This relationship is projected over a total expected production run of 840 units, with direct labor input per unit decreasing from 716 hours for the first unit to 29 hours for the last. These forecasts were based on management's judgment that the hours per unit would follow a 71.4 percent learning curve. Observe that as cumulative production doubles from 10 to 20 units, the direct labor hours per unit decline from 240 to 173. The ratio of 173 to 240 is 71.4 percent. Any other doubling of production results in a similar ratio.

The data of Table 8-1 are plotted in Figure 8-1a on conventional graph paper (based on linear scales), where the vertical axis represents labor hours per unit and the horizontal axis represents the cumulative units produced. For each sequential unit produced the curve describes the labor hours required to produce it. The passage of time is reflected only indirectly.

When the data of Table 8-1 are plotted using logarithmic scales (often referred to as log-log paper), as in Figure 8-1b, the result is a straight line. Since logarithmic scales are constructed using constant proportionate distances, each doubling of either labor hours or cumulative volume causes the same increment to be marked off on the respective axis. An exponentially decreasing relationship plotted using linear scales becomes a straight line when plotted on logarithmic scales, since $\log(an^{-b}) = \log(a) - b\log(n)$.

Learning curves (and experience curves, to be discussed in the next section) usually are plotted on logarithmic scales because this makes it easier to estimate the learning rate from observed data. It also emphasizes the constancy

Table 8-1

Basic Data for Developing a Learning Curve for Insight Optical

Cumulative Production	Hours This Unit	Cumulative Production	Hours This Unit
1	716	150	67
2	516	200	58
10	240	250	52
12	221	300	48
15	198	400	42
20	173	500	38
40	125	600	35
60	103	700	32
75	93	800	30
100	81	840	29

Source. "Insight Optical Equipment Co.," Harvard Case Services, 9-675-168.

Figure 8-1   Learning curve plot for Insight Optical (data of Table 8-1)

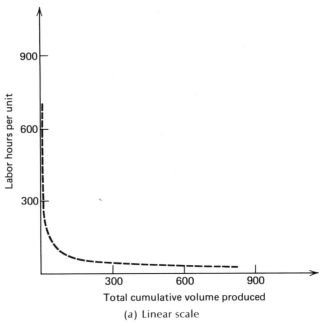

(a) Linear scale

Figure 8-1 (*continued*)

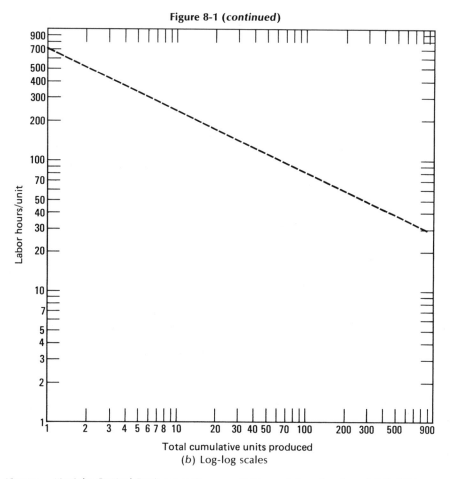

Total cumulative units produced
(*b*) Log-log scales

(*Source.* "Insight Optical Equipment Company," Harvard Case Services, 9-675-168.)

of the cost reduction pattern associated with doublings of cumulative output. In many applications, however, it is useful to plot a curve on both linear and logarithmic scales, since the former reflects what is actually observed through the firm's cost accounting system (which is usually time period-based), whereas the latter highlights the learning rate and its implications for competitive behavior and future management actions. In practice, most learning curves are estimated either visually or using a statistical regression technique. Both approaches are outlined in Appendix 8A.

8-2.2   Relating Learning to Productivity Improvement

Labor productivity improvement in a manufacturing operation is usually measured by the ratio of the average labor hours required per unit produced during a given time period (typically a year) to the average labor hours per unit required during the prior period. Thus, while a learning curve measures the improvement in the labor hours per unit achieved during a *specified increase in cumulative volume,* labor productivity improvement measures the reduction in labor hours per unit achieved during a *specified time period.*

The link between the rate of productivity improvement, as defined here, and the learning rate is contained in the time period required to double cumulative output. For example, if only one year was required to double the cumulative output of a product on an 80 percent learning curve, then only 8/10 as much labor would be required for the last unit produced that year as compared with the last unit produced during the preceding year. In productivity terms, this would be stated as a 20 percent improvement in labor productivity. However, if the product's cumulative production volume had increased by only 50 percent, the observed productivity improvement during that year would have been just over 10 percent, slightly more than half the rate of learning.

There are several different ways to express the conceptual relationship between learning curves and productivity improvement; two particularly useful ones are illustrated in Figure 8-2. The top portion of this figure indicates the position of a product or firm on a given learning curve over a five-year period, assuming two different production growth rates. The greater the growth rate, the farther down the learning curve the product will be after a given period of time. Put another way, volume growth affects the time period over which doubling occurs but not the rate (slope) of learning.

The second approach, outlined in the lower portion of Figure 8-2, depicts the average annual productivity improvement that occurs with each doubling of cumulative production volume for different combinations of growth rates and learning rates. As we will see in Section 8-5, the relationship among the learning rate, the volume growth rate, and the average productivity growth rate has implications for cost reduction programs, for the role that learning plays in formulating manufacturing and business strategies, and for national industrial policy.

8-2.3   The Experience Curve

The experience curve is simply an extension of the manufacturing progress function/learning curve, where the relationship of interest is that between the *cost* (rather than the labor hours) per unit and cumulative volume ("experience"), as illustrated in Figure 8-3. In constructing an experience curve, two data adjustments are required which are not necessary when calculating a learning curve. First, the cost per unit must be adjusted for price inflation, so that costs at one point in time can be compared fairly with costs at another point. Second, the experience curve concept is usually applied to the *value added* by the organization rather than to the total cost per unit. This means that

Figure 8-2 Link between learning curves and productivity

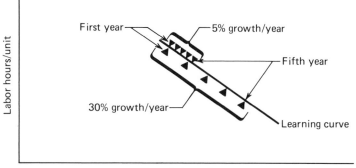

(a) A product (or plant) on a specified learning curve but with different growth rates

Growth Rate (years to dou-ble cumulative volume after first year)	Rate of Learning (% improvement with each doubling of cumulative volume)						
	100%(0%)	95%(5%)	90%(10%)	85%(15%)	80%(20%)	75%(25%)	70%(30%)
0% 1st doubling—1 yr	0	5%	10%	15%	20%	25%	30%
2nd doubling—2 yr	0	2.5%	5%	7.5%	10%	12.5%	15%
3rd doubling—4 yr	0	1.25%	2.5%	3.75%	5%	6.25%	7.5%
4th doubling—8 yr	0	.625%	1.25%	1.875%	2.5%	3.125%	3.75%
5% 1st doubling—0.95 yr	0	5.25	10.50	15.75	21.00	26.25	31.50
2nd doubling—1.80 yr	0	2.78	5.56	8.33	11.11	13.89	16.67
3rd doubling—3.15 yr	0	1.59	3.17	4.76	6.35	7.94	9.52
4th doubling—5.20 yr	0	.96	1.92	2.88	3.85	4.81	5.77
10% 1st doubling—0.91 yr	0	5.50	11.00	16.50	22.00	27.50	33.00
2nd doubling—1.62 yr	0	3.09	6.17	9.26	12.35	15.43	18.52
3rd doubling—2.66 yr	0	1.88	3.76	5.64	7.52	9.40	11.28
4th doubling—4.20 yr	0	1.19	2.38	3.57	4.76	5.95	7.14
15% 1st doubling—0.87 yr	0	5.75	11.50	17.25	23.00	28.75	34.50
2nd doubling—1.48 yr	0	3.38	6.76	10.14	13.51	16.89	20.27
3rd doubling—2.29 yr	0	2.18	4.37	6.55	8.73	10.92	13.10
4th doubling—3.10 yr	0	1.61	3.23	4.84	6.45	8.06	9.68
20% 1st doubling—0.83 yr	0	6.00	12.00	18.00	24.00	30.00	36.00
2nd doubling—1.38 yr	0	3.62	7.25	10.87	14.49	18.12	21.74
3rd doubling—2.01 yr	0	2.49	4.98	7.46	9.95	12.44	14.93
4th doubling—2.62 yr	0	1.91	3.82	5.73	7.63	9.54	11.45

(b) Average annual productivity improvement during each doubling

Figure 8-3 The experience curve plotted on logarithmic scales

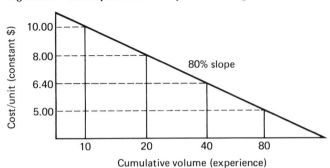

in addition to the cost of direct labor, such value-adding organizational activities and resources as indirect labor, overhead, and capital equipment should be included, but the cost of outside purchased materials should not be included.

Sometimes experience curves based on *total* cost rather than value added appear to fit a straight-line pattern. This usually occurs when a company's suppliers are reducing their costs in accordance with their own experience curves and are translating these lower costs into lower prices. However, since different suppliers may be experiencing very different rates of learning, and the time required for them to double their cumulative volume may also be different, it is generally preferable to separate supplier prices from manufacturing costs.

Although redirecting one's attention from direct labor hours (the "learning curve") to inflation-adjusted value-added costs (the "experience curve") broadens the usefulness of the concept, it introduces two new problems. For a number of reasons, many firms choose to collect costs not by product but by department. Even when costs are collected by product, they often are based on data obtained from several production batches rather than from an individual unit. It is sometimes possible to translate such aggregated costs into approximate unit costs, but an alternative approach may be called for. One usually can estimate the slope of an experience curve using the *cumulative average* cost per unit instead of the *incremental* cost per unit (see Appendix 8A).

Another potential problem is encountered in situations where costs are gathered by time period, but the production of a unit (or batch of units) is spread over several time periods. Using cumulative average cost may be more appropriate in such situations, but this figure may be biased because of the lag between the time when many costs are incurred and when the unit or batch is completed. One approach to handling this situation is to estimate the percentage of total costs that is incurred in each period prior to shipment. This can be used to allocate the total costs in a given period to the different stages of a product's manufacture, and thereby estimate its incremental unit cost.

Since the learning curve can be considered to be a special case of the experience curve, we use the terms interchangeably in the remainder of this chapter. However, we generally prefer to use the term experience curve since it has broader applicability.

8-3   APPLICATIONS OF LEARNING AND EXPERIENCE CURVES

Hundreds of investigations of experience curves have been published in the past few decades. Examining a few of these will illustrate the range of situations in which the concept has been applied and some of the practical problems associated with using it. The following examples have been selected to highlight what we consider to be some of the more interesting managerial applications of the concept.

8-3.1   Experience Curves for a Whole Industry: Steam Turbine Manufacturers

Actual cost data are available for estimating both industry and individual firm experience curves in the U.S. steam turbine industry. From 1946 through 1963 there were three primary competitors in that industry: Allis-Chalmers, General Electric, and Westinghouse. While competitors would not normally make their cost data public, these companies were forced to do so during court proceedings resulting from allegations of price fixing in the early 1960s. Figure 8-4a shows each firm's direct cost per megawatt of generating capacity produced plotted against its cumulative production of generating capacity.

Several issues in Figure 8-4a are worth commenting on. First, the unit of production has been defined as a single megawatt so that different-sized steam turbine generators can be combined when estimating the impact of experience on cost per unit. Second, the firms appear to have followed somewhat different experience curves during this period. General Electric's curve was somewhat steeper (more improvement with each doubling of cumulative production) than were those of Westinghouse and Allis-Chalmers. Third, an experience curve can be estimated not only for each individual firm but for the industry as a whole. An examination of this composite curve suggests that all three companies had roughly comparable rates of learning, but they were at different points on the composite curve because of differences in their cumulative production volumes.

Whereas the costs plotted in Figure 8-4a are direct costs, those plotted in 8-4b are overhead costs. The graph of these overhead costs suggests some experience curve behavior, but the slope is not nearly as steep as is that for direct costs. This might be explained by the fact that overhead costs are usually spread over several products, so that overhead per unit may be related not only to cumulative megawatts of steam turbine production but also to the growth in the cumulative output of other products produced by these firms. If those other products were growing more slowly, total overhead costs would be expected to show a slower rate of improvement.

Another explanation of the behavior of overhead cost per unit is that much of the improvement in overhead probably is due to what we earlier termed static economies of scale, specifically the ability of each firm to keep its overhead from growing as fast as its production volume. This might explain why General Electric, the largest firm in the industry, had a much lower over-

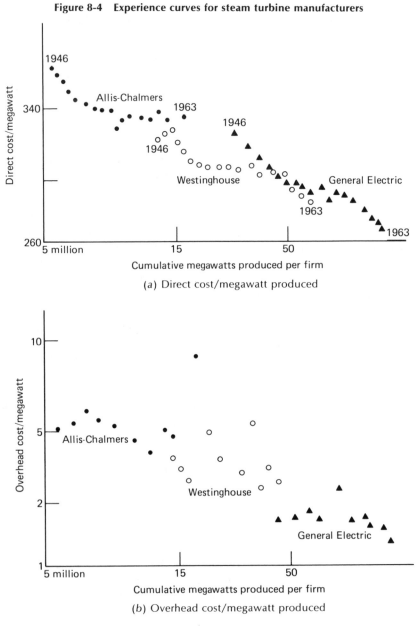

Figure 8-4　Experience curves for steam turbine manufacturers

(a) Direct cost/megawatt produced

(b) Overhead cost/megawatt produced

(*Source.*　Boston Consulting Group/court records.)

head cost per unit than did Westinghouse, and why Westinghouse, in turn, had a much lower overhead cost per unit than Allis-Chalmers.

8-3.2   Learning Curve in a Single Business: Portable Turbines

In the preceding example each order represented a major project, typically requiring some customization for each customer (public utility). In this second example, identical small portable turbine units were being made for the military in a single facility designed for that purpose. The data presented in Figure 8-5 show a pattern that is strikingly similar to that in the preceding example (note that here we are dealing with a learning curve—tracking direct labor hours—rather than an experience curve). Cumulative average labor hours per unit were plotted because individual unit labor hours were not available. As outlined in Appendix 8A, however, the number of units produced (well over 400) and the fact that the manufacturer dedicated a plant to this particular

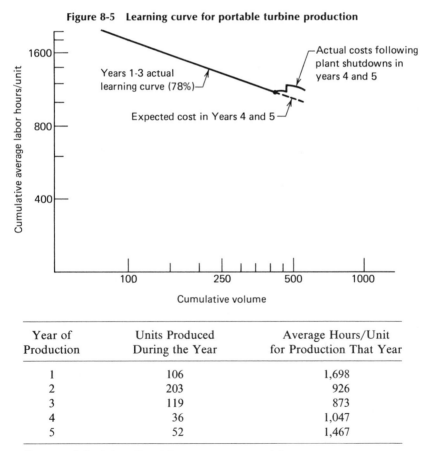

Figure 8-5   Learning curve for portable turbine production

Year of Production	Units Produced During the Year	Average Hours/Unit for Production That Year
1	106	1,698
2	203	926
3	119	873
4	36	1,047
5	52	1,467

(*Source.*   Solar International, Inc., company records.)

product during the five-year life of the contract makes it likely that cumulative average hours provide a satisfactory estimate of the rate of cost improvement.

Figure 8-5 provides some insight about the cost of production interruptions. In Year 4, and again in Year 5, the U.S. Air Force—the plant's only customer—forced it to stop production because of a failure to provide a continuous stream of orders for the product. This substantially increased the manufacturer's cost. These data became available through public hearings, in which the company claimed that the Air Force owed it additional money because of its erratic ordering procedures and failure to observe the spirit of the contract. (The manufacturer interpreted the contract to imply that the Air Force would provide continuous demand, and therefore allow it to reduce its costs and prices in keeping with a predetermined schedule.) The company's claim for reimbursement was based largely on estimating the learning curve achieved during the first three years and extending it through Years 4 and 5, then calculating the difference between the actual labor hours incurred in Years 4 and 5 and the labor hours that would have been incurred had the firm maintained its progress on the original learning curve.

8-3.3   Using Price as a Surrogate for Cost When Plotting Experience Curves.

Unfortunately, it is seldom possible to obtain cost data for competing firms within the same industry. In many instances, however, observed prices can be used to estimate the underlying costs. It is important to understand, however, that the price curve may not parallel the cost curve. Two of the most common price patterns observed empirically are shown in Figure 8-6. In the first of these, price falls steadily (presumably proportional to the decline in costs) so that the slope of the price curve approximates the slope of the cost (experience) curve. The second example illustrates "umbrella pricing"—where the industry's dominant company reduces its price more slowly than its costs are decreasing, thereby increasing its margin—early in the life of the product. At some point, competitive pressure leads to a "price break," where prices drop rapidly back into a more reasonable relationship with cost. After this, prices tend to parallel the experience (cost) curve. The Boston Consulting Group reports that it has plotted such price curves in hundreds of situations, and that price declines roughly parallel cost declines in approximately two-thirds of them. In the remaining third, prices follow the umbrella pricing pattern. Some examples will illustrate these two types of behavior.

Two situations where industries appear to have followed constant margin pricing policies are seen in Figure 8-7. The first of these shows the price per pound of crushed and broken limestone; the second, the price per unit of integrated circuits. In both instances prices followed a fairly constant rate of decline: 20 percent for each doubling of crushed and broken limestone, and 25 percent for each doubling of integrated circuits. It can be seen from the graph of integrated circuit prices that when the industry growth rate slowed during

**Figure 8-6   Relation of prices to costs
for experience curve analysis**

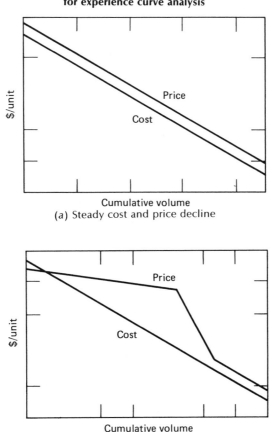

(a) Steady cost and price decline

(b) Umbrella pricing, followed by more rapid price declines

the early 1970s, the time required to double cumulative volume lengthened, but prices (and presumably costs) continued to track the same curve.

Freestanding gas ranges and polyvinyl chloride provide examples of umbrella-pricing patterns. Data for these two industries are plotted in Figure 8-8. In both instances, a kink (price break) occurred in the price curve during the mid-1950s, with steeper slopes after that point than before. For that faster rate of price decline to continue, of course, costs would have to decline at the same rate; otherwise, price declines would eventually flatten out as prices approached costs.

The purpose of this section has simply been to illustrate the breadth of the learning/experience curve concept and the need to address a range of issues when applying it. Appendix 8B discusses the strategic implications of the experience curve concept for such decisions as pricing.

Figure 8-7   Industry experience curves with uniform price reductions

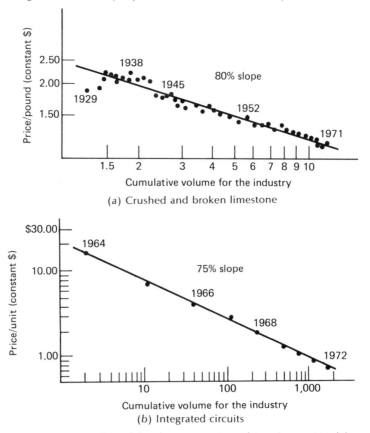

(a) Crushed and broken limestone

(b) Integrated circuits

(*Source.* Data collected by the Boston Consulting Group. Used by permission.)

8-3.4   Additional Practical Concerns in Applying Learning/Experience Curves

A number of practical considerations can make it difficult to estimate an experience curve in a particular situation. One of these was alluded to previously in connection with the U.S. steam turbine data: the notion of "shared experience." This can be particularly troublesome in situations where there is some doubt as to what should be considered the first unit of production. The question is whether earlier units, made for different customers with perhaps somewhat different product specifications and configurations, should be considered as equivalent to later units when calculating cumulative volume. If not, it will be necessary to divide total production into two eras, and plot a second curve beginning with the first unit of the later era.

For example, in Figure 8-9*a* two experience curves with the same rate of

Figure 8-8 Industry experience curves with umbrella pricing

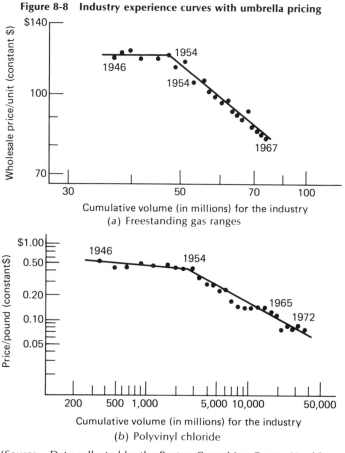

(a) Freestanding gas ranges

(b) Polyvinyl chloride

(*Source.* Data collected by the Boston Consulting Group. Used by permission.)

learning are depicted; their only difference is that in the left-hand graph the firm is assumed not to have produced any units previously. Therefore, by the time the firm produces 10,000 units it will have doubled cumulative volume 13 times, enabling it to reduce its costs dramatically. In the right-hand graph, however, if it began with 10,000 units of previous experience, it will double cumulative volume only once when producing another 10,000 units. Therefore its cost will not be reduced nearly as much.*

Another case where shared experience can make it difficult to analyze and understand cost behavior is seen in Figure 8-9b. After seeing its costs de-

* If the firm does have 10,000 units of prior experience, and incorrectly assumes it is starting with unit 1 instead of unit 10,000, the cost reductions it achieves will be much less than those predicted by the incorrectly plotted curve. This may cause considerable turmoil if the firm responds with strenuous and expensive attempts to improve its learning rate, because it is doing as well as should be expected.

Figure 8-9   Impact of past related production on the experience curve

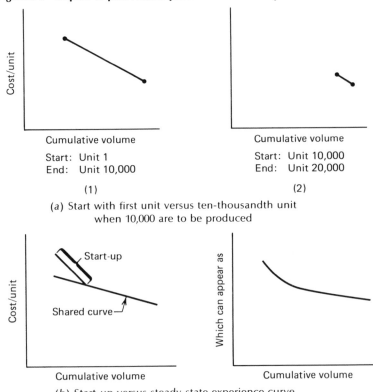

(a) Start with first unit versus ten-thousandth unit
when 10,000 are to be produced

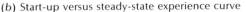

(b) Start-up versus steady-state experience curve

cline at a rapid rate for a while, a firm may find that the rate of improvement
slows markedly. While this may be due to specific management or workforce
actions (which will be examined in Section 8-4), such behavior can also reflect
the start-up phase for a product that is benefiting from prior (shared) experience. As shown in the left-hand portion of the graph, during the start-up phase
the product's learning curve displays a steep rate of descent. But as the start-up
phase evolves into "regular production," the learning rate approaches one that
is more typical of related products. This is one explanation for the frequently
observed "hockey-stick experience curve." Separating out shared experience is
critical if the experience curve is to be used as a reliable planning and control
tool.

Another practical consideration has to do with the sensitivity of forecasts
based on experience curve estimates to changes in certain assumptions (see
Figure 8-10). For instance, suppose a "reference unit" approach is followed:
it is assumed that start-up problems have been overcome, and a reasonable
degree of production stability attained, after a certain number of items have
been produced. The experience curve is therefore assumed to pass through
the point representing the number of this item and its observed cost. If curves

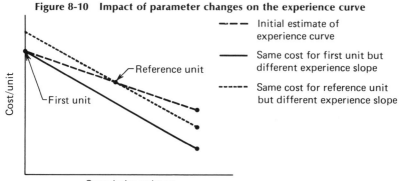

Figure 8-10   Impact of parameter changes on the experience curve

– – –   Initial estimate of experience curve

———   Same cost for first unit but different experience slope

------   Same cost for reference unit but different experience slope

with different slopes are drawn through that same point, the amount of variation will be significantly less than would be observed if, say, the *first* unit of production had been used as the reference point. But choosing which unit to use as the reference unit introduces some subjective judgment into the analysis and can lead to conflicts between various groups, each arguing the merits of "its" curve.

A final important consideration in the application of experience curves involves the use of constant cost data. It is easy to recommend that all costs should be stated in "comparable units" rather than inflated units; all one has to do is remove the effect of inflation from the observed costs. Unfortunately, estimating the correct deflator for each cost category during each time period is seldom easy. The attempts by many companies to implement various approaches to "inflation-adjusted accounting" during the 1970s suggest that it is not always easy—either conceptually or practically—to compensate for the subtle impact of inflation. Therefore, it often makes sense to look both at current dollars and constant dollars when seeking to figure out what the data are trying to tell you.

8-4   MANAGEMENT ACTIONS THAT AFFECT COST IMPROVEMENT

Some technical distinctions between learning and experience curves were discussed in Section 8-2. In this section we look at some of the management actions that can affect the rate of improvement in both types of curves. As a starting point, it is important to differentiate between *individual* learning—the learning that takes place for an individual worker—and *organizational* improvement. A simple example using the game of golf raises several issues that we then explore in more detail.

If a person had never played golf, it is reasonable to assume that the scores achieved should tend to decrease, following some roughly systematic improvement pattern, as the number of rounds of golf played increased. Some of the physical and mental causes of improvement in an individual's golf game are summarized in the upper-left quadrant of Table 8-2.

TABLE 8-2
Actions That Affect Individual "Learning" and Group Improvement

Factors That Cause Improvement	Factors That Impede Improvement
Individual Learning (e.g., Golf)	
Strengthening muscles	Frustration
Feedback: avoiding errors and encour-	Loss of motivation
aging effective approaches	Interruptions and forgetting
Coaching: better techniques	Constraints imposed by:
Better tools and equipment	Other workers
Motivation and incentives	Rules of the game
Practice (translate conscious into uncon-	Shortage of resources
scious behavior)	Physical and mental limits
Group or Organizational Learning	
Individual learning	Slowdown in individual improvement
Selecting and training new members	Constraints imposed by:
Improved methods	Limited capital
Better equipment and technology	Changes in products and markets
Division of labor, specialization	Government regulation
Product design	Work rules and labor contracts
Economies of scale	Inertia, preference for the status quo
Substitution of materials and/or capital	Lack of motivation
for labor	Lack of leadership
Incentives, motivation	
Leadership	

As they reflect on their own experience playing golf, however, most people conclude that never-ending improvement is unlikely. Most would expect that their score (for 18 holes, say) would stabilize at some level and vary only slightly thereafter. What causes such leveling off? Several factors can be identified, including a lack of motivation to improve further (perhaps because one feels that the costs or effort required outweigh the potential benefits), the individual's physical limits, and the "forgetting" that is due to long interruptions between games. These and other factors that may impede individual improvement are summarized in the upper right quadrant of Table 8-2.

In contrast to an individual playing golf, consider the possibilities if a *group* of people were allowed to play golf over a long period of time in a highly competitive environment. Rather than relying simply on one individual's capabilities for the entire game, it would be possible to have different members of the group specialize in various aspects of the game—one person in tee shots, another in putting, and so on—and to make changes in the rules of the game and the equipment used (assuming these were not rigidly specified). This might be expected to lead to much lower game scores than would be possible for a single individual. Similarly, any business organization faced with ongoing pressure to improve its activities (caused, for example, by a competitive market) could reap the benefits not only of individual learning but also of such other factors as economies of scale, materials and capital substitution, and even changes in the product itself. A number of the factors that support group or organizational learning are highlighted in the lower left quadrant of Table 8-2.

Just as a variety of factors can cause a slowdown in individual learning, organizational improvement can be impeded by such things as union work rules, lack of management pressure for further improvement, and the implicit decision that the benefits of such additional improvements are no longer worth the costs. These and other factors that may impede organizational improvement are summarized in the lower right quadrant of Table 8-2.

As one considers the various factors that support or hinder both individual and organizational improvement, as summarized in Table 8-2, it becomes clear that several major categories of possible activities profoundly affect the rate of improvement, as well as the variation in that improvement over extended periods of production activity. Management pressure appears to be the most significant influence determining the extent to which these factors act to improve performance, or become roadblocks to further improvements. Various ways that management action can affect the rate of improvement, and other issues that can have a significant impact on the rate and extent of organizational improvement, are discussed in the remainder of this section.

8-4.1　Labor Efficiency

Direct labor efficiency is highly dependent on the quality and stability of the workforce that performs the production tasks. In cases where labor turnover becomes excessive and/or it is impossible to obtain workers with the required skills, anticipated improvements from experience can evaporate. A clear example of this occurred at Douglas Aircraft (now McDonnell-Douglas) in connection with its production of the DC-9 airframe. The original planning for this plane's production took place in the early 1960s when there was considerable slack in the U.S. economy. Therefore, the company anticipated little problem in obtaining qualified workers and retaining them over several years. Unfortunately, by the time volume production began the labor market in the Los Angeles area had tightened significantly, and it was not possible to obtain the workforce quality and stability that had been expected. Between the beginning of 1965 and mid-1966 Douglas hired approximately 35,000 workers—but it soon lost 12,000 of them. Since the price of the DC-9 had been based on achieving a certain rate of improvement, the inability to "get down the learning curve" resulted in substantial losses and, ultimately, a forced merger. (See Macklin, 1966.)

The compensation and incentive programs developed by a company can also have a major impact on labor efficiency. Unfortunately many wage incentives are designed or applied in a manner that inhibits performance improvements rather than encouraging them. In one study it was observed that substantial improvements occurred during the start-up phase of a new steel-making process, during which time the work crew was given bonuses for improving performance. However, after about four months the temporary incentive plan was converted to a permanent one based on higher standards. This led to labor dissatisfaction, which resulted in a "pegging" of production output. Within a month productivity fell to about 70 percent of previous levels and remained there for almost a year. When management became aware of this, it sought to encourage greater output by altering the standard hours beyond which incentive bonuses were paid. There was an immediate jump in labor efficiency when the workforce recognized it was no longer locked into the compensation levels established under the previous plan and could obtain a larger share of the value it was creating. (See Baloff, 1970.)

Another important influence on labor efficiency can be the way the workforce is organized and supervised. Walton (1979), among others, has reported on a range of companies (including Volvo, General Foods, Procter & Gamble, and Alcan Aluminum) that have experimented with new approaches to workforce organization in the hope of achieving productivity improvements. Generally these new workforce structures have sought to expand workers' responsibilities by moving away from monotonous, traditional production-line technologies toward more group-oriented technologies, and by having groups of workers take on many low-level management tasks. While the limits and benefits of such organizational changes are not yet fully known, some of the results achieved to date are intriguing.

8-4.2   New Processes and Methods

Changes in production technology can be another important source of performance improvement. As discussed in Chapter 7, the process life cycle describes the direction that such changes traditionally follow. Movements along the process life cycle are prompted largely by the desire of firms to improve manufacturing efficiency (move down the experience curve). While a product might initially be manufactured in small batches, using a job shop flow process and general purpose equipment, as it matures the production process tends to evolve toward more of a line flow structure, perhaps even with a moving conveyor in final assembly.

An example of the benefits that can be obtained by such changes in processes and methods is Texas Instruments' experience in the digital watch business. Initially, the TI digital watch was produced using a decoupled line flow process and sold for $69.95, retail. Its next, more standardized, watch design was introduced two years later. Produced with a new production process and more advanced components, it had a selling price of $19.95. A year later TI was able to reduce its costs to the point where it could offer essentially the same watch for $9.95. The approach it followed, including the substitution of capital equipment for direct labor, methods improvements, and value engineering of component parts, is a classic method for improving productivity. (See *Business Week,* May 31, 1976.)

8-4.3 Technical Conservatism and Incremental Capacity Expansion

When a company builds a new manufacturing facility, or an equipment supplier develops a new piece of process equipment, it generally exercises considerable technical conservatism. That is, since one seldom knows in advance exactly what the limitations of the equipment will be, it is usually designed to surpass its required specifications, often by a considerable margin. This frequently makes it possible for the managers of the new facility or machine to gradually increase its overall production throughput rate by expanding the capacity of critical bottleneck operations. Over time this can result in a substantial increase in the total output of the facility without the necessity for major investment. For example, it has been reported that during the 1950s the catalytic cracking units used in oil refineries typically "grew" to about 150 percent of their design capacity over a 10-year period. That is, a unit that might have been designed to produce 100 units per period was producing 150 units per period a decade later without any major outlay for additional capacity. (See Hirschmann, 1964.)

8-4.4 Product Redesign

Just as changes in the production process can be a major source of cost improvement, so can changes in the product being produced. For example, the substitution of lower cost materials or more cost-effective parts can do much to reduce the total cost of a product. In addition, design changes that make the product more producible can lead to increased labor productivity and at the same time increase the capacity of an existing facility. Typically, the second and third generations of a product provide equal or superior performance while requiring substantially fewer production inputs. (See *Business Week,* June 11, 1979.)

8-4.5 Product Standardization

Management actions that increase product standardization have an impact similar to product redesign. For example, redesigning a product line so that it uses a common set of materials and component parts can substantially reduce unit costs. Such standardization frequently goes hand in hand with new processes and methods. In the case of Texas Instruments' digital watch, cited earlier, the product design that enabled the use of an assembly-line production process incorporated a standard module (internal electronic workings) that was the same for all forms of the product. Only the external parts—the band and the watch case—differed among units. During its first year of production, TI produced 5 million essentially identical watches. (See *Business Week,* May 31, 1976.)

8-4.6   Scale Economies

As outlined in Chapter 3, economies of scale can be obtained through a variety of management actions. These include higher utilization of existing facilities, using higher volume facilities which have lower capital cost per unit of capacity and permit increased throughput without a proportional increase in manpower, and reducing changeover costs by dedicating specific production facilities to certain high-volume products. In highly capital-intensive industries such activities may be some of the most important sources of continued cost improvement.

8-4.7   Shared Experience

A common experience base can be an important source of continued cost improvement, particularly in a multiproduct company. Two things are critical if the full benefits of shared experience are to be realized. One is that the organization must be structured in such a way that experience is concentrated in integrated organizational units. If a firm splits its production of a certain component between facilities that are geographically distant, assigns those facilities to different divisions, and restricts the flow of personnel between these divisions, it is unlikely that shared experience will be significant. Communication and feedback are essential if people throughout the organization are to share in the experience gained by various subunits. (See *Business Week,* May 7, 1979.)

8-4.8   Growth Rates

As pointed out in Section 8-2, the rate at which an organization moves down a given experience curve depends on the time it takes for its cumulative production volume to double. The faster the rate of growth, the less time it will take for cumulative volume to double and the faster costs will decline per unit of time. A number of management actions can be taken that directly affect this growth rate. Most of these are marketing activities, but manufacturing may also be able to affect indirectly the demand growth rate by aggressively working to lower costs, improve quality, and speed delivery times. Other activities, such as negotiating long-term contracts with important vendors, can make it possible for the firm's manufacturing organization to benefit from the experience and cost reductions of others.

It should be apparent from the preceding paragraphs that a variety of management actions can support systematic cost improvement in a manner consistent with experience curve theory. The most appropriate actions for a given situation depend on the individual firm's resources, strategies, and competitive environment. It is important to take into account a broad range of possibilities for improving costs and increasing experience, and to direct resources and attention into those avenues that promise the best results over the long term. Developing such coordinated programs is the subject of the next section.

8-5 MANAGEMENT USES OF LEARNING/EXPERIENCE CURVES

With many of the basic elements related to estimating and using experience curves as background, the primary purpose of this section is to examine how top management might apply the concept at two different organizational levels, each with important implications for manufacturing. The first concerns the development of cost reduction programs as part of the firm's budgeting and long-range planning process. Conceptually, the experience curve concept appears to be well suited for helping develop such programs; our experience, however, is that it is seldom exploited. Instead, cost reduction tends to be viewed as a short-term or tactical activity, whereas experience curves are regarded as having longer-term, strategic impact. We believe that cost reduction should be approached as part of a long-term program, and that the experience curve concept provides a natural starting point for developing such programs. Section 8-5.1 discusses one company's approach to using the concept this way.

A second use of experience curve theory is in developing a manufacturing strategy. We discuss some alternative manufacturing strategies that take explicit account of this concept, as well as some of its implications for such strategic issues as vertical and horizontal integration. Whether the same concept should be applied at an even higher level—to the development of corporate strategy—is a hotly debated topic, and a brief summary of some of its implications at that level is presented in Appendix 8B.

Finally, the concern with productivity improvement (at the national level) in the United States, Europe, and elsewhere, motivates us to devote a few paragraphs to national industrial policies in light of experience curve theory. Thinking about national productivity in this context suggests policies that might have a substantial impact on a country's overall productivity, particularly in its industrial sector.

8-5.1 Basing Cost Reduction Programs on Experience Curve Concepts

Whatever its conceptual basis, if a cost reduction program is to be effective over an extended time horizon a set of characteristics like those outlined in Table 8-3 must be met. One of the most important implications of this list is that cost reduction is an ongoing process, and therefore managing it should take into account an assessment of the annual cost improvement that can be sustained over the long term (while, of course, taking full advantage of shorter-term opportunities).

Table 8-3
Characteristics of an Effective Cost Reduction Program

Covers commitments for one year and projections for five years.

Included as a line item in both the annual budget and the long-range plan.

Applies to a majority (e.g., 75+ percent) of manufacturing operations.

Consists of a mix of projects taken from a portfolio of available cost reduction activities.

Promises adequate annual cost improvement to help offset inflation, improve margins, and establish a competitive advantage.

Reflects a reasoned judgment regarding the maximum annual cost reduction that can be sustained as part of a long-term program.

Sufficiently accurate that corporate resources can be allocated based on promised cost reductions.

Includes a mechanism for tracking and evaluating actual cost performance over time.

Developing a systematic cost reduction program is usually a challenging responsibility for a manager. First, a rich set of possible projects must be identified, so that one can choose among them and combine them in imaginative ways rather than having to pursue every project that is proposed. One way to accomplish this is to maintain a backlog of four kinds of potential projects:

Committed Projects that are defined and included in this year's budget
Defined Projects that are completely approved and in the process of being scheduled, but are not yet in the budget
Under study Projects under consideration which require additional engineering and financial analyses
Maybe's Possible opportunities that have not been examined carefully

Separating projects in this manner, and monitoring the flow of projects through the various stages, makes it possible to manage the cost improvement process. Resources can be targeted toward developing specific kinds of projects, and one has control over the mix of cost reduction activities being pursued. Through trial and error a manufacturing organization can develop its own guidelines as to the desired size of this project portfolio. In one company, for example, a backlog of projects promising 300 percent of the current year's budgeted cost reduction seems to work.

A second major challenge in making cost reduction programs effective is to anchor them to a sufficiently distant time horizon so that both near-term and long-term projects can be handled effectively. It is common in many firms to concentrate cost reduction programs on near-term goals, in the expectation that tomorrow will take care of itself. No attempt is made to develop projects that span more than a single budget period, or that cannot be undertaken until a year or two after their evaluation begins. A systematic program based on an extended time horizon and a portfolio of potential projects can do much to prevent cost reduction efforts from becoming too myopic.

A third major challenge is to specify a reasonable improvement goal and then develop sufficient confidence in the organization's ability to achieve that goal that marketing policies and other strategic activities can be based on it. If historical data are available, an experience curve can be estimated and extrapolated (using forecasts of sales volume a few years into the future) to assist in developing reasonable expectations about the amount of cost reduction that is possible.

Figure 8-11 illustrates how a cost reduction program might meet the challenges just described. Developed by a major industrial products firm, this

Figure 8-11   Six steps for developing a cost reduction program for a planning unit

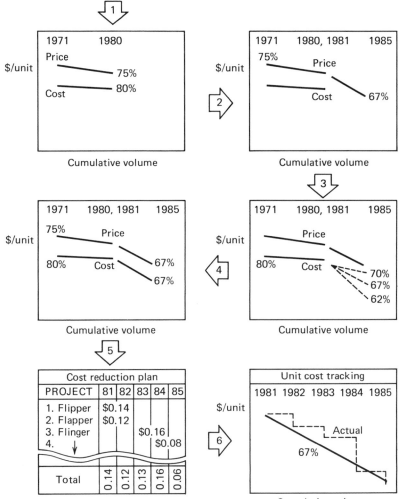

approach encompasses six steps. The first begins by analyzing historical price and production cost patterns in order to develop cost (experience) and price curves, as shown in Step 1. The second step requires that marketing estimate future prices (in constant dollars) and volumes over a five-year time horizon.

In Step 3 manufacturing uses marketing's volume projections to develop alternative cost improvement curves, representing different assumptions about capital investment and the allocation of other manufacturing resources. In Step 4 manufacturing commits to a specific set of assumptions, resource allocations, and the cost improvements they imply. Thus by the end of Step 4 the organization has projected the experience and price curves for the business five years into the future.

In Step 5, a set of projects that will provide the promised annual reductions in cost is selected from the project portfolio. These may span a wide range of activities involving, say, direct labor efficiency, production process changes, product design changes, and scale economies. The final step consists of tracking actual costs and comparing them with the projections. This makes it possible to identify additional projects in the cost improvement portfolio that need to be pursued.

An illustration of the application of this approach is given in Table 8-4 and Figures 8-12 and 8-13. As a starting point, Table 8-4 summarizes the historical data for Product ABC, including annual sales volumes, cumulative volumes, price deflation indices, selling prices, and production costs through 1980. The product's historical (constant dollar) price and cost curves are plotted in Figure 8-12; they have slopes of 96.4 and 70.5 percent, respectively. Figure 8-12 also contains the price, volume, and cost projections for the period 1981–1985 that were agreed to as part of the six-step process outlined in Figure 8-11. Observe that the slopes of the expected selling price (in constant dollars) curve is 69.6 percent, and the experience curve committed to by manufacturing as the basis for its five-year cost reduction program for that product also has a slope of 69.6 percent.

In this example, manufacturing and marketing have projected different future price and cost patterns for the product from those experienced before 1980. Marketing anticipates that constant dollar prices will drop dramatically from their levels of the previous eight years, and production has responded by agreeing to achieve cost improvements equal to the expected price declines, slightly better than those achieved in the past. Another important observation from Figure 8-12 is that despite the absence of significant price pressure on product ABC during most of the 1970s, manufacturing had continued to achieve significant cost improvements; as a result, the company's profit margins grew steadily. The goal for 1981–1985 is to maintain that margin (in percentage terms), implying parallel price and cost curves.

To help it monitor this cost reduction program for Product ABC, the company developed Figure 8-13. It chose to review its cost reduction program semiannually, so those review dates have been added to Figure 8-13. The sys-

Table 8-4
Product ABC—Cost Reduction Program Based on Experience Curve Analysis

Year	Annual Volume	Cumulative Annual Volume	Deflation Index, 1980 = 100	Selling Price/Unit Current $	Selling Price/Unit Constant 1980 $	Production Cost, Current $	Cost/Unit, Constant 1980 $
Actuals							
1971	7294	7294	54.6	$33.00	60.43	$20.60	37.72
1972	685	7979	57.3	34.30	59.86	19.60	34.21
1973	1035	9014	60.4	35.20	58.28	20.10	33.28
1974	1725	0739	63.2	35.63	56.38	20.20	31.96
1975	3201	13940	65.3	37.50	57.43	14.30	21.90
1976	3805	17745	68.8	39.10	56.83	14.90	21.66
1977	3852	21597	76.0	40.90	53.82	14.50	19.08
1978	2750	24373	82.6	49.00	59.33	17.40	21.06
1979	2550	26923	90.9	51.40	56.55	17.40	19.14
1980	2831	29754	100.0	52.70	52.70	18.10	18.10
Projections							
1981	3255	33009	110.0	55.30	50.27	18.46	16.78
1982	3278	36287	120.8	58.10	48.10	19.75	16.35
1983	3378	39665	133.0	61.00	45.86	20.74	15.59
1984	3494	43159	146.3	64.10	43.81	21.84	14.93
1985	3605	46764	159.1	67.40	42.36	23.01	14.46
1981–1985 experience curve slope				139%	69.6%	139%	69.6%

Figure 8-12   Product ABC—historical and projected experience curves

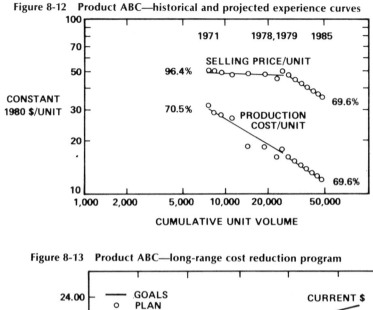

CUMULATIVE UNIT VOLUME

Figure 8-13   Product ABC—long-range cost reduction program

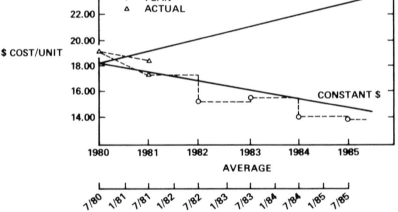

tematic nature of this program makes it possible to assign management responsibility and evaluate ongoing performance in a way that is consistent with long-term strategies and objectives.

8-5.2   Experience Curves and Manufacturing Strategy

One of the earliest documented business strategies based on the experience curve was developed by Henry Ford for his Model T. Figure 8-14 summarizes the selling price for the Model T between 1908 and 1926. Ford's approach was to minimize manufacturing cost and maximize sales volume. Over the years Ford Motor Company's total profits increased steadily, despite lower margins

Figure 8-14 Experience curve for the Ford Model T

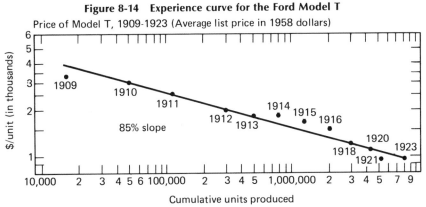

Price of Model T, 1909-1923 (Average list price in 1958 dollars)

Cumulative units produced

(*Source.* Abernathy and Wayne, 1974. Used by permission.)

per unit. As described by one author who studied that period (Abernathy, 1978), there were six major elements in Ford's approach:

1. **Product stability.** Standardization was increased, model improvements were made less frequently, and the product line offered had less diversity than those of competitors.

2. **Capital equipment specialization.** Vertical integration was pursued and processing equipment and facilities were made more specialized. The rate of capital investment increased, and the flexibility of those investments decreased.

3. **Process rationalization.** The production throughput time was reduced, the division of labor increased and the production process rationalized and oriented toward line-flow operations. The amount of direct supervision decreased as labor input fell, and indirect support functions, such as materials handling, grew in importance.

4. **Scale economies.** The process was segmented to take advantage of economies of scale. Some facilities (such as engine plants) were centralized as volume increased, while others (such as assembly plants) were dispersed to trim transportation costs. Spreading overhead over larger production volumes further decreased unit costs.

5. **Material specialization.** Material input costs were decreased through vertical integration and by exercising increased control over suppliers. Suppliers were requested to develop parts and materials that would reduce processing costs.

6. **Labor specialization.** The increasing rationalization of the process led to greater specialization in labor skills. Ultimately this began to lessen workers' pride in their jobs and their concern for product quality. Process changes also altered the type and balance of worker skills required.

Several other companies have successfully pursued similar manufacturing strategies for cost minimization. In order for this type of strategy to be effective, it is necessary that the strategies pursued by the firm's other functions complement manufacturing activities:

1. *Aggressive Pricing.* By pricing in anticipation of expected cost reductions, it is often possible to discourage new competitors from entering the market while simultaneously encouraging the growth of the market. Aggressive pricing, and other sales-stimulating activities, by the firm with the most cumulative experience (volume) can help strengthen its competitive advantage, enabling it to grow faster than the market and move down the experience curve faster than its competitors.

2. *Coordinated Engineering.* Rapid cost declines can also be encouraged by standardizing both production processes and product designs. To accomplish this, engineering must work closely with manufacturing to design products that can be produced efficiently using processes which permit the gradual substitution of capital for labor. (In contrast, the usual product design engineer devotes most of his or her attention to developing innovative new products, with only a secondary concern for their producibility, and manufacturing engineering—designing production equipment—is generally considered the least glamorous of engineering activities.)

3. *Financial Resources.* To support the desired volume growth and facilitate process improvements, the company must often expand capacity well in advance of demand. If the market is growing rapidly, it is often necessary to invest substantial amounts of money in order to minimize manufacturing costs and maximize market share.

Texas Instruments is often cited as using a cost minimization manufacturing strategy and a market share maximization marketing strategy. It is not uncommon for TI to lower its quoted price more than once even before the production of a product begins, and then continue to reduce it as the market grows. The company followed this approach with semiconductors, calculators, and digital watches, seeking to preempt competitors and gain an advantage based on market dominance and low cost. The same approach in home computers, however, was thwarted by competitors who sought cost reductions through improved product designs rather than through production rationalization and economies of scale.

While the publicity surrounding the so-called experience curve strategy might suggest that a cost minimization manufacturing strategy is always the most effective one, there are a number of very successful companies that do not follow this approach. This does not imply that such firms ignore opportunities for reducing manufacturing costs but that total dedication to moving down the experience curve is not the primary means by which they seek to develop a competitive advantage. At least two rationales are commonly used by such firms to explain why cost minimization is not their highest priority.

The first is that pursuit of competitive advantage through aggressive cost reduction requires a market environment that allows a firm to maintain a dominant position once it is achieved. Small specialized firms that focus all their attention on specific market segments may be able to take sales away from a firm that is pursuing a high-volume strategy. They are frequently as profitable as large, broad-product-line firms. Thus a niche strategy sometimes is more successful than is a market domination/cost minimization strategy.

A second counterargument to cost minimization can be tied directly back to some of Ford's problems with the Model T. Ford pursued the experience curve to such a degree that when more comfortable closed-body vehicles, introduced by General Motors, began to be popular in the early 1920s, it was impossible for Ford to respond incrementally. It had become so inflexible that further production of vehicles had to be stopped in 1926 for almost a year in order to reorganize and retool its operations for a new line of cars. Although it recovered market leadership briefly after the introduction of the Model A, its years of domination of the U.S. auto market came to an end with that shutdown. General Motors soon countered with another series of improved designs and gradually moved ahead of Ford.

Committing oneself to a strategy based single-mindedly on cost reduction tends to limit one's flexibility and innovative capabilities. This tradeoff between flexibility/innovation and efficiency was studied in detail by Abernathy (1978). As we emphasized in Chapter 2, low cost is just one of the criteria around which a competitive strategy can be crafted. One can design an effective counterstrategy—as did GM—around one of the other criteria. None of these criteria, or the strategies built around them, is "best" in any absolute sense.

One of the most frequently cited examples of a company that has successfully followed an innovation (as opposed to an efficiency) strategy is Hewlett-Packard. (See Wheelwright, 1984.) While HP clearly understands experience curves and works to extract cost reductions from volume increases, it has chosen to seek its primary competitive advantage through developing innovative, top-of-the-line products. Such a strategy requires that its manufacturing organization be highly flexible, since it is likely to change or replace products sooner than would a company that pursues a cost minimization strategy. In addition, it tends to put more emphasis on new product R&D and pursue an umbrella pricing strategy in the early stages of a product's life cycle. Rather than continually lowering prices simply to build volume, an innovation strategy seeks a substantial return on the product's initial investment early in its life so that funds will be available for developing new products. A cost minimization strategy tends to require longer paybacks on investments, with benefits coming after the product matures and the firm has a dominant market and cost position in the industry. As pointed out in Chapter 2, whether a firm follows a strategy based on efficiency, innovation, or some other criterion, it should tailor the key tasks and skills of its people to the express needs of that strategy.

8-5.3   Implications of Experience Curve Theory for Vertical Integration and Diversification

The experience curve also has significant implications for both vertical integration and horizontal diversification. With regard to the former, determining which components and subassemblies are likely to offer the best opportunities for cost improvement can be key to the long-term success of a business. Texas Instruments entered the hand-held electronic calculator business relatively late, but it was soon able to displace Bowmar as industry leader. One major reason for its success was its greater vertical integration. Bowmar was strictly an assembler of calculators; therefore, once it had reduced its assembly cost substantially it was unable to reduce its total cost faster than permitted by its suppliers' price reductions. TI, on the other hand, being a vertically integrated semiconductor producer (it was one of Bowmar's suppliers of calculator chips), was able to pass through its reductions in component costs faster than did Bowmar's outside suppliers. By pushing aggressively down the experience curve, TI was able to price its calculators below Bowmar's and grab market share away from it. Eventually Bowmar was forced to leave the industry, as were others who were neither integrated nor moving fast enough down the experience curve. Bowmar blamed TI directly for some of its difficulties, in fact, claiming in a $240 million damage suit that TI had curtailed shipments of chips during a period of peak production. (See *Electronic News,* February 17, 1975.)

A simple arithmetic example illustrates how important choosing the right vertical integration strategy can be. Table 8-5 presents information for a single product made up of three basic components: Items A, B, and C. Each finished unit requires one unit of Item A, four units of Item B, and two units of Item C (A could be regarded as the assembly process for components B and C). If it is assumed that each of these component items is on its own experience curve, with a specified rate of learning and a beginning level of cumulative volume, it is possible to project the costs of the various components, and that of the finished unit, over future production volumes. Using the assumptions in Table 8-5, as the cumulative production of the finished product goes from 1,000 units to over 1 million units, the cost of the finished product drops from $360 to $61.98.

It is interesting to observe the cost patterns for the individual items, and the percentage of the total cost represented by each component, as cumulative volume builds. Item A's cost will go from $80 per unit to $4.50 per unit; Item B will go from $55 per unit to $5.91; and Item C will go from $30 per unit to $16.92. It can be seen that even though Item C is on a 70 percent curve, compared with 75 and 80 percent curves for Items A and B, respectively, the cost of Item C declines by less than half during this buildup in volume because of its previous production history. The costs of the other two items, which are unique to this product, are reduced ten to twenty times.

In anticipation of our discussion of vertical integration in the next chapter, we point out that a nonintegrated manufacturer of this product might be able to achieve many of the same cost reductions by buying its components from independent suppliers who were able to achieve similar rates of learning. But producing one or more of these components in-house may permit faster cost reductions and better designed products in certain cases.

Item A initially accounts for almost a quarter of total cost, but it only represents about 7 percent of total cost after 1 million finished units have been produced. Similarly, the four units of component B, initially accounting for over 60 percent of total cost, account for only 38 percent after 1 million units. On the other hand, the two units of Item C, which initially account for slightly less than 17 percent of total costs (the smallest percentage of the three components), represent approximately 55 percent of total costs after 1 million units. Thus what was initially the least important cost component eventually becomes the costliest component.

Another important point demonstrated by Table 8-5 is that if one had attempted to develop an experience curve for the total cost per unit (rather than deriving it from the costs of individual components), one would have arrived at very different total cost projections. In applying the experience curve concept to a specific situation, therefore, it is critical to identify the most appropriate level for defining the "unit of experience" and to concentrate data gathering and analysis efforts there.

While the foregoing illustration suggests the role that the experience curve concept can play in addressing issues of vertical integration, the notion of "shared experience" can also help one think about horizontal diversification

Table 8-5
Impact of the Unit of Analysis on Experience Curves

Component Items	Cumulative Volume (Experience)					
	1,000 Units	4,000 Units	16,000 Units	64,000 Units	256,000 Units	1,024,000 Units
Item A (1 per unit) Assume 75 percent curve						
Component experience	1,000	4,000	16,000	64,000	256,000	1,024,000
Cost/item ($)	80.00	45.00	25.24	14.24	8.00	4.50
Percent of total cost	24.2	18.3	14.5	11.1	8.6	7.3
Item B (4 per unit) Assume 80 percent curve						
Component experience	4,000	16,000	64,000	256,000	1,024,000	4,096,000
Cost/item ($)	55.00	35.20	22.53	14.42	9.23	5.91
Percent of total cost	66.7	57.3	51.6	44.9	39.5	38.1
Item C (2 per unit) Assume 70 percent curve						
Component experience	1,002,000	1,008,000	1,032,000	1,128,000	1,512,000	3,048,000
Cost/item ($)	30.00	29.91	29.56	28.22	24.27	16.92
Percent of total cost	9.1	24.4	33.9	44.0	51.9	54.6
Total finished unit cost ($)	330.00	245.62	174.48	128.36	93.46	61.98

alternatives. Firms frequently use the same component (or, more broadly, the same capability) in several products. Figure 8-15 demonstrates the degree to which this type of "shared experience" permeates an integrated firm like Texas Instruments. Such information can be helpful in anticipating which new products and markets might be most attractive as well as in developing cost projections for a proposed product.

For example, suppose TI wants to make cost projections for a new product (such as its Speak-and-Spell unit). It needs to consider not only the operations and components unique to that product but also the opportunities it has to exploit its experience with other products. Cumulative experience in component distribution, integrated circuit manufacturing, and consumer product distribution are probably all relevant to the new product. This other experience may not only benefit the new product but it, in turn, may add significantly to the cumulative experience in some of these shared tasks, thereby improving the costs of older products (such as calculators). In one sense, shared experience is an approach to accounting for synergy. Texas Instruments has developed a computer model that allows it to identify "experience centers," each having its

Figure 8-15   Potential impact of shared experience in a multiproduct firm

Product flows and experience centers at Texas Instruments

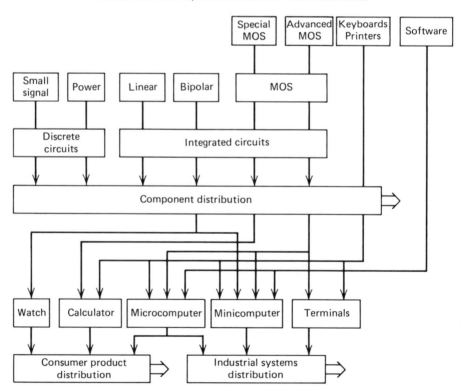

own experience curve and history of cumulative production. This model can be used to evaluate proposed new products or extensions of existing products. Appendix 8B provides a fuller discussion of how the experience curve concept might be used as a basis for assembling "business portfolios" and allocating resources among them.

8-5.4 The Experience Curve and National Economic Policy

One final aspect of experience curve theory that deserves comment is its relationship to public policy issues. As discussed in Chapter 1, the rate of productivity improvement in the United States during the 1970s did not keep pace with those of its major industrial competitors.

In searching for the cause of this national problem, it is instructive to develop a list of the U.S. industries that have experienced particularly low productivity growth rates and compare it with the list of those whose productivity has grown rapidly. The former would include shoes, textiles, and steel; the latter would include computers, consumer electronics, semiconductors, and instant photography. One major difference between the industries on these two lists is that the sales growth rates of the first group are significantly less than those of the second.

Experience curve theory can shed some light on this apparent relationship between slow growth and low productivity improvement. An experience curve analysis for the steel industry, for example, indicates that it has continued to move down about an 82 percent curve over the past several decades. However, since domestic industry production has been growing at an average rate of less than 2 percent per year since 1970 (and cumulative volume is growing at about the same rate), it will take over three decades to double cumulative U.S. domestic steel production. Even if it continues on an 82 percent learning curve, its annual cost improvement will be less than 1 percent a year (18 percent divided by 30 years). Furthermore, since this improvement is in constant dollars, inflation completely masks any cost declines. The high inflation of the 1970s caused actual steel costs and prices to increase dramatically in the United States.

The Japanese steel industry, on the other hand, has grown much more rapidly, both because of the high growth rate of its domestic economy and its success in gaining an increased share of the world market for steel. A faster rate of growth in cumulative volume (and therefore a shorter period between doublings) enabled the Japanese to achieve much greater annual cost improvements (productivity) than the United States. A similar pattern is observed when comparing Japanese and U.S. growth rates in many other industries.

Part of the explanation for the contrasting national productivity growth rates in the United States and Japan may lie in the differing government policies they have developed—implicitly or explicitly—for dealing with low-growth and high-growth industries. In the United States the tendency is to protect mature low-growth ("sunset") industries in order to prevent bankruptcies and massive unemployment. The effect of indirect subsidies, such as import restrictions, orderly marketing agreements, and guaranteed loans is to maintain, and even increase, the investment in such industries. On the other hand, these and other U.S. policies tend to penalize younger, high-growth ("sunrise") industries—both directly through policies that limit incentives for risk capital formation and indirectly through the taxes that are required to finance the support of the low-productivity, "endangered" industries.

In contrast, Japan (through MITI, its Ministry for International Trade and Industry) has systematically attempted to shift financial resources from low-priority (low potential growth) industries to high-priority (potential high-growth) industries. This has contributed to the rapid growth of the Japanese economy and strengthened its competitive position in world markets. An illustration is provided by the textile industry, which was one of Japan's preferred industries in the early 1950s, when it was growing rapidly. Additional investment in that industry has been discouraged since the mid-1960s, however, so that resources could be allocated to high-growth industries such as semiconductors and consumer electronics. Japanese economists often use experience curve concepts to argue in support of such government policies. The United States, on the other hand, has acted repeatedly to shield its textile industry— and the jobs it provides—from foreign competition. In 1961, for example, it unilaterally acted to remove cotton textiles from international agreements for trade liberalization; 10 years later it did the same with synthetic fibers.

8-6 SUMMARY AND CONCLUSIONS

Learning/experience curve theory has received considerable attention since the early 1970s. A number of firms have based their approaches to strategy formulation on this theory, and some have found it to be quite instructive. Others, while seeking to understand the concept, have tended to be skeptical of its value and have used other concepts as the basis for their business and corporate strategies. The concept provides guidance in certain cases and confusion in others. Like any theory, however, it can serve to expand the alternatives considered when formulating a business or manufacturing strategy. If one recognizes its limits and the questions it cannot answer, and uses it primarily as a source of ideas and insight, it can be very useful.

SELECTED REFERENCES

Abernathy, William J. *The Productivity Dilemma.* Baltimore: Johns Hopkins Press, 1978.

Abernathy, William J., and Phillip L. Townsend, "Technology Productivity and Process Change." *Technological Forecasting and Social Change,* Vol. 7, No. 4, August 1975, pp. 379–396.

Abernathy, William J., and Kenneth Wayne. "Limits of the Learning Curve." *Harvard Business Review,* September–October 1974, pp. 109–119.

Baloff, Nicholas. "Extension of the Learning Curve—Some Empirical Results." *Operational Research Quarterly,* Vol. 22, No. 4, 1971, pp. 329–340.

Baloff, Nicholas. "Start-Up Management." *IEEE Transactions on Engineering Management,* EM-17, No. 4, November 1970, pp. 132–141.

Baloff, Nicholas. "Estimating the Parameters of the Start-Up Model—An Empirical Approach." *Journal of Industrial Engineering,* No. 18, April 1967, pp. 248–253.

Bodde, David L. "Riding the Experience Curve." *Technology Review,* March–April 1976, pp. 53–59.

Business Week. "Harnischfeger's Dramatic Pickup in Cranes." June 11, 1979, pp. 114E–114F.

Business Week. "White Consolidates New Appliance Punch." May 7, 1979, pp. 94–98.

Business Week. "Fairchild's Problems: More than Watches." August 15, 1977, pp. 117–118.

Business Week. "How TI Beat the Clock on Its Twenty-Dollar Digital Watch." May 31, 1976, pp. 32–63.

Conway, R. W., and Andrew Schultz, Jr. "The Manufacturing Progress Function." *Journal of Industrial Engineering,* January–February 1959, pp. 39–54.

Dutton, J. M., and A. Thomas. "Progress Functions and Production Dynamics." New York University Working Paper 82–29, May 1982.

Electronic News. "Bowmar Files Chap. XI Petition; White Resigns." February 17, 1975, p. 1.

Henderson, Bruce D. "The Experience Curve Revisited." Boston: The Boston Consulting Group, Perspective No. 229, 1980.

Hirschmann, W. "Profit from the Learning Curve." *Harvard Business Review,* January–February 1964, pp. 125–139.

Janzen, Jerry L. "The Manufacturing Progress Function Applied to a Wage Incentive Plan." *Journal of Industrial Engineering,* Vol. 17, No. 4, pp. 197–200.

Macklin, J. "Douglas Aircraft's Stormy Flight Path." *Fortune,* December 1966.

Pagels, Carl C. "On the Start-Up of Learning Curves: An Expanded View." *AIIE Transactions,* Vol. 1, No. 3, September 1969, pp. 216–222.

Rohrbach, Adolph. "Economical Production of All-Metal Airplanes and Sea Planes." *Journal of the Society of Automotive Engineers,* Vol. 20, 1927, pp. 57–66.

Utterback, James M., and William J. Abernathy. "A Dynamic Model of Process and Product Innovation." *Omega,* Vol. 3, No. 6, 1975, pp. 639–656.

Walton, Richard E. "Work Innovations in the United States." *Harvard Business Review,* July–August 1979, pp. 88–98.

Walton, Richard E. "Explaining Why Success Didn't Take." *Organizational Dynamics,* Winter 1975, pp. 3–22.

Wheelwright, Steven C. "Strategy, Management, and Strategic Planning Approaches." *Interfaces,* Vol. 14, No. 1, February 1984.

Wright, T. P. "Factors Affecting the Cost of Airplanes." *Journal of Aeronautical Science,* Vol. 3, 1936, pp. 122–128.

Young, Samuel L. "Misapplications of the Learning Curve Concept." *Journal of Industrial Engineering,* Vol. 17, No. 8, 1976, pp. 410–415.

Appendix 8A.   Computing Learning Curves

Algebraically, the learning curve can be written as

$$Y_I = AI^{-B} \tag{8A-1}$$

where Y_I = direct labor hours required to product the Ith unit

I = cumulative production count beginning with the first unit

A = a parameter of the model equal to the labor hours required for the first unit produced

B = a parameter that measures the rate at which Y_I is reduced as cumulative production increases

Because learning curves are frequently stated in terms of the percent reduction in labor associated with each *doubling* of cumulative volume, it is useful to consider an alternative form of the learning curve relationship:

$$Y_J = Y_I \left(\frac{J}{I}\right)^{-B} \qquad \left\{ = AI^{-B} \left(\frac{J}{I}\right)^{-B} = AJ^{-B} \right\} \tag{8A-2}$$

where I is again the number of units produced up to some prior point in time, and J is the number of units produced up to the current point in time. (Thus the ratio J/I is the ratio of cumulative production at two different points in time.)

The exponent B which appears in both of these equations can be directly related to the rate of learning that characterizes each doubling of production. Representative values of the exponent B and the corresponding rate of learning are listed in Table 8-6.

Predicting the future cost of a given product using actual data requires estimating the shape (slope) of the curve that most closely fits its historical cost behavior over time. This estimated curve can then be used to plan future labor requirements, given anticipated volumes of production. Both such forecasts may be based, in part, on an analysis of the learning curves observed previously with related products, but the second requires the input of considerable subjective judgment as well.

The procedure for estimating a learning curve, given a set of historical data on labor inputs per unit of production, is outlined in Figure 8-16. There are two commonly used methods for estimating the rate of learning. The first is simply an informal graphical method: visually fitting a straight line through the actual data plotted on log-log paper. In many instances, the approximate results so obtained are sufficiently accurate for management planning.

In some instances, the amount of data available and the need for greater accuracy may dictate the use of a more formal statistical line-fitting technique, such as regression analysis. As outlined in Figure 8-16, this requires some sim-

Table 8-6

The Exponent B and the Rate of Learning

B Exponent Value	Rate of Learning (Labor hours for item $2n$, as a percentage of the labor hours for item n)
0.000	100%
0.074	95
0.152	90
0.235	85
0.322	80
0.415	75
0.515	70
0.623	65
0.738	60

Note. These are computed using Equation 8A-2 with J/I equal to 2.0. For example, for an 80 percent learning curve, $Y_J/Y_I = 0.8 = 2.0^{-0.322}$, and for a 72 percent learning curve, $0.72 = 2.0^{-0.474}$.

ple transformations of the original data, the application of a mathematical procedure to obtain estimates for the values B and $\log(A)$, and then translating the estimate of $\log(A)$ back into an estimate of the parameter A.

When the labor requirement per *incremental* unit of production is not readily available, the *average* labor per unit can be used to approximate the learning curve. This can be done as follows.

The *cumulative* number of direct labor hours required to produce I units is expressed as

$$T_I = Y_1 + Y_2 + \cdots + Y_I = \sum_{n=1}^{T} Y_n \qquad (8A\text{-}3)$$

An approximation of this sum is given by the integral

$$T_I \cong \int_0^I Y_n \, dn = A \int_0^I n^{-B} \, dn = A \left(\frac{I^{1-B}}{1-B} \right) \qquad (8A\text{-}4)$$

Dividing this expression by the cumulative number of units I gives an approximation for the *cumulative average* number of labor hours per unit:

$$A_I = \frac{T_I}{I} \cong \frac{A}{I} \left(\frac{I^{1-B}}{1-B} \right) = \frac{AI^{-B}}{1-B} \qquad (8A\text{-}5)$$

Notice that the slope of this curve (plotted on log-log paper) is determined by the same value of the exponent B as the marginal cost curve (Equation 8A-1).

A learning curve can therefore be estimated by calculating the cumulative average hours per unit for a variety of values of cumulative output I and plotting them on a logarithmic scale. As the number of units completed

Figure 8-16   Computing (estimating) a learning curve

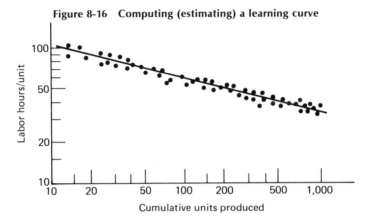

Cumulative units produced

(a) Graphical method of estimating the rate of learning:

1. Fit a straight line to the actual data plotted on log-log paper.
2. Identify two levels of cumulative production, where one is twice the other (i.e., $J/I = 2.0$).
3. Identify the estimated hours/unit for each of these two cumulative production volumes, i.e., Y_J and Y_I).
4. Compute the ratio Y_J/Y_I and convert to a percentage. This is the rate of learning.

(b) Regression analysis method of estimating the rate of learning:

1. Convert the learning curve equation (8A-1) to a linear form by taking the logs of both sides (i.e., $\log Y_I = \log A + (-B) \log I$).
2. Transform the actual observed data to $\log Y_I$ and $\log I$.
3. Apply regression analysis to estimate a and b in $y = a + bx$ where $y = \log Y_I$ and $x = \log I$.
4. Transform regression estimates of a and b to obtain $A = \log^{-1} a$ and $B = b$.
5. Convert B to a rate of learning using the relationship illustrated in Table 8-16.

increases, the cumulative average curve becomes asymptotically parallel to the unit learning curve. Thus the slope of the former becomes equal to the slope of the latter. This approximation typically yields insignificant errors for values of I greater than 50 units but large errors in estimating B can occur for small values of I.

Returning to the Insight Optical data in Table 8-1 and Figure 8-1, the hours per unit and the cumulative average hours per unit are as follows:

Cumulative Production	Hours This Unit	Cumulative Average Hours Per Unit
1	716	716
2	516	616
10	240	371
12	221	347
15	198	319
20	173	285

Cumulative Production	Hours This Unit	Cumulative Average Hours Per Unit
40	125	214
60	103	180
75	93	163
100	81	144
150	67	120
200	58	106
250	52	96
300	48	88
400	42	77
500	38	70
600	35	64
700	32	60
800	30	56
840	29	55

These data are plotted in Figure 8-17. It can be seen that even by the tenth unit, the rate of learning is roughly approximated by the slope of the cumulative average hours slope. By the time 100 units have been produced, the slopes of the actual and average hours curves are identical for most practical purposes.

Figure 8-17   Cumulative average and unit labor data—Insight Optical

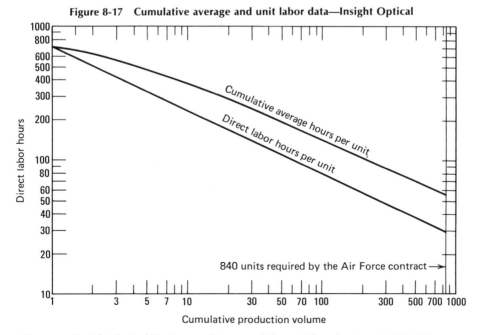

(*Source.* "Insight Optical Equipment Company," Harvard Case Services, 9-675-168.)

Appendix 8B.   Experience Curves and Corporate Strategy

Although the bulk of this chapter has dealt with the applications of experience curve theory to business and manufacturing strategy formulation, some corporations have used it in developing their overall corporate strategy. Using experience curve concepts to understand where each business unit in a corporation is positioned relative to its competitors can offer insight into resource allocation decisions at the corporate level.

In most industries it is not possible to get cost data, or even cumulative volume data, about all competitors, and thus some adjustments and assumptions are needed when using the experience curve as a planning tool. On the cost side, the adjustment normally made is to estimate your own firm's experience curve and then assume that the slope of the curve for the industry is similar to your company's slope. The surrogate most often used for cumulative volume is market share, the rationale being that if your market share never changed, it would be proportional to your cumulative volume. Even when market shares do change, the effect on cumulative volume takes place over several years, so that market share may still be a reasonable surrogate for cumulative volume.

Given these two adjustments, experience curve theory can be used to evaluate a corporation's portfolio of businesses, as illustrated in Figure 8-18 for Texas Instruments. Each of TI's businesses is plotted using a matrix that com-

Figure 8-18   Corporate Business Portfolio—Texas Instruments (1978)

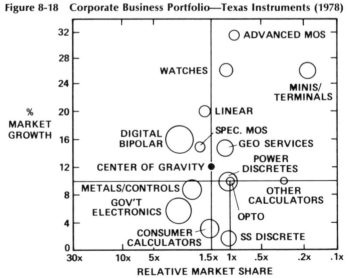

(*Source.* "Texas Instruments: Business Portfolio and Corporate Strategy Analysis," a Mitchell, Hutchins Inc. Status Report written by Thomas H. Mack, March 15, 1977.)

pares market growth rates with relative market share (i.e., relative cumulative experience). The vertical axis represents the (real) market growth rate and the horizontal axis measures (from larger to smaller numbers) the position of the company/business relative to that of its *largest competitor:* greater than 1.0 when the company's market share is larger than that of its largest competitor, and less when its market share is some fraction of the industry leader's share. The area within each circle is proportional either to the assets in that business or, more commonly, to the annual sales the company realizes in that business.

Since growth rates change over time, and the company may be able to alter both its own market share and those of its major competitors, the business portfolio chart will gradually shift over time. Understanding the nature of such shifts is important because various locations on the matrix have different cash flow characteristics.

As demonstrated in Figure 8-19, businesses in the upper right quadrant—high growth markets where the company does not have a dominant position—generally require substantial inputs of cash. Businesses in the lower left quadrant usually generate substantial amounts of cash since the market growth rate is slow (little cash is required) and the company dominates that business (profitability is high). Businesses in the upper left quadrant—with high market growth and high market share—may have a slight positive or negative cash flow, because the cash generated by the dominant market position will generally be needed to maintain growth at the rate of market expansion. The lower right quadrant consists of businesses with low growth, and thus limited capital needs. But since such businesses have low market shares, they probably have low margins and thus generate little cash.

The different cash flow characteristics of each of these quadrants has led people to assign suggestive names to businesses that find themselves in each quadrant. Those in the lower left often are referred to as "cash cows," since

Figure 8-19   Corporate business portfolio—cash flows

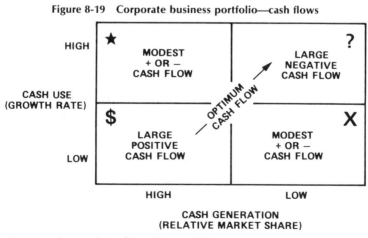

(*Source.*   Boston Consulting Group, 1980.)

they generate substantially more cash than they require. Those in the upper left-hand quadrant, on the other hand, are often referred to as "stars" since they are likely to become cash cows as their market's growth rate slows (assuming the company maintains its dominant position). Those in the lower right-hand quadrant often are referred to as "dogs" because it is difficult for a company to increase its relative market share in a market that is not growing very rapidly. Finally, a business in the upper right frequently is termed "question mark," since it is unclear whether its future movement on the matrix will be downward as market growth slows, or to the left (if it is able to increase its market share).

Some of the behavioral characteristics and strategic choices that generally are associated with businesses that fall into each of these four quadrants are as follows:

1. *Low Growth/Dominant Share* (*Cash Cows*). Such businesses tend to generate more cash than required to maintain their dominant share positions. That excess cash can be used to support growth opportunities elsewhere in the fire. An appropriate strategy for such businesses is generally to *maintain* market dominance through investment in cost reduction and technological leadership, exercise price leadership, and resist proposals to "grow" the business substantially.

2. *High Growth/Dominant Share* (*Stars*). These businesses tend to report substantial profits but often need significant cash to finance their growth. An appropriate strategy is one which seeks to protect the existing market position through product improvements, increased market coverage, and price reductions, all designed to *maintain* (rather than expand) market share.

3. *Low Growth/Low Share* (*Dogs*). These businesses tend to be at a cost disadvantage because they are not nearly as far down the experience curve as many of their competitors. In addition, given the lack of growth in the market, it is difficult to gain share except by taking it directly from a competitor—and thus leaving that competitor with excess capacity. Appropriate strategies for such businesses range from focusing all activities on a specialized market niche, to gradually harvesting the business in order to convert its assets into cash, to selling the business to other companies that have the skills or resource necessary to increase its market share.

4. *High Growth/Low Share* (*Question Marks*). A lack of a dominant competitive position in a rapidly growing market generally means poor profits and substantial cash requirements. If these businesses are not funded in excess of their market growth rates, they will evolve into "dogs" as their markets mature. Thus the appropriate strategy may range from getting out of the business to investing heavily in it in order to gain market share before market growth slows. Such investment may include acquiring competitors and solidifying one's position in niches promising higher growth.

One of the keys to formulating a strategy for an individual business is to develop a good forecast of its industry growth rate over the next several years,

Figure 8-20   Industry growth and the product life cycle—calculators

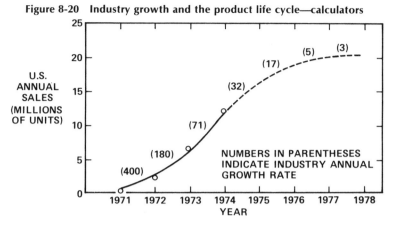

(*Source.*   Based on data taken from case "Electro Industries (A)," Harvard
Case Services, 9-176-268.)

because the investment required to increase market share (as in the case of a
question mark business) or to maintain share (as for a star or cash cow) is heavily dependent on the annual rate of growth of the market. As illustrated in Figure 8-20, the annual growth rate of the hand-held calculator market was
several hundred percent in the early 1970s but had slowed to only 3 percent a
year by the end of that decade. Therefore, a firm that sought to develop a
question mark calculator business into a market leader would have needed to
make a massive investment in order to turn it into a cash cow during that relatively short time span.

Balancing and managing the total portfolio of businesses also requires accurate projections of market growth rates. These guide the allocation of cash
flows among businesses in the various quadrants. Figure 8-21*a* suggests one
"successful" pattern for such cash flow allocations. It consists of taking excess
cash from businesses in the lower left quadrant and using it to move the selected question mark (upper right) businesses to the left, converting them into
stars. Thus when market growth slows, they will become the cash generators
for future reinvestment cycles.

In contrast, some firms have followed "disaster sequences" with regard to
the allocation of their cash flows. Two of these are illustrated in Figure 8-21*b*.
In the upper one, a dominant market position in a high-growth business is allowed to deteriorate because the firm fails to invest sufficient resources to keep
it growing as fast as the market. This may occur either because the firm does
not have good competitive data or because its emphasis on high ROI causes it
to limit its rate of investment. When this happens, the star evolves into a question mark and then, as growth slows, a dog. Another disaster sequence occurs
when a cash cow is milked too quickly (as RCA did in the late 1960s with its
color TV business), so that it loses its dominant position and its ability to generate cash for other businesses. Another way to lose a dominant position is to
allow competitors to segment the market by targeting different products for
each segment. Even though the firm may continue to have the largest market

Figure 8-21   Product dynamics—success and failure patterns

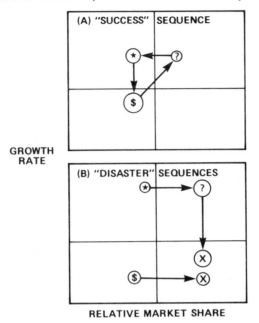

GROWTH
RATE

RELATIVE MARKET SHARE

share in the total (unsegmented) industry, it may have secondary market positions in several of the most important segments.

General Electric, among others, has taken another step in the development of this approach by identifying the skills and behavioral characteristics which are most appropriate for the managers charged with implementing each kind of strategy. Their evaluation and compensation systems can then be customized to the chosen strategy. An invest-and-grow business, for example, is assigned managers who are entrepreneurs and whose evaluation is based mainly on long-term objectives rather than short-term profits. Alternatively, a business in the harvest/divest category is staffed with conservative, experienced managers whose performance is measured more in terms of near-term profit and return on investment.

Vertical Integration and Sourcing

9-1 INTRODUCTION AND OVERVIEW

One of the most critical strategic decisions a firm faces is how to "position itself" in its competitive environment. From the viewpoint of the marketing function, the alternatives are usually expressed in terms of *product* position: the mix of product design characteristics, pricing, distribution arrangements, and promotional/communication approaches that differentiate the firm's product (and related services) from competitive offerings and make it more or less suitable for different market segments. From the point of view of the manufacturing side of the business, on the other hand, positioning alternatives usually are expressed in terms of "vertical integration and sourcing" decisions, or what might be referred to broadly as *process* positioning. The broad panoply of issues encompassed by this term includes such fundamental concerns as:

1. What boundaries should a firm establish over its activities?
2. How should it construct its relationships with other firms—suppliers, distributors, and customers—"outside" its boundaries?
3. Under what circumstances should it change its boundaries or these relationships, and what will be the effect on its competitive position?

Almost every company at some time faces the question of whether to broaden the "span" of its operations, that is, to become responsible for more of its products' final market value. Opportunities to increase span occur in a variety of ways, from a simple decision to make internally a part that currently is being purchased from an outside supplier, to a decision to set up one's own regional warehouses rather than selling through independent distributors.

9-1.1 Decisions That Define Vertical Integration

In approaching decisions relating to the span of operations, it is important to differentiate and consider separately three concepts:

1. The *direction* of such expansion.
2. The *extent* of the process span desired.
3. The *balance* among the resulting vertically linked activities.

To help clarify these concepts, consider a typical small manufacturing business. It buys parts from independent suppliers, assembles them, and sells its products to independent wholesalers. In reality, it is just one link in a larger sequence of transactions that are sometimes called the *commercial chain*. A simplified form of this chain is depicted in Figure 9-1. Our initial focus is on link 4 of the chain, the manufacturer/assembler. An actual commercial chain is, of course, much more complicated since most manufacturers have a number of suppliers, each using a variety of materials and providing everything from commoditylike products (such as plastic pellets or metal sheets) to specially designed motors or electronic control devices. Distribution and sales activities may be similarly complex. The simple linear flow in Figure 9-1, however, illustrates several of the points that are discussed in this chapter, beginning with those concerned with the direction, extent, and balance of vertically linked activities.

Figure 9-1   Links in the commercial chain

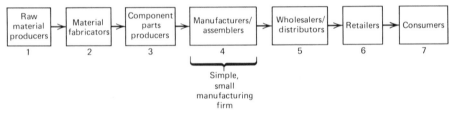

Decisions Regarding Direction

A manufacturer can integrate vertically in one of two directions: "downstream" (or forward), toward increased control over its markets, or "upstream" (backward), toward increased control over its suppliers. It may do both, of course, but usually a manufacturer directs its attention and resources primarily in only one direction. Such decisions reflect both its manufacturing strategy (conscious or unconscious) and the personal preferences and orientation of its management. Backward integration is sometimes regarded as primarily a defensive move whose main purpose is to reduce costs or protect the firm against exploitation by its major suppliers, whereas forward integration is considered to be more of an offensive move, motivated by a desire to gain greater market power. As we will see subsequently, however, the motivation and issues to be considered in making moves in either direction are too complex to be captured by such simple words as "defensive" and "offensive."

A study of Livesay and Porter (1969) of the vertical integration moves of the 100 largest U.S. manufacturing companies between 1899 and 1948 revealed that forward integration moves were almost three times as numerous as backward moves (increasing to almost four times as numerous during the latter part of the period, from 1920 to 1948.)* Given the attention directed at backward integration by economic theorists (who sometimes use the term "vertical integration" synonymously with "backward integration"), it is useful to keep these data in mind. In fact, the *first* vertical integration move made by a manufacturing company is typically a forward one: to establish its own sales organization rather than continuing to sell through independent manufacturing representatives and distributors.

Decisions Regarding Extent

A firm also has to decide how far forward or backward it wants to integrate. Some companies prefer to keep their operations as clean and simple as possible, confining themselves to link 4; others take a couple of steps in one direction or the other; still others go all the way, becoming "fully integrated." The major oil companies, which engage in everything from exploration for crude oil reserves to the manufacture of plastic cups, are familiar examples of the latter approach. Some companies integrate fully with one material but not at all with others.

Decisions Regarding Balance

Finally, a manufacturing firm must decide how to balance the capacities of its various stages of production. Should it, for example, try to maintain "perfect balance," that is, have one captive supplier produce 100 percent of its requirements for a given part while it, in turn, consumes all of the supplier's output? Alternatively, it may prefer to allow each stage in its vertical organization to have different capacities. If so, it will have to manage the complexities created by "outside customers" and "outside suppliers," and establish policies governing their handling relative to the "inside" customers and suppliers. Such complexities and ambiguities may damage its relationships with other suppliers or customers and cause it to lose partial control over its own "captive" suppliers/customers.

As a starting point for addressing the issues arising from different positioning strategies on the commercial chain, Section 9-2 looks at some of the characteristics of specific links in the chain and relates these characteristics to issues of direction and extent. Section 9-3 briefly reviews some of the vast literature that has sprung up about vertical integration and explains how the views of the business manager and the public policymaker can come into conflict. With these differences—in the requirements, benefits, and risks associated with managing different links in the chain—firmly in mind, Sections 9-4 and 9-5 consider the pros and cons of vertical integration from the point of view of a business manager.

Section 9-6 then discusses various alternatives to vertical integration: dif-

---

* Neither Laffer (1969) nor Tucker and Wilder (1977), however, were able to detect any trend toward increased vertical integration among U.S. manufacturing firms as a whole.

ferent forms of sourcing or selling, other than outright ownership and control. The final section of this chapter provides guidelines for developing and pursuing a firm's chosen vertical integration/sourcing strategy. The general framework outlined stresses the need to define clearly the "position" desired on the chain and base that choice on a careful assessment of the organizational capabilities that are likely to have a significant impact on the firm's competitive position. Determining how best to acquire those capabilities—through vertical integration or through some other sourcing or distribution arrangement—can then be addressed within this context. Using a number of examples, the final portion of Section 9-7 outlines a procedure for pursuing and implementing a selected vertical integration and sourcing strategy.

9-2   IMPORTANT CHARACTERISTICS OF DIFFERENT LINKS IN THE COMMERCIAL CHAIN

At the risk of oversimplification, as one moves from the upstream end of the commercial chain (raw material suppliers) toward the downstream end (the ultimate consumer), product variety increases and highly standardized commoditylike products evolve toward specialized consumer-oriented products. This evolution is accompanied by important differences in the production processes used at different points in the chain and the cost structures associated with them. Some of the more significant differences among various links of the chain are summarized in Table 9-1. Because of these differences, manufacturing firms can encounter certain types of problems when they decide to integrate vertically.

Table 9-1
Differences Among Links in the Commercial Chain

Issue	Upstream	Downstream
Product	More standardized	More specialized
Extent of product line	Narrower	Broader
Length of production runs	Longer	Shorter
Type of production process	Automated, connected	Labor-intensive, disconnected
Capital intensity of production	Higher	Lower, then higher
Breakeven utilization point	Higher	Lower
Typical response to market downturns	Reduce prices	Reduce production
Variability of profit	Higher	Lower

9-2.1 Implications for Demand Volatility

Conventional wisdom suggests that the closer a firm gets to the ultimate consumer, the more volatile the nature of demand that must be serviced. However, no matter how fickle these consumers seem to the companies who produce goods and services for them, the companies themselves are generally even more fickle customers for their suppliers. This is largely because of the "accelerator effect" created by the amplifications and delays that are built into the typical supplier–customer "pipeline."

A simple example can illustrate this accelerator effect. A company that services a consumer market produces 100 units monthly of a particular product to meet an apparently steady demand. Each unit contains three component parts of a certain type which the company purchases from an outside supplier. To avoid any possibility of missing a delivery to its consumers because of internal production problems or delays in the delivery of these parts from its suppliers, the manufacturing firm keeps on hand one month's supply (at the current rate of demand) of the finished item and two weeks' supply of component parts. It adjusts its production and supplier requisition rates monthly to maintain these desired inventory levels in the face of demand fluctuations. The supplier usually is able to make deliveries within one week of receiving an order.

If consumer demand suddenly dropped 10 percent, the impact of this decline on the firm's production level and on the orders it places on its suppliers could be dramatic. Table 9-2 describes one possible (and logically justifiable) reaction. It shows that even though ultimate demand dropped only 10 percent, the manufacturer had to reduce its production rate 20 percent to work down its inventory to the new target inventory level. Not until Month 4 does it regain equilibrium with the market. Its supplier is not as fortunate: the supplier's order rate plummets 50 percent in Month 2, then rises rapidly to a rate greater than its initial rate, and does not regain equilibrium until Month 5. This whiplash pattern (commonly referred to as an accelerator effect) is made more pronounced by adding other inventory-carrying agents, such as distributors/wholesalers and retail stores, to the system. Needless to say, the supplier's supplier, who is one link farther out on the whip, experiences even greater volatility of demand.

In practice, therefore, it is not surprising to observe a 10 percent reduction in consumer demand for television sets, say, translated into a 20 or 30 percent reduction in the demand for integrated circuits and, after several months, a catastrophic decline in the demand for integrated circuit manufacturing equipment.

9-2.2 Implications for Asset Intensity

As outlined in Table 9-1, upstream producers tend to produce narrower product lines which permit longer runs utilizing capital-intensive continuous

Table 9-2

Possible Impact of Demand Change on a Single Manufacturer and Supplier

Month	During Month—Consumer Demand	Beginning of Month—Finished Goods Inventory		During Month—Production Rate	End of Month		
					Parts Inventory		Parts Order to Supplier
		Actual	Desired		Actual	Desired	
0	100	100	100	100	150	150	300
1	90	100	100	100	150	150	300
2	90	110	90	80	210	120	150
3	90	100	90	80	120	120	240
4	90	90	90	90	90	135	315
5	90	90	90	90	135	135	270

process production methods. In terms of the product–process matrix described in Chapter 7, upstream producers tend to be located in the lower right quadrant of the matrix. As a consequence, these producers tend to exhibit pronounced economies of scale* and their "minimum economic size"—the minimum size a new facility must be to have costs that are reasonably close to those of its large competitors—tends to be higher. Increased economies of scale also lead to high fixed costs because of interest, depreciation, and maintenance charges, and the fact that the number of workers required to run such an operation is relatively unaffected by the output volume. As a result, the breakeven points of such factories tend to be higher than those of downstream producers. Upstream producers tend also to be highly capital intensive as measured by their sales/asset ratios.†

High capital intensity and scale economies can also characterize the marketing side of a company. There the capital is invested in accounts receivable, warehouses, and finished goods inventories rather than in raw material, plants, and equipment. The economies of scale that are observed arise from a national sales organization, nationwide advertising, and brand image creation. The results, however, are similar. Sears Roebuck, for example, had a sales/assets ratio of about 0.8 in 1981 and 1982, less than that of U.S. Steel (about 1.0). Financial institutions such as banks also tend to be capital-intensive, with sales/assets ratios in the neighborhood of 1.25.

As a result, in some industries the sales/assets ratio increases (it becomes less capital-intensive) for a while as one progresses downstream along the commercial chain, but then it begins to decrease (capital intensity increases) as one continues downstream. In any case, the company's decisions with regard to the direction and extent of vertical integration usually have profound implications for its balance sheet.

9-2.3   Implications for Profitability

As described above, upstream producers tend to be highly automated and capital-intensive. Their production processes have large set-up and changeover costs and it is often difficult to alter the production rates of such processes. (A steel blast furnace, for example, can be operated in one of only two modes: either flat out or shut down.) Therefore, the typical response to changes in the demand level is to adjust prices in an effort to maintain a relatively stable rate of production. Since such processes generally have high fixed costs and high breakeven points (the utilization rate at which all fixed and variable costs are just covered), however, relatively small changes in either prices or output can

---

* As observed in Chapter 3, this is caused largely by the fact that the capacity of a continuous-flow production process increases roughly with the cubic volume of the equipment, while its costs increase roughly with the equipment's surface area. The degree of scale economy can be measured by the percent that costs—both initial investment and operating—increase as a plant's capacity doubles. Typically this ranges between 100 percent (no economies of scale) and about 60 percent (the "six-tenths rule").

† The lower the sales/asset ratio, the higher the capital intensity.

Figure 9-2   Cost structure and profit volatility

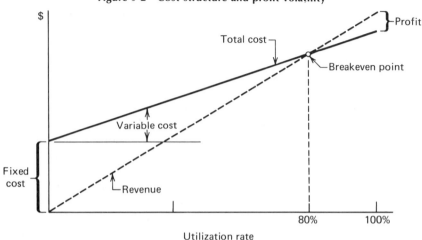

cause major changes in profits. The whiplash effect noted earlier exacerbates
this profit volatility, of course.

These effects on profitability can be illustrated using the cost structure
depicted in Figure 9-2: a company with the capacity to produce 25,000 units
per month of a certain product has fixed costs of $1 million per month and
variable manufacturing costs of $30 per unit. At a selling price of $80 per unit,
the firm must produce 20,000 units a month to break even, implying an 80 percent utilization rate. If the production level rises 10 percent above this breakeven figure, to 22,000 units, the company will achieve a profit before taxes of
$100,000 per month, almost 6 percent of total sales revenue. Similarly, if the
product price rises 10 percent to $88 per unit on the original volume of 20,000
units, the firm will achieve a profit of $160,000 per month, over 9 percent of
sales revenue. Clearly, relatively small changes in the sales price or the utilization rate can result in significant changes in profitability. The higher the fixed
cost (with a compensating adjustment in the variable costs so that the same
total cost results from a given sales volume), the more volatile profitability becomes.

As a consequence, changes in a company's profitability as measured by
its profit/sales ratio tend to exhibit much more short-term volatility (and long-
term cyclicality) in the upstream, commoditylike industries than in industries
closer to the ultimate consumer. In theory at least, over time this ratio tends to
average out at the level required to sustain overall parity with other industries,
as measured by return on equity:

$$\text{return on assets} = \frac{\text{profit}}{\text{assets}} = \frac{\text{profit}}{\text{sales}} \times \frac{\text{sales}}{\text{assets}} = \text{ROA}$$

and

$$\text{return on equity} = \frac{\text{profit}}{\text{equity}} = \frac{\text{profit}}{\text{assets}} \times \frac{\text{assets}}{\text{equity}} = \text{ROA} \times \text{leverage}$$

This rule of rough parity may be violated to the extent that certain industries along the commercial chain are able to maintain high margins through successful product differentiation, by creating barriers to the entry of new competitors, or by following the "price leadership" exerted by a dominant firm.

The combined impact of differences in the capital intensity and profitability associated with various links of the commercial chain can be examined using a "DuPont chart."* Such a chart combines the profitability ratios described above with assets and sales turnover ratios. A DuPont chart for two firms that have selected very different positions in the commercial chain is shown in Figure 9-3. Figure 9-3a is for Hewlett-Packard, which tends to concentrate its assets farther downstream in the commercial chain than does Texas Instruments (Figure 9-3b). Being primarily a manufacturer of integrated circuits, Texas Instruments tends to be much more capital-intensive and experiences much more profit volatility than does Hewlett-Packard.

In general, a manufacturer that decides to integrate backwards accepts higher fixed costs and higher asset intensity in order to achieve lower variable costs and greater control over its operation. Paradoxically, although the improved operations control should increase the firm's ability to predict and control its profitability, just the opposite is generally true: the adoption of a cost structure in which fixed costs are higher, together with a greater degree of demand variability, often leads to higher profit volatility.

9-2.4 Implications for Technological Change

The decision to integrate vertically often is made on the basis of information or design criteria. For example, companies sometimes justify forward integration on the grounds that such moves give them better information about both their immediate customer (the one acquired) and their ultimate market. Conversely, companies justify backward integration as a means for developing competence in the technology of a critical component, to develop proprietary products, or to stay abreast of technological change. In addition, firms may desire to integrate the design of components and final products.

The evidence as to whether backward integration encourages or discourages technological innovation is conflicting. For example, Bowmar failed when it was unsuccessful in integrating backward into semiconductor production and diverted resources too rapidly from its core business of hand-held calculator assembly. Conversely, other companies have failed by not even seeing the competitive need for such shifts in emphasis.

A common mistake of many managers is to behave as if the markets they serve are the source of most important changes, even though history has shown that the fatal assaults usually come from *behind*—from new products and new functions rather than from changing consumer tastes. For example, none of the electronics companies that dominated vacuum tube production was able to

---

* DuPont charts are used here as a way to examine the impact of capital intensity and profitability on a firm's performance. They are also used frequently to evaluate manufacturing's leverage on the overall financial performance (return on equity) of a firm.

**Figure 9-3   DuPont charts for Hewlett-Packard and Texas Instruments
(1980 data, dollars in billions)**

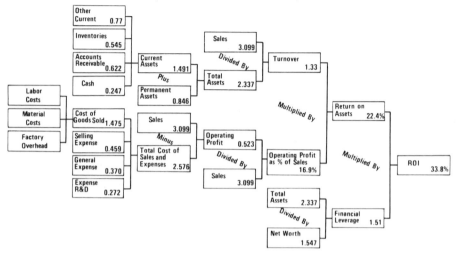

(a) Hewlett-Packard

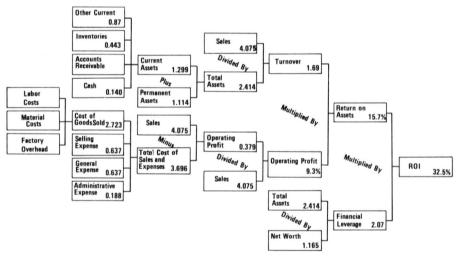

(b) Texas Instruments

(*Sources:*   Hewlett-Packard 1980 Annual Report and Texas Instruments 1980 Annual Report).

dominate the transistor industry. Similarly, none of the dominant producers of mechanical calculators moved quickly enough to develop solid-state electronics capabilities, and they were left behind by the growth of electronic desk and hand-held calculators.

   Since the opportunities and threats stemming from technological change typically originate from material and component innovations that start far back in supply channels, firms attempt to monitor such developments by investing in backward integration. However, as these changes move forward, they often cause such investments to become obsolete. Hence the quandary.

9-2.5 Implications for Scale and Balance

Most manufacturers purchase materials from a number of suppliers and sell their products to a number of customers. Few firms desire to absorb *all* their downstream outlets or upstream sources of supply, so a decision to integrate vertically requires choices. These choices typically reflect the company's assessment as to which materials and markets are most critical for it to control. Even after such choices have been made, a question remains:

> How big should the owned supplier (say) be relative to the parent company?

If the parent and the owned supplier are subject to different scale economies, sizing one to match the capacity of the other may be grossly inefficient. Since progression upstream along the commercial chain generally leads to increased scale economies, the issue is one of balancing the capacities of a materials supplier whose costs may obey the "six-tenths rule" with an assembler that exhibits few economies of scale and has a market of a given size.

The assembler could be sized to meet the needs of the market, but this may mean that the materials supplier is too small relative to its competitors to be efficient. On the other hand, if the assembler decides to match the minimum economic size of the materials supplier, it may have to increase its own operations (and market) substantially. Therefore, if the firm permits both the supplier stage and assembler stage to "find its own level" in order to achieve acceptable profits, the materials supplier may want to produce much more than the assembler can utilize. This raises the issue of how to dispose of the excess output. One obvious way to do that is for the materials producer to find outside customers. This requires setting up a sales force and a marketing program—even though one of the arguments used to justify the decision to integrate backward is that it will eliminate the cost of the supplier's marketing organization—and introduces new customers whose desires may conflict with those of the in-house assembler.

In summary, in choosing the scale and balance of vertically integrated stages, one must consider not only the economics of each link but the other four issues described in this section as well.

9-3 IS VERTICAL INTEGRATION GOOD OR BAD (FOR WHOM)?

Among the issues that have long divided economists, business executives, lawyers, and public policymakers, none is more thorny, contentious, and marked by suspicion of hidden motives than the question of whether vertical integration is good—both for the companies involved and for the public welfare. Classical economic theory appears to provide little guidance in resolving these issues. Consider, for example, the contrasting comments of two very reputable economists:

> Under conventional assumptions [vertical integration] is an anomaly: if the costs of operating competitive markets are zero, "as is usually assumed in our theoretical analysis," . . . why integrate? (Williamson, 1971, p. 112)

> For such firms [that behave competitively, operate in unregulated and untaxed industries, and utilize a technology that provides constant returns to scale] there will be an advantage to integration in the absence of some adverse technological consequences of this action. Always having the option of duplicating the behavior they would have followed separately, integration can hardly be harmful. . . . Without a condition ensuring decreasing returns to integration there appears to be no reason for any producer to remain nonintegrated. (Green, 1974, pp. 3, 6)

Without being familiar with such economic theorizing, companies are usually attracted by vertical integration opportunities for one of two reasons: to increase their profit margins or to improve their control over some part of their business environment. The profitability motive, usually the most obvious, is a natural extension of the familiar make-versus-buy argument: one can absorb the profit margin of the merged supplier/customer, eliminate the purchasing/marketing costs (economists refer to them as "transaction costs") incurred under the normal buyer–seller relationship, and often reduce the logistics costs as well. The control motive is somewhat more subjective but is usually a combination of "We are good managers so we should be able to run that operation better than somebody else" and "If we run it, it will be much more supportive of our constraints, objectives, and strategies than if we leave it to someone else whose objectives are bound to differ at some point."

Before exploring these two major arguments—the one economic and the other more administrative—we review briefly the traditional literature on vertical integration. This literature has been generated primarily by economists and legal scholars and has seldom been "translated" for business managers, nor is it widely appreciated by them. There are benefits, however, to understanding some of the perspectives taken by these scholars and the conclusions they draw.

9-3.1   A Brief Summary of the Literature

The forward and backward integration of firms has been studied from two fundamentally different perspectives. One is that of microeconomic theorists, who are interested in the motivations of "rational profit maximizing firms."

The other is that of welfare economists whose concerns are with social welfare and public policy.

The concerns of the microeconomists generally fall into one of three subcategories. One has to do with information sharing and the reduction of production uncertainties. Recognizing the fundamental interdependence of firms that position themselves at different stages of the same commercial chain, economists like Arrow (1975) and Carlton (1977, 1978) have considered the benefits that a downstream firm can obtain through backward (upstream) integration. Such benefits include better information about the price and availability of materials, which helps the integrated firm make decisions about production levels and capital investment. Similarly, uncertainty about final demand may lead to expensive idle capacity in upstream operations. Forward (downstream) integration may help a firm avoid this by providing it with loyal (captive) customers and thereby stabilizing demand.

A second subcategory involves the notion of "transaction costs," which are defined broadly to include all of the costs associated with conducting business between two independent parties. Such microeconomists as Williamson (1971, 1975) tend to concentrate their attention on the costs associated with free market bargaining, ranging from reliance on spot commodity markets to negotiating long-term contracts. To the extent that integration reduces these "transaction costs" without adding other costs that more than offset them, vertical integration tends to be attractive.

The third subcategory involves the notion of "market power." According to Schmalensee (1973) and Perry (1978), among others, the profit motive leads firms to seek control of those stages in the commercial chain that will give them the greatest leverage over price and volume. Forward integration by basic material manufacturers can provide "guaranteed" outlets for their production, for example, and backward integration can enable them to corner the market on critical components or materials.

The other perspective is that of social welfare economists. They tend to agree that when the rationale for vertical integration is based on reducing uncertainty or lowering transaction costs, the effect on society as a whole is positive. While some redistribution of wealth between producers and consumers may result from such integration moves, the use of more efficient means of production and the elimination of unnecessary costs should result eventually in lower prices for consumers.

But vertical integration that results from the pursuit of market power may not lead to an increase in social welfare. In cases where the nature of the market itself is changed by such integration, the profits of the firm may increase without any improvement in the welfare of consumers. For example, greater control over markets or critical materials may allow a producer to increase its profits by raising prices and reducing production quantities. The public policy concerns with vertical integration are almost always tied to such welfare considerations.

9-4   THE CASE FOR VERTICAL INTEGRATION

As we pointed out earlier, most business managers considering a vertical integration move are heavily influenced by considerations of cost and control. Improved control is achieved by reducing the uncertainty that usually surrounds the free market operations of independent firms and by gaining power over suppliers or customers—the first and third of the microeconomists' concerns described in the previous section. As far as transaction costs are concerned, managers can exploit a wide range of cost-reducing activities.

9-4.1   Arguments for Lower Costs

A firm that links together two succcessive stages of production can act in a variety of ways to "rationalize" the combined operation.

1. It can combine and centralize certain overhead functions such as payroll, billing, production scheduling, and market research, which would not be possible if the two stages of production were not part of the same firm.
2. It can achieve greater efficiency by coordinating the design, production, and marketing of both the end product and its components as a single system.
3. Certain logistics costs incurred in making, storing, and moving the upstream component can be reduced or eliminated by coupling upstream and downstream activities.
4. Design and production changeover costs can be reduced because the integrated firm's natural inclination is to optimize the performance of the combined system rather than its individual parts.
5. Closer contact between the upstream operation and its "customer" permits more accurate forecasts (or, at least, faster feedback), thereby facilitating longer runs, smoother materials flows, and less need for expediting and overtime.

All of these profit opportunities are normally considered when firms analyze make-versus-buy decisions. Most cost accounting textbooks (for example, see Horngren, 1982) recommend that each of the cost-reducing opportunities described above be quantified and balanced against the investment required. While the data to do this may not always be readily available, the techniques for performing such analyses are well understood and widely applied.

9-4.2   Arguments for Improved Control

Although usually much harder to quantify and analyze objectively, improved dependability (of output, price, delivery, quality, etc.) and better control over a firm's environment are often possible if it integrates vertically. Although reducing the level of uncertainty is generally expected to lead eventually to increases in profitability, that is a secondary motivation. Specific ways by which an integrated firm can achieve better control include:

1. Protection from being shut off from critical supplies (or ultimate markets), or otherwise exploited (unfair delivery requirements, price gouging, etc.), by powerful suppliers/customers who accord the firm's needs lower priority than those of other, usually larger, firms.

2. Reduced susceptibility to destructive competitive practices of supplier/customer firms that are themselves divisions of vertically integrated competitor firms.

3. Better measurement of, and hence increased influence over, management performance because of access to information that otherwise would not be available to the firm.

4. Freer communication and more cooperative behavior, since upstream and downstream operations are now members of the same organization.

5. Reduced likelihood that new competitors will enter its business, because of its increased size, reduced costs, and greater control.

6. Greater control over ultimate customers by modifying products to meet the specific needs of different market segments (which often requires tight control over the designs of critical component parts).

7. Increased control over the product quality, delivery time, and price charged by the in-house supplier, as well as the opportunity to differentiate itself from its competitors by developing proprietary materials, components, or technological approaches.

Finally, vertical integration enables the firm to increase the "value-added" component of its total revenue: the difference between its sales revenue and the cost of all purchased items that are used in manufacturing (and distributing) its products, and that contribute to this revenue. Stated another way, the firm's value added is the sum of its cost of direct and indirect labor, manufacturing overhead, selling and administrative activities, and its profits before tax. As its value added increases, the firm can exercise greater control over its costs, final selling prices, and ultimate profitability.

Moreover, the higher the firm's value added, the more strategic freedom it has to differentiate its products and mode of competition. For example, an independent gas station has relatively little flexibility to differentiate itself: it buys gasoline at wholesale and sells it at retail. The oil company that sells the gasoline, however, can position and differentiate itself in a rich assortment of ways. This freedom usually permits the oil company to achieve higher profit margins, lower risk, or both, than the gas station to which it sells.

In the case of forward integration, reducing costs is usually a less important means of increasing profitability than is the possibility of increasing the market prices of one's product. A company's control of a nationwide marketing organization, combined with a strong in-house distribution system and brand image advertising, often can support premium prices. The price differential between "private label" or "house" brands and branded merchandise on a grocer's shelf (although they may be identical products manufactured in the same factory) provides everyday evidence of this approach to augmenting the selling price, and hence the profitability, of a manufacturer's product. It is part of what we earlier referred to as "market power."

All these motivations probably lay behind the philosophy expressed over 60 years ago by Konosuhe Matsushita, the founder of the giant Matsushita Electric Company: "Look after the components and the products will look after themselves."

Given such powerful arguments in favor of vertical integration, why doesn't everybody do it? There are two answers to this question. First, many firms do not experience the increased profitability and improved control that might be expected from vertical integration, for reasons to be explored in the next section. Second, vertical integration can impair the performance of the firm along other important competitive dimensions, even though its total costs may be reduced.

9-5   THE CASE AGAINST VERTICAL INTEGRATION

The arguments against vertical integration can be grouped into two categories that are rough complements to the two arguments just described that favor it. Firms that vertically integrate can experience *higher* costs (lower profitability) as well as a *loss* of control, particularly in terms of their ability to react to changes in their environment.

9-5.1   Arguments Against Lower Costs

As noted earlier, firms often justify decisions to integrate vertically (particularly backwards) on the grounds that it will enable them to reduce their total production costs. Many companies, however, find to their surprise that the expected cost reduction does not materialize and that overall costs may actually increase. To understand why, consider the case of a manufacturer (Company M) that is exploring the possibility of making in-house a part that is currently purchased from an outside supplier (Company S). This part is one of many similar components that Company S produces for a wide range of customers. Company S uses a highly capital-intensive mass-production process specially tailored to the production of these parts.

On what grounds might Company M expect to achieve a lower cost for this part by making it internally? Let us deal with this question by breaking its total factory price into five major components:

1.   Purchased materials.
2.   R&D/design costs.

3. Manufacturing costs.
4. Transportation/distribution costs.
5. Margin (overhead and profit).

It is unlikely that Company M's costs for purchased materials, if it decides to produce the part itself, would be less than what Company S pays for those same materials. Company S, which probably purchases much greater volumes than Company M would, is in a position to coordinate those purchases with its purchases of similar products from the same suppliers. The "clout" that Company S has with its suppliers because it purchases large volumes from them, combined with the fact that they are one step farther up the commercial chain (and therefore usually even more sensitive to changes in their sales volume) than it is, should allow Company S to achieve lower purchasing costs than could Company M if it integrated backward.

Similarly, since Company S has an R&D group experienced in designing these parts, and those designs can be coordinated for a number of related parts, Company S's design costs would probably also be less than Company M's. Moreover, Company S can amortize those R&D costs over a much greater production volume. This does not mean that Company M will not be able to copy the design of the part it currently buys from Company S more cheaply than it cost Company S to design it originally. However, should Company M ever want to redesign the same part, it will probably cost it more to accomplish that redesign than it would Company S.*

The conversion of purchased materials into the part itself also probably would be less for Company S than it would be for Company M for a variety of reasons.

1. Company M's own requirements for the part may not be great enough to permit the economies of scale enjoyed by suppliers like Company S who sell to a number of customers and can afford to use highly specialized and automated equipment. As outlined in Chapters 3 and 8, both static and dynamic (learning curve) economies of scale suggest that the total manufacturing costs of an in-house supplier that is one-fourth as big as its largest (external) competitor might be as much as 50 percent higher than its competitors' costs, even after incurring the start-up expenses associated with beginning production.

2. The high production volume that enables Company S to negotiate favorable purchasing prices for its raw materials from its suppliers may also make it possible for Company S to obtain materials that have already un-

* Commodore International's 1976 purchase of MOS Technology, a failing manufacturer of calculator chips, is sometimes credited with Commodore's later success in small computers. MOS had developed the 6502 processor, which was to become the heart of many small computers, including the Apple II and the Commodore Pet. The jury is still out, however, on whether MOS will be equally innovative as part of a vertically integrated organization.

dergone some preprocessing, such as specially designed castings, nonstandard thicknesses, and unique colors. This preprocessing, which may not be equally available to Company M, reduces manufacturing costs at Company S.

3. A lack of experience in and understanding about the newly acquired business may cause Company M to be an inefficient manager of its new in-house supplier. Moreover, Company M cannot spread its overhead expenses over the high production volumes enjoyed by Company S. The combination of both factors may result in higher total overhead costs for Company M and its in-house supplier than were experienced by Company M and Company S when they had a buyer–seller relationship; that is, transaction costs plus total manufacturing costs may be lower when the firms are separate than when they are integrated.

4. The in-house supplier may be regarded as a "secondary business," and therefore Company M might be unwilling to commit the attention and resources necessary to keep it abreast of its competitors. Or the dedicated in-house supplier may not have the same incentive to reduce costs and improve quality as an independent supplier operating under the threats and incentives provided by a competitive free market.

The only places where Company M may be able to achieve lower costs than Company S are in the last two categories: distribution costs and manufacturing margin. These are part of what were called "transaction costs" in our earlier discussion, with one important difference: if Company S were obtaining an *unreasonable* profit from its sales to Company M, then Company M (which will "charge itself" a more reasonable price to produce these same parts) may accept a lower total margin than Company S is willing to accept.

The important question is: Will the savings from cost categories 4 and 5 (transportation/distribution and profit margin) outweigh the cost disadvantages from categories 1, 2, and 3 (purchased materials, design, and manufacturing costs)? Unless Company S is obtaining extravagant profits from its sales to Company M, or unless Company M has developed a superior process or product design that will enable it to achieve a lower manufacturing cost than Company S, it is unlikely that they will. Even if Company M is able to develop a superior process or product, it may be possible for Company S to copy it, which would make the resulting cost advantage only temporary.

The same kind of argument can be raised against the claim that costs will be reduced by integrating forward. Again, the advantages the firm's current customer gains from its specialized process (distribution and/or marketing), higher volumes, and close relations with its own traditional customers and suppliers can be offset only by the hope of reduced transaction/coordination costs and improved control over one's environment.

As one might expect, these transaction costs tend to be lowest in highly fragmented and competitive industries—characterized by low economies of scale and rapid changes in market preferences. In such environments it is also more difficult to gain any significant market power or enduring technological advantage. As a result, companies in industries like textiles, furniture, recreational boats, and home construction tend to avoid vertical integration. Textile manufacturers, for example, were appalled by Texfi Corporation's decision to integrate backward into synthetic fiber production in the mid-1970s. As they expected, the move was not successful.

Apart from the impact of vertical integration of a firm's profit margin, there may be an impact on its ROI because of changes in its capital intensity and breakeven point. As discussed in Section 9-2.2, integrating backward usually causes both to increase. As a result, ROI may be reduced and become more sensitive to fluctuations in market demand.

A number of studies have attempted to measure the impact of the degree of vertical integration on a firm's reported profit. Most of these have led to inconclusive or contradictory results. Moreover, the findings appear to be highly sensitive to the time period and industry involved. Bowman's (1978) study of 46 computer equipment manufacturing firms arrived at the surprising conclusion that higher profits are associated with *either* a high level of vertical integration or a low level. The least profitable position seemed to be in the middle. Buzzell (1983), in a more recent study involving 1,742 SBU's (strategic business units), arrived at a similar conclusion about the relationship between vertical integration and ROI. Perhaps this explains the difficulties experienced by other studies, many of which tried to fit straight lines through the data.

9-5.2   Arguments Against Increased Control and Flexibility

Most of the arguments outlined in Section 9-4, to the effect that vertical integration will reduce costs and improve control, assume that a manufacturer and a supplier who are members of the same organization will be able to coordinate their activities more closely than they could (or would) if they were independent companies. For example, the "whiplash effect" described in Section 9-2.1, where relatively small changes in the demand level experienced by the downstream company cause large fluctuations in the orders placed with upstream suppliers, can be ameliorated somewhat if the production rates of both companies are centrally controlled. Similarly, the economies and market opportunities available from coordinating the design of parts and finished products as a total system are possible only if the design activities of the two groups are tightly integrated. But many companies find that they actually have less control over an in-house supplier than when they operated under an independent buyer–seller relationship.

Two companies that are adjacent on the commercial chain may be characterized by very different processes and product structures, and they may espouse incompatible operating policies and philosophies. For example, the upstream company may require long runs of relatively few products with very little fluctuation in day-to-day output in order to maintain process stability and high plant utilization. The downstream company, on the other hand, may desire short runs of many products and may continually adjust output to reflect market fluctuations. Each firm may be behaving optimally in its particular situation. How should one integrate these two companies, these two management mentalities, into a single organization?

Changing one company to conform to the needs or desires of the other invites disaster. To choose a "middle strategy" may result in an organization that meets the needs of neither party (we discussed this in Chapter 4 in connection with the dangers of losing focus). And to do nothing—to run the two companies as if they were completely independent—would frustrate entirely the desire for increased control that constituted one of the major motives for integrating in the first place.

We know of one independent trading company, in fact, that found to its surprise that it was buying a material from one division of a giant multinational company and selling it to another division of same company in a different country. After wrestling with the ethical issue involved, the trading company's sales manager decided to approach the customer division, explain what was going on, and suggest that he would understand if the customer preferred to deal directly with its sister division in the future. "Absolutely not," responded the customer, "if we did, both the price we pay and our delivery time would suffer!"

Backward integration can also lead to a loss of control over the technological developments in various businesses, even though management expects just the opposite to occur. While the vertically integrated business may have greater access to technological information than it did before it was integrated, it may not be able to incorporate this new information very easily into its decision-making processes. Its "corporate mentality" is more likely to reflect (perhaps unconsciously) the technology of its original core business and may distort its perspective when it confronts a new, very different technology. In terms of the product–process matrix described in Chapter 7, the distance between the position on the matrix represented by the original core business and that represented by the new business is such that a single corporate mentality may not be able to run both businesses effectively.

After cutting itself off from access to the R&D efforts of its former supplier, it may be difficult for an organization that has integrated backward to stay on top of rapid advances in several different areas, especially the less visible R&D efforts of its new (one step farther back in the commercial chain) suppliers. Even when the expected operating benefits are achieved, backward integration may lead to unforeseen costs. The organizational commitment needed to keep on top of the final product's current technology may actually hinder the commitment and learning associated with mastering a new component technology, unless the two engineering groups are separated organizationally—but this would thwart one of the primary motives for integrating. The failure of the large producers of electronic equipment (who had integrated backward into vacuum tube production) to make the switch to producing transistors fast enough was probably due to this lack of commitment.

Vertical integration may also impede information transfer, even though increased information may now be available to the firm. In the buyer–seller relationships of independent firms, selected focal points exist for the contact and passing of information among the two organizations. Following a vertical integration step, such focal points may increase in number and become blurred, making it even more difficult for design engineers and manufacturing managers to assign priorities to the information coming to them.

Finally, size itself may reduce the degree of managerial control that is possible after integration. The number of communication channels are increased and all of the diseconomies of scale cited in Chapter 3 must be managed within the firm. Moreover, efforts to avoid those diseconomies by restructuring the organization into smaller profit-oriented entities may inhibit the firm from achieving the cost and control benefits that motivated vertical integration. Or they may lead the firm to add other "coordinating" overhead layers to achieve those benefits, which, in turn, would slow responsiveness and increase costs.

Vertically integrating may lead to less control in another form: reduced organizational flexibility to respond to market, product, or technological changes. It is usually much easier for a company to cut back on orders to an independent supplier that produces for a number of companies than to an in-house supplier that is totally dependent on it. It is also much easier to switch suppliers when an improved product or processing technology appears than it is to reequip and retrain one's in-house supplier. Similarly, it is far more expensive in terms of both operating and overhead costs to alter the marketing strategy and distribution methods of one's wholly owned downstream subsidiary than it is to shift one's selling efforts to an independent retailer or distributor who is prevailing in the marketplace by utilizing a new concept or approach. The natural tendency in most organizations is to protect obsolete resources.

Responding to volume changes also tends to be more difficult as a result of vertical integration, particularly if one stage has a different production cycle time, capacity planning horizon, or breakeven point than another, as is usually the case. In its simplest form, this loss of responsiveness occurs when the optimal production batch for a given part is much larger than the optimal batch size of the product into which it is assembled. The combined operation tends to have both large parts inventories and relatively rigid production schedules which, if altered, upset the entire product mix. Similarly, if a certain material or subassembly takes much longer to acquire or produce than the ultimate product, the manufacturer may find itself locked in by decisions made by its in-house supplier months or even years earlier.

Yet another loss in flexibility may occur as a result of union activities across a vertically integrated firm. One of the tenets of the U.S. auto industry for many years was that vertical integration was the key to success. Indeed, the average profitabilities of the three largest U.S. manufacturers were strongly correlated with the ratios of their value added to total sales. The UAW's strong position in the industry eventually led to strong unions, and roughly comparable wage scales, among the auto companies' in-house suppliers. For example, as the average hourly wage at GM increased rapidly during the 1970s—to the point where, by the early 1980s, it was almost double the average rate for U.S. manufacturing as a whole—the average wage at such wholly owned subsidiaries as Delco (which supplies it with car radios and shock absorbers) and Packard Electric (which supplies it with electrical systems) increased proportionally. GM soon discovered the disadvantages of purchasing parts produced by its own subsidiaries' unionized workers, who earned over $20 per hour, compared with buying them from outside, often nonunionized, suppliers whose workers earned less than half as much.

9-6 ALTERNATIVES TO VERTICAL INTEGRATION

Thus far we have talked about vertical integration—either forward or backward—in terms of the ownership and management of a series of linked stages on the commercial chain. While the benefits of vertical integration, in terms of profitability and control, can be substantial, the different market characteristics, process characteristics, financial characteristics, industry structures, and competitive practices can cause pressures, problems, and questions in every aspect of such an integrated firm's activities. Often it is possible to avoid many of these problems, and still achieve the majority of the benefits, by pursuing one of various alternatives to vertical integration.

There is a broad middle ground between buying or selling the firm's products on the open market and owning and managing the supplier or customer. Collectively referred to as "quasi-vertical integration" by Blois (1972) and others, several of the most important alternatives in this middle ground are worth serious consideration before one of the two extremes is accepted.

9-6.1 Holding Inventory

To the extent that the purpose of a backward integration step is to achieve better control over suppliers or to avoid being squeezed out of the market by larger competitors during periods of tight supply, a company can achieve similar results simply by carrying large inventories of the item in question. These inventories can be used as a buffer against temporary shortages and delivery delays and, through volume purchases and careful market timing, they may permit reduced purchasing costs as well.

The investment and effort required by this approach are usually much smaller than those involved in integrating backwards, and the benefits are often comparable. The disadvantage, of course, is that one's flexibility to change the design of one's product (to the extent that this requires a change in the purchased item) is reduced. But, as we have seen, this loss of flexibility may be just as great if one integrates backward.

Another approach that is possible if commodity markets exist for key materials is to purchase forward contracts for, or options to purchase, some portion of a firm's predicted future requirements. This locks in both the material's availability and its price.

9-6.2 Modified Vendor Relations

U.S. companies have traditionally restricted themselves to extreme options: either open market, arm's-length bargaining, which permits maximum flexibility, or full vertical integration, which promises maximum control. As a result, vendor relationships tend to be characterized by short-term agreements, emphasis on price, and multiple sourcing. However, longer-term relationships (not necessarily involving legal contracts), with a smaller number of suppliers or customers, offer certain advantages.

Since the advantages and disadvantages (in terms of cost, quality, control, and flexibility) are often roughly proportional to the length of the contract or working relationship, one test of whether a company should integrate vertically is to ask if it would be willing to commit itself instead to a ten-year relationship with a single supplier or customer. If it objects on the grounds that this would place undue constraints on it, it probably should not integrate. However, a five-year commitment to a close working relationship with either a customer or supplier might be much better than opting for the extreme of open market, arm's-length bargaining. Ownership remains separated under such alternative "middle-ground" relationships, but over time the two organizations grow to understand one another's needs and learn to communicate easily about common problems.

U.S. companies tend to avoid such relationships either on the grounds that they want to guard against losing flexibility (through becoming too dependent on a single supplier or customer), losing power over suppliers or customers (by not being able to play one off against the others in the hope of achieving better terms), or that without formal contractual relationships that cover all important contingencies the other party is not to be trusted. In the eyes of European and Japanese companies, this characteristic of their U.S. counterparts makes them tough customers, but they question whether too much is sacrificed through such hard-nosed dedication to obtaining the best possible terms each year—from firms to which one is inextricably linked.

In contrast, as we discuss in Chapter 12, Japanese companies tend to look upon key suppliers as partners in a joint venture, even though there is seldom a legal document establishing such an arrangement. (They often use the term "co-destiny" to refer to their interlinked fortunes.) One does not disappoint a supplier–partner by not buying from it if its price is somewhat out of line or if quality or delivery problems arise, although one certainly does work with it to solve those "temporary" problems. On the other hand, the supplier–partner is expected to work unceasingly to create improved products and services and to bend over backward to satisfy the needs and strengthen the competitive position of its "customer–partner." The objective is a mutually beneficial, long-term relationship, just as it is in most partnerships.

Through such relationships, Japanese companies are able to exercise almost the same degree of control over delivery schedules that they would if they owned the supplier directly. Delivery contracts usually cover several months and are changed automatically every time the producer alters its production schedule. Often these contracts specify frequent "call-offs" of materials—where the supplier agrees to make deliveries several times a day—so as to allow the producer to keep its raw material inventories low.

There are at least two important prerequisites to making such middle-ground relationships effective. First, both parties must accept the fact that the relationship will be to their mutual benefit. Each must make a credible (in the eyes of the other) commitment to maintaining that relationship and resolving the normal short-term difficulties that arise. Second, each must commit itself to learning about and helping the other organization improve its performance. In the process their joint performance will be improved. Thus, if such a relationship is to work effectively, a manufacturer must take a personal interest in the success of its suppliers/customers. Moreover, it must be willing to invest its resources in activities whose immediate benefits are likely to be experienced first by these suppliers/customers, and which will filter back to benefit the manufacturer itself only indirectly and over the long term.

9-6.3   Long-Term Contracts, Joint Ventures, Minority Equity Investments and Licensing Arrangements

In one sense these intermediate arrangements are simply more formal versions of the long-term supplier–customer agreements just outlined. Through the establishment of joint ventures and licensing arrangements, or simply long-term contracts, legal force is given to the desired operating arrangement. Such arrangements can require less investment than would be required for full vertical integration, yet give a firm substantial leverage with its supplier (at the expense of some flexibility). Both parties rely on legal mechanisms regarding their individual responsibilities to keep them working toward their mutual benefit.

A long-term contract, perhaps containing escalation clauses to permit price changes as costs evolve, allows a company to gain added predictability over its operations. Such an agreement can also help the company gain leverage over material specifications, delivery times, and availability (particularly during supply shortages). Most firms quickly learn, after entering into such long-term contracts, that such nebulous factors as trust and cooperation have much more impact on the overall satisfaction of both parties than does the actual wording of their formal contract.

9-6.4   Investment Integration (as Opposed to Operating Integration)

Moving one step closer to full vertical integration, some companies seek reduced cost and increased control over suppliers without taking on operating responsibility. This can be accomplished, for example, by purchasing tools, dies, and sometimes even the production equipment required to produce an item, and then assigning those resources to a single supplier who becomes the sole source for that item. In effect, the firm integrates backwards in terms of the equipment and tools investment but avoids being involved in the actual production.

Compared with the alternative of increasing raw material inventories, this tactic may allow the firm both to increase its clout with its supplier—the threat of moving production equipment to another supplier is a potent one—and give it more flexibility in facilitating design changes. In situations where the current outside suppliers for an item are few in number and unresponsive to a company's specific needs, offering such an arrangement can enable it to induce another company to become its supplier; the investment required to enter the (supplier) business is reduced and it is guaranteed a certain amount of business.

A similar type of arrangement involves the use of consignment inventories. The producer agrees to pay the cost of the customer's inventory of its product if the customer (usually a wholesaler or distributor) agrees to service that inventory and use it to meet customer needs. As with investment integration, this arrangement often allows the firm to gain better information about final customer markets, expand its distribution network by reducing the investment required for independent distributors to carry its products, and gain control over decisions to change inventory levels.

9-7 DEVELOPING AND PURSUING A VERTICAL INTEGRATION STRATEGY

In keeping with the central message of this book, the most important step in developing and pursuing an integration strategy is to identify the capabilities that are required to support the firm's desired competitive advantage. In formulating its strategy a firm must position itself along two key dimensions—one relating to products and the other to production processes. Vertical integration decisions should be guided by the choices made in both dimensions and also reflect the behavioral preferences and competitive choices outlined in Chapter 2.

Once the issue is defined in terms of acquiring and maintaining control over certain key capabilities, vertical integration can be addressed in a different light. It becomes one—but only one—means for carrying out a given strategy, not an independent decision that reflects a sudden opportunity, industry practice, or the firm's previous history. For example, under certain circumstances it can enable a firm to gain better control over the cost of a critical resource. But, as we have seen, other approaches may achieve a similar degree of control. Moreover, not all competitive strategies are based on the need to control tightly, or minimize, costs.

This point of view, it should be noted, is not universally reflected in practice. Economic costs and benefits tend to be given much greater weight by managers, possibly because they are more quantifiable. Also, arguments based on economic considerations tend to have more credibility in financially dominated companies.

9-7.1   Assessing the Impact of Vertical Integration

On the basis of our experience and the published observations of others, the following generalizations regarding the advantages and disadvantages of integration can be made:

1. Vertical integration may or may not reduce a firm's costs or increase its profits, depending on (among other things) the size of the firm compared with the size of the companies it will now have to compete against, how successful the firm is in coordinating the activities of the merged operations, its skill in managing the acquired business (particularly if it is perceived as a "secondary" business), and the extent to which the firm is willing to accept a lower rate of profit than the previous supplier/customer.

2. Vertical integration may or may not make possible an increase in the quality (defined in terms of performance characteristics) of a company's product. If bringing a supplier in-house enables the company to use specially tailored input parts and materials that would not be obtainable on the open market, and these improved inputs can be incorporated into superior products, quality may increase. On the other hand, to the extent that vertical integration robs the company of some of its ability to use improved materials as they appear on the market, the performance of its products (compared with those of competitors) may decrease.

3. To the extent that the company can coordinate successfully the activities of the new, vertically linked subsidiary, it ought to be able to gain greater control over delivery schedules, costs, customer promises, and other dimensions of competitive performance. On the other hand, if a natural or man-made catastrophe (such as a flood or strike) disrupts either of the two operations, the whole organization can be paralyzed. If it does not have an ongoing relationship with independent suppliers, and its in-house supplier becomes incapacitated, the firm will probably find it difficult to obtain on the open market materials that it normally obtains in-house.

4. Vertical integration usually leads to a loss of flexibility. In the case of backward integration, it becomes more difficult to change production levels and product mix (because these must be coordinated with in-house suppliers rather than accomplished simply by changing the level of purchases from independent suppliers) and technologies (which no longer can simply be purchased as soon as they appear on the market). Nor can the company easily escape an in-house supplier that asks higher prices and offers poorer service than that available in the open market.

These and other advantages and disadvantages are summarized in Table 9-3. A somewhat different approach to assessing how vertical integration might affect a firm's competitive position is the framework developed by Porter (1980) and summarized in Table 9-4. Using competitive interactions and drawing on much of the work of industrial organization economists, Porter developed a list of issues, costs, and benefits that the individual firm might address in evaluating different vertical integration options. Note that only a few of the entries in this table relate directly to profitability improvement. The vast majority reflect issues relating to control in the context of a competitive strategy.

9-7.3 Formulating and Executing the Integration Strategy

As outlined at the outset of this chapter, three important issues must be addressed as part of a firm's vertical integration strategy:

1. The direction of integration.
2. The extent of the process span desired.
3. The balance between the vertically linked activities.

Implementing an integration strategy requires the development of a set of administrative procedures to ensure that the pattern of decisions made in each of these areas is consistent with overall guidelines and policies. Our experience is that most senior managers are not as explicit or comprehensive as they ought to be in communicating these general guidelines and related administrative decision-making procedures to their organizations.

Before making a vertical integration move a firm should be sure that its existing relationships with customers and suppliers are appropriate in light of its chosen competitive strategy. On the upstream side, both the vendors them-

Table 9-3

Possible Advantages and Disadvantages of Vertical Integration

Key Dimensions	Advantages	Disadvantages
Cost	Reduces marketing and transaction costs, including sales commissions and taxes on intermediate goods. Reduces risk premium demanded by supplier because of increased predictability of demand. Allows supplier/distributor's margins to be absorbed.	Increases overhead costs because of difficulties of managing different technologies, control systems, people, etc. Increases logistic costs because of increased need/desire to coordinate shipments, production, distribution, and inventories, and flexibility in choosing the location of sources of supply. Inefficiencies arise out of imbalances between capacities and operating characteristics of vertically linked production stages.

Table 9-3 (*continued*)

Key Dimensions	Advantages	Disadvantages
Control	Makes possible better measurement of performance because of better access to information. Increased control over costs that are rising rapidly or subject to temporary supply–demand imbalances.	Measurement becomes more difficult and less objective because of vested interests and intracompany politics; people have greater confidence in the objectivity of market prices and decisions than in those resulting from bureaucratic processes. More performance measurements become necessary, often adding to the complexity and confusion of the common control system.
Communication	Facilitates communication with respect to complex matters because of common training, experience, and codes of behavior/value systems—particularly in industry environments characterized by low trust.	When the organization is structured according to process stages, each tends to attract its own specialists, who often have more allegiance to their professions than to their company because of their separation from ultimate products and customers.
Organization climate	Helps resolve potentially acrimonious bargaining between buyer and seller because both are on "same team."	If protracted bargaining between buyer and seller occurs, continual mediation may be required; this may lead to intraorganizational acrimony.
Operations management	Simplifies and facilitates purchase or sale agreements, particularly when these require investment in long-lived special-purpose equipment or specialized know-how. Ensures availability of critical materials, permitting full or most efficient utilization of facilities.	If company "forces" its in-house supplier to undertake long-term investments without compensating long-term commitments, it will increase its vulnerability to losses and/or its sense of persecution and "secondary status." Creates more rigidity because company is locked into single supplier and is less able to take advantage of technological changes, price reductions, etc.
Competitive differentiation	Permits better control over and exploitation of proprietary technology.	Causes organization to lose its sense of focus. "Not invented here" syndrome may blind company to advantages of other companies' technological advances.

Table 9-4

A Competitive Analysis of Vertical Integration

Potential Benefits	Potential Costs
Economics of integration	Cost of overcoming mobility barriers
Access to technology	Increased operating leverage
Assure supply and/or demand	Reduced flexibility to change partners
Offset bargaining power and input cost	Higher overall exit barriers
distortions	Capital investment requirements
Enhance ability to differentiate	Foreclosure of access
Elevate entry and mobility barriers	Maintaining balance
Enter a higher-return business	Dulled incentives
Defend against foreclosure	Different management requirements

Source.   Porter, 1980, Chapter 14.

selves and the form of the relationships that have developed with them should be reviewed to ensure that the firm is taking full advantage of essential capabilities and performance characteristics. Similarly, its existing customers and markets should "fit" its competitive strategy. While most firms spend considerable time on this latter (downstream) activity, few devote equal attention to upstream considerations. Many manufacturing problems could be avoided (along with many unsuccessful vertical integration moves) if more attention were paid to this step. This kind of preliminary analysis is important because sometimes the problems that a firm is seeking to solve through a vertical integration move could be corrected simply by improving its existing, nonintegrated relationships.

Once a firm does decide to increase its span in the commercial chain, it must decide whether to acquire an existing organizational unit or develop its own. The advantage of integrating through acquisition is obvious: it allows the company to get into the business much more quickly than it could through a "do-it-yourself" approach. Plants do not have to be built, equipment does not have to be purchased. Even more important, people—both workers and managers—do not have to be hired and trained. The organization is already in place, equipped with a "memory bank" and information network relating to technological know-how, suppliers, and competitors.

The disadvantages of integration through acquisition tend to be more subtle but basically they are the mirror image of the advantages: one is stuck with all of the weaknesses of the acquired company as well as its strengths. Such weaknesses might include poor plant locations, old equipment, obsolete (or inappropriate) product designs, weak managers, dissatisfied or inefficient workers, counterproductive work practices, an adversarial union, and incompatible organizational policies and philosophies. One also faces the myriad problems associated with trying to integrate a new organization into an existing one.

The question of internal development versus acquisition is further complicated by the paradox alluded to earlier: most manufacturers use a variety of purchased parts and materials that come from a large number of producers, but they use only a small percentage of the total production of any one of them. Therefore, if a manufacturer buys an existing supplier, it may be utilizing only a small portion of that company's capabilities for its own products. Should it strip away or spin off the other products and services and retain only those aspects of the supplier's activities that serve its own needs? Focusing its activities in this way may enable the firm to reduce the new in-house supplier's costs, but this could also tend to isolate it in the marketplace, reducing the information and motivation that enable it to maintain its competitiveness with other independent suppliers. This narrowing of focus also may impair the in-house supplier's interest and ability to experiment with, develop, and introduce new products.

Alternatively, if the company decides to allow the acquired company to operate much as it did before, it may not be able to take advantage of the potential benefits of focus. Worse—it may find itself being distracted from its primary business in trying to deal with such questions as: Should this in-house supplier be treated as a profit center or a cost center? Should transactions between stages be conducted through arm's-length bargaining or centrally managed through coordinated planning and preestablished transfer prices? How much independence should the management of the in-house supplier be allowed? Should it be allowed to expand capacity, add new products, integrate backwards itself? Some companies find that if the new supplier is given too much independence, the "tail begins to wag the dog": they lose the control they sought to gain. Many companies soon learn that purchasing a company to assure a predictable source of supply at a reasonable cost is one thing; being in, say, the plastics business itself over the long term is quite another.

Such questions must be addressed before a company decides whether to integrate vertically through acquisition or through growing its own organizational unit. Closely linked, cost center–oriented operations are usually much easier to establish through internal development, whereas more arm's-length, autonomous subsidiary relationships are easier to set up through acquisition. Some firms have been successful, however, at establishing this latter type of relationship by setting up "new venture" groups composed of relatively autonomous in-house personnel.

The way a company chooses to resolve these issues depends on its management's responses to questions like: What business are we in? What kind of company do we want to be—a corporate family or a corporate army? What kinds of motivations and values do we want to support among our individual managers and workers? What pressures and opportunities are offered by the marketplace and by competitors?

9-7.4   Avoiding the Common Pitfalls of Integration

Most of the major pitfalls that a firm can encounter in pursuing a vertical integration strategy can be grouped into three categories. The first is letting apparent (short-term) profitability become too dominant in deciding when and where to integrate vertically. If control is considered the primary issue, and economics a second-level issue, most of these pitfalls can be avoided. Make-versus-buy decisions that go awry are almost always the result of decisions that are driven by profitability considerations rather than the desire to expand and control critical capabilities.

The second common mistake is falling prey to the self-delusion that one can manage any kind of business successfully. All too often a firm's real, though unstated, justification for integrating vertically is the belief that it can manage the other business better than can its current managers. While this is sometimes true, particularly if the firm is very successful in some similar activity, vertical integration often requires a company to undertake activities that are very different from those it is accustomed to. Thus vertical integration usually requires developing superior management skills in a new area, not simply applying existing skills. As indicated in Section 9-6, there are usually a variety of alternatives to vertical integration, one or more of which may provide the desired capabilities and improved control without having to become "better managers" in new areas.

A third potential pitfall serves as an appropriate closing note for this chapter. In analyzing the vertical integration moves in a number of U.S. companies, one is struck by their lemminglike behavior: industries tend to be dominated by firms that are either highly vertically integrated or are characterized by very little integration. Smaller firms in highly integrated industries often exhibit a greater degree of integration than do large firms in less integrated industries. Given our analysis of the advantages and disadvantages resulting from vertical integration and the range of alternatives to it, one wonders whether this apparent agreement within industries is a reflection of rational assessment or a follow-the-leader mentality. How a firm decides to position itself on its commercial chain necessitates choices from a rich assortment of possibilities, each of which involves important strategic challenges and opportunities. The variety of positions that a firm can occupy in its strategic environment is too large and seeded with opportunities to be left to the dictates of conventional industry wisdom.

SELECTED REFERENCES

Armour, Henry O., and David J. Teece. "Vertical Integration and Technical Innovation." *Review of Economics and Statistics,* Vol. 62, No. 3, August 1980, pp. 470–474.

Arrow, Kenneth J. "Vertical Integration and Communication." *Bell Journal of Economics,* Vol. 6, No. 1, Spring 1975, pp. 173–182.

Bain, J. S. *Essays in Price Theory and Industrial Organization.* Boston: Little, Brown, 1972.

Blois, K. J. "Vertical Quasi-Integration." *Journal of Industrial Economics,* July 1972, pp. 253–272.

Bork, Robert H. "Vertical Integration and Competitive Processes," in *Public Policy Towards Mergers,* J. F. Weston and S. Peltzman (eds.). Santa Monica, CA: Goodyear, 1969, pp. 139–149.

Bowman, Edward H. "Strategy, Annual Reports, and Alchemy." *California Management Review,* Vol. 20, No. 3, Spring 1978, pp. 64–71.

Buzzell, Robert D. "Is Vertical Integration Profitable?" *Harvard Business Review,* January–February 1983, pp. 92–102.

Carlton, D. W. "Market Behavior with Demand Uncertainty and Price Inflexibility." *American Economic Review,* September 1978, pp. 571–587.

Carlton, D. W. "Uncertainty, Production Lags, and Pricing." *American Economic Review,* February 1977, pp. 244–249.

Caves, Richard. *American Industry: Structure, Conduct, Performance,* 4th ed. Englewood Cliffs, NJ: Prentice-Hall, 1977.

Comanor, William S. "Vertical Mergers, Market Powers, and the Antitrust Laws." *American Economic Review,* Vol. 57, No. 2, May 1967, pp. 254–265.

Gort, Michael. *Diversification and Integration in American Industry.* Princeton, NJ: Princeton University Press, 1962.

Green, Jerry R. "Vertical Integration and Assurance of Markets." Discussion Paper No. 383, Harvard Institute of Economic Research, October 1974.

Harrigan, Kathryn R. *Strategies for Vertical Integration.* Lexington, MA: Lexington Books, 1983.

Horngren, Charles T. *Cost Accounting: A Managerial Emphasis,* 5th ed. Englewood Cliffs, NJ: Prentice-Hall, 1982.

Kaserman, David L. "Theories of Vertical Integration: Implications for Antitrust Policy." *Antitrust Bulletin,* Vol. 23, No. 3, Fall 1978, pp. 483–510.

Laffer, Arthur B. "Vertical Integration by Corporations, 1929–1965." *Review of Economics and Statistics,* Vol. 51, No. 1, February 1969, pp. 91–93.

Livesay, Harold C., and Patrick G. Porter. "Vertical Integration in American Manufacturing, 1899–1948." *Journal of Economic History,* Vol. 29, No. 3, September 1969, pp. 494–500.

Maddigan, Ruth J. "The Measurement of Vertical Integration." *Review of Economics and Statistics,* Vol. 63, No. 3, August 1981, pp. 328–335.

May, George A. "An Economic Analysis of Vertical Integration." *Industrial Organization Review,* Vol. 1, 1973, pp. 188–198.

Mueller, Willard F. "Public Policy Toward Vertical Mergers," in *Public Policy Towards Mergers,* Weston and Peltzman, (eds.). Santa Monica, CA: Goodyear, 1969, pp. 150–166.

Perry, M. K. "Vertical Integration: The Monopsony Case." *American Economic Review,* September 1978, pp. 561–570.

Pfeffer, Jeffrey, and Gerald R. Salancik. *The External Control of Organizations: A Resource Dependence Perspective.* New York: Harper and Row, 1978.

Porter, Michael E. *Competitive Strategy.* New York: Free Press, 1980, Chapter 14.

Scherer, F. M. *Industrial Market Structure and Economic Performance.* Chicago: Rand McNally, 1970.

Schmalensee, R. "A Note on the Theory of Vertical Integration." *Journal of Political Economy,* March–April 1973, pp. 442–449.

Stigler, George J. "The Division of Labor Is Limited by the Extent of the Market." *Journal of Political Economy,* Vol. 59, No. 3, June 1951, pp. 185–193.

Tucker, I. B. and R. P. Wilder. "Trends in Vertical Integration in the U.S. Manufacturing Sector." *Journal of Industrial Economics,* Vol. 26, No. 1, September 1977, pp. 81–94.

Westfield, Fred M. "Vertical Integration: Does Product Price Rise or Fall?" *American Economic Review,* Vol. 71, No. 3, June 1981, pp. 334–346.

Williamson, Oliver E. *Markets and Hierarchies: Analysis and Antitrust Implications.* London: Free Press, 1975.

Williamson, Oliver E. "The Vertical Integration of Production: Market Failure Considerations." *American Economic Review,* Vol. 61, No. 2, May 1971, pp. 112–123.

Managing Changes in Manufacturing's Technology and Structure

10-1 INTRODUCTION AND OVERVIEW

Among its other attributes, the human species is endowed with a sense of history and a curiosity about its place in that history. Having identified various epochs in human development—and given them such names as the Stone Age, the Iron Age, the Dark Ages, the Age of Discovery, and the Age of the Industrial Revolution—one might well wonder what future historians will call the age in which we now live. Alternatives being proposed include Atomic Age, Computer Age, and the Age of Mass Communication.

Note that all these terms describe manifestations of the same force: technological change. The sweep and scope of technological change shape everybody's lives today, but often they affect business managers most quickly and directly. Long before the average consumer is exposed to (and slowly changes his or her patterns of life to adjust to) a new technological development, managers concerned with that development have been forced to adapt to its peculiar ambiguities and imperatives. Technological innovation simultaneously creates the future and triggers the eventual destruction of the present. Existing equipment becomes obsolete; workers' experience and skills become less valuable; and management instincts and systems that had previously been successful come into question. By its very nature, therefore, managing technological change involves trying to establish order over the unknown, and, at the same time, it can trigger internal conflict in an organization.

Just as physicists use the concept of "half life" to measure the rate of deterioration of a radioactive substance (the half life is the length of time that elapses before half its radioactivity is dissipated), some professions use the same term to measure the rate of obsolescence of their own skills. The half life of the knowledge of a newly graduated electrical engineer, for example, is now estimated to be about seven years. That is, within seven years of graduation, half of what he or she knows about electronics will have become obsolete. In such a changing environment, experience can be as dangerous as ignorance. Business managers must be similarly concerned about the half life of their own expertise. Managing technology in today's world requires the ability not only to keep abreast of an existing technology (and incremental changes in that technology) but also to mold and manage organizations that are capable of responding to the gradual obsolescence of existing technologies by continually rejuvenating themselves.

Most textbooks about production management properly spend a great deal of time discussing the problems of managing manufacturing structures: systems comprising equipment, people, and procedures. To manage such systems one must understand their capabilities and limitations, provide them with appropriate resources (people, skills, and funds), and make operating decisions that allow the organization to realize its full potential. Managing even a stable process technology, therefore, means managing workers and their interaction with equipment. It means creating effective working relationships between workers and supervisors and between work groups having different sets of skills (such as industrial engineers, process engineers, and quality assurance). Finally, it means modifying equipment, material flows, and individual jobs to use available resources most effectively.

As suggested by the title of this chapter, however, our intention here is to focus on an expanded view of process technology management—one that is more the domain of top management in that it includes designing the manufacturing structure and process as well as shaping their evolution over time. We address the things that top management must do, and the problems it must guard against, in dealing effectively with such questions as:

1. How can an organizational environment be established in which continual improvement in manufacturing capabilities is both broad-based and self-sustaining, so that the firm's production processes become a source of competitive advantage rather than a liability?

2. What kind of process technology is appropriate for a given situation (what particular capabilities must it have and what weaknesses or constraints can it afford to have if tradeoffs are required)? How frequently should changes in process technology be made, and what circumstances or events are likely to trigger them?

3. What procedures should be adopted to help identify, select, and pursue the best opportunities for changing the firm's process technology? How should these changes be implemented, and what organizational strengths are required to carry out the firm's strategy for technological improvement?

Each of these three types of questions is addressed in this chapter. In Section 10-2 we discuss the kind of organizational environment and attitudes that can help a firm exploit technological opportunities in its manufacturing processes, and how top managers' objectives and attitudes toward risk are likely to affect the process changes they select and their probability of success. The following section deals primarily with the second group of questions: the specific decisions that are involved in pursuing a given process technology strategy. The product–process matrix framework outlined in Chapter 7 is used to help understand the dynamic interaction of product and process change. It also offers insight into the role management plays in guiding such changes and how, if it does not do its job, the slow accumulation of operating decisions can inadvertently cripple a firm's competitive strategy and stifle further innovation. The final section deals with organizational procedures—ranging from capital budgeting methods to selecting the test site for a proposed change—that can complement the chosen strategy.

10-2   ESTABLISHING THE ORGANIZATIONAL CONTEXT FOR PROCESS CHANGE

As we argued in Chapter 6, senior managers often define their role in managing manufacturing process technology too narrowly. They confine themselves to passing judgment on capital investment proposals that deal with equipment whose primary purpose is to provide production capacity for specific (and usually existing) products. Having made these investment decisions, they delegate the "technical details" of their businesses to various specialists. In 1981, for example, the consulting firm of Booz Allen & Hamilton polled 800 executives from the thousand largest U.S. corporations and concluded that

> a lack of involvement of top management in the technology process resulted in consistent underfunding of technology-related activities. Instead they emphasized those areas that have a more immediate impact on profits. . . . Three in five respondents said top management's role was limited to either reviewing major development programs above some dollar threshold, or singling out and following programs of key importance . . . This limited involvement of top management may be a major reason why technology functions are perceived to be significantly and chronically underfunded. (Harris et al., 1983)

At about the same time, on the basis of an analysis of attitudes toward productivity and technology in 96 U.S. companies (along with 25 U.K. and 25 Japanese manufacturing companies), McInnes (1983) worried that such delegation of operational responsibility, together with profit-oriented control strategies, "has created an organizational centrifugal force; a force which is inimical to the required concentration of expertise and resources to cope with the systemic problems of managing organizational adaptation to radical technological change."

In counteracting this "centrifugal force," top management must b directly involved with technological change, keeping in mind that ever cess technology embodies a set of organizational capabilities that affoi merous opportunities for competitive differentiation and superiority. We will expand on the nature of this broader role for top management later in this section, but first we will explore two subsidiary issues that underlie it: how managers' attitudes toward technological risks are formed, and why they often become so preoccupied with the search for "breakthroughs" in process improvement.

10-2.1 Managers' Assessment of Technological Risk

Most managers think of "risk" in terms of the possibility that something will turn out worse than expected. Sometimes, but not often, they separate out the risks they incur because they have taken a certain action from those they expose themselves to because they did not. We will argue in this section that if top managers adopt too narrow a view of process technology, they may avoid the first kind of risk but increase their exposure to risks of the second kind.

No business is without risk. Although sometimes managers can take actions that reduce the level of some of the risks they are exposed to, they usually do so at the expense of increasing other risks. In effect, then, all they are doing is substituting one type of risk for another. For example, they can balance the risks associated with not taking an action against those associated with taking the wrong action, or they can substitute a financial risk (more debt, say) for an operating risk (not having enough production capacity). Risk management, therefore, is less a matter of risk avoidance than one of choosing the kinds of risks that one is willing to deal with.

This distinction needs to be stressed because a manager's reaction to a particular type of risk often appears to depend more on his or her familiarity with that risk than on its actual magnitude. Marketing managers, for example, spend much of their time projecting the growth of markets and estimating the share of that market that their company should be able to achieve. Feeling comfortable with such estimates, they are willing to live with the kind of errors that result from them. On the other hand, financial or engineering managers might be very uncomfortable with these same risks. The marketing manager, in turn, might be very uneasy about taking on the risks of interest rate changes, currency devaluations, or debt repayment schedules, which are part of the everyday job of the financial manager. Similarly, many people smoke cigarettes or fail to fasten their car seatbelts, yet are afraid to fly.

Such apparently irrational behavior is due in part to the fact that managers' attitudes toward a given risk depend on the amount of control that they feel they can exercise in a particular situation (see Simon, 1979). This sense of control, in turn, is closely aligned with the manager's "familiarity" with those types of risks. Most people, for example, are more concerned about the possibility of being in an airplane crash than an auto accident, even though voluminous statistics indicate that car accidents are much more likely than plane crashes. The difference is that the airplane passenger feels little control over his or her situation, either in terms of the ability to avoid a potential accident or to take corrective action in the event of one. The passenger is totally dependent on another person's skill—and luck. The same person, however, probably has much greater familiarity with driving a car, and a greater sense of control (although it may be unfounded) in the event of an accident.

Marketing managers tend to be less uneasy about market risks because they are familiar with them and feel they have some control over them. More important, they know how to take evasive or corrective actions if an "accident" appears imminent. These same managers, however, generally lack such knowledge or confidence regarding the actions that could be taken in response to financial or technological accidents.

The same technological risks that appear so ominous and uncontrollable to a marketing or financial manager might not be worrisome at all to a technical person. The engineer will instinctively assess the key components of these risks, determine how difficult each component will be to overcome, and juggle his or her skilled personnel and other resources in such a way as to "make things come out right." The engineer knows, or knows how to find out, where the problems lie and where the project can be pushed ahead with little resistance.

Things do not always come out right, of course, any more than exchange rates always move in the expected direction or industry demand behaves as the marketers' charts predicted. But this is of only secondary importance. The point is that the manager who has considerable experience with these kinds of risks tends to have a much more realistic (experience-based) reaction to them. As the old saying goes, "You prefer the devil you know to the devil you don't."

The same notions of familiarity and control are important in establishing an appropriate organizational environment for dealing with changes in process technology. All such changes involve some risk. The extent to which its managers feel comfortable with such risks conditions the entire organization and has a profound influence on its overall attitude toward technological change. If top management has little first-hand knowledge about the firm's process technology and how it has evolved, it may be less willing to accept the technological risks associated with changing that technology. Figure 10-1 suggests graphically the relationship we have observed between senior managers' familiarity with manufacturing technology and their perception of its risks and opportunities.

As suggested by the curve in Figure 10-1a, when management's knowledge of a manufacturing technology is low, the risk they perceive in changing it is relatively high. As they gain more knowledge about that technology, surprisingly, their perception of the risks associated with changing it may actually increase, because they can identify specific problems that have no apparent solutions. As a result, they often become even *more* conservative in making manufacturing technology–related decisions.

Once a certain threshold of familiarity is reached, however, the magni-

Figure 10-1   General management views of manufacturing process technology

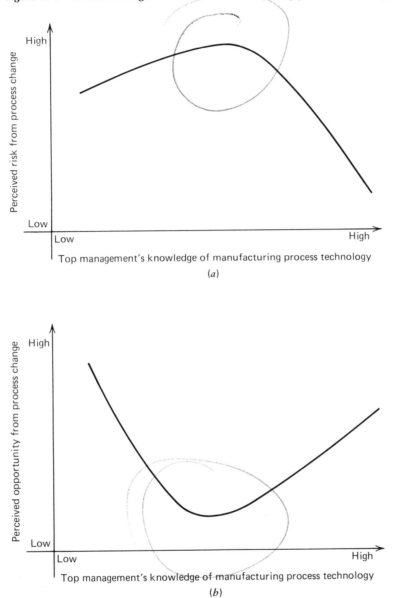

(a)

(b)

tude of the perceived risks associated with pursuing changes in the technology begins to decrease. In short, managers on the left-hand side of the curve (the rising portion) are instinctively apprehensive about making process changes and therefore tend to avoid such changes, whereas those on the right-hand side (the declining portion) tend to deal with their uncertainties by learning more about the technology.

A complementary relationship is shown in Figure 10-1b, where the vertical axis now represents the perceived rewards obtainable from changing (improving) a process technology (and the horizontal axis again represents top management's technological familiarity). This phenomenon is observable today in connection with such process enhancements as material requirements planning (MRP), robotics, and computer-aided design/computer-aided manufacturing (CAD/CAM). Managers on the far left-hand side, knowing little about these technologies, are frequently persuaded to see in them tremendous promise and opportunity. They are likely to experience tremendous disappointment later, just as did managers of the 1950s when computers were first being touted as the solution to all their problems. On the right-hand side, managers who have a solid understanding of their process technologies are likely both to see the potential in a given change and to have a much better understanding of what is involved in making such a change. In such organizations, management does not rely solely on specialists to make the "right" technology decisions.

Figure 10-1 also provides some insight into why such apparently promising technologies as robotics and CAD/CAM have been adopted so slowly by U.S. companies. They are aimed primarily at industries that have traditionally considered innovations in products and marketing strategies more important to competitive success than innovation in manufacturing processes. In these instances, therefore, top management tends to have much greater first-hand familiarity with product innovation, and technical specialists typically are entrusted with assessing new process opportunities. Whatever their recommendations (often they report what they think their bosses want to hear), senior managers in these companies usually overemphasize the risks associated with such changes.

One purpose of this chapter is to make the process of technological change less mysterious (and therefore less threatening) to those who do not have a technological background. By identifying the problems that can occur, placing their associated risks in perspective, and showing how and where a manager can exercise control over them, we hope to alleviate what is a natural uneasiness. Readers who already have successfully managed a technological change in a manufacturing process, on the other hand, may gain a better understanding of what it is they have been doing right all along.

10-2.2   Depending on "Breakthrough" Process Improvements

Just as top management's understanding of and attitude toward technological risk has an enormous impact on the organization's support of process improvement, so do its views regarding the form of such improvements. The term "breakthrough strategy" has a nice ring to it. It sounds like an aggressive, go-for-broke approach based on confidence in both one's technological superiority and in one's organizational strength. In fact, it is usually just the opposite—a desperate attempt to break out of a deteriorating situation. It is more likely to reflect a recognition that one has fallen behind technologically than any sense of technological superiority, a recognition of the need to galvanize a demoralized organization rather than an attempt to exploit its strengths.

Businesses tend to pursue process breakthroughs after a long period during which their desire for stability and control (or their aversion to technological risks) has come to dominate their need for continual evolutionary change. Rather than forcing themselves to endure the ongoing stress and effort associated with continual incremental improvements (like those contributing to organizational learning that were outlined in Chapter 8)—whereby existing skills, equipment, and products are gradually rendered obsolete—they ease back on their oars and drift into the more comfortable waters of the status quo. The process is insidious because it is so popular with everybody: managers do not have to work so hard; workers (and unions) can concentrate their attention on job creation, wage increases, and other means for carving off ever-larger shares of the stable pie; and competitors find that they can relax as well. Stable oligopolylike market structures encourage such lowering of competitive pressure, as do industry-wide wage negotiations. Over time managers lose touch with workers, engineers with manufacturing, manufacturing with customers, and the corporate staff with the line organization.

Suddenly the serene picture is disrupted. A new competitor (often foreign-based, but sometimes a domestic company from outside the industry) enters; companies in other industries find that new forms of their products, based on different technologies, can displace traditional products; or a company (often a smaller one) within one's own industry catches fire under the impetus of a major technological innovation and attempts to carve out a larger role for itself. Companies that have adopted stable, well-understood process technologies suddenly find themselves under attack and alarmingly vulnerable. They do not have the time to get back down the learning curve by following the usual approach based on multiple small improvements. Instead, they must stake their survival on a wild attempt to regain competitive parity—even leapfrog their new competitors—with a major technological breakthrough.

Unfortunately, an organization that has lost its ability and willingness to engage in continual self-imposed obsolescence and renewal is poorly equipped to make such a major breakthrough. It lacks the skills, the resources, and the ingenuity. The U.S. steel industry's battle with foreign imports in the 1970s provides a recent example of such a scenario, as does the U.S. machine tool industry's confrontation with Japanese and European competitors in the early 1980s.

Recognizing how difficult it is to develop their own breakthroughs, companies often attempt to "buy a breakthrough," that is, purchase a new technology from another firm. To get this new technology to work properly, they sometimes have to import people who understand it. Unfortunately, these new people, like any outsiders who enter a stable existing organization, often find themselves distrusted even though they come to help. (We will return to this topic later on.)

Even what appears to outsiders as a "breakthrough," in fact, may simply be the result of an accumulation of small incremental improvements. As Malpas (1983) put it:

> Most big advances are the result of someone persevering with a new idea that initially seems only marginally better than the one it is to replace. Many processes in use today, seen as breakthroughs in retrospect, were judged only barely viable when introduced.

In his study of strategic management in ten major manufacturing firms, Quinn (1980) found that the relentless pursuit of incremental improvements was the key to success even in such major breakthroughs as plain paper copying (Xerox) and the float glass process (Pilkington Brothers). The key motivation behind both these efforts was top management's belief that ever-increasing organizational knowledge about its process technology would ultimately provide it with a competitive advantage. This is reminiscent of our discussion of the broad perspective toward manufacturing technology at the end of Chapter 6. There we emphasized that technical competence is not only profitable, but it can be essential to the survival of a firm and its managers.

10-3   DEVELOPING A PROCESS TECHNOLOGY STRATEGY

The product–process matrix described in Chapter 7 provides a convenient framework for putting the evolution of a given process technology into the context of an industry's evolution from birth to maturity. It also helps one identify the specific decisions that reflect a firm's process technology strategy. Using this framework, we next discuss when and how a company might decide to make a transition from one point on the matrix to another and the management problems associated with such a transition. Finally, we discuss the managerial implications of adopting different types of transition strategies.

Most of this section is concerned with the problems associated with managing the change from a company's existing process technology to one that is new to it, although it may be well known to other companies. We close, however, with some comments about the problems of pioneering a new process technology—one for which there is little experience to serve as a guide. The difference is more of degree than of kind, as many of the problems that confront an organization in pioneering a technological change are simply exaggerated forms of those that face it when it deals with any important process change.

10-3.1   Matching Product Changes with Process Technology Changes

Within the framework of the product–process matrix, the typical evolution of an industry is down the diagonal, and it involves a series of changes in both product structure and process technology. If such diagonal movement *always* occurred, it would be possible to collapse the two-dimensional matrix into a single dimension and base one's analyses and projections on either the product life cycle or the process life cycle. However, even though moving along the diagonal is a composite pattern (the industry average, in a sense), it is a very unlikely pattern for any individual business to follow. Firms tend to make only one kind of change at a time: either adopting an alternative product structure given an existing production technology, or adopting an alternative process structure for producing an existing product structure. Progression down the diagonal (if it occurs), therefore, usually results from a sequence of loosely linked vertical and horizontal steps.

A company's position on the matrix can change relative to its competitors even if it makes no moves of its own. Its competitors may simply move away from it, either toward greater product standardization or less. Many companies, in fact, evolve almost unconsciously to a position above the diagonal because they are so preoccupied with their attempts to improve and standardize products that they neglect to make compensating process changes. Such neglect is even more likely if the firm has the kind of "narrow perspective" toward process technology that we described in Chapter 6.

Just as a position too far above the diagonal can put the firm at a major competitive disadvantage, a position too far below can be equally precarious. The appropriate position for a given company depends both on how rapid and inexorable the product's evolution is along the product life cycle and on the technological constraints and opportunities associated with various stages along the evolution of the process life cycle. For example, moving vertically down a column usually implies an increase in the company's capital intensity as well as its breakeven volume. If the product life cycle progresses too rapidly toward maturity, and this progress is accompanied by major changes in product design, the firm may not receive the return it expected from its investment in process improvement before that investment is made obsolete by the next step along the product dimension. This is one reason why the required payback period on investments in process technology in the electronics industry is typically less than two years, and sometimes as low as six months, whereas it typically exceeds seven or eight years in the steel and oil industries.

Similarly, a company has to worry about the possibility that the product life cycle may "reverse direction" after it has moved toward a more standardized production process. This can occur through a process as simple as the familiar phenomenon of product proliferation, whereby a company tries to stimulate sales in a relatively mature market by developing customized products for different market segments. Or it may take as complex a form as the kind of "industrial de-maturization" described by Abernathy et al. (1983). In either case, as the company's product structure moves horizontally to the left on the matrix, its manufacturing process becomes less and less compatible with its product structure, particularly if it was on or below the matrix diagonal before the shift occurred.

10-3.2   Contrasting Industry Scenarios

Not all companies, of course, will (or should) make the same decision as to how to alter their manufacturing process when they find themselves at a given point on the matrix. The choice each makes must be based on its market situation, technological opportunities, internal organizational competences and resources, and the environment from which it draws its production experience. For example, for many years after World War II, European and Japanese companies usually entered international markets for products some years after American companies had introduced them. When they did enter, they typically used manufacturing processes that were more efficient than U.S. processes in terms of their use of raw materials and capital. This was in part plain common sense: the best method of entry for a latecomer is either to modify the product to meet the peculiar needs of a local market or to find some way to improve the process used in making it. The improvements these competitors chose to make in their processes, moreover, were generally influenced by the fact that the cost of materials historically has been higher in Europe and Japan than in the United States. In addition, Europe and Japan both experienced capital shortages for many years after World War II.

Since 1945, U.S. firms have tended to concentrate their energies on new product introduction—an activity that is typically a heavy consumer of capital and human skills. European and Japanese firms meanwhile concentrated on process improvements. Companies in each country, therefore, appear to have been making the right decision given their environment (see Gruber et al., 1967). This comforting theory may no longer be as persuasive as it once was, given the deepening problems within many U.S. manufacturing industries. We discuss German and Japanese approaches to manufacturing management in detail in Chapters 11, 12, and 13.

The optimum strategy would seem to be to position the firm above the diagonal when the horizontal movement (toward product standardization) is rapid or uncertain and below when it is relatively slow and predictable. Usually this would suggest being above the diagonal early in the product life cycle and dropping below later on. As pointed out in Chapter 7, this is similar to the pattern of innovation that Abernathy and Utterback (1975) identified during their research.

While this pattern—product innovation leading in the early stages of the product's progression through the product life cycle and process innovation leading later on—may hold in the majority of cases, a number of counterexamples can be identified. These suggest that innovations may follow a much more intricate pattern, with process and product interchanging leadership roles more than once. Numerous examples of this can be found in the electronics industry. The common radio is a good one. It followed the traditional life cycle until about 1955, when a process innovation (printed circuit boards utilizing transistors) triggered the introduction of the miniature, battery-powered radio, and product innovation (FM and stereo receivers) followed. In the mid-1970s another process innovation (microcircuitry) led to the development of other products, including the low-cost citizens band (CB) radio (a transmitter as well as a receiver) and the miniature (Sony Walkman, for example) stereo receiver. Maturity in radios appears to have been a transitory phenomenon.

A related issue that is just as interesting has to do with why some products never seem to complete their progression down the matrix diagonal. Instead, they appear to stall at some point. Classic examples are home building and furniture, both of which seem to be victims of an arrested product development. Processes already exist that would carry both products farther down the diagonal if increased product standardization were allowed (or accepted) by the customer. In the case of home building, this appeared to become possible with the popularization of the mobile home. But, if anything, this product became less standardized during the 1970s. The mobile home industry now finds itself in the same frustrating predicament as the standard home industry.

Once an industry stops progressing (other examples would include construction equipment, sailboats, and clothing), a key question is how to get it started again. The answer does not appear to lie in process innovation, given the abortive attempts in both home building (modular homes built from plastic or metal components) and furniture (molded or pressed plastic forms). The failure of these industries to achieve the systemic efficiency of the auto industry is due more to the inability of the market to standardize than to the lack of process opportunities.

10-3.3 Another Perspective on the Learning Curve

Thinking about industry evolution in the context of the product–process matrix also provides new insights about the learning curve. Unfortunately, the term "learning curve strategy" suggests a black or white choice: either one follows it or one does not. Analyzing the actual process of cost reduction in terms of the product–process matrix, however, provides a richer understanding of the options available to a company. Progression along the product life cycle alone, without any change in the process used (that is, proceeding horizontally across the matrix), would still provide numerous opportunities for cost reduction through product redesign, product line simplification, development of improved raw materials and parts, economies of scale, use of less costly distribution channels, and the fact that over time the whole organization learns to do its job better.

Similarly, moving vertically down the matrix provides other cost reduction opportunities: new production processes, improved materials handling technology, and automation. What is called the learning curve is simply the combination of these two effects; it depicts the total improvement in unit cost obtainable by combining product evolution with process evolution.

A company that prefers to follow a path above the diagonal (as seen in Figure 10-2) in effect restricts the cost reduction opportunities available to it. At a given point in the product life cycle, therefore, it may be able to reduce its

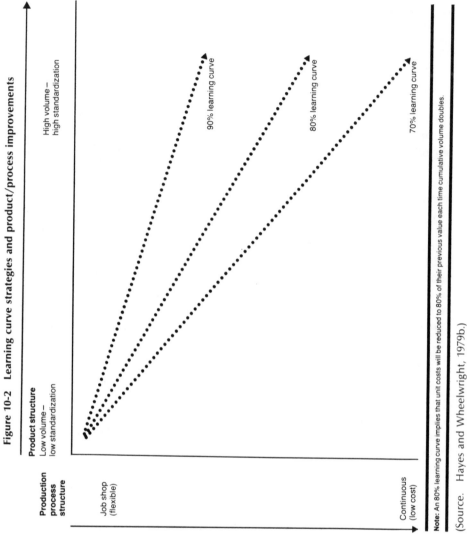

Figure 10-2 Learning curve strategies and product/process improvements

Production process structure

Job shop (flexible)

Continuous (low cost)

Product structure

Low volume – low standardization

High volume – high standardization

90% learning curve

80% learning curve

70% learning curve

Note: An 80% learning curve implies that unit costs will be reduced to 80% of their previous value each time cumulative volume doubles.

(Source. Hayes and Wheelwright, 1979b.)

unit cost only to 90 percent (say) of its previous value after doubling its cumulative volume. It will, however, preserve its flexibility to follow market movements quickly and it will limit its capital investment. A company that chooses to follow a path below the diagonal, on the other hand, may achieve a greater rate of cost reduction (70 percent, say) than do companies that pursue a path along the diagonal. The danger of this strategy is that those cost reductions may make the company less flexible to product changes. Therefore, its advantage may be short-lived.

As noted in Chapter 8, Henry Ford followed an almost incessant pursuit of learning curve economics with his Model T Ford. Between 1908 and 1926 Ford produced more than 15 million Model Ts, and was able to reduce the car's price from $850 to about $290 ($200 in 1907 dollars). Throughput time was reduced from 21 days to 4, and the number of salaried workers was cut from about 5 percent of total employment in 1913 to less than 2 percent in 1921. To provide specially designed and processed materials for his production machine, Ford invested in steel mills, weaving mills, a glass plant, a cement plant, coal mines, rubber plantations, a railroad, and even his own forests and logging operations. (See Abernathy and Wayne, 1974.) When General Motors was able to segment the market by offering a variety of products, however, Ford's sales gradually fell below its breakeven point (which, of course, was much higher than GM's because of Ford's enormous fixed investment in mechanization and vertical integration). This forced it into the traumatic switchover to the Model A, from which it never fully recovered.

During this same period, it should be emphasized, GM was experiencing learning curve benefits with a number of components that were common across models. The real issue, therefore, is not whether learning improvements will be pursued, but rather the *degree* to which cost improvement will drive the firm's competitive strategy. Whether a company decides to pursue product and process movements along the diagonal rather than above or below it will largely determine the rate of learning that it is likely to experience.

10-3.4 The Impact of Process Changes on Organizational Climate

In the light of our earlier reference to the organizational difficulties that arise from various types of product–process transitions, it is not surprising that so many process innovations encounter major difficulties or fail altogether. Consider the case of a company that decides (either as a result of an explicit strategy or in an ad hoc manner) to move to a more standardized product line. Preoccupied with the resulting marketing problems, it may be slow to recognize that its manufacturing organization is not designed or equipped to produce this new product structure efficiently. When it does, it usually has to move rapidly either to change its manufacturing process or to return to its original product strategy.

For example, in the mid-1970s, Hewlett-Packard's pocket calculator division was following HP's usual strategy of offering a wide variety of products using a relatively fluid production process. Through aggressive marketing it found itself obtaining increasing numbers of large orders for more standard calculators as well. The division hesitated to alter its production system to respond to the nature of those orders, which would have required a downward movement on the matrix. As a result, it soon found itself in head-on competition with Texas Instruments, but with a product–process combination that was not nearly as effective as the one that TI had chosen. Under the prodding of its founders (as reported in *Business Week,* 1975), HP decided to back away from this confrontation and return to its more traditional strategy: to develop new products or make major changes in existing products, so that it could periodically return to the upper left-hand corner of the matrix without having to make major changes in its process technology.

Usually a company cannot back away from such a process change, however. If its industry is moving away from it and its previous market segments are eroding, it must move ahead. Unfortunately, this realization often occurs only after a long period of steadily increasing acrimony: marketing complains that "manufacturing is letting us down" and manufacturing complains that "marketing people don't understand that things are not as easy as they think they are." Top management, for its part, keeps asking manufacturing to "fix what it has" before considering additional process investment. It is in this atmosphere of mutual suspicion and a sense of lost momentum that the decision is finally made to introduce a new manufacturing technology. It would be hard to pick a worse time: the company is under competitive pressure, it may be in a cash bind, and top management has lost confidence in its manufacturing organization. That organization, moreover, may be crippled by the loss of key managers who have been let go because of dissatisfaction with their ability to "solve problems" or "be team players" (partially arising out of their frustration with senior managers who did not appear to understand their problems or supply critical resources at the right time).

To avoid such a chain of events, a company should adopt an approach toward both product and process innovation that builds on the kind of organizational competences that were described in Chapter 7. This might lead it to confine itself to some subsegment of the product–process matrix. For example, HP traditionally has tended to keep within the upper left-hand quadrant, while TI has concentrated on the lower right-hand quadrant. Both upper left-hand corner and lower right-hand corner strategies can be successful, as can others. The most dangerous strategy, however, is what might be called a "middle strategy": getting in late, never making the organizational adjustments necessary to compete effectively in a mature market, and being forced to get out early.

10-3.5 Managing More Radical Shifts in Process Technology

Thinking about the set of capabilities that best meets the needs of a specific subsegment of the product–process matrix can provide useful guidance when contemplating either a product or a process change. From time to time, however, top management may be forced to address the need for a shift in its process technology that is more radical than simply balancing product changes with an appropriate process change within an existing matrix. Instead, the firm might find it necessary to define a new matrix.

Both product and process technologies mature over time. Early in the technology's development the improvement that is possible through the commitment of a specified amount of resources can be substantial, but as the technology matures, more and more resources are required to obtain smaller and smaller increments of improvement. This phenomenon is sometimes described in terms of an S-curve, similar to that used to model the product life cycle. (See Foster, 1982.) When the limits, either physical or economic, of a particular technology are approached, management generally faces one of two options.

One is to continue to pursue improvements within that technology. For example, during the 1800s the builders of sailing ships recognized the potential threat posed by steamships soon after they appeared. For a number of years, however, steamships were neither as fast nor as reliable as sailing ships, and conventional shipbuilders concentrated on designing and building ever more efficient sailing vessels. As a result, the average speed (as measured by the time to cross the Atlantic, say) of sailing cargo ships increased more in the 50 years following the introduction of steamships than it had in the previous 300 years. But eventually they came up against the implacable implications of the S-curve: the rate of sailing improvement slackened, while steamship improvements continued. A more recent example of similar behavior can be seen in RCA's strenuous efforts during the 1960s to improve the speed and reliability of vacuum tubes, in an attempt to counter the threat posed by transistors. Because of its preoccupation with the old technology, RCA lost its chance to become a major force in the new one.

The other alternative is to recognize the inevitability of technological obsolescence and to shift the firm's resources gradually from improving the existing technology to developing its successor. One example of such a shift was provided by the Harris Corporation (formerly the Harris-Intertype Company), a Cleveland, Ohio–based producer of printing equipment. In the mid-1960s it came to the conclusion that mechanical typesetting equipment faced a grim future. Ten years were devoted to changing the firm's capabilities from mechanical to electronic technology. By the late 1970s that transition was complete. It encompassed both a change in name and a shift in corporate headquarters (to its electronics operation in Florida). This shift required the development of a whole new product–process matrix into which corporate resources could be channeled while the old matrix (mechanical typesetting and printing equipment) was being phased out.

10-4 IMPLEMENTING CHANGES IN PROCESS TECHNOLOGY

The road to hell, it is said, is paved with good intentions. We suspect that it is also littered with the burned-out wrecks of promising technological innovations that never worked. Why are some companies successful at introducing new process technologies while others have extreme difficulty? Why do some companies that have a history of successful innovations suddenly experience problems with a new one?

It is easy to use limited data (one's own experience, say, or one's casual observation of the experience of others) to construct theories about the secrets of success or failure in process innovation. Unfortunately, few theories have weathered exposure to large amounts of data because so many variables obscure the picture: industries differ, technologies differ (some are inherently more complicated than others or are at different stages of development), companies differ, their vendors and consultants differ, and the people involved differ. When a cake doesn't come out right, who is to blame: the recipe, the ingredients, the oven . . . or the chef? Everybody blames someone else.

As one examines the data contained in a number of surveys and case histories (see, for example, Myers and Marquis, 1969; Olsen, 1975; and Rothwell et al., 1974), one is likely to conclude that much of the advice on "how to succeed in implementing a process innovation" is quite superficial. One reads, for example, that "top management commitment" and the "support of the workforce" are essential, that "interfunctional committees" help deal with the pervasive effects of technological change throughout the enterprise, and that it is important to find someone to "champion" the new technology.

Yet in many instances top management commitment seems to hinder the innovative process (particularly when top managers force an innovation on an unwilling organization). Similarly, interfunctional committees can complicate, frustrate, and bureaucratize the implementation process as easily as they abet it. And the "wrong" technological champion can do irreparable damage. Worse, these supposed answers are not really answers; they are more like questions. *How* does one obtain the commitment of top management and the support of the workers? *Who* should be on the interfunctional committee, and whom should it report to? *Where* does one find a technological champion, and how does one know—before it is too late—whether one has found the right person?

Our own views—based on personal observation, a number of case histories, and an analysis of the growing body of literature on technological innovation—are discussed under four headings: focusing the organization's efforts, selecting a test site, selecting and nurturing key human resources, and establishing a set of administrative procedures that reinforce desired changes.

10-4.1 Focusing the Organization's Effort

A process innovation appears to have a high probability of success if there is consistency among the answers to three questions:

1. What is the organization's manufacturing mission? (What must it do well if it is to succeed, given its chosen strategy?)
2. What is the technological innovation really good at doing? (What kinds of

things will it allow the manufacturing organization to do easier or better, and what will it make more difficult to do?)

3. To what extent do the characteristics of the test site—the place where the new technology is to be tested—match the characteristics of the rest of the organization?

As discussed in previous chapters, successful organizations tend to concentrate their attention and effort on doing a few things very well. They set priorities, allocate resources, and measure results according to the importance of different types of activities. Their ability to maintain these priorities depends largely on how successful they are in transmitting the same sense of focus (and understanding of priorities) throughout the organization. Workers, group leaders, production specialists, plant managers, and corporate staff personnel should all respond instinctively to the question, "What is the most important thing for this company to be doing?" with roughly the same answer, and they must understand how their own activities complement this overall goal.

One sometimes hears the argument that large companies should be more innovative than small ones. This is because they can spend more on R&D (companies employing over 5,000 people spend well over three-fourths of all the R&D dollars spent in the United States), and they have greater staying power when trying to overcome the difficulties associated with a particularly difficult technological transition. But no serious study has shown any relationship between size and technological innovativeness. Size is much less important than commitment, and unity of purpose often becomes increasingly difficult to achieve as an organization grows.

When there is confusion over priorities in an organization, one might expect people to work at cross-purposes and make decisions that are not in keeping with the real needs of the business. On the other hand, when a shared sense of priorities exists, the organization tends to make good decisions regarding which technological innovations to pursue and then works hard to implement those decisions. This is crucial to understanding why some firms demonstrate great commitment—from workers to top management, and everybody in between—to doing certain things and little commitment to other things. If a proposed process change does not help the company do something that is important for its competitive success, it is unlikely to be supported wholeheartedly throughout the organization.

It is also important to understand that process technologies do not appear out of thin air. They are designed by individuals who have certain constraints and objectives in mind. Since no technology is equally good at everything, tradeoffs must be made by those who design and implement it. No plane yet built can fly at twice the speed of sound, carry 400 passengers, and land in a cow pasture. No one is even trying to invent such a process. Instead, they focus on one criterion or another and develop Concordes, 747s, and helicopters.

Every new process technology reflects the compromises that some person or group has made as they wrestled with conflicting criteria. It is not surprising, therefore, that technological innovations that help the organization do the things it feels to be important are more likely to elicit broad support and commitment among workers and managers than those that do not assist the organization in doing the important things. Organizations that lack *any* clear sense of purpose have difficulty almost every time they try to do something new. Success in these companies appears to be almost random, and it depends critically on the ability and commitment of a small group of individuals who band together—for whatever reasons, usually personal ones in an atmosphere of crisis—to try to make it work.

Therefore, an organization is more likely to be successful at introducing a new process technology when, first, it has a clear sense of priorities and, second, the attributes of the new process are consistent with these priorities. It should not be surprising that many companies that attempted to "computerize" their operations (through various types of process control systems or material requirements planning systems, for example) have encountered difficulty. Depending on the computer, the process, and the specific application, some computerized processes or procedures are good at producing long runs of standard products within tight tolerances while others are good at making fast changeovers from one product to another. Some are very predictable and "robust" in changing environments; others are finicky and get out of adjustment easily. No single technology is best for every environment or every strategy.

10-4.2   Selecting the Test Site for a Process Improvement

A second set of issues that one encounters when implementing a process change involves the location where the initial application of the new process technology takes place; this is sometimes referred to as the "test bed." On the one hand, one would like to provide an environment that promises the highest probability of success for that technology. One might choose, for example, a particularly simple product or production facility, or one that is relatively new and therefore more closely related to the new technology than older products and facilities. One might even decide to use a semiartificial test bed: a pilot plant or specially designed process, say.

The problem with such an approach is that, while it maximizes the innovation's chances of success, it also makes it more difficult to transplant the supposedly successful innovation to the corporate mainstream. Technological innovation is not unusual in this regard. Companies that have attempted to implement new forms of work organization or new approaches to the worker–manager relationship have found that these tend to work best when implemented in a new plant with a newly recruited labor force. But no matter how well they work in such surroundings, it is very difficult to transfer these new approaches to environments that are more typical of the rest of the company. (See Walton, 1975.)

The test bed should be representative of the corporate mainstream for another reason. As we argued in the previous section, an innovation tends to succeed when workers and managers see it as contributing to the key competitive strengths of the business. Test beds that lack a sense of identity with the company's competitive needs (and its competitive priorities) lose some of this potential support.

Therefore, selecting a test bed represents a delicate choice. It must "fit" the technological innovation in the sense that it provides an environment in which the innovation has a good chance of success. On the other hand, it must also be representative of the broad mainstream environment in the company. Test beds that excessively sacrifice one set of advantages to the detriment of the other are less likely to be successful than those where an appropriate balance exists.

When all three links of this triangle are firm—when the firm's *competitive needs* (as captured by its sense of priorities) are well-served by the *capabilities* (and constraints) *of the new technology,* and the *test bed* chosen is compatible with both—technological innovation is well positioned to succeed. However, even a perfect fit does not guarantee success. It must be complemented by the selection and assignment of key human resources.

10-4.3 The Technological Entrepreneur and Other Key Personnel

Whether or not the foregoing prerequisites are met, the success or failure of a technological innovation can sometimes be traced to the personality and abilities of the project leader, the person responsible for making the innovation work. Students of management are just beginning to understand what the attributes are that make for a successful project leader, but the available evidence suggests that these attributes conform generally to those implied by the title "technological entrepreneur." (For other definitions, and a different perspective, see Maidique, 1980.)

A technological entrepreneur is not just a glorified nine-syllable equivalent for "project leader." It is someone who possesses certain specific skills that are not necessarily suggested by the simpler, four-syllable term. First, he or she must have technological curiosity and empathy. This is not to say that they have to have a technological background (even though most do). What is more important is that they have an innate curiosity about how things work and are able (relish, in fact) to communicate and work effectively with engineers, scientists, computer specialists, and so on.

Nor is it just a matter of being a "quick study." Even more critical than the ability to grasp the essentials of a technology quickly is a certain kind of imagination and insight that allows one, within the constraints imposed by that technology, to think of ways of modifying it to better meet the needs of the existing process, or of modifying the existing process to better meet the demands of the new technology.

Good technological entrepreneurs have enough inner confidence to be willing to ask "dumb" questions and keep asking them—plowing through the jargon, implicit assumptions, and unstated relationships that often surround technology—until they are satisfied that they really understand at a gut level what goes on and why. It is also helpful to have a certain amount of interpersonal skill, so that throughout such questioning they can preserve cooperative relations with the technologists upon whom they are so dependent for information.

Moreover, the technological entrepreneur must be tough. Even trained scientists do not necessarily understand everything about a new technology, yet their status (and self-image) suggests that they should. When asked a question by a less-informed person about an issue that they do not clearly understand, rather than admit ignorance or uncertainty they may, like all of us, feign understanding and respond with an evasive answer that is obscured by jargon and edged with impatience. They hope that the questioner, chagrined at the apparent stupidity of his or her question and afraid to take more time from such an important and informed person, will retreat without any further attempt to plumb the depths of the issue. Good technological entrepreneurs—in fact, good managers in general—are not so easily discouraged.

Other important qualities are suggested by the second half of the term: entrepreneur. In case after case, we have been struck by the ability of some people to surmount the confusion that surrounds any innovation and to manage it into reality. Sometimes these people have little or no managerial experience and yet they instinctively do the right thing. Other people with impeccable managerial credentials, with proven records of administrative success, fail miserably. Why?

Again the evidence is fragmentary, but it seems to point toward the fact that the qualities that make for a good technological entrepreneur are more like those of someone who starts up his or her own business than like those of someone who is successful at managing an existing business. For example, the technological entrepreneur must be able to:

1. Thrive in the ambiguity that surrounds working in an unstructured environment without clear lines of authority or specific resources.
2. Operate through interpersonal ad hoc agreements and understandings, on the basis of personal credibility, good will, and mutual advantage rather than relying on organizational loyalty or "rank" in that organization.
3. React instinctively to opportunities and crises, and thus maintain the credibility of the project and keep it progressing inch by inch, rather than waiting for studies, committee reports, and clearance from higher authorities.
4. Identify the people whose support is crucial to the success of the project and win their allegiance.

The key question for top management is, "How does one know if a prospective project leader has these characteristics?" Unfortunately, there are no very good tests, only a warning: the personality attributes one is looking for are not necessarily those that we commonly associate with a "good manager." In fact, we have seen good managers fail miserably in this kind of assignment, as well as technological entrepreneurs whose success prompted them to undertake more traditional management assignments only to find they were unable to cope with the structure, lines of communication, and time lags associated with formal ongoing organizations. Burgelman (1982) carried out an extensive systematic study of these project leaders and was able, at its conclusion, to provide only a few general guidelines and comments on pitfalls to be avoided. There simply is no sure-fire test.

At this point we would not presume to offer a formal recipe for success since we still understand only dimly the chemistry among the various ingredients. But it seems clear to us that, once the three legs of the triangle described in the previous section are in place, the organization should seek out a certain kind of person to manage the project. Often a very wide net must be used, since the best person may be someone who is not much appreciated in his or her current assignment. They are sometimes loners who chafe under existing rules and persist in making proposals or organizing informal groups to pursue activities that are outside the mainstream of their department's interests.

To complement the efforts of the technological entrepreneur, the organization must provide other skills and resources: R&D specialists, process engineers, industrial engineers, and so on. Even the best technological entrepreneur would be unable to make progress without access to such basic technical skills. One of his or her first tasks, therefore, is to assess the existing skills of the organization and identify any essential ones that are missing. Then a way must be found to acquire them, either through contacts with external organizations or by selective hiring.

10-4.4 Establishing Administrative Procedures That Reinforce Process Innovation

It is one thing to implement projects that have been clearly identified as appropriate ways to improve a process technology. It is quite another to put procedures into place that will guide this identification and ensure that the projects chosen will receive the human resources and capital resources they need. With regard to human resources, it is much more likely that the necessary capabilities will be available if the firm has access to a full range of them. Rather than waiting for a project to come along before hiring individuals with certain skills, firms should ascertain the mix of skills that is likely to be needed, hire to that mix, and then assign experienced people to projects as they arise.

It is also important for manufacturing firms to establish attractive career paths for people who have critical technical skills. Some firms that have been particularly successful at process innovation have a practice of rotating engineers through several parts of the organization. New hires are typically assigned to what some firms call "sustaining engineering" (keeping existing operations running smoothly). Then they move, perhaps, to field service engineering, then to new process engineering. Once such career paths are established, a reasonable balance—both in numbers and in prestige—must be maintained between design engineers and manufacturing/process engineers. If

/process engineers begin to feel that they are second-class citi-
o in too many American companies), they will either leave or
ey do.

pital budgeting system can encourage or hinder its rate of im-
ocess technology. If its top management regards the risks associated with changing its process technology as generally being greater than
product or market risks, say, then they will, consciously or not, tend to raise the
hurdles applied to proposed investments in process improvements. As a result,
few of these projects will get approved. No matter how good the firm may be at
identifying opportunities for process improvement, the capital and (more important) the leadership necessary for implementation will not be available. To
overcome this problem, management's mindset regarding technological risk
must be changed, as we discussed at the beginning of this chapter.

Another common procedure that discourages process innovation is cred-
iting a proposed process change only with the benefits that result from its use in
connection with the first product it produces. No credit is given, as far as the
capital budgeting system is concerned, for the longer-term capabilities the process change will provide the entire organization. For example, consider a firm
that plans to expand its manufacturing capacity and is trying to decide whether
to use its existing process or a new one. The profits that result from the additional sales are typically credited to the *existing* process, and the new process
receives credit only for the incremental cost savings it provides over that existing process. The follow-on products that it might be able to build as a result of
those capabilities are not taken into account. In the words of one experienced
manufacturing manager:

> Some managers recognize that such a project is usually the first of a series,
> and that it is the series, not the prototype alone, they must evaluate. But
> many do not . . . [This may explain why] today's best process for making
> propylene oxide was offered to seven established producers, all of whom
> turned it down. All but one are now out of business. (Malpas, 1983)

In the firms that have been most successful at making significant and
sustained improvements in process technology, top management has conditioned the whole organization to believe that the risks of process innovation are
inherently no greater than the risks of product or market innovation. New
technologies frequently are approved in connection with facilities expansion,
not only because they are justified by incremental cost savings but also because
they improve the firm's manufacturing capabilities and provide a stronger
foundation for future product and market development.

10-5 SUMMARY AND CONCLUSIONS

In this chapter we tried to make the risks associated with changing process
technology less threatening by putting them into a framework that helps man-

agers to understand when and how certain changes might be necessary, the kinds of strains that an organization often undergoes when it contemplates or implements such a change, and the kinds of issues that seem to be the key to successful implementation. Being able to predict the dilemmas one might face often makes the reality less unsettling when it arrives.

It is important that general managers be familiar with their process technologies for another reason, and that causes us to be concerned about the capability of many manufacturing companies to keep their processes up to the standards set by their international competitors. The same kind of experience that makes it possible for managers to put technological risks into proper perspective is, for similar reasons, essential in choosing the people to be given technological assignments within a company. With experience comes a "sixth sense" that helps one assess the ability of an individual to do a particular kind of job. Consider, for example, the following quote from a marketing consultant:

> I think I can tell a good sales rep just by being around him or her. If the person is experienced, confident, well prepared, speaks well, maintains control of situations, and seems to have a time plan, I assume I have a good one.

Whether this marketing consultant is always right is not the issue. What is important is that he feels more competent with his assessment than would a design engineer who is asked to hire a good sales person. In an important sense, "It takes one to know one." Therefore, a person with sales experience will make his or her decision about the competence of another salesperson more confidently—and probably with a greater likelihood of being correct.

In this light, it is not surprising to see companies that are dominated by managers who have certain backgrounds almost inevitably gravitate toward attracting more of the same kinds of people, and doing more and more of the things they are already good at doing. This can be dangerous, as many U.S. companies are beginning to realize. As we pointed out in Chapter 1, the executive suites of the largest American corporations have come to be increasingly dominated since the 1950s by people with financial, control, and marketing backgrounds.

We do not mean to imply that these people are not of the highest caliber. What we *are* saying is that they, like everybody else, tend to be good at certain things and weak at others. Most people unconsciously favor the activities they are good at and avoid those they feel less confident about. If there is nobody with a manufacturing or engineering background in the top group—someone who has the same level of credibility and authority as the others—almost inevitably the company will fall behind in terms of its technological capabilities.

If one's background is primarily financial, moreover, one tends to formulate issues in terms of financial alternatives: rather than do something for one's self, one always has the alternative of buying it from someone else. For example, rather than inventing, developing, testing and debugging new products or processes in-house, the obvious alternative (to someone whose work experience has given him or her confidence in the workings of free competitive markets) is to wait until some other organization has developed a similar product or process and then buy it. If one's top management group does not include anyone with a thorough understanding of the process skills required to develop technology internally, the option of buying it already developed looks even more attractive.

We have observed that as the proportion of people with nontechnical backgrounds increases in a company's top management group, that company tends to purchase more and more of its manufacturing equipment from external suppliers instead of designing and developing this equipment itself. Similarly, it tends increasingly to purchase new products and processes from other companies—by seeking licensing agreements, hiring away the people in those companies who helped develop the new technology, or simply acquiring the company as a whole.

All of these activities increased in popularity in the United States during the 1970s. They reflect the implicit assumption that technology is something that can easily be brought in from outside the firm—an assumption we feel is fundamentally incorrect. Such activities ultimately destroy both a company's willingness and its capabilities to develop its own proprietary technology, and thus to use technology as a competitive weapon.

Technological capability is not something that can be bought and sold easily. If it were, it would not constitute an enduring competitive advantage. It is not an *object,* it is an *objective;* something that one must seek and perfect continuously or it will erode. A technological object (a new product or process) is simply the embodiment of an organization's technological capabilities. For this reason managing technology within a company—developing and exploiting its technological capabilities—is more like playing tennis than like buying a new tennis racquet. If one does not develop the skill and the strength to use the new racquet properly (in business terms, the management and technical infrastructures), one will not be able to compete successfully against opponents who have those skills even though they may use older racquets.

To build an organization that is skilled at converting technological advances into actual products and manufacturing processes, one must ensure that the entire organization is involved. Experience in dealing with technological issues of the type that we have been discussing must be diffused throughout the firm so that all managers develop a technological sixth sense to go along with their marketing and financial senses. Technological expertise cannot be delegated or confined to a single group, such as R&D. If it is, the organization soon will discover that it is unable to translate the technological outputs of the R&D group into well-engineered products. Even if it could design such products, it would be unable to produce them efficiently in its factories or sell them effectively through its sales organization.

If the technology is imported from another company (even when the developers and skilled implementers come with it), but the necessary support systems and organizational empathy do not exist, then it is likely that the new technology will ultimately fail to be assimilated properly. In this sense, organizations are like the human body, which tries to reject a heart transplant even though the new heart is essential to its survival. Despite its life-saving potential, it is perceived to be a "foreign" object. The new technology is similarly starved of nutrients (resources) and attacked by those who see their role as one of protecting the traditional activities and capabilities of the organization.

Developing a broad-based technological capability takes time, patience, and resources. Funds and attention cannot be turned on and off according to the current economic environment. The best, most innovative people will leave an organization if they are made to feel that what they are doing is less important than meeting the financial community's current expectations.

This commitment to the long-term nurturing of technological competence must start at the top. Top management must be willing to accept personally the risks associated with major technological change. It cannot delegate that responsibility to "experts." The specialized technological skills of engineers and scientists, however valued, may be used against them at some point because such expertise implies that they lack the "broad management perspective" required to make the critical decisions upon which technological success ultimately depends. To take on these risks themselves, even to become champions of a technological venture, requires top managers to develop an intimate understanding of the technology and to be involved in all stages of its development.

SELECTED REFERENCES

Abernathy, William J., Kim B. Clark, and Alan M. Kantrow. *Industrial Renaissance.* New York: Basic Books, 1983.

Abernathy, William J., and Phillip L. Townsend. "Technology, Productivity, and Process Change." *Technological Forecasting and Social Change,* Vol. 7, 1975, pp. 379–396.

Abernathy, William J., and James Utterback. "A Dynamic Model of Product and Process Innovation." *Omega,* December 1975, pp. 639–657.

Abernathy, William J., and Kenneth Wayne. "Limits of the Learning Curve." *Harvard Business Review,* September–October 1974, pp. 109–119.

Burgelman, Robert. "Corporate Venturing." Graduate School of Business, Stanford University, Working Paper, 1982.

Business Week. "Hewlett-Packard: Where Slower Growth Is Smarter Management." June 9, 1975, pp. 50–58.

Dhalla, Nariman K., and Sonia Yuspeh. "Forget the Product Life Cycle Concept." *Harvard Business Review,* January–February 1976, pp. 102–112.

Foster, Richard N. "A Call for Vision in Managing Technology." *Business Week,* May 24, 1982, pp. 24–33.

Gold, Bela. *Productivity, Technology and Capital.* Lexington, MA: Lexington Books, 1979.

Gruber, William H., Dileep Mehta, and Raymond Vernon. "The R and D factor in International Trade and International Investment of U.S. Industry." *Journal of Political Economy,* Vol. 74, No. 1, February 1967.

Harris, J. M., R. W. Shaw, Jr., and W. P. Sommers. "The Strategic Management of Technology." *Planning Review,* January 1983.

Hayes, Robert H., and Modesto A. Maidique. "The Technology Gap." *The New York Times,* June 2, 1981.

Hayes, Robert H., and Steven C. Wheelwright. "The Dynamics of Product–Process Life Cycles." *Harvard Business Review,* March–April 1979, pp. 127–136.

Kidder, Tracy. *The Soul of a New Machine.* Boston: Little, Brown, 1981.

McInnes, J. "Corporate Management of Productivity—An International Comparison." Sloan School of Management, Massachusetts Institute of Technology, Working Paper, WP1398-83, January 1983.

Maidique, Modesto. "Entrepreneurs, Champions and Technological Innovation." *Sloan Management Review,* Winter 1980, pp. 59–76.

Malpas, R. "The Plant After Next." *Harvard Business Review,* July–August 1983, pp. 122–130.

Myers, S., and D. G. Marquis. *Successful Technological Innovations.* Washington, D.C.: National Science Foundation, NSF 69-17, 1969.

Olsen, R. Paul. "Equipment Supplier-Producer Relationships and Process Innovation in the Textile Industry." Ph.D. dissertation, Graduate School of Business Administration, Harvard University, 1975.

Quinn, James Brian. *Strategies for Change: Logical Incrementalism.* Homewood, IL: Richard D. Irwin, 1980.

Quinn, James Bryan. "Technological Innovation, Entrepreneurship and Strategy." *Sloan Management Review,* Spring 1979, pp. 19–29.

Rosenberg, Nathan. *Perspectives on Technology.* Cambridge: Cambridge University Press, 1976.

Rothwell, R., O. Freeman, A. Horlsey, F. T. P. Jervis, A. B. Robertson, and J. Townsend. "SAPPHO Updated—Project SAPPHO Phase II," *Research Policy,* Vol. 3, 1974, pp. 258–291.

Schumpeter, Joseph A. *The Theory of Economic Development.* Cambridge, MA: Harvard University Press, 1934.

Simon, Herbert. "Rational Decision-Making in Business Organizations." *American Economic Review,* Vol. 69, September 1979, pp. 493–513.

Walton, Richard E. "The Diffusion of New Work Structures: Explaining Why Success Didn't Take." *Organizational Dynamics,* Winter 1975, pp. 3–22.

11
German Approaches to Manufacturing Management

11-1 INTRODUCTION

The publication of *Le Defi Americain* (*The American Challenge*) by Jean Jacques Servan-Schreiber, a Frenchman, in 1967 ironically coincided with the high-water mark of admiration for America's management methods and style in other countries. Servan-Schreiber's argument, in fact, was that America's key advantage in international markets over European* companies was its managerial and technological superiority. He argued that unless strong measures were taken by European governments, the efficiency and aggressiveness of U.S. firms would give them increasing control over Europe's economy.

Within four years of the publication of that book, observers were expressing concern about the slowdown in long-term productivity growth and R&D spending that appeared to be taking place in America. In addition, the United States experienced its first trade deficit in manufactured products since 1893. Reflecting its weakening position in international markets, the dollar was cut free from the gold standard and allowed to float (mostly down during the ensuing ten years) against other currencies.

In the first chapter of this book we argued that a major portion of the responsibility for this decline lies with the way many U.S. manufacturing companies are managed—that a new management philosophy and set of approaches for dealing with certain types of decisions had led U.S. managers to underinvest in and underexploit their technological capabilities. But another major reason for the relative decline of U.S. manufacturing in the 1970s might

---

* At that time Japan was considered a minor nuisance by most people; it was designated, in effect, as a "semi-less-developed country" during the Kennedy Round of international tariff negotiations in the late 1960s.

be simply that their competitors got tougher. Therefore, whereas in the 1960s European and Japanese managers were asking themselves what they could learn from U.S. companies, the 1980s is the time to begin asking what U.S. manufacturing managers can learn from their world class competitors in Europe and the Far East.

11-1.1 Overview of the Next Three Chapters

In this and the following two chapters we concentrate on the two countries, West Germany and Japan, that have proven to be the United States' most effective competitors in international markets for manufactured products. This chapter describes some of the characteristics and management practices we have observed in well-run German factories; the next summarizes our observations about well-run Japanese factories. Finally, in Chapter 13 we pull together some of the common threads and speculate about their implications for manufacturing companies around the world.

We do not spend much time commenting on aspects of foreign management that are dominated by so-called national characteristics: the ingrained patterns of managerial behavior that are caused by cultural traditions, societal expectations regarding individual behavior, and the institutional relationships that have grown up over the years (for example, among government, organized labor, and business). There are three reasons for this.

First, we have found that national stereotypes often break down when one looks closely at what actually goes on inside a company. Within a given manufacturing industry, companies around the world face very similar problems; they must draw on similar resources in solving them; and they must operate within similar constraints imposed by technology, markets, and competitors. We believe that success in operating within these constraints, solving these problems, and using these resources effectively is influenced much less by the unique aspects of the home culture than most people think.

Second, to understand a culture and its impact on behavior thoroughly, one has to spend considerable time studying it. We cannot claim to be experts about either German or Japanese culture and national psychology, and we would prefer not to display our ignorance in print. We do think that we are well-informed about manufacturing management, and we therefore concentrate our attention on that topic.

Finally, commenting on such "national characteristics" would lead us to an intellectual dead end. If significant differences in the ways that companies are managed were due simply to "ingrained" national differences, there would be little opportunity to learn from others without instituting massive (and probably impractical) changes in child-rearing, education, family structure, cultural mores, and institutional structures. Our intent here is to focus on those issues and differences that might lead our readers to think about changes in management practices that are implementable and potentially effective within their own cultures.

Many attributes of both German and Japanese industrial and managerial practice are not at all incompatible with those normally considered to be "American." The Germans and the Japanese have obviously learned much from the United States since World War II. It is no slur on American traditions and values to assert that now Americans can learn something in return. And now is not the first time for such learning—many American industrial practices owe their origins to British industrial technology and traditions. Having said this, we do not ignore national differences entirely, in the sense that Chapter 13 focuses on those managerial approaches that are *not* driven primarily by national differences. Presumably, such approaches would be the easiest ones for other companies to adopt within their own cultures.

11-1.2 West German Industry's Enviable Record

In spite of the upward pressure on the Deutsche Mark during most of the 1970s and the economic stagnation and political turmoil the Germans have faced in recent years, the German economy remains remarkably strong in its most important area, the manufacturing sector. Although the overall German balance of payments has been up and down in recent years, throughout the 1970s its balance of payments for manufactured products was always in the black (see Table 11-1).

Table 11-1 also shows how vigorous the growth of German manufactured exports was during the 1970s. Even though German industrialists have been beset by many of the same problems as their U.S. counterparts (slow economic growth, rapidly escalating energy prices, and a perceived decline in the "work ethic," particularly among younger workers), Germany's productivity growth rate in the manufacturing sector actually increased in the 1970s—from a level of about 5.1 percent in the 1960s to about 5.5 percent—whereas it dropped

Table 11-1

Total German Exports and Imports of Manufactured Products

(DM in billions)

Year	Exports	Imports
1974	193	83
1975	188	92
1976	219	112
1977	234	122
1978	242	133
1979	265	155
1980	292	174

Source. Statistiches Jahrbuch: 1981 (Fuer die Bundesrepublik, Deutschland) [Statistical Yearbook: 1981 (for the Federal Republic of Germany)], p. 245.

precipitously in the United States. As a result, despite relatively high labor rates and energy costs (one recent study indicates that energy accounts for about 22 percent of the total cost of German manufactured products, compared with about 14 percent for U.S. manufactured products), during the early 1980s orders for German capital goods were increasing rapidly in areas such as Latin America and the Pacific Basin, where traditionally the United States has been a major supplier.

The Germans know that their economic strength lies in their heavy industrial manufacturing sector. As energy prices have risen and international competition has toughened, the Germans have turned to their strength and concentrated their efforts on improving their foreign exchange-earning performance. For their traditional competitors this means even tougher competition in the future.

11-2 GERMAN MANUFACTURING MANAGEMENT

11-2.1 Gründlichkeit

It is commonly believed that the Germans' greatest virtues are their discipline and willingness to work hard. Neither is necessarily true, as is clear to anyone who has seen the enormous traffic jams immediately after lunch on Friday afternoon, as millions of Germans begin to get an early start on the weekend. Absenteeism is endemic in German industry; in 1981 it was more than 12 percent (including "planned" absences) and among the highest in the world. But two other German traits *are* generally observable: with relatively few exceptions German workers are neat and meticulous. From the point of view of the manager of industrial production, these traits may be much more important than discipline and hard work. But they are not exclusively German, as is attested to by their transference to "guest workers" from other countries. Nor do they occur without considerable managerial encouragement.

At the very least, the German obsession with neatness and meticulousness leads to a well-ordered workplace and to a constant concern with *Gründlichkeit:* getting everything "just right" on the technologically complex manufactured goods which form the foundation of German industrial strength. This meticulousness drives German workers to take extra care and insist that what goes out of their shops is as close to perfect as possible. Perhaps even more important is the fact that managers traditionally share this "inbred" concern with getting the product made right.

One hears regularly that neither American workers nor American managers care sufficiently about the quality of their product. Whether this is true or not is not necessarily important. What is important is that it is widely perceived to be true—by America's foreign competitors and, more critically, its foreign customers. German products have an enviable reputation for quality around the world. Therefore, a look in some depth at certain German practices that foster and strengthen concern with quality may provide clues to how other companies can improve their own.

11-2.2 German Attitudes and Management Practices

Most successful German manufacturing companies exhibit five conspicuous traits that probably constitute the basis for many of their strengths:

1. They foster a management system that seeks consciously to maintain technical strength throughout the managerial hierarchy.

2. They use a traditional apprenticeship system, which provides a broad base of what some German scholars call "low-level competence" (not competence *of* a low level but competence *at* lower levels). This gives them a pool of skilled, technically proficient workers who maintain an "Old World craftsmanship" attitude toward their work, and who are so well versed in the theoretical fundamentals of their trades that they adapt rather easily to new process technologies.

3. They exhibit an intense product and customer orientation which both focuses on the individual needs of each customer and stresses on-time delivery, solid engineering, careful workmanship, and reliable after-sales servicing.

4. They feel themselves to be under intense competitive pressure and, as a result, they are willing to accept lower profit margins and returns on capital.

5. The orientation of their management is toward the long-term growth and stability of the firm. Instead of being rewarded primarily for short-term "bottom line" results, managers are expected to engage in activities, such as research and development, which have long-term payoffs.

Although we focus our attention largely on the positive benefits of these attitudes and practices, we do not wish to convey the impression that they are unequivocally good, or necessarily superior to practices in other countries. Many have a darker side that must be acknowledged. For example, the strong allegiance that German (and Japanese) workers tend to show toward their geographic districts, companies, and professions can undercut the ability of their economies to adjust to major changes in the competitive environment. It also tends to dampen entrepreneurial activity, particularly that associated with "spinoffs"—the establishment of a small new firm by a group of managers who leave the constricting confines of an older, larger one.

11-2.3 Management and Supervisor Training

The Germans do not seem to have developed the concept of management, as a profession in and of itself, that has grown up in the United States. The graduate-level business school—designed specifically to train people to go directly into positions of managerial authority, armed only with a theoretical education in the "science" of management—does not exist in Germany. As a result, managers who hold responsible positions in German manufacturing plants are normally people who received their undergraduate and graduate training in the technical professions and who remain well versed in the technical operations they manage. (More than 35 percent of all university degrees awarded in Germany in the late 1970s were engineering degrees, compared with less than 6 percent in the United States and 20 percent in Japan.) A surprisingly high percentage of them hold multiple degrees (often a combination of engineering and economics) and/or doctoral degrees. Typically, they have considerable practical experience as line engineers as well as theoretical familiarity with the technologies of their business.

To a considerable extent this difference is due to the high regard that Germans hold for *Technik,* their word for a concept that is profoundly different from those implied by such English words as "technique," "technology," and "science." *Technik* refers specifically to the "art [involving both products and methods] of manufacturing" (see Lawrence, 1980, esp. pp. 96–100), and it encompasses manufacturing techniques, production equipment technology, and what Americans prosaically call "production management." The concern with *Technik* exerts a pervasive influence on German managers' thinking, to the point where other managerial activities—such as planning, control, and strategy formulation—are relegated to secondary status.

A company's, or a manager's, skill in *Technik* is accorded great prestige in Germany, where it is regarded as the primary basis for industrial and personal success. Compared with the relatively low appreciation for manufacturing skill and the lack of appeal of careers in manufacturing to college and business school graduates in their own countries, American and British observers are fascinated by the high regard that Germans have for *Technik.* They are similarly impressed by German managers' "product mindedness": their detailed knowledge about their products and their interest, almost their preoccupation, with how they function and are used.

A typical example of this management expertise is found in an electrical equipment fabrication plant operated by a subsidiary of Siemens. The plant employs 2,000–3,000 workers, most of them highly skilled machinists. Its manager in 1979 held a doctorate in engineering and had spent all of the 20–25 years since he was graduated from university with the same company. While he had received no special training in management either in school or at mid-career, he had spent his entire career working as both line and staff engineer with the products and processes he was now in charge of. During our tour of his plant it rapidly became apparent that this manager was not only familiar, but completely at home technically, with what was going on. The relatively easy communication between him and the skilled factory workers suggested that his technical expertise was recognized by them and that it contributed significantly to his authority and acceptance in the plant.

At the same time, our discussion later in his office made clear that this manager was not simply a "technical type" left to run an engineering plant while isolated from front office strategy and planning. He was as well versed about the firm's international, financial, and political problems as he was about his own plant's operations. The maintenance of technical expertise at all levels in management seems to be fairly typical of German manufacturing companies.

First-line supervisors, moreover, are seldom young trainees who are expected to move up rapidly after only a brief experience on the shop floor. Rather, they are skilled workers with long experience; often they are also natural leaders among their fellow workers (see Fores et al., 1978). Daimler-Benz, for example, requires that all of its foremen pass the "master" level examinations in the trades they supervise. Other automakers in Germany do not insist that foremen be masters, but they must be *gelernte*—qualified journeymen.

The problems that many American firms have with low morale among their supervisors, and their difficulty in recruiting them (see Sasser and Leonard, 1980), hardly exist in Germany. Moreover, American companies frequently offer first-line supervisory positions to recent university graduates as part of a management training program. While of necessity these people become operationally familiar with the processes they supervise, most of them expect to move beyond the shop floor relatively quickly.

German firms have not adopted the practice of moving managers from place to place and from job to job every two or three years, as do many American firms. They appear to have consciously avoided developing the expectation that promising young managers must be constantly on the move within the company if they are to have a chance to rise to the top. Occasional movement is to be expected of potential top managers in large companies, but such movement typically comes every six or eight years rather than every two or three years. It is our observation that the gulf between plant management and the shop floor, which exists to some degree in every factory, tends to be widest at those companies that do move managers frequently from location to location.

11-2.4 Developing Low-Level Competence

Quality production requires more than just a solid work ethic, high morale, and good management. While all these are necessary, they are not sufficient; real technical competence at the factory floor level must also exist. If the Germans have had any "secret weapon" during Europe's economic difficulties since 1973, it is the technical competence at lower levels that is the product of their apprenticeship system.

Under the German apprenticeship system more than half of all young people leave full-time schooling by age 16 to enter three years of apprenticeship (over 430,000 apprenticeships were being served in 1981). During this period they spend approximately four days of each week on the job in their chosen trade. The fifth day is spent in a state-run vocational school learning the "theoretical" aspects of the trade. The subject matter taught the apprentices is closely regulated, both by the state and by the trade associations of the various industries, to assure that workers receive uniform training nationwide.

The apprenticeship system enjoys wide approval from government, the unions, and industry, and is also supported by an educational system that permits only a small fraction of young Germans to go on to college. Apprenticeships are required for more than 450 different job classifications. The government and the unions favor it over other training systems (such as longer programs of general education, with job training taking place somewhat later in life, as is common in the United States) because it offers a partial solution to the problem of youth unemployment and provides most apprentices with a marketable trade. Industry strongly supports the system because, by training youths in needed trades at an early age, society is provided with a workforce that is not only highly skilled but also well motivated, disciplined, and responsible. As one union official phrased it, "They learn to be on time . . . and what a working environment is." The apprenticeship program is particularly responsible for maintaining the skills required by the high-technology heavy industries that are so crucial to Germany's export success. These are skills that the public schools usually do not have the resources to teach properly.

Note that youths are trained by industry itself, not the state. Moreover, they are given considerable experience and responsibility in the real-life workplace at an early age. Employers are eager to hire and even, if necessary, retrain those who have been through the apprenticeship system. They have found through long experience that those who have been apprentices are fairly easy to retrain and adapt well to different work environments. As evidence of this employability, in mid-1981 the unemployment rate for teenagers in Germany was 5.1 percent, somewhat *less* than the country's overall unemployment rate. In the United States, by contrast, the teenage unemployment rate was above 18 percent—almost three times the unemployment rate of other age groups.

One German, now the executive vice president of an American bank, commented in a letter (*The Wall Street Journal,* September 22, 1981):

> While I am receiving a satisfactory return on my investment in an academic education, I recognize that as a banker I draw most of my daily job needs from my German apprenticeship during which I was paid $15 per month.
>
> Youth unemployment should rarely be a national problem in Germany, for the simple reason that the world continues to use any surplus skilled laborer or tradesman, technician or engineer, especially when they are also trained in foreign languages. Could that be the reason why there are so many German nationals making a reasonably good living in every corner of the world?

The law does not require German companies to maintain apprenticeship programs, but an unofficial discipline is applied by trade associations and generally supported by private industry. More than 350,000 German companies offer them, and few large companies (even those with parent firms outside Germany) are without an apprenticeship program. In fact, until about 1970 a completed apprenticeship was a prerequisite for courses leading to a *Gymnasium* engineering degree (the German *Gymnasium* is roughly equivalent to the last two to three years of a U.S. high school plus the first year of college), which is the steppingstone for a university degree in engineering. It is still not uncommon to find university-trained engineers who have done apprenticeships.

One of the best known apprenticeship programs is run by Ford of Germany at its large Cologne works. Each year Ford has several times as many applicants as the 210–250 apprentices it takes in. Within the three-year program, Ford's attrition rate is less than 5 percent, even better than the national rate of about 20 percent. (Both young people and their parents fear that there will be little opportunity for them to obtain skilled work if they do not complete an apprenticeship.) Ford's program is unusually costly to the firm because, unlike most companies, it does not permit its apprentices to perform work on the shop floor until the last six months of their apprenticeship. But the company still feels that its "gold-plated" program pays off in the long run, since about 97 percent of its graduates remain with Ford for the bulk of their working lives. Not only are these people skilled tradesmen, but they have inculcated in them from an early age the work habits and attitudes that Ford believes underlie the building of quality products.

Most American executives who have examined the German system are highly impressed with it. They lament the attitudinal problems of young American workers, as well as their lack of basic technical skills, and express regret that American trade associations do not have the clout to impose a similar system on U.S. companies. Few companies are willing to finance such programs because they fear that, once trained, their graduates would be enticed away by other companies that are unwilling to pay for training programs of their own. Unfortunately, this argument is self-fulfilling: as more and more American companies accede to it, and cease investing in training their own workers, the more attractive the workers trained by the remaining companies become.

11-2.5 Customer Orientation, German Style

Most American firms pride themselves on their "customer orientation," by which they typically mean their emphasis on aggressive selling and their responsiveness to customer complaints. Customer orientation to German managers, however, means something quite different: the delivery, on schedule, of finely engineered products. This kind of customer orientation rests on the belief that the reputation earned by quality products, timely delivery, and excellent after-sales service is the best possible marketing tool (see Turnbull and Cunningham, 1981).

Germans believe that for a manufacturing company to be customer oriented in this sense, it must have technical strength throughout the organization and managers who are willing to spend a major portion of their time in the field. This enables them to be close to their customers so that they can understand and anticipate their needs, and to communicate those needs effectively back to the organization. All this sounds trite and obvious, but the realities of bureaucratization and routinization within manufacturing organizations make it extremely difficult to maintain such customer closeness consistently over time, particularly if sales managers do not have technical training and manufacturing managers do not have a firsthand understanding of customers' problems and needs.

When a firm is developing a product for which a large market does not yet exist, the larger German corporations tend to rely on the engineering reputations and customer relationships they have already developed in the countries where they expect to market the new product. With this expectation in mind, it is common for the Federal Research and Technology Ministry (BMFT) in Bonn to subsidize German firms' development of products for which it believes significant worldwide demand will ultimately arise.

As one example, Maschinenfabrik Augsburg–Nürnberg (MAN) has been involved in a number of R&D contracts of this sort, many focused on developing solar and wind energy hardware. The eventual intended market is not foggy West Germany but North Africa, where MAN has already established a successful sales operation. MAN expects that the reputation built for it in those countries by its trucks and heavy industrial equipment will work to its advantage when they become interested in buying "alternative energy" hardware. Similarly, MAN's success over the longer term will depend on whether this new generation of products lives up to the reputation gained by its current products.

In contrast, some American companies—even apparently successful ones—often suffer in international competition because of an incomplete vision of what their customers need. They are willing to customize their products to the specific requirements of each customer (admittedly a strong selling point), but they have problems with reliability and, perhaps more important in the long run, have failed to develop adequate service/support systems for their products. Consequently, they find themselves vulnerable to competitors who provide such peace of mind, for one of the first questions any potential customer asks when contemplating buying a product from a distant company is, "Can I depend on its working as it is supposed to?"

German companies, while respecting their customers and trying to be good suppliers, do not subscribe to the notion that "the customer is always right." They believe that sometimes the customer does not necessarily know what is best for it or its supplier, and that therefore the supplier must sometimes—politely but firmly—say "no." They are horrified by companies that are so full of pride or hungry for business that they never back down from a customer demand, no matter how complex the design problems that result or how soon delivery is required. Such companies often are unable to live up to their promises and ultimately generate increasing customer dissatisfaction—rather than appreciation for "bending over backward" on customers' behalf.

To the Germans this is not customer orientation at all. Despite all the scurrying and scrambling to meet the customer's unmeetable demands, it does not produce what the German industrialist believes to be the customer's *real* need: a product so well engineered and reliable that the customer will wait for it if necessary and will return to its manufacturer for more in the future.

11-2.6 Fighting for Survival

Although most German companies feel confident about their own prospects, they believe that German industry as a whole is under far greater pressure than is U.S. industry. The most important form of pressure comes from the necessity to compete in export markets. Most German manufacturing firms *must* export to survive; products manufactured for export represent about half of total German (and Japanese) manufacturing output; in the United States the figure was under 10 percent in 1981. Their problems have been compounded by the fact that the prices of their products in these export markets are not totally under their control because of the wild fluctuations in the exchange rates that have occurred since 1970. In fact, during most of that period their own currency was strengthening against the currencies of their major competitors.

In these foreign markets, moreover, they must compete against "world class" competitors, including the Japanese and the giant U.S. multinationals. Since Germany has experienced relatively slow growth rates since 1973 (generally less than 2 percent, compared with more than 4 percent previously) and looks forward to similar or even lower internal growth rates throughout the 1980s, corporate growth will continue to depend largely on success in these export markets.

To make matters even more difficult, real labor costs in Germany more than doubled during the 1970s; its average annual wage of over $16,000 in 1981 was close to the highest in the world. "We must increase our sales and reduce our other costs simply to stay even" is a typical complaint of the German manufacturing manager.

Finally, German firms tend to be much smaller than U.S. firms. Each of the 20 largest (in terms of sales) German companies is about 40 percent of the size of their U.S. counterparts, and the hundredth largest German firm is only about one-sixth as large as the hundredth largest in the United States. This is not true in every industry, of course. The sales of Hoechst, which was Germany's fourth largest company in 1982, were somewhat greater than those of DuPont (before its acquisition of Conoco), its largest U.S.-based rival in the chemical industry. This kind of size comparability is rare, however. More typical is the auto industry, where Daimler-Benz (Germany's largest auto company) was comparable in size to Chrysler (the third largest in the United States).

How can one compete against world class competitors when one is small, has higher cost labor than most of one's competitors, and cannot easily lay off workers? The not-so-glib answer is that in order to compete effectively one must first survive, and long-term survival is a much more important goal for German firms than it is for U.S. companies. Who can grow the fastest or show the highest return on equity are, to them, secondary and somewhat frivolous issues.

Given the enormous success of German manufacturers since the 1960s, American observers are sometimes startled by German managers' pessimism and their envy of their U.S. counterparts. With Russian tanks and missiles just across the border, few natural resources, increasingly stiff competition from Japan and other countries, relatively little flexibility with regard to labor–management issues, high debt ratios, and low profit margins—no wonder the United States still appears to them to be the land of opportunity.

11-2.7 A Long-Term Orientation

Observers often comment on the differences between American managers, who are typically under pressure to produce high short-term profits, and German managers, who are expected to plan for the long term. Relatively modest returns over several years are accepted if a German company's top management believes this is necessary to building a solid long-term position in a market.

To some extent this long-term orientation is due to the fact that German stockholders, in contrast with those in the United States, have a relatively minor influence on management. This lesser stockholder influence, in turn, is partially due to tradition: stockholders do not expect to have much influence on company management and do not invest with the expectation of spectacular short-term results. Partly it is also due to the influential role that banks play in German industry. German bankers sit on corporate boards and play an active role in influencing corporate strategy. Typically they are primarily interested in the long-term financial strength of the firm. Finally, it must be acknowledged, a long-term orientation is encouraged by accounting and reporting practices that obscure short-term performance results.

Another important cause is that, while it is not the German style to make overt demonstrations of company loyalty, both workers and managers do tend to identify their own futures with the future success of the corporations for which they work. In practice, this means that employees are not laid off or threatened with dismissal for poor performance as much as are American workers. It also means that managers do not feel under pressure (or put themselves under pressure) to perform outstandingly in a short period of time in each job position they hold.

Neither workers nor managers tend to be as mobile as their American counterparts, either from job to job or from region to region. They tend, early in life, to seek work at the larger, more prestigious German-based multinational firms, and typically they stay there throughout their working lives. National labor legislation recognizes and supports this tendency, making it extremely difficult for firms to lay off permanent workers. Nor do managers, at either higher or lower levels, have a tradition of moving from company to company. They tend to finish their careers with the same organizations they started with. To close the loop in this self-sustaining system, companies typically put such effort into training their own people that they prefer to promote mostly from within.

11-3 THE CAUSES AND IMPLICATIONS OF THESE CHARACTERISTICS

Each of these managerial practices contains implications about the likely behavior of managers and workers in certain situations. They also interact to produce other distinctive attributes of the German management style.

11-3.1 The Worker–Manager Relationship

The combination of technical competence at both the managerial and the worker level makes possible a strong bond between management and the shop floor. This is a totally different kind of bond from that achieved by periodic, highly publicized attempts designed to show that management "cares" about the welfare of workers, or is interested in what workers think about quality control, process improvements, and so on. Such attempts, however sincerely motivated, come across as Band-Aids that disappear as soon as the current manager tires of them or moves on.

In German plants it is not uncommon for very senior managers to talk directly with workers about their specific tasks. Because managers normally are at home technically with most of the tasks performed in their plants, they can do more than just listen intently and pat the worker on the back for a job well done. They are able to engage workers in an intelligent discussion about the technical aspects of their work. One of the side products of the apprenticeship system (and the German admiration for *Technik*) is that workers typically take great pride in the tasks they perform and love to discuss them at length, often going into considerable theoretical depth about them. It stands to reason that if workers get a truly substantive technical response from senior managers, they are going to be stimulated to continue the dialogue with others at lower management levels in the plant. In addition, they will develop a level of respect for management that goes beyond "they actually care about me as a person." The much more significant and effective message is, "They understand and care about the job I do and are as interested in working to improve it as I am."

Several conditions must be present for such a relationship to work as we have outlined it: (1) technically competent managers, (2) managers who deliberately take the time to initiate serious dialogues with workers about their work, and (3) a skilled, competent workforce that has a tradition of pride in what it produces. The long-term orientation of most German industrial enterprises helps to foster this kind of relationship, as does the expectation that managers should be fully competent in every aspect of their plant's operations—not just passing through the plants on their way up the ladder.

11-3.2 Consensus-Seeking Decision Processes

German managers do not have nearly as much freedom of action as U.S. managers. The large corporations, in particular, have little choice but to make major decisions through a slow, consensus-seeking deliberative process that takes into consideration both worker interests and the public welfare. The most important limitation on management is the German codetermination system, which, among other things, legally mandates that German managers negotiate major decisions with worker-dominated works councils at the plant level. These decisions are then subject to the overall scrutiny of supervisory boards (roughly equivalent to the outside directors on an American board of directors), 50 percent of whose members, since 1976, are elected by the company's workers. The necessity to seek the approval of these worker representatives, together with other restrictions imposed by law, makes it very difficult for German managers to lay off large numbers of workers or move production to a new location, even within Germany.

In one German firm we visited, management indicated that during the worldwide recession of 1979–1982 it took a full nine months to cut the production capacity of their German plants, even though it was apparent to all concerned that such cuts were inevitable. Their U.S. plants were able to implement such cuts within four weeks of when the need to do so was fully recognized. Even to go to temporary short (less than 40 hour) work weeks, German manufacturers are required by law to provide, as a minimum, a two-week period for negotiations with labor and an additional two weeks lead time for the announcement of the agreed-upon cutback.

Consensus decision making also may be a carryover from the postwar "we're all in this together" spirit of reconstruction which permeated German society at all levels and which still probably exists at a subconscious level. The German practice of extending this consensus-building process to industry–government relations enables them to face external competition in each industry with a unified industry policy and a minimum of industry–government bickering.

There is no law that requires firms to respect the federal government's industrial policies in formulating their own competitive strategies. Most do so most of the time, however, largely because of an unwritten understanding that leaders of government, industry, and labor should work closely together to devise policies designed to protect the economic and export strength of the nation. In return for a sympathetic and helpful ear in government, German industry normally aligns itself with the industrial policies being promulgated. This leads to a decision-making structure that can be slow moving but that eventually gets most important groups lined up behind a company's plans. The result is a minimum amount of labor strife and less foot dragging by lower levels of management. Consensus-seeking decision making is also essential in matters concerning capital investment and R&D spending, since the firm's banks must be brought into the process.

Plant managers are usually also involved in this consensus-seeking process, and therefore they do not tend to feel the isolation that we often observe in American plant managers. Either because they have been trapped through overspecialization into roles that preclude meaningful cross-functional interchange ("We'll tell you what to do; your job is to do it"), or because they carry the stigma of temporary passers-through, who, the workers believe, will be moved to another job within a short period of time, U.S. plant-level managers often feel distant both from their workers and from corporate officers. Also, unlike German managers who know that they will not be abandoned if things go awry, American managers often characterize their role as "fall guys": there to take the blame if things go wrong but not given sufficient authority (or, perhaps, not listened to enough upstairs) to make sure the job is done right.

One of the benefits of such consensus-seeking at the factory level is the relative ease with which German manufacturers seem to coordinate and direct complex production sites. Facilities that employ 5,000 to 10,000 workers, produce a variety of product families, and utilize several production technologies seem to be effectively controlled and managed. U.S. plants of the same size in the same industry, on the other hand, often are considered to be too big, too complex, and too chaotic, if not completely "out-of-control." German managers maintain control by dividing up such large facilities into effectively focused departments and subplants, and then coordinating them in such a way as to realize both the benefits of focus *and* the benefits afforded by size (which makes it easier, for example, to manage the capacity imbalances that arise from product mix shifts). This balancing act appears to be facilitated by both management's technical competence and its use of consensus-seeking approaches.

11-3.3 Technological Incrementalism

Because of their emphasis on developing the technological expertise of both workers and managers, their reliance on slow consensus-seeking decision making processes, their commitment to building enduring customer relationships, and their willingness to measure results over a long time frame, the most successful German companies tend to concentrate on products that will be in demand well beyond the foreseeable future, not just in Germany but elsewhere in the world as well. Moreover, they prefer to pursue state-of-the-art products through a series of incremental improvements within the same basic product or process technology, rather than through dramatic leaps to new technologies that would make obsolete the skills and reputation that they have built up painstakingly over the years.

The fact that they do not generally seek breakthroughs in technology does not mean that they *lag* in technology. Far from it; their high labor costs induce strong pressures for continual improvement. But their research and development emphasis tends to be less on basic research than on exploiting and expanding the breakthroughs made in other countries.

The technological development of both products and processes capitalizes on the technical skills and competencies shared by workers and managers in German firms. Continued investment in those skills is complemented by continued investment in plant and equipment. The objective in both cases is to upgrade capabilities incrementally rather than replacing old assets with new ones. The German firms we studied invest 8–12 percent of their annual sales revenue in plant and equipment; most of this investment goes into enhancing manufacturing performance, not simply increasing capacity. This tends to be two to three times the rate of plant and equipment investment observed in these companies' U.S. counterparts, who give primary emphasis to capacity expansion.

Such continual investments in the technical capabilities of both people and facilities appear to be motivated by a recognition of the synergies that result when product designs are linked to improvements in process technologies, the need to enhance the value that workers can add to the product (in order to offset their high wages), and a belief that technology is the key to long-term productivity gains—in fact, the solution to most competitive problems. As a consequence, at least one fulltime member of the executive committee in most German firms is assigned to oversee manufacturing technology as his primary responsibility. This top-level perspective continually encourages technical projects and plans, a major ongoing activity in the German firms we studied.

This sort of technological development appears to be particularly well suited to the type of company that dominates the German economy, especially its export markets: huge, diversified heavy manufacturing concerns that sell industrial components, machine tools (the German machine tool industry is the largest in the world), chemicals, turnkey transportation and communications systems, and complete industrial plants. In most of these fields major technological breakthroughs occur only occasionally, but there is an ongoing process of incremental technological improvement that makes the difference between market leadership and also-ran status.

The combination of technically proficient management, a well-trained work force, and consensus-seeking decision processes also encourages German managers to work closely with their workers and supervisors in refining and perfecting process technology, although they do so without the colorful cheerleading that is common in Japanese firms. It seems to be a natural by-product of the works council system.

11-4 SOME CONCLUDING THOUGHTS

We summarize this chapter and integrate it with the next chapter's discussion of Japanese manufacturing management approaches in Chapter 13. We would like to make three final observations at this point, however. First, being smaller than one's major competitors is not so big a disadvantage if one focuses all one's attention and resources on a single industry or set of related businesses. German firms tend to have this kind of focus: they are not distracted by the greener pastures that seem to so fascinate U.S. managers; nor do they seek to cover over difficulties in individual businesses by averaging them in with a diverse set of unrelated businesses. Their managers try to do what they do better than anyone else in the world. German singlemindedness is a national stereotype that is often both accurate and effective.

Second, German manufacturers do not see any quick fixes or easy solutions to what they perceive as ongoing, long-term competitive challenges. Continued investment in people, technology, and capital assets, following the long-term directions established and agreed to by labor, management, and government, is required. We have yet to meet a German manager who viewed any part of his firm's business as a "cash cow"—an area where one could get ahead of the competition and then coast, siphoning funds to other, more promising, businesses. Their competitors are investing most of their cash throwoff back into the same business; they must do the same, or fall slowly behind.

Third, German business and government leaders are well aware of both their industrial strengths and their weaknesses. They do not forsee a reduction in the German wage rate or a massive shift in emphasis to the newer, high-technology industries. Instead, their strategy is to build on their strengths in highly engineered mechanical-electrical products by rapidly exploiting the latest advances in production technology: group manufacturing, CAD/CAM, robotics, and flexible manufacturing systems. These will allow them, they hope, to defend and expand their position as producers of small lots (often one-of-a-kind) of sophisticated industrial products for international markets.

SELECTED REFERENCES

Child, J., M. Fores, I. Glover, and P. Lawrence. "A Price to Pay? Professionalism and Work Organization in Britain and West Germany." *Sociology,* Vol. 17, No. 1, February 1983, pp. 63–78.

Fores, M., P. Lawrence, and A. Sorge. "Germany's Front Line Force." *Management Today,* March 1978.

Lawrence, P. *Managers and Management in West Germany.* New York: St. Martin's Press, 1980.

Limprecht, Joseph, and Robert Hayes. "Germany's World Class Manufacturers." *Harvard Business Review,* November–December 1982, pp. 137–145.

Sasser, W. Earl, and Frank Leonard. "Let First Level Supervisors Do Their Jobs." *Harvard Business Review,* March–April 1980.

Servan-Shreiber, J. J. *The American Challenge.* New York: Atheneum, 1968.

Turnbull, P., and M. Cunningham (eds.). *International Marketing and Purchasing.* London: Macmillan, 1981.

Japanese Approaches to Manufacturing Management

12-1 INTRODUCTION

During the 1970S the world's image of the Japanese factory underwent a total reversal. In the 1960s the stereotype was that of a sweatshop, teeming with legions of low-paid, low-skilled workers trying to imitate by hand, with great effort and infrequent success, what skilled Americans and Europeans were doing with sophisticated equipment and procedures. Today, shocked and awed by the success of Japanese manufactured products around the world, and recognizing that their competitive prices are almost invariably accompanied by superior quality, the United States and Europe look for explanations of Japan's prowess in terms of gleaming modern factories peopled by skillful robots—both human and otherwise—all under the benevolent dictatorship of "Japan, Inc."

Our firsthand observations of more than a dozen Japanese manufacturing facilities suggest that this new stereotype is probably just as incorrect as the old one. The Japanese factory of today is not a premonition of the factory of the future. If it were, U.S. and European managers, with their technical ability and resources, should be able to duplicate it. Instead, it is something much more difficult to copy. The Japanese present the world with an image of the factory of *today*—running as it should. They have achieved their current position by doing relatively simple things, but doing them very well, and slowly improving them all the time.

12-1.1 Questioning the Conventional Wisdom about Japan

The Robot Theory

Japanese factories are *not* the modern structures filled with highly sophisticated equipment that many Americans expect them to be. Although we encountered

352

a few "intelligent robots" in the early 1980s, they were largely experimental in nature and the general level of technological sophistication observed was not superior to that found in U.S. factories in the same industries. The kind of automation that was observed generally consisted of materials handling equipment that was used in conjunction with standard processing equipment—just as it is in the United States.* Nor do the Japanese tend to run this standard equipment at higher rates or longer hours than do manufacturers in other countries. Because of government regulations against women working after 10 P.M., very few Japanese factories operate more than two shifts.

The Quality Circles Theory

Nor do the famed "quality circles" appear to be the key to Japanese success, as some believe. Quality circles were not widely adopted until the early 1970s, more than five years after the Japanese Union of Scientists and Engineers (JUSE) gave them its official support, and long after most companies had already built enviable reputations for high-quality products. Most Japanese companies appear to have experienced problems with them during the first three to four years after their introduction, and it was not until the late 1970s that they began achieving the results that were originally anticipated. Even then they were confined primarily to the large, elite companies. (See Wood et al., 1983.)

   Some companies we visited treated quality circles as secondary, noncentral activities; another had eliminated them altogether ("temporarily," it said). But the quality levels at these plants, as measured both by their success in the Japanese market and by the evaluations of American competitors, were apparently just as high as those in companies where quality circles were active (see Garvin, 1983). In most companies, by the way, quality circles devoted the majority of their time to issues and problems that were not (at least directly) related to quality; productivity improvement, working conditions, absenteeism, and the like, were their primary focus.

   One American manager observed that there appears to be a growing gap between the concerns of workers and those of managers in the United States: managers have focused their attention upward, toward more strategic issues, whereas workers have tended to narrow their attention to the job at hand. As a result, little "low-level management" or, perhaps worse, "low-level engineering" is being done in U.S. companies. Such activities appear to be the *real* purpose of quality circles in Japan.

   In short, quality circles are not the driving force behind the high quality of Japanese products. They are the last step in a long process. To paraphrase a well-known advertising slogan, "The quality was in before the circles came on."

The Japan, Inc. Theory

Finally, most U.S. managers are somewhat surprised to find little evidence of the famous "Japan, Inc."—the term often used to describe the supposedly close

---

* Increasingly, however, one sees "flexible automation of assembly tasks," a phrase used by Japanese to describe the step-by-step automation of assembly processes.

working relationship between Japanese business and government, in which the government acts to protect, coordinate, and reinforce the activities of Japanese companies. Although the Japanese government does subsidize certain industries, as we pointed out in Chapter 8, and there is some cooperation between companies (with governmental support)—particularly in the large, mature cyclical industries such as steel and aluminum—what impresses most visitors more is evidence of one of the most fiercely competitive domestic arenas in the world.

Japanese companies must deliver quality products because Japanese customers demand quality and their competitors are able to deliver it to them. The pressure on prices is such that the profit margins after taxes of Japanese companies are generally about half those of U.S. companies in the same industries. And pressure by their industrial customers for fast deliveries often forces these companies to maintain high inventories of finished goods. More than one Japanese manager told us that "if we prove that we can compete successfully in this market, we can compete anywhere." Another commented, "You wonder why Japanese companies are so successful in your [the U.S.] market. But the only ones you see are the ones that succeeded here. They had to be good. They survived." And McInnes' survey (1983) of 25 Japanese manufacturing companies indicated that the single greatest factor behind their emphasis on productivity improvement was their perception that domestic competition would become increasingly brutal.

The Japanese government does attempt to protect and assist young industries, as do most other countries (through tariffs, subsidies, import restrictions, etc.), and the uniqueness of Japanese society, language, and commercial arrangements erect other subtle yet effective barriers against imports in general. Moreover, certain industries that are thought to have high potential for growth and exports are targeted for special assistance. But if a particular company—even within a favored industry—cannot compete, it gets little help from the government, whose apparent philosophy is to encourage the winners rather than protect the losers. Therefore, despite the Japanese ideal of lifetime employment, one often meets young managers who have changed companies either because their original company went bankrupt or because its business had deteriorated to the point where it was in the company's best interests, as well as their own, to seek their fortunes elsewhere.

Few General Rules

Although one can talk about general tendencies, such as the practice of promoting individuals on the basis of seniority rather than achievement or ability (at least during the early stages of their careers), factories in Japan are characterized by just as much diversity as is found in other countries. The exotic, strikingly different "Japanese way of doing things" is not what struck our eyes.

One does not, for example, see uniform compensation systems. We had been led to expect wage systems based on seniority, bonuses based on corporate profitability, no incentives based on individual performance, and no time clocks. Yet at one company we found wages based on skill levels and commuting distance as well as seniority, others where (by agreement with the union) bonuses were equal to a certain number of months of regular salary *independent* of recent corporate profitability, and another where the general manager talked about his plans to tie individual compensation more directly to individual performance measurements—almost a piecework incentive concept. Most companies did not use time clocks, but some did. Most put considerable emphasis on employee suggestion plans, but one did not (because it claimed this would undermine the concept of group cooperation in solving problems).

It is also important to keep in mind that the sophistication and management practices observed in Japanese companies are highly dependent on their size and past record of success. Small manufacturing establishments (with fewer than 50 employees) play a much bigger role in Japanese industry than they do in the United States, and many of the larger companies cater only to the Japanese domestic market. The following observations are based on what we saw at a number of the *elite* Japanese manufacturing companies—those world class competitors whose names are household words around the world, and with whom American and European companies find themselves increasingly grappling in international markets.

12-2   JAPANESE MANUFACTURING ATTITUDES AND PRACTICES

12-2.1   Cleanliness and Orderliness

The most striking aspect of Japanese factories, at least initially, is their exceptional cleanliness, quiet, and orderliness. These characteristics seem to transcend the type of industry, the age of the company, its location, or whether or not it is a subsidiary of a U.S. company. Clearly, this is not accidental. Nor is it simply a reflection of the cultural norms of Japanese society, which place a high value on cleanliness and orderliness. (Japanese baths, hot towels, and the practice of removing one's shoes before entering a house are well known; the exceptional cleanliness of the people, the cars they drive, the streets they drive on, and the buildings in which they congregate in great numbers must be seen to be appreciated.)

That this deep-rooted concern for orderly surroundings should be transferred to the workplace is not surprising. Yet it comes as a pleasant shock to most American managers when they step into a Japanese factory. The workers' uniforms (provided, of course, by the company; sometimes white gloves and work shoes are part of the ensemble) are clean, their machines are clean, and the floors around their machines are clean. Rest areas are centrally located, tastefully decorated (often with plants and flowers), and immaculate. One American manager recounts with wonder being asked to put plastic covers on his shoes before being allowed to walk out on the floor of a plant that was at least 30 years old! His verdict: "When you clean up the plant like that, you tend to clean up the thought processes in the plant at the same time."

Possible sources of litter and grime are carefully controlled: boxes are placed to catch metal shavings, plastic tubs and pipes are positioned to catch and direct oil away from the workplace, spare parts and raw materials are carefully stacked in specified storage areas. Moreover, machines and workplaces are continually cleaned and swept by the workers themselves. One even sees production workers sweeping the aisles (clearly marked and laid out with geometric precision, one might add) near their work group "in their free time." As more than one Japanese manager responded, when some American manager expressed surprise at this or asked what additional compensation was involved, "One does things out of pride as well as for money, doesn't one?"

We have come to the conclusion, however, that the personal attitudes of the Japanese worker, as impressive as they are, are not the major reason behind the almost total sense of order that is observed. Instead, it is more a reflection of the attitudes, practices, and systems that the managers of those plants have carefully put into place over a long period of time. The evidence of management ingenuity and hard work is everywhere.

12-2.2   Caring for Equipment

The job definition of the typical Japanese worker is much broader than that of his or her U.S. counterpart. It includes responsibility not only for output, quality, and helping fellow workers, but also for cleaning and maintaining his or her equipment. Moreover, he or she is trained to correct minor problems that arise in the course of the day, conduct regular preventive maintenance, monitor its operation and make compensating adjustments, and continually search for ways to eliminate potential disruptions and improve overall performance. The object is to avoid, if at all possible, any breakdown of equipment during working hours.

To this end, tools, dies, and production equipment are not overloaded. There appears to be excess machine capacity at most plants and, in fact, it is not unusual to see machines running at slower rates than they were designed for (and often slower than the usual rate in U.S. factories). What might explain this apparent overinvestment? One U.S. manager proposed that "the typical U.S. cost structure, with its high variable costs and relatively low fixed costs, tends to cause manufacturing managers to focus their attention on variable costs and underemphasize investment. Often, in fact, major investments are not even under their control, but are paid for out of a different cost center, higher in the organization." Another explanation, which we expand upon in a later section, is that the Japanese tend to use smaller, less expensive machines that they design and build for their own specific needs. Also, the design of this equipment places higher importance on reliability and ease of maintenance than on throughput rate.

Lower operating speeds not only reduce the possibility of jams and breakdowns but also reduce the wear on machine parts and dies. The combination of regular preventive maintenance, constant cleaning and adjustment, and reduced rates of usage has another side benefit: machines last longer. Our expectation before visiting Japan was that we would be impressed by the newness of Japanese machine tools, compared with those in use in the same industries in the United States (where the average age of machine tools in all industries is about 20 years, versus about 10–12 years in Japan). But Japanese machines do not appear to be that much newer; they just *look* newer. And they appear to "run newer." One American manager who studied the Japanese companies in his industry estimated that even though they use equipment similar to that found in the United States, their machines and tools last two to three times as long. Another summarized the difference as follows: "They use their machines; we abuse ours."

In most factories we have seen extensive use of rather elaborate equipment monitoring and early warning systems. These devices monitor the process flow and signal when jams occur, measure dimensions and other characteristics of finished parts, indicate when these characteristics begin to approach tolerance limits, keep track of the usage (number of strokes, shots, or impressions) of dies or fixtures, and signal when it is time to adjust or regrind them.

One result of this extensive monitoring, together with the widespread use of simple materials handling equipment and the Japanese practice of packing machines close together (discussed in the next section), is that the typical Japanese worker is able to oversee the operation of more machines than U.S. workers in the same industry. American managers, when first walking out onto the floor of a Japanese factory, are often struck by the image of a forest of machines—virtually untended. Sometimes they *are* untended. The Japanese have such trust in the error-free functioning of their equipment that it is not uncommon for them to load up a machine with work at the end of the last shift and let it run through the night.

It is well known that the Japanese spend a much higher proportion of their national income on capital investment than does the United States (in fact, more than twice as much). What is less well known is the difference in the way this money is spent. In 1980, for example, only about 40 percent of the total capital invested by Japanese manufacturing companies was spent on replacing old equipment, expanding capacity for existing businesses, building capacity for new businesses, or meeting environmental regulations. The majority of their investment was devoted to upgrading the capabilities of *existing* equipment and processes: introducing materials handling and other process rationalization measures, rebuilding and improving equipment, adding monitoring devices, and reducing the number of workers through automation. In most U.S. companies, by comparison, more than three-fourths of the capital investment dollar is spent on the first category; the term "capital investment," in fact, has almost become synonymous with "capacity expansion."

12-2.3   Eliminate the Root of All Evil

Another factor that markedly improves the general neatness and orderliness of the plants we visited is the almost total absence of inventory on the plant floor. Raw materials are doled out in small batches. In many cases these raw materials and purchased parts are stored by vendors and called off as needed; frequently three to four deliveries a day are made to avoid stockpiles within the plant at any one time. Finished goods are removed quickly from the floor as well. They are either transferred immediately to a separate finished-goods warehouse or shipped directly to customers or to a distributor organization. The inventory that is observed is carefully placed in special boxes in specified places around the plant—marked, like the aisles, with painted lines.

In between, work-in-process inventory is kept to a minimum. Material moves along in a steady flow, assisted by materials handlers, by automated materials handling equipment, and by the workers themselves. There is little need for buffer inventories of partially completed work before individual work stations to avoid stoppages caused by breakdowns at earlier process stages, because such stoppages almost never occur. The careful preventive maintenance, monitoring of machine performance, and optimized machine speeds mentioned earlier see to that. Nor do rejects pile up, in separate baskets or on the floor, because the incidence of rejects is very low (more on this later). In short, most of the companies we have seen appear to have developed materials movement systems that are similar in results to Toyota's now-famous "just in time" system: inventory is minimized when every part arrives just when it is needed, or just when a machine is available.

Less work-in-process inventory reduces overall investment, speeds up the production cycle time, and makes it easier to monitor the progress of work through the plant; it also makes it possible to move machines closer together. This, in turn, makes it easier for operators working at adjacent machines to communicate with and help one another. The next step is to link machines together through automatic materials handling devices (or even to pass parts manually from worker to worker) and then to increase the number of machines under each worker's supervision. Eventually it may allow the company to automate entirely the operation of closely coupled groups of machines. (See Schonberger, 1982, esp. Chapter 5.)

Why do U.S. companies have such high work-in-process inventories? One major reason is their emphasis on the production of "economic batches," which seek to balance inventory costs against the setup costs associated with the changeover from one item to another. The Japanese believe that inventory is bad in principle, and therefore seek to eliminate the attractiveness of large batches by reducing setup costs. Toyota, for example, estimates that the time required to change over a heavy press in the hood and fender stamping department at one major U.S. auto company was six hours in 1979. It was about four hours at Volvo and at a German company. Toyota's own changeover time was 12 minutes (see Monden, 1981a,b).

One senior manager asserted to us that "inventory is the root of all evil," and he and his managers had been working from 1975 to 1980 to eliminate this evil from their production system. When questioned as to whether the benefits of such an approach outweighed its costs, he answered with an emphatic affirmative. "You would be surprised at how much you simplify problems and reduce costs when there are no inventories," he argues. "First, if you have no inventories, you don't need any inventory managers or inventory control systems. Nor do you need expeditors, because you can't expedite. And, finally, when something goes wrong, the system stops. Immediately the whole organization becomes aware of the problem and works quickly to resolve it. If you have buffer inventories, these potential problems stay hidden and may never get corrected."

Over those five years his organization had used a variety of approaches to implement this inventory reduction program. They:

1. Encouraged marketing and engineering personnel to standardize parts and components.
2. Increased the frequency of vendor deliveries to one to four times a day, instead of one to four times a month.
3. Developed a mixed-model assembly line for low-volume models.
4. Reduced setup and changeover times through equipment and procedure modifications.
5. Reduced lot sizes and increased the frequency of model changes.
6. Promoted discipline and commitment to the policy throughout all operations and over time.

Over a period of years, these systematic efforts to implement operations policy achieved impressive results:

	1975	1980
Production quantities	100 index units	300 index units
Production models	120	350
Warehouse space	80,000 square feet	20,000 square feet
Inventory level (of raw and in-process inventories)	10 days	1.5 days
Lot sizes	2–3 days	1 day

12-2.4   Keeping Murphy Out of the Plant

This attitude toward inventory requires iron discipline and total control, not just on the plant floor but also in the plant's managerial infrastructure: vendor relations, production planning, industrial engineering, manufacturing/process engineering, and quality assurance. This discipline is attributable, at least in part, to the orderly way of accepting direction (from below as well as above) that characterizes Japanese organizations. But self-discipline is not enough; there must also be a determination at all levels of management to prevent problems from occurring and making sure that the ones that do arise are resolved before they get to the plant floor.

"Before you can increase productivity or improve quality, you must have stability and continuity in your manufacturing process," argued one manager. "How can you have stability when crises are occurring? Our job is to keep crises from developing on the production floor so that our production workers can focus their attention on quality and productivity."

As a result, production schedules typically are based on capacity measures that are derived from actual performance data (not theoretical or obsolete standards) and are established at least a day in advance, generally several days. Moreover, they are iron-clad. (How can you change a production schedule when the inventory required to produce something different is not available?) No expediting and no overloading are allowed. Work is metered out to the plant in carefully controlled doses instead of being "dumped on the floor so the foreman can figure out what to do with it." As a result, we seldom detected any sign of a crisis atmosphere in any of the plants we visited. Nor do they appear to be subject to the "end-of-the-month push" that characterizes so many American factories.

One plant that produces electronic instruments in low volumes uses a different approach. Production schedules are made up two weeks in advance, and at the beginning of each two-week period all the materials required for that schedule are distributed along the production line. At the end of the two weeks the inventory is gone and a new batch of materials is brought in. Workers, therefore, not only have the satisfaction of "cleaning up the floor" every two weeks, but also are exposed to continual, controlled pressure.

Another company, which had a very broad product line, sought to reduce the frequency of equipment changeovers (which, it was felt, both reduced machine utilization and, worse, by disrupting the orderliness of the flow of work through the plant, increased the sense of pressure on the workers) by imposing a simple constraint on its production schedulers: no more than eight product changes a day. Salesmen might complain, and the schedulers might be pushed to the limit of their ingenuity, but the rule was firm. If it became impossible to operate within this rule, the solution was to reduce the product line or increase the size of the minimum orders that customers could place—not to burden the factory with added confusion.

This "accident-prevention program" extends to a company's suppliers. It is not unusual to find that a supplier's forecast of deliveries to the plant is established several months in advance. Almost no changes in the plant's production schedule are made after the final supplier delivery schedule is issued. This tight and stable linkage is reinforced by the fact that Japanese companies tend to favor nearby suppliers, even to subsidize their formation or relocation.

As one American manager put it, "Doesn't 'Murphy's law'* work here? Where is Murphy now that we need him?" Perhaps part of the reason that Murphy lives in America is because American managers actually *enjoy* crises; they often get their greatest personal satisfaction, the most recognition, and their biggest rewards from solving crises. It is part of what makes work fun for them. To the Japanese manager, however, a crisis is evidence of failure. The objective is crisis-free, disruption-free, error-free operation: it is one aspect of the Japanese ideal of *wa* (group harmony).

12-2.5 Quality Consciousness

The attention to detail, precision, high reliability, and durability of Japanese products have achieved worldwide renown—to the point where German auto manufacturers, who claimed as recently as 1978 that their position was almost impregnable in their home market because of the German consumer's obsession for high-quality products, found within two years that Japanese imports were taking over 10 percent of that market and were threatening to inundate them. Most Americans find this reputation for quality somewhat incongruous because not too long ago "Made in Japan" was synonymous with cheap, shoddy products. But those who focus on the stunning reversal that has been made miss the real point. What is important is not that Japanese manufacturers have made a remarkable transition, but that it took them 25 years of hard, dedicated work to make that transition.

The reason this is so important is because high quality is not something that results from a few management decisions; it requires the creation of a complex, all-encompassing, interacting "system." Developing such a system requires a long-term, uncompromising top management commitment. Again and again in Japan we heard the terms "quality consciousness" and "quality mentality," as Japanese managers struggled to explain how they achieved high quality. The Japanese have taken the familiar American slogan, "You don't inspect quality into a product; you have to build it in," one step farther: "Before you build it in, you must 'think it in.' "

You "think it in," first, by carefully preplanning in the product design stage. Interminable discussions between engineering, production, quality assurance, and marketing take place before the design is finalized. While the product design is being completed, manufacturing engineers are developing machine specifications and industrial engineers are developing methods and standards. Everything is done as part of a total product–process system (see Garvin, 1983).

Once production begins, the objective is to hold to these standards. Therefore, another aspect of thinking quality in is training workers so they become capable of delivering consistently high quality, and developing expectations of high quality in them. Production workers automatically check the parts they receive to make sure that they are defect-free. They work meticulously,

* The most common statement of Murphy's law is "If something can go wrong, it will go wrong."

knowing that any defects that arise from their operation will be spotted and ultimately tracked back to them, which will result in a serious loss of face. More important, producing high-quality products is a source of pride, and it is constantly reinforced by management attitudes and actions.

A third way of thinking quality in is by developing a working environment in which everybody is encouraged to discuss the quality problems that arise (even when they are so minor that the product passes final inspection) and to work together to ascertain their causes and to develop corrective measures. In many U.S. companies there is a "we against them" attitude between production workers and quality control personnel; as a result, potential problems are kept hidden, defects are shunted off to be reworked, and the pressure to meet delivery deadlines makes it psychologically difficult for quality inspectors to delay delivery because of "minor" quality problems. In Japanese companies the "we" is everybody, and "them" is defects. Feedback from everybody—production workers, quality assurance workers, salesmen, vendors, and customers—is encouraged. Field service organizations often report directly to the manufacturing manager rather than to the sales manager, as they do in most U.S. companies. Cross-functional training and fluid functional boundaries also encourage the identification and resolution of quality problems in Japanese factories.

A fourth way of thinking quality in is recognizing that even the most carefully designed and stable production process will not be able to maintain high quality if the materials that enter that process are defective. Therefore, intensive effort is devoted to screening incoming parts and materials (100 percent inspection is often used) and to feeding the results back to suppliers. The pressure put on suppliers to improve their quality is incredible, but Japanese manufacturers do not think that simple pressure is sufficient. Instead, they work with the supplier to try to ascertain *why* problems have arisen in his organization and help him develop approaches for solving these problems. Often they will conduct seminars for personnel within the supplier company, the message of which is: "If you follow these steps, you will learn to meet our requirements." Given the long-term relationship between suppliers and customers in Japan, it is unthinkable for the supplier to refuse such assistance and advice—or to take lightly such a commitment of resources from the customer.

Developing this system of mutually reinforcing skills, expectations, group processes, and systems took a long period of time and was possible only because of the enormous importance that Japanese top management placed on it. Driving them, in turn, long before Japan's determined assault on export markets, were the requirements of their own domestic market. One senior Japanese official explained why: "A 1 percent defect rate may sound okay in the United States, but it is not acceptable in Japan. It means that if you sell 100,000 units of a product, 1,000 of them will be defective. In a country as small geographically and as crowded as ours is, it is simply unacceptable to have that many dissatisfied customers 'unselling' your product to their friends."

The American concept of an "acceptable quality level" (AQL) has not been adopted by the Japanese—because they believe that *no* defect is acceptable. Moreover, the practice in some U.S. companies of shipping off-spec products to remote or less favored customers is unthinkable to them.

Following de Gaulle's advice, the Japanese make a virtue out of necessity. Over time they came to realize that the resources and management attention that were being poured into improving quality were paying off in unexpected ways. One group vice president of a large American company, who carefully studied the relationship between productivity and quality in plants around the world, observed that the same conditions that promote defect-free operation also promote productivity improvement. "We have found that a 2 percent reduction in defects is usually accompanied by a 10 percent increase in productivity," he stated. And one noted authority on quality management (Crosby, 1979) estimates that American firms spend 15–20 percent of their sales revenue on quality-related activities; he includes prevention costs, appraisal/inspection costs, and failure costs in this "total cost of quality."

This apparent relationship between productivity and quality (which counters the usual notion that higher quality should lead to higher costs) may not simply be caused by the fact that fewer defects mean more output without a corresponding increase in costs. As one Japanese manager pointed out, "If you eliminate the production of defective items, things become much simpler and less costly to manage. You don't need as many inspectors as before. You don't need to have production workers doing rework, or systems that manage the detection and flow of rework through the process. Waste goes down. Inventory goes down. But morale goes up. Everybody feels very proud when you produce only perfect products."

12-3   THE CAUSES AND IMPLICATIONS OF THESE CHARACTERISTICS

Cleanliness, orderliness, quality, lack of inventory: all this strikes the eye of any visitor to a Japanese factory. We have tried to describe why and how they have pursued each of these goals, but the more we analyze Japanese manufacturing methods and philosophies, the more we have come to realize that they are all interconnected. This is because there are certain aspects of Japanese management philosophy and practice that seem to underlie everything that we have observed.

12-3.1   A "Lifetime" Perspective

Japanese companies tend to speak in terms of "philosophies of business" and "corporate visions" rather than about "strategies" and "tactics." Americans are often taken aback by the tendency of Japanese managers to answer specific questions by quoting a simple general rule, or principle, that was apparently embedded deeply in their corporate culture and consciousness. Usually such maxims stress some abiding virtue like "create satisfied customers," or "serve society." At first one suspects they are attempting to avoid a direct answer, using a philosophical principle as a smokescreen. But then one begins to see a pattern emerge.

For example, one of the most thought-provoking aspects of Japanese companies for an American is their emphasis on long-term commitments. U.S. companies jealously guard their "flexibility" and "responsiveness," which leads them to use terms such as "sales," "hourly workers," "vendors," and "stockholders." Elite Japanese companies, on the other hand, are more likely to think in terms of "everlasting customers," "lifetime employees," "suppliers–partners," and "owners." The implications for both action and attitude are enormous.

One does not go about developing an "everlasting customer" in the same way that one goes about "making a sale," for example. Completely different expectations are involved, and a long period of mutual information gathering is required. One does not disappoint an everlasting customer by delivering defective products or by not meeting delivery promises. Nor does one disappoint a supplier–partner by turning to another supplier if the price quoted is somewhat out of line (although one certainly does begin to work with the supplier–partner in an effort to get that price back into line with those of competitors). The objective of Japanese companies, like that of all partnerships, is a mutually beneficial long-term relationship.

The Japanese custom of lifetime employment has been widely commented on. Briefly, it works somewhat as follows: a young man (only very recently were women included) joins a company immediately after graduation from high school or college. From then until his retirement at about age 55 (there are now pressures to increase this to 60) he is guaranteed a job with the company. In return for this guarantee, together with company-subsidized pension plans, medical care, dormitories, vacation packages, and the like, he offers his total allegiance to his employer. Usually he marries within the company. When he does marry, it is understood that the company's needs come first, then his family's, then his own. (In this sense the worker's relationship with his company is similar to that between men and their clan, or *Han* in feudal Japan.)

Two points are worth emphasizing, however. First, although this practice has historical roots, its current form dates only to the end of World War II and it is still not practiced by the majority of Japanese companies. Only the "elite" companies practice it extensively, and they tend to dilute it by employing, at the same time, both subcontractors and large numbers of "temporary workers," hired on a monthly or annual basis. In 1980 less than a third of all Japanese workers enjoyed lifetime employment.

Second, its main impact on Japanese companies has little to do with either the constraints it imposes on management or the total dedication to the needs of the company that it encourages in workers. Rather, it forces a company to think about workers in a completely different way. They become, in a very real sense, "human capital," and expensive capital at that; a male worker will earn something in excess of ¥100 million ($500,000 in 1981 purchasing power) in salaries and bonuses during the 35 years of his employment, and another ¥30–50 million in fringe benefits. In 1981 the total package of salary, bonuses, and benefits for a skilled worker often exceeded $25,000 annually.

As in the case of any similarly expensive capital equipment, therefore, considerable planning and screening go into the selection of workers and managers. Once "acquired," careful thought goes into getting the most value out of the workforce; often this requires putting more value (through skill-building activities) into it over time: training programs, job assignments, and so on. A Japanese factory worker will typically spend at least a quarter of his or her first half-dozen years with a firm in various kinds of training programs, both during working hours and in the evenings. In addition, whereas Americans tend to keep job definitions narrow, explicit, and geared to one or two summary measures of performance, the Japanese approach is to define job responsibilities very broadly. Workers are expected not only to meet production (and cost) goals but also to take care of their equipment and continually look for ways to keep improving the productivity and quality of their operation.

Japanese managers consistently emphasize the importance of getting the opinions and recommendations of workers whenever a problem surfaces in their sphere of concern. "They are the experts," these managers insist. This is not lip-service or false modesty; in Japan the workers *are* experts on the subject of their jobs. Management sees to it that they are.

The Japanese emphasis on continually building the skills of their production workers has an enormous impact on American manufacturing managers who have studied it. "Our whole philosophy has been to 'deskill' our work force through automation, so we end up having relatively unskilled people overseeing highly sophisticated machines. The Japanese put highly skilled people together with highly sophisticated machines and end up with something better than either," commented one manager. "American managers are preoccupied with increasing their responsibilities; the Japanese are more concerned with increasing their *capabilities.*" Another observed that "U.S. industry has divided up the total work that has to be done and assigned various parts of it to specialists. This has resulted in production jobs that are repetitive and uninteresting, while the skilled jobs are centralized and removed from the production floor where they are needed, and where corrective action must be taken." A third put it more succinctly: "Our whole approach has been to design 'foolproof production systems,' but the fools always win. The Japanese simply try to eliminate the fools from their operation."

Finally, the discipline of lifetime employment provides a powerful inducement for Japanese companies to restrict their workforce by continually searching for ways to avoid hiring new people and to increase the productivity of existing people. Several of the companies we interviewed, when asked to describe their capital budgeting procedures, couched their explanations in terms of such familiar concepts as payback and return on investment. "Unless," they would hasten to add, "the proposal permits one to reduce the number of workers required. Then almost no rate of return is required. That is automatically in the company's best long-term interests." One manager put it more bluntly:

"You can't lay off a worker, but you can shut down a machine." There is another, longer term, motive behind this insistence on not adding workers: the emerging shortage of skilled labor in Japan as its economy expands faster than its population.

It is important to remember that this commitment to their workers also leads to a reciprocal commitment from workers to their company. Recognizing that a no layoff policy requires a workforce level that lags behind sales demand, Japanese workers in companies we visited were willing to work up to 60 hours of overtime per month (roughly three hours per day) when demand required it. Their willingness to make this commitment is encouraged by their knowledge that their managers understand intimately the difficulties and pressures they operate under and are working just as hard as they are.

This is because potential managers typically begin their careers with a year or so in relatively low-level occupations—the shop floor or the trading desk—to learn about the day-to-day concerns of operating people, and another sojourn in the accounting department to learn their company's information and control systems. Over time they work their way up the ladder, step-by-step. In the plants we visited, all personnel, from the youngest production worker to the plant manager, wore the same company uniform.

Just as the elite Japanese companies are constrained from laying people off, they find it almost impossible to move their facilities. Partly this is a result of the Japanese tradition of not liking to move from one's home district. It is also a reflection of the current housing shortage in Japan, which forces most young unmarried workers to live with their parents and therefore robs them of some of their mobility.

McInnes' survey (1983) indicated that Japanese manufacturing managers are significantly less optimistic about the future than are American managers. They also believe that this future will be characterized by a much higher rate of technological turbulence than do their American counterparts. But they do not believe that they can escape their problems by changing either their workers or the locations of their factories. They must forge ahead, working with what they have. And "forging ahead" is critical. As one Japanese manager put it, "Life is long, but success in business short. It is not something that one achieves quickly or forever. One must continually strive to succeed further, or success will go away."

12-3.2   The Team Approach

The importance of "group consciousness" in Japanese society has been widely commented upon,* and it is highly visible in manufacturing environments. We

* "First, it refers to a value concept in which behavior for the benefit of the group is rated more highly than behavior for the individual's own benefit. Secondly, it refers to a pattern in which division of work is made on a group basis rather than an individual basis, and both decision making and responsibility are shared among the whole group. Thirdly, it refers to the tendency of group members to orient themselves to the group and to make a clear distinction between the group and outsiders." (Ishida, 1980.)

have already noted the emphasis placed on continual communication and feedback, the careful planning and coordination required in order to prevent crises from arising on the production floor (in connection with both production schedule changes and new product introductions), and the close relationship between manufacturing companies and their suppliers, customers, and unions. The term "co-destiny" often is used to indicate the close interdependence and the shared expectations that exist between a company and *all* its affiliated organizations—the "productive confederation" we described in Chapter 1.

Participative management styles, marked by mutual respect and a mutual desire to work toward the common interest, are also the norm (see Pascale and Athos, 1981). Many American managers have commented on the tendency of Japanese managers to negotiate with representatives of other companies through long, exhausting group meetings. During these meetings the Americans generally find themselves inundated with questions, not only about the agreed-upon topic of discussion but also about issues that appear to be only tangentially related: technological developments, the strategies being followed by various competitors, and the social and political developments taking place in various parts of the world. One U.S. marketing manager observed, "When I visit a U.S. customer, I am allowed to present my product and then out I go. When recently I visited [a Japanese customer], on the other hand, I was told we would meet with a group of four people—which turned into a group of twelve. I was told we would probably be there for an hour, but we were there for four hours as they questioned and probed me for information about what was happening in other areas and with other manufacturers. All the time I was speaking they were making notes frantically; then, after I finished, they had a discussion in Japanese to ensure that they had all the necessary information. I was then asked to tour their factory and make suggestions and recommendations for improving their product. I think," he concluded, "that the Japanese approach is more fruitful."

When asked to comment on this difference in their treatment of vendors, American managers usually justify their short, directed meetings on the grounds that they are "too busy" to spend time in such meetings. One wonders where Japanese managers get the time to be so thorough. Perhaps they do such a good job of organizing their own operation that it can run without their active supervision and intervention. Or perhaps they have a different notion of what is really important to the ultimate success of their business, and therefore allocate their time differently. McInnes (1983), for example, found that Japanese managers are more likely to be held accountable for the attainment of specific productivity improvements than are American and British managers.

This group sense and willingness to help each other has, of course, another side: there is considerable peer pressure to meet group norms. Japanese workers do not like to have their mistakes noticed, or to be the recipient of "helpful suggestions," any more than American workers do. But if this is done in a polite and impersonal way, the guilty party's sense of shame and resentment at being identified is reduced. If a problem is corrected quickly, both the person who points it out and the person who "might" have caused it are praised. The focus is always on the problem itself—not who caused the problem. When the problem is eliminated, everybody wins.

As might be expected, the relationship of the work group to its supervisor is much closer and marked by respect than is the case in the United States. In Japan, as in Germany, a supervisor has a position of considerable status in a manufacturing company. Most have at least ten years' experience and a proven reputation as an excellent worker before they are promoted. Once in this position they have the responsibility for their workers' overall performance and well-being—both during and outside working hours. They hold daily meetings (usually before the shift begins) with their work group to review the situation and plan their activities. If a worker has to leave his or her work station unexpectedly, and nobody else is available, the supervisor fills that place. If workers have a problem either on the job or at home, they go first to their supervisor. The supervisor is also expected to spend freely of his time and income (although expense money is often provided) in entertaining his workers after working hours.

Japanese express the view that the ability to influence the behavior of others is related to the closeness of the relationship between them. "If you are too remote," one remarked, "it is difficult to get someone to make an *extra* effort. Therefore, in a worker–manager relationship, a '1' (worker) plus a '2' (supervisor) may equal a '3' or even a '4' in results, whereas a '1' and a '5' will often equal less." Another pointed out, "To be recognized as a leader, one must show humility . . . and politeness. Arrogance and rudeness will invite immediate sanctions no matter how able one may be." Contrast this with the American ideal of a "tough," "hardnosed," "decisive" decision maker—the kind who is sometimes characterized as a "no-toes" manager (because he tends to pull the trigger before his gun clears the holster)!

In keeping with this philosophy, Japanese managers believe in bestowing (often extravagant) praise in public and (delicately worded) reprimands in private. As an example of such a reprimand, one Japanese made the following comment in the privacy of an office: "I get the impression that American managers spend more time worrying about the well-being and loyalty of their stockholders, whom they don't know, than they do about their workers, whom they do know. This is very puzzling. The Japanese manager is always asking himself how he can share the company's success with his workers."

12-3.3   Do It Yourself

Another aspect of Japanese manufacturing companies that often surprises American managers is their insistence on designing and producing their own production equipment in-house. Most of the companies we visited claimed that at least 50 percent of their production equipment was built by their own people, and much of the remainder was at least designed in-house. (It should be mentioned that the forerunners of much of this equipment were probably imported; over time they were copied, modified, and improved to the point where they are effectively new machines.) In the same industries in the United States, the percentages were less than one-third as great. One Japanese magazine has estimated that 40 percent of the R&D money spent by Japanese companies is for process or equipment improvement.

The conventional wisdom in the United States is that equipment manufacture is best left to "experts": the equipment producers who can afford the high fixed costs associated with specialized engineers and machinery, and who can amortize these fixed costs and other developmental expenses over relatively long production runs.

The Japanese will have none of this. "Every machine represents a compromise between various uses and, therefore, various users," said one manager. "We prefer to design equipment that is specifically directed toward our own needs. Not only do we get more appropriate equipment, but our costs are lower and our delivery times are less." Why is this so? "We always need machines when business conditions are good," he explained, "which is the same time that everybody else wants machines. The equipment manufacturing industry is notorious for its cyclical behavior. During these periods of high demand, they stretch out their lead times and they raise prices. If you are dependent on them, you soon regret it." The cost of machines designed in-house is further reduced by the fact that one does not need to incorporate the safety margins and "design cushions" that equipment manufacturers have to build into the general-purpose machines they design for broadly defined markets.

This may help Japanese companies during the boom times of capital equipment, one might reason, but wouldn't they have to pay a price during slack times: forced to carry underutilized manufacturing engineers and skilled machine makers? Not at all, according to the Japanese managers. That is when the attention of these skilled resources is directed to upgrading the company's existing equipment: new drive mechanisms, computerized controls, materials handling equipment, and the equipment monitoring and warning devices that we remarked about earlier. "The advantage of having highly skilled people (like manufacturing engineers) around is that they are always able to find something useful to do!" The argument is plausible—but still alien to the American ear.

As one U.S. manufacturing manager recently observed: "U.S. managers analyze, rationalize and agonize until their office walls are covered with paper before committing to a piece of equipment requiring an investment of $500,000—and therefore an annual depreciation charge of $50,000. Yet the process of evaluating and making recommendations regarding the training, compensation, and career-path of a $50,000 a year (including benefits) engineer typically requires one-half piece of paper, reluctantly prepared in one-half hour once a year!" This difference in priorities is puzzling, particularly when it is recognized that a machine is simply the embodiment of an engineer's skill.

12-3.4   Pursuing the Last Grain of Rice

"Pursuing the last grain of rice in the corner of the lunch box" is a Japanese saying that describes, somewhat disparagingly, someone's tendency to be finicky. But it conveys volumes about the combined Japanese attributes of frugality, orderliness, and persistence. Not only are they smart and industrious; they are never satisfied. And they regard *all* problems as important.

The concept of "zero defects" is an example. As one Japanese academic phrased it, "If you do an economic analysis, you will usually find that it is advantageous to reduce your defect rate from 10 percent to 5 percent. If you repeat that analysis, it may or may not make sense to reduce it further to 1 percent. The Japanese will make that improvement, however. Having accomplished this, they will attempt to reduce it to 0.1 percent. And then 0.01 percent. You might claim that this obsession is costly, that it makes no economic sense. They are heedless. They will not be satisfied with less than perfection."

Indeed, in most of the Japanese factories we have visited the quality charts on the walls measured the defect rate not in terms of percentages but in "parts per million": 1,000 parts per million represents a 0.1 percent defect rate. In 1980 these companies seemed to be achieving defect rates in the range of 300–500 ppm, and their "near-term goals" were to reduce the rate to 100–200 ppm (0.01–0.02 percent). And long term? "Zero, of course." One manager smiled and added, "It's not just that we are idealistic, but we realize that other companies' willingness to stop at 95 percent, coupled with our unwillingness to accept 95 percent, is what makes us such able competitors."

Another Japanese manager, with perfect sincerity, informed us that "a defect is a treasure." So few of them occurred in his company that each could be studied individually and mined for the information it contained about the remaining bugs in his production process. One of the companies we visited, in making almost a million of a certain high-precision metal part, had produced exactly three defects. All three were still in the quality control manager's office, where they were being examined in the hope that their causes could be eliminated in the future.

It is important to add that when a Japanese manager talks about a "quality problem" in his operation, he is almost as likely to be talking about a design problem, a productivity problem, an inventory problem, a delivery problem, or an absenteeism problem as about defective products. All of these problems are interrelated, and all are manifestations of underlying problems in the management of the production process itself. "Quality," in its broadest sense, means "error-free operation." Any defect in any part of the operation, therefore, becomes a "quality problem" as far as management is concerned. Therefore the whole organization is encouraged to locate the "remaining grains of rice" in the operation, and work persistently to eliminate them, one by one. At Matsushita, for example, the stated goal was to receive 1 million written suggestions from their employees during 1980. Each would be responded to. Rewards would be given even for proposals that were not accepted.

One U.S. manager who has worked closely with his company's Japanese subsidiary noted with admiring exasperation that the Japanese never seem to be satisfied with the new product designs developed by his company's U.S.-based R&D group. "They will criticize the design interminably," he sighed, "and offer many reasons why it should be changed. But if you break down and let them modify the design 'for the Japanese market,' they usually do come up with a better one!"

The insistence on neatness, on reducing inventories to the bare minimum, and on eliminating defects from the process has another, more economic, justification in Japan as well. Industrial land is prohibitively expensive. In Nagoya, an industrial city about the size of Philadelphia located more than 100 miles from Tokyo, buildable land cost roughly ¥250,000 per "tsubo" (somewhat more than 4 square yards) in 1980. This works out to about $27 per square foot, or $1.2 million per acre. In the city of Tokyo and its immediate surroundings, the cost was up to five times as much. Every square foot is precious, and therefore every nonproductive square foot of factory space—whether it be space tied up with unneeded inventory, with the storage and rework of defective products, or with unneeded people—becomes an obvious target for elimination.

12-3.5   Stability *and* Flexibility

Up to this point we have described a number of Japanese management practices which, while encouraging high productivity, asset utilization, and quality, might be expected to make Japanese factories relatively inflexible. For example:

1. *Lifetime employment* for a sizable percentage of the workforce (up to 80 percent of the workforce in the elite Japanese companies have it) might be expected to reduce Japanese companies' ability to respond to protracted downtimes. Conversely, a reluctance to add workers to whom one must offer additional lifetime employment guarantees should limit their response to rapid increases in demand.

2. *Low work-in-process inventories* should restrict their ability to respond to rapid changes in the product mix demanded by customers.

3. *Long-term relationships with a limited number of suppliers* similarly should prevent them from being able to respond quickly to rapid increases in demand or changes in component technology (for reasons that were discussed in Chapter 9).

4. *Emphasis on stable, repetitive flow processes* should cause inefficiency and delays when changing the product mix or introducing new products.

5. *Designing and producing equipment in-house* should further restrict their ability to respond to a significant increase in production level, or a major change in product design.

In spite of these apparent sources of rigidity, Japanese factories appear to be at least as flexible—in terms of their ability to respond to changes in production volume, product mix, and product/process design changes—as those in other parts of the world. This apparent paradox is explained both by the reverse sides of the same coins, and by some of the other management practices described earlier in this chapter:

1. Employees to whom a company has made a commitment of lifetime jobs tend, in turn, to have a stronger commitment to their companies. Therefore, they usually are willing to work considerable amounts of overtime when the success of the enterprise demands it. The same is true of suppliers to whom one has made a long-term commitment, and who therefore have a vested interest in your success.

2. Lifetime employment also eliminates workers' fears of losing their jobs because of market or technological changes. Combining this with Japanese companies' emphasis on continual skill enhancement and job rotation produces workers who are willing and able to shift work assignments rapidly in response to market or production needs. Moreover, they willingly assist in the introduction of new process technology.

3. Low work-in-process inventories imply shorter production cycle times, which, combined with suppliers who also have short cycle times, allows Japanese companies to respond quickly to product mix changes and to the introduction of new products.

4. Production equipment that is designed in-house can be customized for the kinds of changes in product mix that the company expects to encounter. The preference of Japanese companies for machines that are smaller and cheaper than those usually supplied by outside equipment makers also allows them to expand or contract production in relatively small increments. Finally, companies are able to produce the equipment they need when they need it, unhampered by the constraints of some outsider's product design decisions and delivery schedules.

5. The management training programs and organizational structures adopted by Japanese companies add to their flexibility. Broadly trained managers who operate without rigid job definitions in a mutually cooperative environment communicate better and find it easier to make the adjustments necessary during periods of rapid change.

Managers who are generalists, who have considerable flexibility to define their own jobs, and who adopt a "we're all in this together" attitude might also be expected to shorten the time required to develop new products or production processes. Indeed, American managers in a number of industries are finding that their Japanese counterparts can design a new product and get it into production in about half the time that it takes them. In fact, the senior manager of one superbly run American production facility confided to us, "I think I can match my Japanese competitors' productivity and quality levels. What concerns me is whether I will be able to match their product development cycles."

12-4 SOME CONCLUDING THOUGHTS

The sudden onslaught of Japanese companies into world markets, where they have overcome competitors who were once thought to be invincible, has precipitated a frantic search for explanations and remedies. Too many people, we feel, have focused their attention primarily on dramatic "solutions" (particularly those that appear to be easy to copy), such as quality circles, government assistance based on a National Industrial Policy, and robots.

Our observations suggest that these are not the major factors behind Japan's manufacturing process. It appears to be due more to a cooperative relationship among managers, workers, suppliers, and customers that is based on mutual respect and mutual commitment—the kind of commitment that comes from the recognition that they are all in the same boat in a large, hostile ocean, and a rather small, fragile boat at that. If any part of the boat springs a leak, the whole boat will sink.

The combination of this cooperative spirit, coupled with the fierce competition in their domestic environment, drives Japanese companies to accept lower profitability and to search continuously for opportunities to improve performance throughout the manufacturing organization: improved equipment, better systems, higher worker skills. This grassroots activity is nourished by the best managerial talent available. No magic formulas are involved, just steady progress in small steps, paying attention to manufacturing fundamentals, patiently laying the foundations that will allow them to exploit future opportunities, always pressing against the boundaries of what one can do, and persistently looking for the opening, the crack in the competitive resistance that will allow one to break out.

In fact, many of the things that Japanese companies have done to improve their strategic competitive position appear to outsiders to be relatively simple "operational details." But the cumulative impact of these details can be substantial. The success stories at Toyota, Sony, and Japan's other world class manufacturing companies are the result of setting long-term goals that were closely linked to short-term operational improvements. As a result, lower level managers could understand clearly the strategic significance of what they were being asked to do. By refusing to separate the strategic from the operational, Japanese managers have made their manufacturing operations into strategic competitive weapons.

SELECTED REFERENCES

Abernathy, William J., Kim B. Clark, and Alan M. Kantrow. "The New Industrial Competition." *Harvard Business Review,* September–October 1981, pp. 68–81.

Christainsen, Gregory B., and Jan S. Hogendorn. "Japanese Productivity: Adapting to Changing Comparative Advantage in the Face of Lifetime Employment Commitments." *Quarterly Review of Economics and Business,* Vol. 23, No. 1, Summer 1983, pp. 23–39.

Cole, Robert E. "Learning from the Japanese—Prospects and Pitfalls." *Management Review,* September 1980, pp. 22–42.

Cole, Robert E. "Permanent Employment in Japan: Facts and Fantasies." *Industrial and Labor Relations Review,* Vol. 26, October 1972, pp. 615–630.

Crosby, Philip B. *Quality Is Free.* New York: New American Library, 1979.

Davidson, William H. *The Amazing Race: Winning the Technorivalry with Japan.* New York: Wiley, 1984.

Drucker, Peter. "The Price of Success: Japan Revisited." *Foreign Affairs,* August 1978, pp. 28–35.

Drucker, Peter. "What We Can Learn from Japanese Management." *Harvard Business Review,* March–April 1971, pp. 110–122.

Garvin, David. "Quality on the Line." *Harvard Business Review,* September–October 1983, pp. 64–75.

Hayes, Robert H. "Why Japanese Factories Work." *Harvard Business Review,* July–August 1981, pp. 56–66.

Ishida, H. "The Japanese Style of Management." *Sumitomo Quarterly,* Vol. 1, No. 3, 1980, p. 19.

Juran, J. M. "Product Quality—A Prescription for the West." *Management Review,* June–July 1981.

McInnes, J. M. "Corporate Management of Productivity—An International Comparison." Sloan School of Management Working Paper 1398–83, January 1983.

Monden, Yasuhiro. "Kanban System." *Industrial Engineering,* May 1981, pp. 29–46. (a)

Monden, Yasuhiro. "What Makes the Toyota Production System Really Tick?" *Industrial Engineering,* January 1981, pp. 36–48. (b)

Nakane, Chie. *Japanese Society.* Berkeley: University of California Press, 1970.

Ouchi, William. *Theory Z.* Reading, MA: Addison-Wesley, 1981.

Pascale, R. T., and A. G. Athos. *The Art of Japanese Management.* New York: Simon and Schuster, 1981.

Schonberger, Richard. *Japanese Manufacturing Techniques.* New York: Free Press, 1982.

Van Zandt, Howard F. "How to Negotiate in Japan." *Harvard Business Review,* November–December 1970, pp. 45–56.

Vogel, Ezra F. *Japan as Number One: Lessons for America.* New York: Harper & Row, 1979.

Vogel, Ezra F. "Guided Free Enterprise in Japan." *Harvard Business Review,* May–June 1978, pp. 161–170.

Wheelwright, Steven C. "Japan—Where Operations Really Are Strategic." *Harvard Business Review,* July–August 1981, pp. 67–74.

Wood, Robert, Frank Hull, and Koya Azumi. "Evaluating Quality Circles: The American Application." *California Management Review,* Vol. 26, No. 1, Fall 1983, pp. 37–53.

Learning from Your World Class Competitors

13-1 INTRODUCTION

What lessons can manufacturing managers learn from their world class competitors in Germany and Japan? Concentrating on those issues that do not appear to be primarily "cultural" in nature, we offer six suggestions for corporate managers to contemplate as they adapt their business strategies to a world where they will be increasingly engaged in hand-to-hand combat with foreign competitors. We discuss five of them briefly in this section. The sixth, which summarizes and expands these first five, is discussed in Section 13-2.

13-1.1 Build the Skills and Capabilities of Your Workforce

Many companies, by default, relegate the training of new workers to the public (and vocational) school system, and to the few companies that *do* emphasize thorough in-house apprenticeship programs. These latter companies—such as IBM, Hewlett-Packard, and Procter & Gamble, which have been admiringly referred to as "corporate universities"—see many of the graduates of their training programs go on to successful careers in other companies. Surprisingly, this does not appear to undermine the effectiveness of such programs; the companies that sponsor them usually continue to be the most successful in their industries. Other companies, while willing to subsidize the continued education of those workers who seek advancement, tend to emphasize white-collar training (in accounting, selling, and public speaking, say) for workers in their twenties and thirties, rather than the improvement of the technical skills of younger workers.

Expanding the nature of worker training, like the Japanese, or instituting apprenticeship programs along the German model, is likely to be expensive, however, because of stringent fiscal limitations on what public schools can do. Such expenditures may be easier for a company to absorb once it begins to view its skilled workforce as a capital investment no less valuable than its plant and equipment. Recent research suggests, in fact, that more than half the skills acquired in on-the-job training are company-specific (Mincer and Jovanovic, 1982).

The shortage of highly skilled workers, particularly in its defense industries, is becoming an issue of national concern in the United States. In mid-1981, when 8 million Americans were collecting unemployment checks, there were more than a million openings for high-skilled workers. A government study has found that there are eight times as many openings each year for skilled machinists as there are graduates from apprenticeship programs. Arthur Webner, executive vice president at Pratt & Whitney Aircraft, estimates that his company will lose approximately 75 percent of its machinists through attrition by 1987 (*Aviation Week & Space Technology*, July 20, 1981).

Similarly, Charles Bradford, the director of apprenticeship programs for the Machinists Union, has pointed out that because the average tool and die maker is over 45 years old, many will begin to retire just as the number of young people entering the U.S. workforce nosedives. "The combination of the two is something we're worried about," he admits (*The Wall Street Journal*, September 10, 1981).

In addition to the industry- and company-specific arguments for increased worker training, there are also major benefits at the national level. Unemployment is almost always a much greater problem for untrained, unskilled workers than for those skilled in specific trades. More important, most developed countries face the following basic dilemma: over the long term, their unskilled workers invariably end up competing with unskilled workers in less developed countries, even though the wages in the developed countries are much higher. The United States simply cannot pay high wages for unskilled work while others pay low wages for equivalent work, and expect to maintain employment levels and competitive parity. Japan and Germany seem to have recognized this fact, as have such rapidly developing nations as South Korea, Singapore, and Taiwan.

Over the longer haul American managers need to rethink their entire concept of training. They have long tended to focus on the *content* of training programs, assuming that motivation and work habits were developed elsewhere or that they would develop naturally as the worker matured on the job. The Germans and Japanese do not make that assumption. One of the greatest strengths of the systems they have adopted is that, by training workers thoroughly when they are still young, they are able to instill the discipline and pride of workmanship that are essential to producing high-quality products.

If industry is serious about improving the skills and attitudes of its workforce, it must begin to think about ways to encourage the intensive training of younger workers, as well as retraining the older workers in dying industries. Those who doubt that such programs can work on American soil may be unaware that Germany's highly successful government-sponsored Job Retraining Program was modeled after America's own "G.I. Bill" education program after World War II. Firms in industries that lack sufficient discipline to enforce industry-wide apprenticeship programs might consider joining forces with local technical or high schools in setting up programs for technically oriented nonacademic students—with part of each week spent in school and part training at the company.

An additional benefit of extensive entry-level training is that it provides the foundation for subsequent enhancement training and even retraining. Most German and Japanese firms do much more ongoing training than their U.S. counterparts, both to develop general skills (such as reading circuit diagrams) and such specific skills as those associated with introducing a new piece of equipment or a new production technology. Their motivation for doing so is not simply their inability to lay off excess workers. Rather, they view additional training as an attractive investment that has a relatively quick payback.

Even the Japanese concept of lifetime employment is not totally foreign to other countries. In most large U.S. companies, for example, most production workers who have worked for more than ten years have a form of a lifetime employment, in that because of seniority they are almost never laid off. Rather than exploit that fact by making it explicit, and using it to increase their workers' sense of self-worth and commitment to the company, however, American managers continue to refer to them as "hourly workers." This implies that these workers are expendable—which they are not. And it blinds companies to the opportunities for increasing their workers' value-generating capabilities (through retrofitting, computerizing, etc.) comparable to those that are routinely employed to upgrade the capabilities of expensive capital goods—which they are. Managers often complain about workers who "don't have any commitment to the company," conveniently ignoring the fact that most companies make no commitment to their workers.

13-1.2 Build Technical Competence Throughout Management

Foreign observers, who usually admire the marketing and financial skills of American managers, often fault their lack of technological expertise. They point out that only one-sixth of U.S. high school students take a senior level science course and that more than half require remedial training in mathematics when they enter college. In Germany, by contrast, students encounter biology in the third grade, physics and chemistry in the fifth, and—for those on a university preparatory track—increasingly advanced math and science courses each year. As a consequence, Germany has half again as many engineers per 100,000 people as does the United States; Japan has more than twice as many. This sad state of affairs has led to what Robert Henderson, former chairman and CEO of Itek Corporation, calls "today's most common phobia in America: technophobia. At the highest level it is threatening the economic and political leadership in the U.S." (*Enterprise,* March 1981).

Moreover, by not developing the managerial capabilities of their technical people, companies also fail to exploit a large pool of potential leaders. The belief that very few technical people make good managers is a self-fulfilling prophecy. The Germans and Japanese have not fallen prey to it: not having a business school tradition of educating people to be managers, they simply expect that their best engineers will become successful managers. They often do there, just as they do at Hewlett-Packard and other U.S. high-tech firms.

Our experience with German and Japanese firms, as well as with a handful of U.S. companies that regard technical literacy as a prerequisite for a variety of management careers, suggests that they encourage such literacy through the adoption of at least two widely held policies. First, such firms tend to believe that a college student's choice of a "major" is an effective screen with regard to his or her likely interest in, and comfort with, technology. MBA students frequently complain that companies are "biased" if they refuse to interview anybody who does not have an undergraduate engineering degree— even for finance or marketing jobs. They are absolutely correct. Such companies have found that the undergraduate major is a good indicator of a potential manager's long-term prospects for integrating technical considerations with other management perspectives.

Second, these firms believe in training potential managers early in their careers in the basics of the firm's technologies. This is an essential part of their "management development program." Such training also involves exposure to a variety of functions—marketing, manufacturing, field service, and product design—at fairly low levels in the organization. Becoming familiar with the basic technologies used by the firm's customers is also encouraged. These and other practices greatly enhance the likelihood of technical competence throughout a firm's management.

13-1.3   Compete Through Quality

True customer orientation is an attitude, not of a series of quick fixes. It requires a complete rethinking of what one's customer's needs are and how they can best be satisfied. Usually this means a redoubled commitment to an essentially old-fashioned value: the production of quality goods, augmented with quality service. Too many managers define "customer orientation" in terms of firefighting—trying to respond to customers' complaints or special requests with fast corrective action. They would do better to rebuild in their organization a dedication to generating long-term customer loyalty through their products themselves. This kind of thinking is at the heart of the German and Japanese competitive philosophy. It had much to do with the continued strength of their economies during the difficult inflationary years of the 1970s.

Underlying this emphasis on quality is the recognition that it is not simply a task for the manufacturing function or the quality department. Rather it involves all parts of the organization, as well as the customer's organization, and the degree to which it results in a competitive advantage is largely dependent on how well the various functions and organizations work together. Particularly important is the coordination among marketing, manufacturing, and design engineering: marketing shares information about what is required by and is potentially attractive to customers; manufacturing indicates what is possible in terms of features, sustainable tolerances, and reliability; and engineering provides suggestions for product enhancements and monitors the linkages between manufacturability criteria and product performance.

A good example of this type of coordination, and the important role of design in improving quality, is provided by the recent experience of Nippondenso, a Japanese manufacturer of components for the worldwide automotive industry. Gauges and dials (such as fuel and temperature indicators for the dashboard of an automobile) comprise one of its major product lines. This company recognized that it could significantly improve product quality and reduce costs through automation if product options could be standardized and its entire product line redesigned. Working with customers and their own manufacturing staff, Nippondenso's design engineers developed a new family of gauges that offered improved features and performance in the customers' products and that could be produced using more cost-effective manufacturing processes. While the entire project took almost four years, within six months after completion the company was turning out over 250 different models (500,000 gauges per month) on an automated production line whose changeover time between models was one second and whose cost per unit was significantly lower than that of the old process. More important, its two largest customers—Toyota and Ford U.S.—were so impressed by the quality of these gauges that they eliminated all incoming inspection. This further reduced their costs and led them to increase their purchases from Nippondenso.

13-1.4 Develop *Real* Worker Participation

Prodded by the German and Japanese examples, many senior manufacturing managers are exhorting their manufacturing organizations to involve the workforce in improving production operations through quality circles, productivity programs, and the like. But the implementation of such programs will not be easy or enduring given the ingrained management–shop floor atmosphere of mutual distrust and hostility in many traditional industries.

True worker–manager participation does not occur simply by holding meetings and asking workers for their opinions. A long period of preparation and confidence building is required before workers and managers can interact naturally and productively within a company. First, they have to develop a common vocabulary, knowledge base, and set of competences. The skills of workers have to be augmented so that they can understand the nuances of the technologies that they deal with and the kind of management and marketing problems that are encountered in such technologies. The technical skills of managers have to be similarly encouraged, so that they can interact directly with workers on technical problems. Finally, production workers, engineers, and managers have to be brought together so that interaction is natural and, in fact, unavoidable. (This practice has historical roots in both Japan and Germany. The German army, for example, has traditionally believed that commanding officers should be at the front with their troops. However, when General Douglas MacArthur adopted this practice at the French front in World War I, he was criticized by his superiors back at headquarters.)

When technically competent workers, engineers, and managers are placed together in a competitive environment that demands continual improvement in productivity and quality, they tend to cooperate instinctively and with a minimum of organizational friction. In German and Japanese factories the closeness of managers and engineers to the production process is striking. Their offices frequently are right next to the production lines, and they are continually circulating on the plant floor. The engineering groups of many American companies, on the other hand, have become too specialized over time. Often they have been moved away from the production floor—even to separate buildings and remote locations. As a result, engineers and managers have lost the habit of dealing directly with production problems and the motivation to ferret them out before they flare up into open crises. Almost inevitably they tend to spend most of their time contemplating the next generation of products, rather than devising ways to improve the current ones.

Germany and Japan are not alone in recognizing the value of teamwork and of close bonds between functions and organizational levels. For example, although Americans pride themselves on their "rugged individualism" (and criticize, in the same breath, the fact that "everybody is out for themselves"), they love to work in smoothly functioning teams. Baseball is Japan's national pastime, but they did not invent it. An American did.

Similarly, the "we're all in this together" attitude of Japanese and German companies is reminiscent of the American management tradition of "let's roll up our sleeves and get it done." The lack of managerial elitism in the U.S. used to be a source of wonder to Europeans, who long suffered from a management tradition that reflected the deep divisions between social classes there. It is with some shock that Americans are beginning to recognize the emergence of elitism and lack of trust in their own country—managers who isolate themselves from workers, both physically and emotionally, who have no direct experience in the businesses they manage, and who see their role as one of managing resource allocation and other organizational processes rather than leadership by example.

There is growing evidence of the importance of and opportunity for this kind of ongoing worker–management cooperation in the United States. For example, the following vignette is provided by Professor Robert Cole at the University of Michigan. Knowing that all major Japanese consumer electronics firms had established active Quality Control Circle programs in Japan, in 1981 he contacted the five Japanese-owned television plants in the United States to learn about whether and how they were using such circles. Somewhat unexpectedly, he found that none of these subsidiaries had yet instituted Q.C.

circles. They all explained that, for different reasons, they were not yet "ready" for them. Training workers, solving process problems, developing organizational trust, and building expectations had to come first. Ironically, at about that same time dozens of U.S. companies were plunging into Q.C. Circle programs without having gone through such preparation. A number of these programs were later abandoned.

Another piece of evidence supporting the benefits of such programs, when they are managed as part of a long-term effort, comes from Ford Motor Company's Employee Involvement Program. Over a five-year period, worker roles, expectations, and relationships with management have changed dramatically in a number of plants. Equally dramatic has been the change in Ford management's attitude toward workers, and their appreciation of the contribution they can make.

13-1.5   Rebuild Manufacturing Engineering

Americans are inveterate tinkerers, and they have a tradition of self-reliance that springs from their frontier roots. Therefore, many observers have been surprised to discover how far American companies have fallen behind their German and Japanese counterparts in terms of their ability to design and manufacture equipment for their own factories.

Too many U.S. companies have allowed their manufacturing engineering skills to atrophy as their managers increasingly relied on independent equipment suppliers for their needs. They no longer can design and produce their own production equipment, or even carry out major repairs (or modifications) of the equipment they purchase. Having allowed themselves to become overly dependent on outside suppliers, they have essentially lost their ability to compete on the basis of *unique* process technology—something that is not available "off the shelf."

Most world class German and Japanese manufacturing companies have large, well-staffed, very active machine shops. Much of the success of these companies is a result of the proprietary production processes that are incubated in these shops and therefore unavailable to their competitors. One American company, with a mixture of pride and chagrin, recently showed us a series of new machines with which they were reequipping one of the largest departments in their plant, and which would increase the productivity of their workers threefold. This equipment was not designed and produced by an independent supplier, because no supplier had decided to make such a product. Instead, it was manufactured by this company's own Japanese subsidiary. Dissatisfied with the standard production technology it had received from its parent, this subsidiary had decided to improve it. It had retained the skills and capabilities that its American parent had gradually lost over time.

We know of one privately held German manufacturing firm, employing about 5,000 hourly workers (80 percent in Germany and 20 percent in the United States), which in the mid-1970s perceived that its manufacturing engineering capabilities had begun slipping. As one means for counteracting this slippage, its Vice President of Manufacturing hired four direct recruits over a two-year period; each had a Ph.D. and more than ten years of experience managing various aspects of manufacturing technology. Within five years the company felt it had regained worldwide leadership in manufacturing technology in its industry. More important, its product designers had been able to build on that strengthened base of expertise to improve product quality and reduce costs. As a result, the company was able to strengthen its market position despite the economic downturn of the early 1980s.

A disgruntled European manager wrote us that

> For too long U.S. managers have been taught to set low priorities on mechanization projects, so that eventually divestment appears to be the best way out of manufacturing difficulties. Why?

> The drive for short-term success has prevented them from looking thoroughly into the matter of special manufacturing equipment, which has to be invented, developed, tested, redesigned, reproduced, improved, and so on. That's a long process, which needs experienced, knowledgeable, and dedicated people who stick to their jobs over a considerable period of time. Merely buying new equipment (even if it is possible) does not often give the company any long-term advantage over competitors.

13-2   TORTOISE AND HARE APPROACHES TO INDUSTRIAL COMPETITION

The competitive difficulties now being experienced by a number of highly visible U.S. industries surprise and puzzle many Americans. Americans invented the transistor and the color television receiver, yet today American companies produce only about half of all the (transistorized) color television sets sold in the United States, and their world market share continues to slip. Americans invented the numerically controlled machine tool in the 1950s, yet within 25 years, over one-fourth of the machine tools sold in the United States were imported. Why is a nation that put a man on the moon and invented genetic engineering unable to produce a consumer videocassette recorder (all VCRs sold by American companies are imported, even though an American firm produced the first commercial videotape machine in 1955), or even a better car than Toyota?

Perhaps at least part of the answer is contained in the question. One reason Americans do not make a better (that is, less expensive and higher quality) car than Toyota is *because* they can put a man on the moon. The same skills and managerial psychology that enabled them to conceive and carry out projects like that may hamper them in a competitive environment where success is based more on a series of small steps than on a few dramatic breakthroughs.

13-2.1   Alternative Paths to Competitive Progress

In the face of free market competition, a company's "competitive effectiveness" (lower cost, better quality, more features, longer product life, etc.) should steadily improve over time. In fact, if it does not, it will soon find itself outpaced by those competitors who do continue to improve. A combination of two very different approaches can be employed in advancing a firm's effectiveness. They are shown graphically in Figure 13-1.

One extreme approach is through a series of "strategic leaps": a few major steps forward at critical points in time. Such an approach is depicted in Figure 13-1a. These "leaps" might take a variety of forms: a major product redesign, a major factory modernization or expansion, a move to another location that promises major improvements in wage rates or labor relations, the acquisition of a supplier of a critical material or component, or the adoption of an important new manufacturing technology. Between these giant steps, only incidental improvements in competitive effectiveness are sought, as the company digests its last step and contemplates the next.

At the opposite extreme, a company can try to progress through a series of relatively small steps whose cumulative impact is just as great. (See Figure 13-1b.) Instead of relying on a series of major discontinuities in its organization, such a company continually strives to strengthen its competitive position through a variety of incremental improvements, such as methods improvements, reject reduction, faster production cycle or delivery times, and improved product reliability.

Which approach is best? Theoretically, both can get you to the same point. But each places different demands on an organization and exposes that organization to different risks.

13-2.2   Strategic Leaps

For example, each step in Figure 13-1a is highly visible and usually requires a major expenditure of funds. Therefore, people at all levels in the organization are involved in analyzing and critiquing it. A great deal of staff involvement is required, and the expertise of many highly specialized people—financial analysts, strategic planners, legal experts, scientists, outside consultants, and public relations personnel—must be tapped. Such experts often have more allegiance to their "professions" than to the company itself.

Because each step is so big and so visible, the persons or groups proposing the change are exposed to a great deal of risk. But they also can reap great rewards: if they succeed, they are heroes; if they do not, they suffer the consequences. As a result, those who rise to the top of such organizations tend either to be those who were successful in conceiving and implementing two or three of these major leaps during their careers (the "lucky gamblers") or those who were able to avoid being involved in any major failures (the "corporate kibitzers").

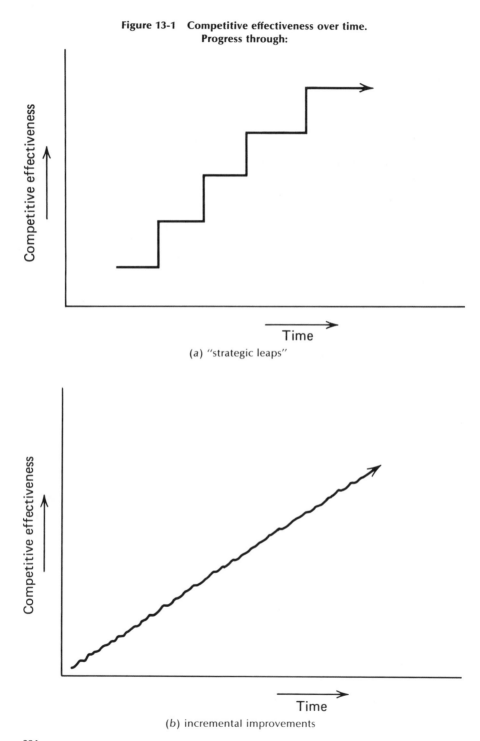

**Figure 13-1   Competitive effectiveness over time.
Progress through:**

(a) "strategic leaps"

(b) incremental improvements

Finally, because of the magnitude of the funds required, the timing of the change becomes important. A decline in profits, a potential acquisition, a sudden surge of orders that pushes the whole organization to the limit of its resources—all can delay the project or put it on "hold."

On the other hand, such a strategy does not require outstanding, highly trained people at lower levels in the organization. Their job is simply to operate the structure that top management and its staff of experts have created for it. It is not necessary to put a lot of time and effort into training and upgrading factory workers or lower level managers, because their newly developed skills may be made obsolete by the next strategic leap (to a new location or a new technology, say). Personnel policies that reward employee longevity are not particularly desirable because they reduce the company's flexibility—its ability, for example, to pull up stakes and move to a new location, to sell the business, or to make a significant reduction in employment because of a major automation program.

Similarly, it is not necessary for workers or lower level managers to have a detailed understanding of how their own operation affects, and is affected by, other parts of the organization, because these relationships may change entirely during the next major transition. Nor are employee suggestion programs particularly useful. Workers cannot possibly understand how the changes they are proposing would fit in with the company's overall strategy (or even the next leap it is contemplating), and they do not have the skills or expertise required to develop ideas for meaningful changes.

Finally, it is not necessary to have strong manufacturing engineering skills, especially at the local plant level, since any significant changes in manufacturing technology are expected to be provided by outside experts. Significant improvements in process technology usually come about in association with the introduction of major new products, which often necessitate replacing substantial portions of the existing manufacturing process (requiring a major investment of corporate funds) rather than the upgrading of existing processes. Since continuous incremental productivity improvements are not expected, the only local manufacturing engineering inputs required are largely of a maintenance or sustaining nature.

13-2.3   Incremental Progress

As suggested by Figure 13-1b, few of the steps taken by a company that follows a "continued incremental improvement" approach are very visible or risky. Because major capital authorization requests seldom are necessary, there is little need for much staff assistance or the advice of outside experts. Rather than putting massive resources into developing elaborate plans and projects in the rarified atmosphere of a remote headquarters building, such a company expects the bulk of its improvements to bubble up from lower levels in the organization.

This approach requires a great deal of the kind of "low-level expertise"

we talked about in Chapter 11. Developing this kind of expertise is a long process. Great effort must be spent on recruiting workers and managers who are
both loyal and educable. Once these people are hired, their capabilities must be
continually improved and expanded, both through formal education programs
and through job assignments that provide a broad understanding of the company's products, processes, and competitive environment. Top management
tries to augment this understanding, and to keep it up to date, by disseminating
information about current financial results, market behavior, and the activities
of competitors. Finally, once this investment in low-level expertise has been
made, it is important to retain the people who have it within the company.

Long-time employees have another advantage: over time, through their
multiple job assignments, they develop personal relationships with a number of
people in different parts of the organization. These relationships make it easier
to implement small changes that require communication between, and the cooperation of, several different groups. This is important since such changes are
typically so small that senior corporate managers and their staffs seldom get
involved in implementing or coordinating them.

Finally, such projects generally require so little capital that often they can
be funded out of a plant's annual operating budget. Plant managers will be
more supportive of such efforts if they are intimately familiar with the plant's
production systems and people and are deeply committed to their plant's long-
term success because they expect to stay there for a fairly long period of time.
And such changes are more likely to work if workers, plant engineers, and
lower level managers participate in developing them—through suggestion programs, quality circles, and the like—and if they identify the company's long-
term success with their own.

Firms that adopt the incremental approach must develop measurement
systems that can track this kind of progress, compensation and promotion systems that encourage it, and resource allocation systems that support it.
Throughout such organizations, workers and managers develop a common understanding of the operating approaches that are most likely to generate such
improvements and the rewards that accrue to the individuals and organizational units that make them happen.

13-2.4   The Choice and the Risks

Up to this point we have been describing, rather abstractly, two highly contrasting "pure" strategies. Few companies choose approaches so extreme; most
fall somewhere along the broad spectrum between them. However, we are
willing to make the following generalization: U.S. firms tend to adopt approaches on the "strategic leap" side of this spectrum, whereas the firms of
America's two most powerful international competitors, Germany and Japan,
tend to seek "incremental" improvements within an existing structure and
technology. They are the tortoise; the United States is the hare.

In the fable, Americans might recall with some apprehension, the tortoise won the race. Is this the fate of the United States as well? To answer that question, let us examine the risks and rewards of each approach.

The great risk of the incremental approach is that one will be leapfrogged (to mix our metaphors) and left behind by a competitor who abandons its traditional technology, location, or corporate strategy and adopts a new and more successful one. The folklore of business is full of such examples: piston engines being surpassed by jet engines, vacuum tubes being surpassed by transistors, ditto machines being supplanted by xerography, New England textile companies that moved south; the list goes on and on.

Conversely, the great risk of the strategic leap approach is that a new breakthrough may not be available exactly when it is needed. That is, after seizing a major competitive advantage, a company may see it nibbled away by competitors who gradually adapt themselves to the new technology or strategy and then push it beyond the limits the first company was able to achieve. This is the time when it would like to take another leap forward, but what if its laboratories and strategists reach into their hats and find nothing there?

An obvious response to such a predicament is to adopt an incremental approach, like that of one's competitors, until a breakthrough does come. But this is not so easy for a firm that has configured itself around the expectation of repeated breakthroughs. As we have seen, the kind of organization that can pursue this latter approach well bears little resemblance to one that takes the incremental approach. Managers and workers have different skills, instincts, and psychological mindsets.

Fortunately, the reverse is not as true. As the German and Japanese companies that we examined in Chapters 11 and 12 are demonstrating all too well, companies that adopt an incremental approach *can* eventually accommodate themselves to a new technology. They may not be as fast, but, given the time, they can do it. In other words, the ability to progress through incremental change does not preclude a firm's ability to master a major change, although it may slow it down.

In fact, our recent experience with a handful of leading firms in different countries suggests that developing the capabilities to make ongoing incremental improvements may actually enhance an organization's ability to make occasional leaps. This is particularly true in industries where improvements are complex, resource intensive, and multidisciplined in nature. Many of the most successful Japanese and German firms seem firmly committed to the notion that broad-based technical skills, tied together through consensus-based management processes, can lead to better designs, shorter product development cycles, and more efficient resource utilization. It also characterizes rapidly changing, process-intensive American industries (like semiconductors) in which process and product improvements have to be linked together integrally.

This, then, provides another, and somewhat sobering perspective on the problems that many American firms are facing in today's unforgiving competitive world. In the fable, the tortoise won the race simply because the hare fell asleep. One can argue that many U.S. industries fell asleep, starting in the late

1960s. Astride an apparently insurmountable technological advantage and blessed with limitless resources, their huge domestic market was supposedly secure behind its protecting oceans. Although they awoke with a jolt in the late 1970s, in the 1980s they still find themselves falling behind. Why?

In most mature industries the development of markets and technology is not discontinuous; rather, it moves forward in a steady, almost predictable manner. Even in such high-technology industries as semiconductors and computers, for example, the progress of the 1980s is taking place within technological frameworks that were essentially established more than 15 years earlier. Such industries play a larger role in the world economy today than they did 20 years ago; therefore, the opportunities for dramatic breakthroughs are fewer.

Nor are strategic "end runs" as easy as they were a decade ago. Today's sophisticated multinational companies have identified most of the major potential markets, and they have uncovered most of the unexploited pools of low-cost labor in the world. U.S. companies are running out of islands to jump to.

In effect, then, the path of the race has led our hare into a competitive swamp. Only infrequently will it encounter a piece of solid land large enough to provide firm footing for another jump. In such an environment, its jumping ability alone is no longer sufficient to allow it to prevail against the tortoise. To do so, it will have to learn to swim as well as jump.

13-3 CONCLUSION

As one reviews the approaches that world class German and Japanese manufacturing firms have taken in achieving their present strong positions, three facts become apparent. First, they base their competitive assaults not on financial or marketing ability but on their manufacturing and technical ability. They believe that however sophisticated one's organization may be in various ways, success depends ultimately upon the production of reliable, well-engineered products.

Second, to emulate them, a company must build a variety of organizational capabilities, and this requires a long and sustained effort. There are no shortcuts along this road, which is precisely why the investment in these organizational capabilities permits one to achieve a *sustainable* competitive advantage—the subject of this book. Moreover, once gained, such an advantage must be continually reinforced. Japanese and German managers often describe their U.S. counterparts as being too complacent and comfortable. The very notion that a competitive advantage, once gained, will remain unassailable, even for a short time, is totally foreign to them. No matter how great the advantage, it requires continuous attention; over time such attention will lead to additional improvement.

Third, while German and Japanese firms seem to have adopted many of the same philosophies and approaches, they adapt and tailor them to fit their unique organizational, political, cultural, and competitive settings.

1. Both encourage extensive training and human resource development, but German firms tend to emphasize engineering-technical skills while Japanese firms tend to emphasize problem-solving skills, especially in small groups.

2. Both relentlessly pursue improvements in production processes, but German firms emphasize equipment technology while Japanese firms emphasize the role that workers and lower level managers play in process improvement.

3. Both pursue excellence in product quality, but German firms tend to place greatest importance on the role of product design in improving quality, while Japanese firms rely on their manufacturing organizations to identify and eliminate the causes of poor quality throughout their processes.

4. Both emphasize the role of manufacturing technology in achieving a long-term advantage, but German firms emphasize flexible systems that can handle low volumes and great variety, while Japanese firms emphasize more automated, high-volume processes.

5. Both recognize the need for stable employment, but in German firms (which must operate under a nationwide co-determination system) technical competence is the primary basis for mutual manager–worker respect; Japanese firms, which are less constrained by national legislation and deal with company unions, expect worker–manager respect to arise more out of continual interaction and cooperative activities.

6. Both view long-term considerations as taking precedence over short-term issues, but German firms see product features and improved productivity (to offset wages) as the keys to survival and success, whereas Japanese firms are more likely to emphasize continual volume growth and cost reduction through standardization and mass production.

These contrasting approaches should serve as a warning that there is no "one best way" to manufacturing excellence, and that approaches adapted to the needs of one environment should not be lifted intact and transplanted to another. This lesson is easily forgotten, as witnessed by Chrysler's successful efforts to reduce its work-in-process inventories in the early 1980s. It did so, however, without gaining the support and full cooperation of its workforce. The consequence: an unexpected strike at a single stamping plant in November 1983, was able to shut down the firm's entire manufacturing network within eight days. Although the strike lasted only a little over a week, it cost Chrysler $80 million.

Despite their differences, well-run factories around the world share many similarities. That is, a well-run German factory is much more like a well-run Japanese factory than German society is like Japanese society. And well-run American factories have important similarities to both. They are clean and orderly. They emphasize quality and dependability. They are characterized by well-trained workers and the kind of high morale that comes from a combination of the workers' sense of their own competence and their confidence in the competence of their managers. And workers and managers engage in continual, open communication at a number of levels on a variety of issues.

One seldom sees posters proclaiming new quality or productivity programs, or managers entrusted with these responsibilities, in German or Japanese factories. Their managers believe that continued improvement in quality and productivity is part of everyone's job. Encouraging that belief, nurturing it over a long period of time so that it develops roots throughout the organization, and working together to translate it into superior products and satisfied customers are at the heart of their industrial success.

This is why their example will be so hard for other companies to emulate. The solution to improving one's manufacturing competitiveness does not, according to this view, lie in the "last-quarter touchdowns," "technological fixes," or "strategic coups" that Americans love so much. Instead, if the United States is to withstand and prevail against the onslaught of its foreign competitors, it will have to use the same approach to competition they use: continually putting its best talent and resources to work doing the basic things a little better, every day, over a long period of time. It is that simple—and that difficult.

SELECTED REFERENCES

Aviation Week & Space Technology, July 20, 1981, p. 15.

Enterprise, March 1981, p. 3.

Hayes, Robert H. "Reflections on Japanese Factory Management." Harvard Case Services, 9-681-084.

Hayes, Robert H. "Tortoise and Hare Approaches to Industrial Competition." Harvard Case Services, 9-683-008.

Hayes, Robert H., and Joseph Limprecht. "Germany's World Class Industrial Competitors." Harvard Case Services, 9-682-081.

Mincer, J. and B. Jovanovic. "Labor Mobility and Wages." Cambridge, MA: National Bureau of Economic Research Reprint 304, August 1982.

The Wall Street Journal, September 10, 1981.

14

Building Manufacturing's Competitive Potential

14-1 OVERVIEW

We began this book by describing the growing challenges facing industry today. Then we described and illustrated a number of the ideas, concepts, and techniques we have found helpful in our work with manufacturing firms around the world. In this chapter, we try to pull together and summarize some of the topics covered.

In Section 14-2 we build on a framework proposed by Abernathy, Clark, and Kantrow (1981) for thinking about today's new industrial competition. This two-dimensional framework provides an overall perspective on the nature of manufacturing's problems and challenges, and allows one to categorize various possible solutions to these problems.

In Section 14-3 we discuss the role of the manufacturing function in the individual firm. Four alternative roles are outlined, and the significant differences among them are described. We illustrate these roles using examples drawn from firms and industries that have adopted each of them. While the ideas contained in the preceding chapters may help improve the performance of a firm that has adopted any one of these four roles, our intent is to encourage companies to move toward more progressive ones. We also describe how two prestigious organizations are doing this.

In the final section of this chapter we touch on two other sets of issues that are critical to developing the manufacturing function's full competitive potential. One of these sets of issues, which is intertwined with a number of the topics covered here, is the primary focus of another book that is already well along in its development.

14-2 FOUR CONTRASTING PERSPECTIVES ON THE NEW INDUSTRIAL COMPETITION

During the early 1980s a surprising number of books about business management have appeared on *The New York Times* best seller list. Most begin with
the same basic premise: a number of important manufacturing-based industries
and firms (especially in the United States) have been hit so hard by foreign
competition that they are now fighting for their very survival. Some of the most
popular of these books include:

> *Japan as Number One,* Vogel (1979)
> *Managing in Turbulent Times,* Drucker (1980)
> *Theory Z,* Ouchi (1981)
> *The Art of Japanese Management,* Pascale and Athos (1981)
> *Megatrends,* Naisbett (1982)
> *In Search of Excellence,* Peters and Waterman (1982)
> *The Next American Frontier,* Reich (1983)
> *Industrial Renaissance,* Abernathy, Clark, and Kantrow (1983)

Although each book starts with essentially similar assessments of the difficulties wracking American manufacturing-based businesses, they point to very
different causes and therefore end with different recommendations. In considering these proposed solutions, it is useful to review the specific problems their
authors are grappling with and the perspectives they bring to the task.

A conceptual framework that we find useful for characterizing the various challenges facing industrial managers as well as the approaches that have
been offered for dealing with them is that proposed by Abernathy, Clark, and
Kantrow (1981). As summarized in Figure 14-1, it divides these approaches
into four categories. Along one dimension of this two-by-two matrix they differentiate between macro (country-level) and micro (company-level) perspectives; along the other, between "hardware" (structural decisions or institutional
relationships) and "software" (human behavior, management policies, and
other infrastructural issues).

Macro issues are essentially national in scope. Tax laws, fiscal policies,
and societal behavior (sometimes intertwined with aspects of national culture)
are examples of the macro issues that writers like Naisbett (1982) are primarily
concerned with. The micro level, on the other hand, includes issues that are
specific to an individual company, including such structural decisions as the
type of vertical integration it chooses, the type of plant and equipment it has
put into place, and the management systems and organizational structures it
has adopted.

The other dimension in Figure 14-1 is somewhat more difficult to characterize. The left-hand column (structure) relates to physical realities: legal and
institutional structures and physical assets. The right-hand column (infrastructure) refers to systems and policies affecting such things as human resources,

Figure 14-1   Key elements/perspectives on manufacturing competitiveness

	Structure ("hardware")	Infrastructure ("software")
Macro (country)	**1** Fiscal/tax policies Monetary policies Trade policies Industrial policies Capital markets Political structure Organized labor	**2** Culture Traditions Religion Values Social behavior
Micro (company)	**3** Business market selection Plant and equipment decisions Capacity/facilities Location/specialization Process technology Vertical integration	**4** Measurement and control systems Workforce policies Vendor relationships Management selection and development policies Capital budgeting/allocation systems Organization structure

personnel management, and company philosophy. Pascale and Athos (1981) pay particular attention to this column.

Many of those writing about industrial competition today fail to distinguish among these various dimensions, and as a result their analyses and recommendations often shortchange important considerations. The four quadrants in Figure 14-1 can help clarify the sources of industrial problems and stimulate thinking about possible solutions. For instance, quadrant 1, the macro/structure quadrant, deals with government institutions, policies, and the laws related to them. Reich (1983) places primary emphasis on this quadrant. The quadrant labeled macro/infrastructure deals with such cultural characteristics as value systems, traditions, religious beliefs, and social behavior. Much of the writing about cultural effects (particularly the Japanese culture), such as the work of Vogel (1979) and Ouchi (1981), focuses on issues and potential solutions in this quadrant.

The quadrant labeled micro/structure deals primarily with the physical facility, technology, and sourcing decisions made within the individual manufacturing firm. Most commentators on business strategy formulation and technology management devote the bulk of their attention to such issues, just as we do in this book. The final quadrant, company infrastructure, has to do with the firm's management systems and controls as well as its organizational and human resource policies. Some people seem to think that such issues simply represent the "implementation" of micro/structure decisions, but Peters and Waterman (1982) show how powerful they can be in determining a company's competitive success.

All four quadrants clearly play a role in the overall success of a manufacturing company. The relative importance of each quadrant varies widely, however, depending on the environment and management's approach to dealing with that environment. We do not believe that the first quadrant—macro/structure—is the dominant cause of most manufacturing companies' competitive problems. Even in such settings as Japan and Singapore, where government policy has been very supportive of industrial development, it is the "frosting on the cake"—complementing strengths that are based primarily on the activities in other quadrants. Companies who believe that their salvation lies in actions taken in this quadrant, particularly those who operate in free market systems (such as the United States), are seriously misdirected, in our view.

Focusing on the second quadrant—macro/infrastructure—is even less productive, we feel. Cultural anthropologists have long known how difficult it is to alter significantly a peoples' cultural characteristics and value systems. While selected values may be accentuated or discouraged at the national level, it is seldom possible to change basic values in any reasonable length of time. Even if such changes could be made, it would be extremely difficult to reach agreement as to the direction in which one ought to move. Thus, although we find some of the work that focuses on this quadrant interesting and insightful, we do not think it holds much promise for managers of firms, industries, or countries who are seeking to rebuild their manufacturing competitiveness during this century.

The micro/structure quadrant has traditionally been viewed as the major source of leverage in manufacturing. That is, if manufacturing had any role to play in a firm's competitive struggle, it was thought to be through the types of structural decisions contained in this quadrant. While such structural decisions obviously do have great impact on manufacturing competitiveness, we think they should be viewed from a broader perspective than has historically been the case.

Keeping competitive, much less "catching up," is not simply a matter of spending money on physical facilities or the latest technology. These decisions have to be carefully integrated with each other, with other functional strategies, and with the firm's overall business strategy. This is the essence of the framework developed in Chapter 2 and, as we described in Chapter 11, it has been a major strength of Germany's world class manufacturing firms. Firms that manage the decisions in this quadrant effectively can, over time, forge their manufacturing operations into powerful competitive weapons. But even making these decisions "right" may not be enough.

The fourth quadrant in Figure 14-1, micro/infrastructure, represents a set of issues that go hand in hand with those included in the previous quadrants. The evidence compiled by Abernathy, Clark, and Kantrow (1981, 1983) and by

Peters and Waterman (1982) suggests that this is a major source of the long-term competitive strength of a number of leading firms. In fact, as outlined in Chapter 12, leading Japanese manufacturers place primary emphasis on the elements in this quadrant. Systematically focusing on, and refining the details of, their manufacturing operations can provide a firm with a competitive advantage that is difficult for competitors to overcome if they have not developed a similarly effective infrastructure (Itami, 1983).

We have not focused our primary attention on quadrant 4 in this book, choosing instead to concentrate on the micro/structure quadrant. This is the appropriate place to begin, in our view, given the perspective and problem-solving approaches of most large manufacturing firms. With that set of decisions in place, issues relating to quadrant 4 can be addressed. The combination of the two can powerfully support and enhance manufacturing's contribution to the firm's competitive struggle. We want to emphasize that the activities in quadrant 4 represent much more than simply implementing, or "cleaning up the details" associated with, quadrant 3. The only sure way to build a long-term competitive edge in manufacturing is by developing a strong infrastructure that reinforces a strong structural base, consisting of facilities, technology, and suppliers.

14-3   STAGES IN THE DEVELOPMENT OF MANUFACTURING'S STRATEGIC ROLE

At the simplest level, one can think of one's manufacturing organization as either making a contribution to one's business strategy or not. Some of the earliest writings about manufacturing strategy essentially adopted that perspective. Useful as they were in raising awareness about the contribution that manufacturing can make to a firm's success, the issues involved are much more complicated than a simple "yes-no" answer would suggest.

Our experience indicates that manufacturing can play at least four major roles in a firm's competitive strategy. These four roles, or stages of development, fall along a continuum and, given the inertia of most large organizations, any enhancement of manufacturing's competitive contribution tends to take place through systematic movements from one stage to an adjacent one. It is seldom possible to skip an entire stage by piling "more resources" on the problem. Given the step-by-step nature of this process, a firm should begin by identifying where it is currently along the continuum, and the factors that have led it to be there, before it embarks on the pursuit of the next stage.

In this section, we identify the characteristics of each of these four stages and provide examples drawn from organizations found at each stage. We devote particular attention to the distinction between stages 3 and 4. While both are "progressive" in terms of the importance of the role they assign to manufacturing, their differences are significant—much more than simply a matter of degree. Even though most world class manufacturing companies are at stage 4, the level of the commitment and the resources required by that stage are beyond the capabilities—and the will—of many companies.

14-3.1   The Four Stages of Development in Manufacturing's Strategic Role

The four stages are outlined in Table 14-1. Stage 1 is the most passive and least progressive view of manufacturing and its competitive role, while stage 4 is the most aggressive and progressive role. We consider stage 1 to consist essentially of an *internally neutral* perspective: management regards manufacturing as neutral at best and seeks simply to minimize any negative impact that it might have. It is not expected (in fact, should not even try) to make any significant positive contribution. Some characteristics of organizations in this stage include the following:

1. They tend to call in outside experts when "obvious" strategic issues involving manufacturing occasionally arise. The implication is clear—the

Table 14-1

Stages in the Evolution of Manufacturing's Strategic Role

Stage 1—Minimize Manufacturing's Negative Potential: "Internally Neutral"

External experts are used in making decisions about strategic manufacturing issues
Internal management control systems are the primary means for monitoring manufacturing performance
Manufacturing is kept flexible and reactive

Stage 2—Achieve Parity (Neutrality) with Competitors: "Externally Neutral"

"Industry Practice" is followed
The planning horizon for manufacturing investment decisions is extended to incorporate a single business cycle
Capital investment is regarded as the primary means for catching up to competition or achieving a competitive edge

Stage 3—Provide Credible Support to the Business Strategy: "Internally Supportive"

Manufacturing investments are screened for consistency with the business strategy
Changes in business strategy are automatically translated into manufacturing implications
Longer-term manufacturing developments and trends are systematically addressed

Stage 4—Pursue a Manufacturing-Based Competitive Advantage: "Externally Supportive"

Efforts are made to anticipate the potential of new manufacturing practices and technologies
Manufacturing is centrally involved in major marketing and engineering decisions
Long-range programs are pursued in order to acquire capabilities in advance of needs

---

manufacturing organization cannot be relied on to handle such important issues by itself.

2. They tend to rely on detailed measurements of and controls over operating performance as the primary means for ensuring that manufacturing does not get too far off track before top management's attention is attracted and corrective action (again usually involving outside experts) is brought to bear. In essence, this detailed performance measurement/evaluation system is viewed as a kind of early warning system that guards against the potentially negative impact of manufacturing.

3. In making structural manufacturing decisions, their goal is generally to keep manufacturing in a flexible and reactive position so that it does not get "locked in" to the wrong set of facilities and processes.

This view of manufacturing is particularly prevalent in large consumer product firms, as well as in companies whose manufacturing process is considered relatively simple and straightforward (and therefore not likely to have much impact on the firm's overall competitive position). Moreover, the manufacturing technology employed is regarded as relatively standard, and therefore something to be acquired from outside equipment suppliers rather than developed (or even enhanced) within the company. Firms that are in this first stage tend to view their production processes as representing a set of "once and for all" decisions—reflecting the "narrow view of technology" described in Chapter 6. Changes occur only when new products absolutely require it or when additional capacity is being added.

This stage is not only prevalent in companies that are highly marketing-oriented (such companies often consider their products and processes to be relatively low technology), but also in high-technology companies that tend to confine their attention to product technology—and exclude process technology. Many consumer electronics and electronic instrument companies view the role of manufacturing as being primarily an assembly and test operation.

The second stage of manufacturing's strategic role also can be characterized in terms of a form of neutrality. Firms in this stage, however, seek *competitive* neutrality (parity with major competitors) on the manufacturing dimension, rather than internal neutrality. Therefore we describe this stage as *externally neutral.* Like the firms in stage 1, firms in stage 2 see manufacturing's role as neutral at best, but they define that role in relation to "industry practice." Competitive neutrality is sought in the following ways:

1. "Industry practice" is followed in matters regarding the workforce (for example, through industry-wide bargaining agreements with national unions), equipment (buying processing equipment from the same suppliers who serve major competitors), and capacity additions (by timing such additions to follow the pattern set by others).

2. The operations planning horizon is extended to include an entire business

cycle (and performance is averaged over that cycle when comparing the competitive success of the major players in the industry).

3. Capital investments are the favored means for gaining a comparative advantage. The only way that manufacturing competence can contribute to this advantage is through judicious timing in these capital investments.

This view of manufacturing is particularly prevalent in many of America's traditional smokestack industries: steel, heavy equipment, automobiles, tires, and major appliances. It is also common in high-tech firms that do not consider manufacturing to be technically sophisticated and expect their product development people to design a new production process whenever a new product requires it. When stage 2 firms do make improvements in their process technology, they tend to adopt the "strategic leap" approach described in Chapter 13. Moreover, they tend to rely on sources outside of manufacturing (often their R&D labs or outside suppliers) to provide these improvements rather than expecting their manufacturing function to develop them itself.

The third stage is one in which the firm expects its manufacturing organization to provide credible and significant support to its overall competitive strategy. We describe this stage as *internally supportive,* in that manufacturing's contribution is derived from and dictated by a business strategy. This is the role that most writers, including Skinner (1969, 1978), seem to imply when describing the concept of manufacturing strategy. In this role, manufacturing would:

1. Screen decisions to be sure that they are consistent with the business strategy.
2. Translate the business strategy into implications and terminology that are meaningful to manufacturing.
3. Actively seek to identify longer-term developments and trends that may have a significant impact on the success of the manufacturing organization. Management recognizes the value of having a manufacturing strategy and begins to employ such devices as plant charters and mission statements in structuring and guiding manufacturing activities over an extended time horizon.

Investigations of robotics, CAD/CAM, and other advanced manufacturing processes are the type of long-term concerns that might be addressed as part of this stage. It is possible to pursue such advanced manufacturing practices while still in stage 2, but firms that do so tend to regard them as strictly defensive moves—as a means for keeping up with their industry. Stage 3 firms, on the other hand, see technological progress as a natural response to changes in the firm's strategy or competitive position.

The transition from a stage 2 to a stage 3 perspective often is precipitous and dramatic: the firm suddenly becomes aware that it is in serious manufacturing trouble—as many U.S. automobile, machine tool, steel, and consumer electronics companies found themselves in the 1970s. The managers of such companies discover that they have to become "enlightened" quickly regarding the actions required to regain their manufacturing competitiveness. Stage 2 firms may also be driven to move to stage 3 when strong new competitors enter their market. If such firms continue to think only in terms of regaining competitive parity, however, over time they are likely to regress to stage 2.

The fourth and final stage of manufacturing's strategic role is when a firm's competitive strategy is based to a significant degree on its manufacturing capabilities. In such firms the role of manufacturing is what we call *externally supportive,* and this book is directed at companies that see this as their goal. Stage 4 firms also put careful thought into developing a manufacturing strategy, but they tend to regard it somewhat differently than do stage 3 firms. Characteristics of stage 4 firms include the following:

1. They anticipate the potential of new manufacturing practices and technologies and seek to acquire expertise in them long before their implications are fully apparent.
2. Manufacturing's credibility and influence within the company make it possible to extract the full potential from such manufacturing-based opportunities, because other functions cooperate with complementary efforts.
3. They develop long-range business plans in which manufacturing capabilities are expected to play a major part in securing the company's strategic objectives. The manufacturing organization is viewed as a strategic resource that is a source of strength by itself as well as a means for enhancing the contribution of other functions. Rather than being derived from its overall business strategy, the firm's manufacturing strategy is developed in an iterative fashion with the business strategy and the other functional strategies. Manufacturing is "externally supportive" in that it is seen as a means for attaining a significant advantage in the firm's external environment.

Firms that pursue a stage 4 manufacturing strategy are generally of two types. One comprises those firms whose business strategy places primary emphasis on a manufacturing-based competitive advantage. That advantage is usually low cost. Such firms as Emerson Electric, Texas Instruments, Mars (candy), United Parcel Service, and Union Camp fall into this category. Some of these firms regard their manufacturing function as the primary source of their competitive advantage and relegate other functions to a secondary or derived role (comparable to the role manufacturing is assigned in most firms).

The other type of stage 4 firm, whose approach is the one we advocate, consists of those that seek a balance of excellence in all of their functions and pursue "externally supportive" roles for each of them. That is, they think that all functions should have comparable (stage 4) roles to play if they are to realize their maximum potential. Such firms are sometimes harder to identify than those that are dominated by their manufacturing functions because all their functions are integrated so well. Some firms of this type that we are familiar with include Hillenbrand Industries, some divisions of General Electric, Caterpillar Tractor, John Deere, and IBM. We describe two of these organizations in more detail in Section 14-3.3.

The leading firms in process-intensive industries are usually in stage 4. In these industries, the evolution of technology, the interaction between product and process technologies, and the sources of both product and process improvement are so intertwined it is almost a prerequisite that a firm be in stage 4 to gain a competitive edge. Such firms can provide useful models for firms that are not process-intensive but want to move to stage 4.

As mentioned earlier, we feel it is useful to think of the four stages outlined in Table 14-1 as falling along a continuum. We want to emphasize, however, that while movements between stages 1, 2, and 3 can be evolutionary in nature and involve progress along a broad range of fronts within manufacturing, the transition from stage 3 to stage 4 requires an effort that is both greater and of a different kind to be successful. Progression from stage 1 to stages 2 and 3 can be handled largely within the manufacturing function. In a sense, it can be thought of as "manufacturing fixing itself." However, moving to stage 4 involves changing the way that the rest of the organization thinks about manufacturing and interacts with it. In the next section we address some of the important distinctions between stages 3 and 4.

One can better understand the stages summarized in Table 14-1 by considering the reasons that impel firms to move from one stage to the next, the form such moves take, and their likely implications. Most young companies assign either stage 1 or stage 2 roles to manufacturing, at least partly because this requires less management attention and knowledge about this function. In the United States, companies tend to start out with a unique product or with the identification of an unexploited niche in a market; hence they tend to place primary emphasis on distribution, product design, or some other nonmanufacturing function. They are likely to remain at that stage until external pressures force a move. As long as no direct competitor successfully develops stage 3 or 4 capabilities, stages 1 and 2 can be comfortable, secure, and apparently effective. A review of the post–World War II history of many U.S. industries (and *Fortune* 500 firms) suggest that such an approach can be satisfactory for decades.

When firms consider moving to stage 3, they appear to do so for one of three, often interrelated, reasons. First, the traditional approach may be perceived as being increasingly ineffective, leading to internal tensions. Second, one or more of the firm's major competitors may move to a higher stage and begin to pose a direct competitive threat. Third, an enlightened management group may recognize the advantages of moving from stage 2 to stage 3 (or the potential perils of not so moving) even though a competitive challenge is not yet apparent.

During the early 1980s, all three of these motivations, reinforced by the admonitions of a number of authors, led literally hundreds of firms to initiate activities that represented shifts toward stage 3. With no end to the competitive pressure in sight, many additional companies are likely to attempt to make similar transitions to stage 3 over the next several years. But this emphasis is likely to be relatively short-lived in a number of them, for reasons outlined in the next section.

14-3.2 Contrasting Stages 3 and 4

While many of the concepts and ideas in this book should be useful to companies contemplating moves from stage 2 to stage 3, and we view stage 3 as a prerequisite to stage 4, the differences between stages 3 and 4 cannot be overemphasized. In stage 3, manufacturing considerations are incorporated in the firm's overall strategy, but the manufacturing function is not viewed as a significant source of potential competitive *advantage*. In fact, manufacturing organizations in stage 3 firms are still largely regarded as being responsive in nature (albeit with better foresight and a broadened perspective), and are simply encouraged to pursue their traditional roles with more ingenuity and somewhat greater resources. As a result, a firm may make a major move that appears to outsiders as being the manifestation of a stage 3 approach (such as building a customized new facility to support a new product), only to find itself back in stage 2 a few years later.

In contrast, stage 4 implies a basic shift in manufacturing's role and self-image. Just as important, it requires a change in the nature of nonmanufacturing managers' understanding and view of manufacturing. In this final stage, manufacturing is regarded as an equal partner in the enterprise, capable of providing input to others as well as managing itself. All levels of management are expected to possess a certain level of technical competence so that they can be aware of how their actions interact with manufacturing activities. More broadly, not only should they have a general understanding of the way products, markets, and processes interact, but these interactions are planned for and coordinated across functions. The traditional approaches that are used to improve manufacturing performance—such as providing flexibility through excess capacity, improving delivery dependability through holding finished goods inventories, and reducing cost through labor productivity improvements—often are reconceptualized in creative ways in stage 4 firms. For example, flexibility may also be achieved through changes in the design of products and/or processes, faster delivery through shorter production cycle times, and low cost through improved product quality and reliability.

In stage 4 firms, manufacturing experience is an efficacious and valued route to general management. In addition, manufacturing resources are looked upon as providing major opportunities for enhancing the firm's competitive strength, not only in the near term but well into the future. A firm that is solidly entrenched in stage 4 values and rewards manufacturing initiative. Such firms evaluate all major manufacturing investments in terms of their potential strategic benefits and expect them to generate returns that are higher than their industry's average return. Our description, in Chapters 11, 12, and 13, of the approaches to (and philosophies of) manufacturing that are being followed by world class German and Japanese manufacturers clearly illustrates the characteristics of stage 4 outlined here.

The way top managers in many companies respond when they are made fully aware of the differences between stages 3 and 4 further indicates the significance of the nature and magnitude of this difference. We know of relatively few American companies whose top managers viewed stage 4 capabilities as their company's obvious goal, and already had begun expanding their manufacturing function's role with the clear intent of moving through stage 3 fully into stage 4.

The majority of firms that move into stage 3, in our experience, do not see a subsequent move to stage 4 as being either essential or natural. Managers in these firms often regard stage 3 as providing 90 percent of the benefits ("so why spend the extra efforts required to go to stage 4?"), or they prefer to "play it safe" by remaining in stage 3 for a sustained period before deciding how and whether to move to stage 4. A sizable number even respond negatively to the prospects of stage 4, viewing it as very risky from an organizational point of view. They feel threatened by the kind of initiatives their manufacturing organizations might propose, once they are unleashed. One firm, for example, saw a move to stage 4 as being potentially destabilizing—particularly to its R&D group, which had historically played the key role in establishing the firm's competitive advantage.*

Three variables often can discriminate effectively between firms that are in stage 4 and those in stage 3. Each might be thought of as a sort of "litmus test" for a firm's real attitude toward the competitive role its manufacturing organization can play. The first variable is the amount of in-house process innovation that is done for future generations of products. Our experience is that firms in stage 4 are continually investing in process improvements, not only because of the resulting benefits for existing products, but because this enhances capabilities that will benefit future generations of products. We referred to this in Chapter 6 as the broad perspective on process technology.

A second discriminator between stages 3 and 4 is the extent to which a firm develops its own manufacturing equipment. In stage 3, a firm can continue to rely on outside suppliers for equipment development. However, in stage 4 the firm insists that it know more than its suppliers about everything that is critical to its business. While the firm may continue to buy much of its equipment, it also produces a substantial amount in-house so that it is close to "the state of the art" in that equipment technology. The German and Japanese manufacturers described in Chapters 11 and 12 follow this practice much more than do most of their American counterparts. It is interesting that even in Germany,

---

* Abernathy, Clark, and Kantrow (1983), on the other hand, suggest that if an industry goes through a period of "dematurization," the resulting technological upheaval may make it absolutely essential to move to stage 4.

where leading firms do a significant amount of their own equipment development, equipment-supplying industries such as the manufacturers of machine tools are strong and innovative. Rather than reducing their market and competitive vitality, this in-house development seems to have stimulated the interaction between manufacturers and their equipment suppliers.

A final variable that can be used to distinguish between stages 3 and 4 is taken directly from Figure 14-1. Our experience is that companies at stage 3 often focus their attention primarily on activities in the "micro/structural" quadrant. To be in stage 4, however, a company must also be able to deal effectively with elements in the "micro/infrastructural" quadrant, and must integrate them effectively with micro/structure decisions. This does not mean that every firm in stage 4 must give both quadrants equal weight, but simply that they look upon both quadrants as important sources of competitive strength.

14-3.3 Two Examples of Transitions to Stage 4 Manufacturing Status

To complete this discussion of what being at stage 4 implies for manufacturing's role in a firm, we now describe how two organizations in the early 1980s made a transition to a stage 4 understanding of manufacturing's strategic potential. The first example is one of General Electric's strategic business units, their dishwasher operation; the second is IBM.

General Electric Dishwasher

Electric dishwashers are one of several types of major consumer appliances that GE has produced for decades. In the late 1970s, GE's dishwasher strategic business unit (SBU) assessed itself and came to the conclusion that its product design was essentially 20 years old, its production processes were from 10 to 20 years old, its workforce was aging (with an average seniority of 15 to 16 years), and it was confronted by a strong union. The company's U.S. dishwasher manufacturing was located primarily at GE's Appliance Park in Louisville, Kentucky, along with five other major appliance operations. A single labor relations group dealt with the entire site, comprising more than 14,000 hourly workers; labor–management relations were viewed as neutral at best and deteriorating.

In spite of all this, the SBU had been very successful. It held the leading position in the U.S. market, accounting for approximately one-third of the dishwashers sold. In late 1977 the division, as part of its normal redesign planning cycle, proposed that $18 million be invested in the incremental improvement of its product and manufacturing process. Senior management normally would have approved such an investment and carried on with the dishwasher SBU's traditional approach to business (largely stage 2, in terms of manufacturing's competitive role).

In this case, however, GE decided that it might be the right time to consider pursuing a very different course. Part of the impetus for this rethinking came from GE top management, who asked several tough questions about the long-term prospects for the business. The idea of making a fundamental change in the dishwasher unit's previous strategy rapidly gained support from some key middle managers, who saw that major opportunities might be created if GE could break out of its traditional mode of thinking.

GE product designers had developed a top-of-the-line product with a plastic tub and plastic door liner that were more expensive than the standard (steel) product but offered significantly better operating performance and used a proprietary material developed by another GE division. In addition, it was apparent that it would be possible to make a substantial increase in the level of dishwasher standardization if the design and marketing functions exercised sufficient self-discipline. Also, since only 55 percent of U.S. households owned electric dishwashers, the business still had considerable long-term growth potential, as well as a large ongoing replacement market. When these factors were combined with GE's strong competitive position, management concluded that if the "right product" were introduced, at the right price and quality level, GE could significantly expand both primary demand and its own market share, particularly in the private label segment. As a result, the dishwasher business's management was challenged not just to "fix" its current problems but to "do it right."

As a result, the modest incremental proposal for product and process improvement was jettisoned and a much bolder proposal adopted. It required an investment of $38 million and, more important, major changes in the product design, manufacturing process, and attitudes of the people involved. The new proposal had three major aspects. The first had to do with *people*. A major commitment was made to improve the working environment through better communication, feedback, and worker involvement in the design of the process. It required almost two years to lay the groundwork in this area but, once in place, the new worker–manager relationship made it possible to enhance significantly manufacturing's contribution to the overall business.

The second aspect of the proposal was a complete rethinking of the *product*. It was redesigned around a central core consisting of a one-piece plastic tub and a one-piece plastic door. To ensure that the product would meet the desired quality standards, extremely tight specifications were established both for GE and its vendors. In fact, both internal and external suppliers were required to reduce their incidence of defects to one-twentieth of their former levels. Those that could not meet the new standards were dropped. To meet the new product's cost targets, as well as its higher quality specifications, it was necessary to coordinate product and process development, rather than separating them as had been the traditional practice.

The third major aspect of this proposal involved the design of the *process*. Automation was pursued aggressively; its goal was not just to reduce costs but also to improve quality, and the product design was modified in accordance with the capabilities and constraints of the new process. In addition, more worker control and shorter cycle times were built into the process, and an entirely new approach was taken to delivering the finished product to customers.

Finally, product testing was integrated more completely with manufacturing rather than assigned to a separate quality control organization.

By late 1980, the basic building blocks of this new strategy had been defined and agreed to. Each of the functions—product design, marketing, and manufacturing—was expected to pursue a stage 4 role in terms of its competitive contribution. Manufacturing management was also asked to cooperate in developing performance measures that—tracked over subsequent years—would indicate how well the manufacturing organization was carrying out its responsibilities.

As outlined in Table 14-2, by 1983 significant improvement had already been achieved in such important areas as service call rates, unit costs, material handling, inventory turns, reject rates, and productivity; substantial additional improvements were anticipated in 1984. Other gains—such as a 70 percent reduction in part numbers, the elimination of 20 pounds of weight in the finished product (which cut freight costs), and significantly more positive worker attitudes—also were experienced. Perhaps most important was the significant jump in market share that occurred during the first 12 months after the new product's introduction. During the summer of 1983, *Consumer Reports* rated GE's new dishwasher as offering the best value among U.S. dishwashers.

Table 14-2

GE Dishwasher—Results

	1980/81	1983	1984 (Estimates)
Service call rate (index) (lower is better)	100	70	55
Unit cost (index)	100	90	88
Number of times tub/door handled	27/27	1/3	1/3
Inventory turns	13	17	28
Reject rates (mechanical/electrical test)	10%	3%	2.5%
Output per employee (index)	100	133	142

Source. Published GE data.

IBM Corporation

We turn now to a description of a global manufacturing strategy that has been implemented by a large organization, and which reflects a transition to a stage 4 approach. This description of IBM's worldwide manufacturing approach is based on a presentation made by its corporate vice president of manufacturing to the company's 50 largest U.S. industrial customers in late 1983.

In the early 1980s, IBM viewed its worldwide activities as comprising 13 major businesses. For example, large computer systems comprised one such business; typewriters, another. In each of these businesses, IBM faced a rapidly changing environment and the need for carefully designed and coordinated strategies if its historical success were to continue. Each business's manufacturing organization was expected to play a major role—equal to those of the other functions—in developing and executing its strategy. This was due not only to the fact that manufacturing was responsible for 49 percent of IBM's assets, 110,000 of its employees, and 40 percent of its final product cost, but also to a strong belief that manufacturing could make a major contribution to the creation of a competitive advantage in each business.

The major aspects of IBM's worldwide manufacturing strategy can be organized and described from two perspectives, which provide a framework for the common elements in all 13 businesses. It is the corporate manufacturing group's responsibility to make sure that both these perspectives are incorporated within each business so that manufacturing can realize its full potential. From one perspective, manufacturing strategy is viewed in terms of the emphasis given to seven major elements:

1. *Low Cost.* IBM firmly believes that it must be the low-cost producer in each business if it is to be successful, where "success" is defined as being regarded by customers as having the best product quality, growing as fast or faster than the market it serves, and being profitable. This low-cost position is pursued by stabilizing the manufacturing environment (reducing uncertainty wherever possible) and linking manufacturing more effectively with marketing and distribution. To this end, marketing is considered to "own" finished-goods inventory, and a 90-day shipping horizon has been adopted to stabilize the factory's production rate. In addition, IBM has decided that it will design products around certain standard modules and, while it will produce different configurations of these standard modules to customer order, it will not manufacture customized modules.

2. *Inventories.* IBM's goal is to reduce inventories significantly. As a first step, inventories are to be measured more carefully and frequently. Production schedules also are to be stabilized to reduce "order churn" (the fluctuation in mix and volume that occurs before an order actually gets into the final production schedule). Lower pipeline inventories also are expected to result from the adoption of a just-in-time philosophy, and from a standardization of components. Within the first 18 months of this effort, IBM was able to reduce its inventories by hundreds of millions of dollars while supporting ever-increasing levels of sales.

3. *Quality.* This is measured in terms of the *total* cost of quality, including prevention, detection, and appraisal. IBM estimates that 30 percent of its products' manufacturing cost can be attributed directly to not "doing it right the first time." Significant improvements in quality, as well as reduced cost, are sought through improved product designs (the design's manufacturability is a major determinant of quality), the pursuit of zero defects (actions taken in this regard included working with fewer vendors having broader responsibility, including performing functional tests), and through systematic stress testing during product design and manufacturing.

4. *Automation.* Automation is being pursued primarily because it is ex-

pected to lead to higher product quality. IBM believes that automation is most effective when it encourages interaction between product design and process design. This requires managing the evolution of the manufacturing process according to a long-term plan, just as product evolution is managed. Reducing overhead—which is felt to result primarily from the variety and complexity of the product line—is another goal of automation.

5. *Organization.* To provide the product design and marketing functions with better interfaces with manufacturing, IBM has defined an additional level of line manufacturing management. This organizational level, referred to as "production management centers," is responsible for all of the plants that manufacture a given product line. For example, the three large system plants (located in France, Japan, and the United States) would all be under a single production management center. That center serves as the primary interface with marketing for that product line, and also with R&D's efforts to design new products. Such centers not only create more effective functional interfaces, they also are responsible for process planning, the defining of plant charters, plant performance measurement, and ensuring that the processes and systems employed by different facilities are uniformly excellent.

6. *Manufacturing Systems.* The intent in this area is to develop integrated systems that provide information, linked directly to strategic business variables, for both general and functional managers. Such systems must be compatible with each other yet flexible enough that each business can select the modules it needs to run itself. As a part of this systems effort, IBM is rethinking its entire manufacturing measurement system with the intent of reducing its historical focus on direct labor while giving more emphasis to materials, overhead, energy, and indirect labor. IBM believes that its manufacturing systems, like its product lines, should be made up largely of standard modules that are based on a common architecture, so that each business can assemble its own customized configuration.

7. *Affordability.* The major intent here is to make external competitiveness, not internal rules of thumb, the basis for evaluating manufacturing performance. Thus, instead of its traditional practice of evaluating manufacturing against its own history, IBM now believes that its manufacturing operations should be better than those of any of its competitors. This requires new information and new methods of comparison, but IBM considers it essential to a realistic assessment of its manufacturing competitiveness. As part of this concern with affordability, IBM is seeking systematically to reduce its overheads, which now exceed 25 percent of total manufacturing cost.

These seven activities represent a rethinking of manufacturing's competitive role at IBM and the types of approaches that must be pursued if its full potential is to be realized. IBM has also identified, as a second perspective, three major themes that seem to run through all of the seven categories. These themes buttress our judgment that IBM has moved to a stage 4 appreciation of manufacturing's potential contribution.

The first is an emphasis on pursuing activities that facilitate, encourage, and reward the effective interface between manufacturing and marketing, as well as between manufacturing and engineering. IBM is convinced that these interfaces should involve people who regard each other as "equals" and who have the ability to make significant contributions to other areas as well as their own. Information, influence, and support should flow across these interfaces in both directions. A number of the actions in the seven categories described above support the development of this type of horizontal interchange.

A second major theme is that product technology and process technology should interact. Process evolution (including automation) should be planned in a systematic manner and communicated to R&D, so that product plans can be developed that take advantage of anticipated process improvements. IBM uses the terms *process windows* and *product windows*. Its goal is to match these windows (encompassing steadily improving opportunities) at critical points in time, so that IBM's products can exploit state-of-the-art products and processes in meeting customer needs and competitive realities. Neither product technology evolution nor process technology evolution should be dominant. Rather, the two interact in such a way that each achieves its full potential.

The third major theme is based on focusing attention and resources on only those factors that are essential to the long-term success of a business. In one sense, enhancing and integrating the seven areas of manufacturing activity outlined above represent one form of this focus. In addition, the emphases on manufacturing, on quality (not only in manufacturing but in all functions), and on overhead reduction are all regarded as keys to the long-term success of the business. The manufacturing organization is expected to ensure that such issues are addressed as effectively as possible.

The results of this worldwide manufacturing strategy are now becoming apparent. Whether one looks at large-scale systems, typewriters, or personal computers, the story seems to be the same: IBM is moving toward its intended competitive advantage, and doing so through a balanced attack across all the functions in each business.

14-4 CONTEMPLATING THE NEXT MOUNTAIN

Our experience suggests that in addition to adopting a broad perspective on manufacturing's potential role in a company, and developing procedures that move the organization in the desired direction, two other elements must be present. One is, simply stated, the need for management vision and leadership. The "logic" of manufacturing strategy does not in and of itself lead organizations to be world class manufacturers. Rather, they must be guided by people who can envision what is possible and can communicate that vision and its implications to their organizations. At least one senior manager has been the driving force in virtually all of the firms we have seen that have advanced to stage 4 in terms of manufacturing's competitive contribution. These leaders spring not only from manufacturing but from all functional backgrounds, and their goal is not simply to elevate manufacturing but to see their companies "firing on all cylinders." Therefore, they seek ways to integrate all functions into an effective whole. They are strong enough, persuasive enough, and tough enough to push beyond the surface logic of conventional management thinking and force their organizations to grapple with the deeper logic of what is required to survive and prevail in the world of the new industrial competition.

A second characteristic of the organizations that are likely to prevail is that they pay great attention to what we referred to at the outset of this chapter as the "micro/infrastructure" aspects of manufacturing (quadrant 4 in Figure 14-1). Our emphasis in this book has been on the micro/structural elements (quadrant 3) because we think this is the appropriate starting point for most companies and most managers. Once these decisions are made correctly, however, they must be buttressed by the appropriate infrastructure: systems for quality control, workforce management, and production planning/materials management. Organizational structure, manufacturing systems, and performance measurement are other important infrastructure elements. Although micro/structure activities frequently can be handled largely within the manufacturing function, infrastructure activities require broad horizontal involvement across functions at fairly low levels of the organization.

We were advised at one point that "you never finish a book, you just abandon it." So, rather than let this book run on, we have chosen to make quadrant 4—and the horizontal activities that link it to quadrant 3—the subject of our next book.

SELECTED REFERENCES

Abernathy, William J., Kim B. Clark, and Alan M. Kantrow. "The New Industrial Competition." *Harvard Business Review,* September–October 1981, pp. 68–81.

Abernathy, William J., Kim B. Clark, and Alan M. Kantrow. *Industrial Renaissance.* New York: Basic Books, 1983.

Drucker, Peter F. *Managing in Turbulent Times.* New York: Harper & Row, 1980.

Itami, Hiroyuki. "Invisible Resources and Their Accumulation for Corporate Growth." Research Paper 682, Stanford University, March 1983.

Naisbett, John. *Megatrends.* New York: Warner Books, 1982.

Ouchi, William. *Theory Z.* Reading, MA: Addison-Wesley, 1981.

Pascale, Richard T., and Anthony G. Athos. *The Art of Japanese Management.* New York: Simon & Schuster, 1981.

Peters, Thomas J., and Robert H. Waterman, Jr. *In Search of Excellence.* New York: Harper & Row, 1982.

Porter, Michael E. *Competitive Strategy.* New York: Free Press, 1980.

Rafii, Farshad, and Jeffrey G. Miller. "The Impact of Strategy Articulation on Manufacturing Performance." School of Management, Boston University, Working Paper, 1982.

Reich, Robert B. *The Next American Frontier.* New York: Times Books, 1983.

Skinner, Wickham. "Manufacturing—Missing Link in Corporate Strategy." *Harvard Business Review,* May–June 1969, pp. 136–145.

Skinner, Wickham. *Manufacturing in the Corporate Strategy.* New York: John Wiley & Sons, 1978.

Stobaugh, Robert, and Piero Telesio. "Match Manufacturing Policies and Product Strategy." *Harvard Business Review,* March–April 1983, pp. 113–120.

Vogel, Ezra. *Japan as Number One.* Cambridge, MA: Harvard University Press, 1979.

Index